Lecture Notes in Artificial Intelligence 2484

Subseries of Lecture Notes in Computer Science
Edited by J. G. Carbonell and J. Siekmann

Lecture Notes in Computer Science
Edited by G. Goos, J. Hartmanis, and J. van Leeuwen

Springer

Berlin
Heidelberg
New York
Barcelona
Hong Kong
London
Milan
Paris
Tokyo

Pieter Adriaans   Henning Fernau
Menno van Zaanen (Eds.)

Grammatical Inference:
Algorithms
and Applications

6th International Colloquium, ICGI 2002
Amsterdam, The Netherlands, September 23-25, 2002
Proceedings

 Springer

Series Editors

Jaime G. Carbonell, Carnegie Mellon University, Pittsburgh, PA, USA
Jörg Siekmann, University of Saarland, Saarbrücken, Germany

Volume Editors

Pieter Adriaans
Senior Research Advisor, Perot Systems Nederland B.V.
Hoefseweg 1, 3821 AE Amersfoort, The Netherlands
Professor of Learning and Adaptive Systems, Universiteit van Amsterdam
ILLC/Computation and Complexity Theory, Plantage Muidergracht 24
1018 TV Amsterdam, The Netherlands, E-mail: Pieter.Adriaans@ps.net

Henning Fernau
University of Newcastle, School of Electrical Engineering and
Computer Science, University Drive, Callaghan, NSW 2308, Australia
E-mail: fernau@cs.newcastle.edu.au
Wilhelm-Schickard-Institut für Informatik, Universität Tübingen
Sand 13, 72076 Tübingen, Germany, E-mail: fernau@informatik.uni-tuebingen.de

Menno van Zaanen
FNWI/ILLC, Cognitive Systems and Information Processing Group
Universiteit van Amsterdam, Room B-5.39, Nieuwe Achtergracht 166
1018 WV Amsterdam, The Netherlands, E-mail: mvzaanen@science.uva.nl

Cataloging-in-Publication Data applied for

Die Deutsche Bibliothek - CIP-Einheitsaufnahme

Grammatical inference: algorithms and applications : 6th international colloquium ; proceedings /
ICGI 2002, Amsterdam, The Netherlands, September 23 - 25, 2002. Pieter Adriaans ... (ed.). -
Berlin ; Heidelberg ; New York ; Hong Kong ; London ; Milan ; Paris ; Tokyo : Springer, 2002
   (Lecture notes in computer science ; Vol. 2484 : Lecture notes in artificial intelligence)
   ISBN 3-540-44239-1

CR Subject Classification (1998): I.2, F.4, F.3

ISSN 0302-9743
ISBN 3-540-44239-1 Springer-Verlag Berlin Heidelberg New York

Springer-Verlag Berlin Heidelberg New York
a member of BertelsmannSpringer Science+Business Media GmbH

http://www.springer.de

© Springer-Verlag Berlin Heidelberg 2002
Printed in Germany

Typesetting: Camera-ready by author, data conversion by Boller Mediendesign
Printed on acid-free paper   SPIN: 10870596   06/3142   5 4 3 2 1 0

Preface

The Sixth International Colloquium on Grammatical Inference (ICGI 2002) was held in Amsterdam on September 23-25th, 2002. ICGI 2002 was the sixth in a series of successful biennial international conferences on the area of grammatical inference. Previous meetings were held in Essex, U.K.; Alicante, Spain; Montpellier, France; Ames, Iowa, USA; Lisbon, Portugal.

This series of meetings seeks to provide a forum for the presentation and discussion of original research on all aspects of grammatical inference. Grammatical inference, the process of inferring grammars from given data, is a field that not only is challenging from a purely scientific standpoint but also finds many applications in real-world problems.

Despite the fact that grammatical inference addresses problems in a relatively narrow area, it uses techniques from many domains, and is positioned at the intersection of a number of different disciplines. Researchers in grammatical inference come from fields as diverse as machine learning, theoretical computer science, computational linguistics, pattern recognition, and artificial neural networks.

From a practical standpoint, applications in areas like natural language acquisition, computational biology, structural pattern recognition, information retrieval, text processing, data compression and adaptive intelligent agents have either been demonstrated or proposed in the literature.

The technical program included the presentation of 23 accepted papers (out of 41 submitted). Moreover, for the first time a software presentation was organized at ICGI. Short descriptions of the corresponding software are included in these proceedings, too.

We would like to thank the members of the technical program committee and the reviewers for their careful evaluation of the submissions, the members of the local organizing committee, Menno van Zaanen, Marjan Veldhuisen, and Marco Vervoort for their help in setting up the event, the invaluable secretarial support, and updating the website.

July 2002   Pieter Adriaans

Technical Program Committee

Pieter Adriaans, Perot Systems Corporation/University of Amsterdam,
The Netherlands (Chair)
Dana Angluin, , Yale University, USA
Jerry Feldman, ICSI, Berkeley, USA
Henning Fernau, University of Newcastle, Australia
Colin de la Higuera, EURISE, University of St. Etienne, France
Vasant Honavar, Iowa State University, USA
Dick de Jongh, University of Amsterdam, The Netherlands
Makoto Kanazawa, University of Tokyo, Japan
Laurent Miclet, ENSSAT, Lannion, France
G. Nagaraja, Indian Institute of Technology, Mumbai, India
Arlindo Oliveira, Lisbon Technical University, Portugal
Jose Oncina Carratala, University of Alicante, Spain
Rajesh Parekh, Blue Martini, USA
Yasubumi Sakakibara, Tokyo Denki University, Japan
Arun Sharma, University of New South Wales, Australia
Esko Ukkonen, University of Helsinki, Finland
Enrique Vidal, U. Politécnica de Valencia, Spain
Takashi Yokomori, Waseda University, Japan
Menno van Zaanen, University of Amsterdam, The Netherlands
Thomas Zeugmann, University of Lübeck, Germany

Organizing Committee

Pieter Adriaans (Chair)
Henning Fernau (Co-chair)
Menno van Zaanen (Local organization and demo session)
Marjan Veldhuisen (Secretariat)

Additional Reviewers

Marc Bernard
Stephan Chalup
Philippe Ezequel
Jean-Christophe Janodet

Table of Contents

Contributions

Inference of Sequential Association Rules Guided by Context-Free
Grammars 1
    C.M. Antunes, A.L. Oliveira

PCFG Learning by Nonterminal Partition Search 14
    A. Belz

Inferring Subclasses of Regular Languages Faster Using *RPNI* and
Forbidden Configurations 28
    A. Cano, J. Ruiz, P. García

Beyond EDSM 37
    O. Cicchello, S.C. Kremer

Consistent Identification in the Limit of Rigid Grammars from Strings
Is NP-hard 49
    C. Costa Florêncio

Some Classes of Regular Languages Identifiable in the Limit from
Positive Data 63
    F. Denis, A. Lemay, A. Terlutte

Learning Probabilistic Residual Finite State Automata 77
    Y. Esposito, A. Lemay, F. Denis, P. Dupont

Fragmentation: Enhancing Identifiability 92
    H. Fernau

On Limit Points for Some Variants of Rigid Lambek Grammars 106
    A. Foret, Y. Le Nir

Generalized Stochastic Tree Automata for Multi-relational Data Mining .. 120
    A. Habrard, M. Bernard, F. Jacquenet

On Sufficient Conditions to Identify Classes of Grammars from
Polynomial Time and Data 134
    C. de la Higuera, J. Oncina

Stochastic Grammatical Inference with Multinomial Tests 149
    C. Kermorvant, P. Dupont

Learning Languages with Help 161
    C. Kermorvant, C. de la Higuera

Incremental Learning of Context Free Grammars....................... 174
    K. Nakamura, M. Matsumoto

Estimating Grammar Parameters Using Bounded Memory 185
    T. Oates, B. Heeringa

Stochastic k-testable Tree Languages and Applications.................. 199
    J.R. Rico-Juan, J. Calera-Rubio, R.C. Carrasco

Fast Learning from Strings of 2-Letter Rigid Grammars................. 213
    Y. Seginer

Learning Locally Testable Even Linear Languages from Positive Data 225
    J.M. Sempere, P. García

Inferring Attribute Grammars with Structured Data for Natural
Language Processing 237
    B. Starkie

A PAC Learnability of Simple Deterministic Languages 249
    Y. Tajima, M. Terada

On the Learnability of Hidden Markov Models......................... 261
    S.A. Terwijn

Shallow Parsing Using Probabilistic Grammatical Inference.............. 269
    F. Thollard, A. Clark

Learning of Regular Bi-ω Languages.................................. 283
    D.G. Thomas, M. Humrosia Begam, K.G. Subramanian,
    S. Gnanasekaran

Software Descriptions

The EMILE 4.1 Grammar Induction Toolbox......................... 293
    P. Adriaans, M. Vervoort

Software for Analysing Recurrent Neural Nets That Learn to Predict
Non-regular Languages 296
    S.K. Chalup, A.D. Blair

A Framework for Inductive Learning of Typed-Unification Grammars..... 299
    L. Ciortuz

A Tool for Language Learning Based on Categorial Grammars and
Semantic Information.. 303
    D. Dudau Sofronie, I. Tellier, M. Tommasi

'NAIL': Artificial Intelligence Software for Learning Natural Language 306
    S. Lievesley, E. Atwell

Lyrebird^TM: Developing Spoken Dialog Systems Using Examples 309
    B. Starkie, G. Findlow, K. Ho, A. Hui, L. Law, L. Lightwood,
    S. Michnowicz, C. Walder

Implementing Alignment-Based Learning 312
    M. van Zaanen

Author Index 315

Inference of Sequential Association Rules Guided by Context-Free Grammars

Cláudia M. Antunes[1] and Arlindo L. Oliveira[2]

[1] Instituto Superior Técnico, Dep. Engenharia Informática, Av. Rovisco Pais 1,
1049-001 Lisboa, Portugal
claudia.antunes@dei.ist.utl.pt
[2] IST / INESC-ID, Dep. Engenharia Informática, Av. Rovisco Pais 1,
1049-001 Lisboa, Portugal
aml@inesc.pt

Abstract. One of the main unresolved problems in data mining is related with the treatment of data that is inherently sequential. Algorithms for the inference of association rules that manipulate sequential data have been proposed and used to some extent but are ineffective, in some cases, because too many candidate rules are extracted and filtering the relevant ones is difficult and inefficient. In this work, we present a method and algorithm for the inference of sequential association rules that uses context-free grammars to guide the discovery process, in order to filter, in an efficient and effective way, the associations discovered by the algorithm.

1 Introduction

With the rapid increase of stored data, the interest in the discovery of hidden information has exploded in the last decade. One important problem that arises during the discovery process is treating sequential data, and, in particular the inference of sequential association rules.

Association rules are a classical mechanism to model general implications of the form X⇒Y, and when applied to sequential patterns they model the order of events occurrence. Some of the main approaches to discover these sequential patterns are based on the well-known apriori algorithm [2], and they essentially differ on the data portions considered to generate pattern candidates [3], [11], [9]. However, the number of discovered rules is usually high, and the interest of most of them doesn't fulfill user expectations. Filtering them after the fact, i.e., after the generation phase, is inefficient and in some cases prohibitive.

In order to minimize this problem, an apriori-base algorithm, termed SPIRIT (Sequential Pattern mIning with Regular expressIons consTraints) [6] constrains the candidate generation with regular expressions. In this way, it is possible to focus the discovery process in accordance with the user expectations, and at the same time, to reduce the time needed to conclude the process. In this paper, we extend this approach to use Context Free Grammars as constraints.

The paper is organized as follows: section 2 describes some applications of sequential data mining. Section 3 presents the objectives of the paper and a summary

P. Adriaans, H. Fernau, and M. van Zaanen (Eds.): ICGI 2002, LNAI 2484, pp. 1-13, 2002.

of the principal apriori-based approaches to discover sequential association rules. Section 4 presents the adaptation of apriori to use context-free grammars as constraints to guide the discovery of frequent sequences. In section 5 an example of an interesting problem, which can be guided by a simple context-free grammar, is presented. Finally, section 6 presents the conclusions and points some possible directions for future research.

2   Applications of Sequential Data Mining

The ultimate goal of sequential pattern mining is to discover hidden and frequent patterns on sequences and sub-sequences of events. One important application is modeling the behavior of some entity. For instance, when using a database with transactions performed by customers at any instant, it is possible to predict what would be the customer's next transaction, based on his past transactions.

Temporal data mining is a particular case of the sequential pattern discovery problem. In the last two decades, the prediction of financial time series was one of the principal goals of temporal data mining [5]. However, with the increase of stored data in other domains and with the advances in the data mining area, the range of temporal data mining applications has enlarged significantly. Today, in engineering problems and scientific research temporal data appears, for example, in data resulting from monitoring sensor networks or spatial missions (see, for instance [7]). In healthcare, despite temporal data being a reality for decades (for example in data originated by complex data acquisition systems like ECG), more than ever medical staff is interested in systems able to help on medical research and on patients monitoring [13]. Finally, in finance, applications on the analysis of product sales, client behaviors or inventory consumptions are essential for today's business planning [3].

Another important application of sequential pattern mining is in bioinformatics, where different characteristics of proteins and other biologically significant structures are to be inferred from mapped DNA sequences. Some important applications in this domain are on molecular sequence analysis, protein structure prediction, gene mapping, modeling of biochemical pathways and drug design [15].

3   Sequential Pattern Mining

3.1   CFG Driven Inference of Temporal Association Rules

The aim of this paper is to present a method that uses context-free grammars as models that match interesting patterns hidden in the database, and uses these grammars to constrain the search. This is done by discovering sequential patterns with an apriori-based algorithm whose search is constrained by the given context-free grammar. Changes in the grammar can then be applied in order to guide the search towards the desired objective, resulting in a methodology that effectively infers a context-free grammar that models interesting patterns in the database.

The first step on the process of inferring a grammar that supports frequent sequences is described, and consists on discovering the frequent sequences on the database that satisfies a given grammar. This problem is technically challenging and the main contribution of this paper is an efficient algorithm for this procedure.

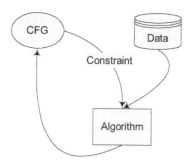

Fig. 1. Grammar inference process

The next step consists on evaluating the number, type and interest of the discovered sequences, and generalizing or specializing the given grammar, in order to adapt it to the obtained results.

Note that if the number of discovered sequences is too large, the grammar used to constrain the mining process is too generic and doesn't put enough restrictions on the discovery process. This means that the grammar should be restricted. On the other hand, if the number of discovered sequences is too small, it is necessary to generalize the grammar in order to accept a larger range of sequences.

Clearly, this is an highly non-automated method for grammatical inference, since the data mining practitioner herself is guiding the inference process. In practice, this may represent a very interesting method, since the use of association rule algorithms is usually encumbered by the difficulty in isolating the useful rules from the useless ones.

3.2 Sequential Association Rules

Sequential association rules are implications of the form $X \Rightarrow_T Y$ which states that if X occurs then Y will occur within T events [4], where X and Y are. Stating a rule in this new form, describes the impact of the occurrence of an event to the other event occurrence, within a specific number of events.

In general, the process of mining sequential association rules is composed mainly by the discovery of frequent patterns. Note that these patterns may be viewed as sequential association rules by themselves, since a sequence imposes an order on its elements. One of the most common approaches to mining frequent patterns is the apriori method [2], which requires some adaptations for the case of sequential data.

Apriori acts iteratively generating the potential frequent k-itemsets (set of items) and pruning them by their support, until there are no candidates. A k-itemset is a set with k elements and is frequent when its support (the number of occurrences in the database) is greater than a user-specified threshold. In step k+1, the algorithm generates the new candidates by combining each two frequent k-itemsets and retaining the frequent ones to the next step.

This process could be used without loosing the property of completeness, because an itemset with length k isn't frequent unless all of its k-1 subsets are frequent. This property is known as anti-monotonicity [10], and allows for reducing significantly the number of candidates for which the support counting is done, reducing the time needed to discover the set of all frequent itemsets.

The AprioriAll [3] and its improvement GSP [14] are apriori adaptations for mining sequential patterns. The main difference to apriori is that candidates are sequences instead of itemsets, which means that the order in which each item appears is relevant. Another difference is that it is necessary to decide the value of T (the maximum gap between consecutive sequence elements), in order to restrict the impact of an element to another. Another important difference is on the notion of support: an entity supports a sequence/pattern if it is contained in the sequence that represents the entity, and there aren't more than T elements between two consecutive pattern elements. Stated in this form, an entity could only contribute once to increment the support of each pattern [3].

However, like apriori, the algorithm suffers from one main drawback: the lack of user-controlled focus.

SPIRIT Algorithms. SPIRIT is a family of apriori-based algorithms that uses a regular expression to constrain the mining process. The regular expression describes user expectations about data and preferences about the type of rules the user is interested on. In this way, it is used to constrain the candidates' generation. Given a database of sequences D, a user-specified minimum support threshold sup and a user-specified regular expression constraint C, the goal is to find all frequent and valid sequential patterns in D, in accordance with sup and C respectively [6].

The main algorithm is similar to AprioriAll, and is presented in figure 2. It consists essentially on three steps: candidate generation, candidate pruning and support pruning.

The candidate generation step, like in AprioriAll, is responsible for the construction of sequences with length k+1. However, the construction method depends on the chosen constraint. Since most of the interesting regular expressions are not anti-monotone, the construction consists on extending or combining k-sequences (that are frequent but not necessarily accepted by the regular expression) ensuring that all candidates satisfy the imposed constraint.

On the candidate pruning step, candidates which have some maximal k-subsequence valid and not frequent are removed, reducing the number of sequences passed to the next step and consequently, reducing the global processing time. Finally, on the support pruning step, the algorithm counts the support for each candidate and selects the frequent ones.

With the introduction of constraints in the mining process, the algorithm restrains the search of frequent patterns in accordance to user expectations, and simultaneously it reduces the time needed to finish the mining process.

```
Procedure SPIRIT (D, C)
begin
   let C':= a constraint weaker than C
   F:=F₁:=frequent items in D that satisfy C'
   k:=2
   repeat{
      // candidate generation
      using C' and F generate Cₖ:={potentially frequent
      k-sequences that satisfy C'}
      // candidate pruning
      let P:={s∈Cₖ: s has a subsequence t that satisfies
      C' and t∉F}
      Cₖ:=Cₖ-P
      // support-based pruning
      scan D counting support for candidate k-sequences in
      Cₖ
      Fₖ:=frequent sequences in Cₖ
      F:=F∪Fₖ
      k:=k+1
   }until TerminatingCondition (F, C') holds
   //enforce the original constraint C
output sequences in F that satisfy C
end
```

Fig. 2. SPIRIT algorithm [6]

4   Using Context-Free Grammars as Constraints

Despite the fact that regular expressions provide a simple and natural way to specify sequential patterns, there are interesting patterns that these expressions are not powerful enough to describe.

Consider for example the following problem: a company wants to find out typical billing and payment patterns of its customers.

So, the specification language should be powerful enough to describe this constraint and exploit the fact that for well-behaved customers there are as many invoices as payments in any given order. If an invoice is represented by an *a* and a payment by a *b*, the language has to accept sequences like *abab* as well as *aabbab*, and rejects *aabbb* or *baab*. Note that, in the real world a payment transaction is always preceded by an invoice and not the other way around.

Note that no regular expression can be used to describe this problem since they are not able to record the number of occurrences for each element. However, context-free grammars are powerful enough to describe most of the structure in natural languages and simple enough to allow the construction of efficient parsers to analyze sentences [1]. For instance, the grammar S→aSbS|ε is able to model the problem stated above, since the first expression imposes that if an invoice occurs, then a payment would also occurs in the future.

Context-free grammars have been widely used to represent programming languages and more recently, to model RNA sequences [12].

The SPIRIT algorithm exploits the equivalence of regular expressions to deterministic finite automata (DFA) to push the constraint deep inside the mining process. Using context-free grammars as constraints implies using non-deterministic push-down automata to do the same.

If we define a push-down automata as the tuple $(Q, \Sigma, \Gamma, \delta, q0, Z0, F)$ where Q is a finite set of states, Σ is an alphabet called the input alphabet, Γ is an alphabet called the stack alphabet, δ is a mapping from $Q\times(\Sigma\cup\{\epsilon\})\times\Gamma$ to finite subsets of $Q\times\Gamma^*$, $q0\in Q$ is the initial state, $Z0\in\Gamma$ is a particular stack symbol called the start symbol and $F\subseteq Q$ is the set of final states[8]. The language accepted by a pushdown automaton is the set of all inputs for which some sequence of moves causes the pushdown automaton to empty its stack. The PDA equivalent to the grammar presented above would be

$$M = (\{q_1, q_2\}, \{a, b\}, \{S, X\}, \delta, q_1, S, \{q_2\})$$

with δ defined as follows:

$$\delta(q_1, a, S) = \{(q_2, push\ X)\},\ \delta(q_2, a, S) = \{(q_2, push\ X)\},$$
$$\delta(q_2, a, X) = \{(q_2, push\ X)\} \text{ and } \delta(q_2, b, X) = \{(q_2, pop)\}.$$

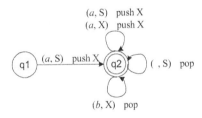

Fig. 3. A push-down automata equivalent to the grammar $S\rightarrow aSb|\epsilon$.

This automaton is represented in figure 3, where, for example "$(a, S)\rightarrow push\ X$" is used to indicate that when the input symbol is a and the top stack symbol is S, then X is pushed into the stack.

4.1   Using CFGs to Constrain the Search

Since a super-sequence of a given sequence s may belong to the CFG, even if s does not belong to the CFG, the anti-monotonicity property is not present. Therefore, using the PDA to restrict the candidate generation process is not straightforward. Four distinct relaxations to the original expression have been used with DFAs, namely:

- *Naïve*: an anti-monotonic relaxation of the constraint, which only prunes candidate sequences containing elements that do not belong to the language alphabet. For example, if we consider the automaton defined in figure 1, only sequences with a's and b's are accepted by the *Naïve* constraint.

- *Legal*: the initial constraint is relaxed requiring that every candidate sequence is legal with respect to some state of the automaton equivalent to the constraint. A sequence is said to *be legal with respect to q* (with *q* a state of the automaton) if there is a path in the automaton, which begins in state *q* and is composed by the sequence elements. For example, if we consider the automaton like before, *a*, *ab*, *aab* or *b* are accepted as legal.

- *Valid suffix*: a constraint relaxation that only accepts candidate sequences valid with respect to any state of the automaton. A sequence is said to *be a valid suffix with respect to q* if it is legal with respect to *q* and achieves a terminal state. With the same automaton, *a* or *aa* aren't valid suffixes, but *b* or *ab* are.

- *Complete*: the constraint itself that imposes that every candidate sequence is accepted by the automaton. For example, *ab* or *aabb* are accepted.

A fifth possibility may be added to the above ones:

- *Valid prefix*: a reverse "valid suffix" relaxation, which requires that every candidate sequence is legal with respect to the initial state. Reversely, *a* or *ab* are valid prefixes but *b* is not.

The application of the naïve and complete alternatives with context-free grammars is straightforward. A sequence is accepted by the naive criterion in exactly the same conditions than before, and is accepted by the complete criterion if the sequence could be generated by the grammar that represents the constraint.

However, these two criteria are ineffective in many cases, for two different reasons. The naïve criterion prunes a small number of candidate sequences, which implies a limited focus on the desired patterns. The complete, can generate a very large number of candidates since the only way to apply it involves generating all strings s of a given length that belong to the language. The other two alternatives are, in many cases, significantly more effective in pruning the candidate list.

The extension of the legal and valid alternatives to context-free grammars is non trivial, since the presence of a stack makes it more difficult to identify when a given sequence is either legal or valid. However, it is possible to extend the notion of legality and validity of a sequence with respect to any state of the push-down automaton.

Consider the basic operations to manipulate stacks:

- $\lambda.push$ X – introduces the element X on the top of the stack λ;

- $\lambda.top$ – returns the element on the top of the stack λ;

- $\lambda.pop$ – removes the element on the top of the stack λ;

- $\lambda.isEmpty$ – verifies if the stack λ is empty.

Definition 1   A sequence s=<s1...sn> is legal with respect to state qi with stack λ, if and only if

- $|s|=1 \wedge \lambda.isEmpty \wedge \exists X \in \Gamma$: $\delta(q_i, s_1, X) \supset (q_j, op)$ with $op \in \{push, pop, no\ op\}$.
- $|s|=1 \wedge \exists X \in \Gamma \wedge \lambda.top=X$: $\delta(q_i, s_1, X) \supset (q_j, op)$ with $op \in \{push, pop, no\ op\}$.
- $\lambda.isEmpty \wedge \exists X \in \Gamma$: $\delta(q_i, s_1, X) \supset (q_j, pop) \wedge <s_2...s_n>$ is legal with respect to state q_j with stack λ.

- $\exists X \in \Gamma \wedge \lambda.\text{top}=X$: $\delta(q_i, s_1, X) \supset (q_j, op) \wedge <s_2...s_n>$ is legal with respect to state q_j with the resulting stack of applying the operation op to λ.

This means that any sequence with one element is legal with respect to a state, if it has a transition defined over the first element of the sequence. On the other cases, a sequence is legal with respect to a state if it has a transition defined over the first element of the sequence, and if the residual subsequence is legal with respect to the resulting state.

Consider again the automaton defined in figure 1:

- a is legal with respect to q_1 and the stack with S (rule i), since there is a transition from q_1 that could be applied $[\delta(q_1,a,S)\supset(q_2,\text{pushX})]$.

- a is also legal with respect to q_2 and the empty stack (rule ii) since there is also a transition from q_2 $[\delta(q_2,a,S)\supset(q_2,\text{pushX})]$.

- b is legal with respect to state q_2 and the empty stack since it has length-1 and there is a transition from q_2 with symbol b $[\delta(q_2,b,X)\supset(q_2,\text{pop})]$.

- ab, is naturally legal with respect to q_1 and the stack with S (rule iii), since from q_1 with a, q_2 is achieved and X is pushed into the stack. Then second symbol b, with X on the top of the stack the automaton performs another transition and a pop. Similarly aba, $abab$, $abab$ and $aaba$ are also legal with respect to q_1.

- ba is legal with respect to q_2 and the empty stack (rule iv). Since, with b, the automaton remains on q_2 and the stack empty, and with input a, X is pushed into the stack. Note that ba is a subsequence of $abab$, and consequently a sequence legal with respect to some state. Similarly, bab, $baab$ and even bbb are legal with respect to q_2. Note that bbb is a subsequence of $aaabbb$, for example.

Note that pop is allowed on an empty stack, because it is possible that the sequence's first element doesn't correspond to a transition from the initial state, or it may correspond to an element for which there are only transitions with pop operations, like the element b in the automaton in figure 1. If pop on the empty stack wasn't allowed, a simulation of every possible stack resulting from the initial to the current state would be necessary, in order to verify if the operation may be applied. This simulation could be prohibitive in terms of efficiency and would require a considerable effort.

Definition 2 A sequence $s=<s1...sn>$ is said to be suffix-valid with respect to state qi with stack λ, if and only if:

- $|s|=1 \wedge \lambda.\text{isEmpty} \wedge \exists X \in \Gamma$: $\delta(q_i, s_1, X) \supset (q_j, op)$ with $op \in \{pop, no\ op\} \wedge q_j$ is a final state.
- $|s|=1 \wedge \exists X \in \Gamma \wedge \lambda.\text{top}=X$: $\delta(q_i, s_1, X) \supset (q_j, pop) \wedge q_j$ is a final state $\wedge (\lambda.pop).\text{isEmpty}$.
- $\lambda.\text{isEmpty} \wedge \exists X \in \Gamma$: $\delta(q_i, s_1, X) \supset (q_j, pop) \wedge <s_2...s_n>$ is suffix-valid with respect to state q_j with stack λ.
- $\exists X \in \Gamma \wedge \lambda.\text{top}=X$: $\delta(q_i, s_1, X) \supset (q_j, op) \wedge <s_2...s_n>$ is suffix-valid with respect to state q_j, with the stack resulting of applying the operation op to λ.

This means that a sequence is suffix-valid with respect to a state if it is legal with respect to that state, achieves a final state and the resulting stack is empty.

Like before, consider the automaton defined in figure 1:

- b is a suffix-valid with respect to state q_2, since it is legal with respect to q_2, achieves a terminal state and the final stack is empty.

- a is not a suffix-valid, since any transition with a results on pushing an X into the stack, which implies a non empty stack.

Note that, in order to generate valid sequences with respect to any state, it is easier to begin from the final states. However, this kind of generating process is one of the more difficult when dealing with pushdown automata, since it is needed a simulation of their stacks.

In order to avoid this difficulty, using prefix validity instead of suffix validity could be an important improvement.

Definition 3   A sequence s=<s1...sn> is said to be prefix-valid if it is legal with respect to the initial state.

Sequences with valid prefixes are not difficult to generate, since the simulation of the stack begins with the initial stack: the stack containing only the stack start symbol.

Using the automaton defined in figure 1 again:

- a is a prefix-valid, since there is a transition with a from the initial state and the initial stack.

- b is not a prefix-valid, since there isn't any transition from the initial state with b.

The benefits from using the suffix-validity and prefix-validity are similar. Note that, like when using the suffix-validity, to generate the prefix-valid sequences with k elements, the frequent k-1-sequences are extended with the frequent 1-sequences, in accordance to the constraint.

Using these notions and an implementation of pushdown automata, it is possible to use context-free grammars as constraints to the mining process.

5 Example

This section exemplifies the application of the proposed algorithm to the discovery of sequential association rules, and simultaneously, to illustrate the process of inferring a grammar that supports the discovered rules. It begins with an example of the grammar inference process and finishes with the comparison of the results achieved with and without the use of context-free grammars to constrain the discovery of sequential rules.

Consider again the problem of identifying billing patterns of some company customers. A first definition of well-behaved customers may be: one customer is well-behaved if he doesn't receive an invoice before paying the previous one, and has done all his payments. This pattern could be specified by the regular grammar (a particular case of context-free grammars) S→abS |ε.

Table 1. Data set used to exemplify the mining process

Data set
<ababab>
<aabbab>
<aababb>
<babaab>
<abaabb>

Supposing that the company has the dataset represented in table 1, the results of running our algorithm over the data set using the complete constraint are shown in table 2. Ck represents the set of candidate sequences with k elements and Fk the set of frequent k-sequences.

Table 2. Results achieved with the complete constraint defined by $S{\rightarrow}abS \mid \varepsilon$.

K	C_k	Support	F_k
1	-	-	-
2	<ab>	1.0	<ab>
3	-	-	-
4	<abab>	0.4	<abab>
5	-	-	-

Comparing the discovered sequences with the existent on the database, it is clear that the first approach to define well-behaved customers is too restrictive and the generalization of that notion is needed.

A simple generalization consists on considering that a well-behaved customer is a customer who always makes at least one payment after receiving one or two consecutive invoices and has made, at the end of the period, all its payments.

This constraint may be modeled by the grammar $S{\rightarrow}ASB|SCS|\varepsilon$ with $A{\rightarrow}aab$, $B{\rightarrow}b$ and $C{\rightarrow}ab$. The push-down automaton presented in figure 4 could be used to push the filtering imposed by this grammar inside the algorithm.

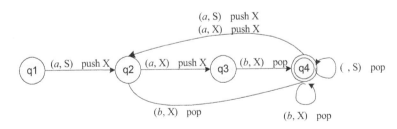

Fig. 4. Push-down automaton equivalent to grammar $S{\rightarrow}ASB|SCS|\varepsilon$ with $A{\rightarrow}aab$, $B{\rightarrow}b$ and $C{\rightarrow}ab$.

The results of running our algorithm over the data set using the new constraint are shown in table 3. We can suppose that, in this toy example, the results obtained are satisfactory in terms of the quality and number of the discovered sequences, and that no grammar generalization or specialization is required.

Table 3. Results achieved with the complete constraint defined by S→ASB|SCS|ε with A→aab, B→b and C→ab.

K	C_k	Support	F_k
1	-	-	-
2	<ab>	1.0	<ab>
3	-	-	-
4	<aabb>	0.4	<aabb>
	<abab>	0.4	<abab>
5	-	-	-

Comparison to Apriori without Constraints

Table 4 presents the candidates generated by GSP and those generated by the algorithm adapted to use the complete context-free grammar constraint.

Table 4. Comparison of the results achieved with GSP and the complete constraint

K	GSP			Complete		
	C_k	Support	F_k	C_k	Support	F_k
1	<a>	1.0	<a>			
	<b>	1.0	<b>	–	–	–
2	<aa>	0.4	<aa>			
	<ab>	1.0	<ab>			
	<ba>	1.0	<ba>	<ab>	1.0	<ab>
	<bb>	0.4	<bb>			
3	<aaa>	0.0				
	<aab>	0.8	<aab>			
	<aba>	0.8	<aba>			
	<abb>	0.6	<abb>			
	<baa>	0.4	<baa>	–	–	–
	<bab>	0.8	<bab>			
	<bba>	0.2				
	<bbb>	0.0				
4	<aaba>	0.2				
	<aabb>	0.4	<aabb>			
	<abaa>	0.4	<abaa>			
	<abab>	0.4	<abab>	<aabb>	0.4	<aabb>
	<baab>	0.4	<baab>	<abab>	0.4	<abab>
	<baba>	0.4	<baba>			
	<babb>	0.0				
5	<abaab>	0.4				
	<ababa>	0.2				
	<baabb>	0.2	<abaab>	–	–	–
	<babaa>	0.2				
	<babab>	0.2				

Note that the number of candidates generated by the new algorithm is significantly less than with GSP. This difference appears because the constraint imposes that sequences are only accepted if they have an even number of elements. Note however, that when k=6 the GSP algorithm finishes, but the algorithm using the complete constraint continues counting the support for generated candidates.

Table 5. Comparison of the results achieved with the constraints "legal" and "prefix-valid"

	Legal			Prefix-valid		
K	C_k	Support	F_k	C_k	Support	F_k
1	<a>	1.0	<a>	<a>	1.0	<a>
	<b>	1.0	<b>			
2	<aa>	0.4	<aa>			
	<ab>	1.0	<ab>	<aa>	0.4	<aa>
	<ba>	1.0	<ba>	<ab>	1.0	<ab>
	<bb>	0.4	<bb>			
3	<aab>	0.8				
	<aba>	0.8	<aab>			
	<abb>	0.6	<aba>	<aab>	0.0	<aab>
	<baa>	0.4	<abb>	<aba>	0.8	<aba>
	<bab>	0.8	<baa>	<abb>	0.8	<abb>
	<bba>	0.2	<bab>			
	<bbb>	0.0				
4	<aaba>	0.2				
	<aabb>	0.4	<aabb>	<aaba>	0.2	<aabb>
	<abaa>	0.4	<abaa>	<aabb>	0.4	<abaa>
	<abab>	0.4	<abab>	<abaa>	0.4	<abab>
	<baab>	0.4	<baab>	<abab>	0.4	
	<baba>	0.4	<baba>			
	<babb>	0.0				
5	<abaab>	0.4				
	<ababa>	0.2		<abaab>	0.4	<abaab>
	<baabb>	0.2	<abaab>	<ababa>	0.2	
	<babaa>	0.2				
	<babab>	0.2				

Note that on the results obtained with the legal constraint (presented in table 5), the difference between the numbers of generated candidates is less notorious. For example, C4 would only have seven elements versus the eight elements generated by GSP. However, using the valid-prefix constraint reduces the number of candidates significantly, focusing the discovered rules according the company expectations.

6   Conclusions

We presented a methodology and an algorithm that uses context-free grammars to specify restrictions to the process of mining temporal association rules using an Apriori-like algorithm.

Context-free grammars can model situations of interest to the data miner practitioner, and restrict significantly the number of rules generated. However, its application is not straightforward, since the restrictions imposed do not satisfy the anti-monotonicity property. We defined and proposed to use several different alternative restrictions that are a generalization of what has been proposed by other authors for regular grammars.

The results show that the additional expressive power of context free grammars can be used without incurring in any additional difficulties, when compared to the use of regular grammars, if the appropriate algorithms are used to restrict the search.

We have implemented these algorithms and tested them in small synthetic data sets with positive results. In the near future, we plan to use this approach in real data sets to empirically validate the efficacy and efficiency of the approach.

References

1. Allen, J.: Natural Languages Understanding, 2ndedition. The Benjamin/Cummings Publishing Company, Redwood City (1995)
2. Agrawal, R., Srikant, R.: Fast Algorithms for Mining Association Rules. In Proceedings of the International Conference on Very Large Databases (1994) 487-499
3. Agrawal, R., Srikant, R.: Mining sequential patterns. In Proceedings of the International Conference on Data Engineering (1995) 3-14
4. Das, G., Mannila, H., Smyth, P.: Rule Discovery from Time Series. In Proceedings of Knowledge Discovery in Databases (1998) 16-22
5. Fama, E.. Efficient Capital Markets: a review of theory and empirical work. Journal of Finance (1970) 383-417
6. Garofalakis, M., Rastogi, R., Shim, K.: SPIRIT: Sequential Pattern Mining with Regular Expression Constraint. In Proceedings of the International Conference on Very Large Databases (1999). 223-234
7. Grossman, R., Kamath, C., Kegelmeyer, P., Kumar, V., Namburu, R.: Data Mining for Scientific and Engineering Applications. Kluwer Academic Publishers (1998)
8. Hopcroft, J., Ullman, J.: Introduction to Automata Theory, Languages and Computation. Addison Wesley (1979).
9. Özden, B., Ramaswamy, S., Silberschatz, A.: Cyclic association rules. In Proceedings of the International Conference on Data Engineering (1998) 412-421
10. Ng, R., Lakshmanan, L., Han, J.: Exploratory Mining and Pruning Optimizations of Constrained Association Rules. In Proceedings of the International Conference on Management of Data (1998) 13-24
11. Ramaswamy, S., Mahajan, S., Silberschatz, A.: On the Discovery of Interesting Patterns in Association Rules. In Proceedings of the International Conference on Very Large Databases (1998) 368-379
12. Searls, D.B.: The Linguistics of DNA. American Scientist, 80 (1992) 579-591
13. Shahar, Y., Musen, M.A.: Knowledge-Based Temporal Abstraction in Clinical Domains. Artificial Intelligence in Medicine 8, (1996) 267-298
14. Srikant, R., Agrawal, R.: Mining Sequential Patterns: Generalizations and Performance Improvements. In Proceedings of the International Conference on Extending Database Technology (1996) 3-17
15. Zaki, M., Toivonen, H., Wang, J.: Report on BIOKDD01: Workshop on Data Mining in Bioinformatics. In SIGKDD Explorations, Volume 3, Issue 2 (2002) 71-73

PCFG Learning by
Nonterminal Partition Search

Anja Belz

ITRI
University of Brighton
Lewes Road
Brighton BN2 4GJ, UK
Anja.Belz@itri.brighton.ac.uk

Abstract. PCFG Learning by Partition Search is a general grammatical inference method for constructing, adapting and optimising PCFGs. Given a training corpus of examples from a language, a canonical grammar for the training corpus, and a parsing task, Partition Search PCFG Learning constructs a grammar that maximises performance on the parsing task and minimises grammar size. This paper describes Partition Search in detail, also providing theoretical background and a characterisation of the family of inference methods it belongs to. The paper also reports an example application to the task of building grammars for noun phrase extraction, a task that is crucial in many applications involving natural language processing. In the experiments, Partition Search improves parsing performance by up to 21.45% compared to a general baseline and by up to 3.48% compared to a task-specific baseline, while reducing grammar size by up to 17.25%.

1 Introduction

The inference method presented in this paper belongs to the subdomain of grammatical inference (GI) that is concerned with the inference of context-free languages from positive data, where to infer a language means to name a grammar or generator-tester for it.

The aim of practical GI in general can be described as creating inference mechanisms G which, given an inference domain of formal languages $\mathbf{L}$, some finite amount of information I about a language $L \in \mathbf{L}$, and a set of admissible languages $\mathbf{L_I}$ for each information set I, produce a guess or set of guesses $G(I) = \{L_1, L_2, \ldots L_n\} \subset \mathbf{L_I}$ about the identity of L. GI methods differ principally in their choice of $\mathbf{L}$ and $\mathbf{L_I}$, the kind of information taken into account, the nature of the mapping from data sets I to guesses, and their ability to identify the members of $\mathbf{L}$ in the limit (i.e. for increasingly large amounts of information). For the standard abstract families of languages[1], Gold showed in his 1967 paper

---

[1] In order of containment, the standard abstract families of languages are the seven language classes containing the recursively enumerable, recursive, primitive recursive, context-sensitive, context-free, regular and finite languages, respectively.

P. Adriaans, H. Fernau, and M. van Zaanen (Eds.): ICGI 2002, LNAI 2484, pp. 14–27, 2002.

that if I contains subsets of L and its complement $\bar{L}$ (positive and negative examples), then there exists a guessing method G that identifies the context-free languages[2] in the limit. However, if I contains only positive examples, there is no guessing method to identify any superfinite language class[3] in the limit.

Identifiability in the limit is important because it means that a GI method can guarantee that its guesses will approximate the target language more and more closely with increasing size of I. Without limit identifiability, GI is a random guessing game unless additional knowledge is used in the inference process. For this reason, GI methods with superfinite inference domains do not generally attempt to infer languages from example strings alone, but enforce additional restrictions on $\mathbf{L}$ and/or $\mathbf{L_I}$, or use prior knowledge to construct an initial grammar. An example of an exception in context-free GI is Wolff's work, e.g. [14].

Even if there was a GI method that could limit-identify the context-free languages, this would not be sufficient for natural languages (NLs). This is so because for each context-free language there exist several context-free grammars (shown by the existence of normal forms, e.g. Chomsky and Greibach), each of which would assign a different set of derivations to the strings in the language. However, the whole point in having grammars for natural language is to be able to assign structure to sentences which can be used as a basis for further (e.g. semantic) analysis. The assumption is that nonterminals should correspond to word and phrase categories, and that there is one (or at least a small number) of correct derivations for each string of words.

An inference mechanism can only learn correct derivations if the data it is given contains derivation annotation. NL samples with derivation annotation are easily obtained, as many large copora of annotated text have been compiled over recent decades. If the annotations in them were objectively correct, that is, if they reflected some definitive grammar for the NL, then inferring that grammar would be as simple as reading production rules off the annotations. Because there are a finite number of such rules in any CFG the method would identify the NLs in the limit. However, each corpus of annotated text reflects only one guess as to what the 'true' grammar of a given NL might be. Moreover, even within one corpus there are errors and inconsistencies. While it is therefore not feasible to read a grammar off an existing annotated corpus[4], such grammars nevertheless form a very useful starting point for NL grammar building.

PCFG Learning by Partition Search makes it possible to use any PCFG as a starting point for grammar building, adaptation and optimisation. Its inference domain $\mathbf{L}$ is the context-free languages. Information I about a language $L \in \mathbf{L}$ comes in the form of elements of L with labelled or unlabelled annotation indicating their correct derivation. A canonical grammar is defined as the starting point for the GI process (either some default grammar, or one derived from I).

---

[2] In fact, the entire class of primitive recursive languages.

[3] Superfinite language classes contain all finite languages and at least one infinite language. There are non-superfinite languages (which do not contain all finite languages) that can be identified in the limit.

[4] Although such grammars perform surprisingly well, as first shown by Charniak [4].

The set of admissible languages $\mathbf{L_I}$ is the subset of $\mathbf{L}$ containing all and only languages for which grammars can be derived from the canonical grammar by a combination of merge operations on the canonical grammar's nonterminal set.

Partition Search PCFG learning has a range of practical applications: (i) grammar building starting from some default grammar; (ii) grammar optimisation using existing grammars; and (iii) grammar adaptation where existing grammars that were created for one task are adapted and optimised for another.

The remainder of this paper is structured as follows. Section 2 gives basic definitions and operations, and outlines the family of grammar learning algorithms that Partition Search belongs to. Partition Search is described and discussed in Section 3. In Section 4 an example application is reported where grammars are learned for the task of noun phrase extraction.

2   CFG Learning by Merging and Splitting Nonterminals

2.1   PCFG Nonterminal Set Operations

This section informally introduces the two operations — nonterminal merging and nonterminal splitting —that form the basis of the family of GI methods that Partition Search PCFG Learning belongs to. The descriptions of the merge and split operations presuppose the following definition of PCFGs.

Definition 1. *Probabilistic Context-Free Grammar (PCFG)*

A (PCFG) is a 4-tuple (W, N, N_S, R), where W is a set of terminal symbols, N is a set of nonterminal symbols, $N_S \in N$ is a start symbol, and $R = \{(r_1, p(r_1)), \dots (r_m, p(r_m))\}$ is a set of production rules with associated probabilities. Each rule r_i is of the form $n \to \alpha$, where n is a nonterminal from N, and α is a string of terminals and nonterminals. For each nonterminal n, the values of all $p(n \to \alpha_i)$ sum to one, or: $\sum_{i:(n \to \alpha_i, p(n \to \alpha_i)) \in R} p(n \to \alpha_i) = 1$.

Nonterminal merging: Consider the two PCFGs G and G' below[5]. Intuitively, to derive G' from G, the two nonterminals NP-SUBJ and NP-OBJ are merged into a single new nonterminal NP. This merge results in two rules from R becoming identical in R': both NP-SUBJ -> NNS and NP-OBJ -> NNS become NP -> NNS.

$G = (W, N, N_S, R),$ $G' = (W, N', N_S, R'),$
$W = \{$ NNS, DET, NN, VBD, JJ $\}$ $W = \{$ NNS, DET, NN, VBD, JJ $\}$
$N = \{$ S, NP-SUBJ, VP, NP-OBJ $\}$ $N' = \{$ S, NP, VP $\}$
$N_S = $ S $N_S = $ S
$R = \{$ (S -> NP-SUBJ VP, 1), $R' = \{$ (S -> NP VP, 1),
       (NP-SUBJ -> NNS, 0.5),   (NP -> NNS, 0.625),
       (NP-SUBJ -> DET NN, 0.5),   (NP -> DET NN, 0.25),
       (VP -> VBD NP-OBJ, 1),   (VP -> VBD NP, 1),
       (NP-OBJ -> NNS, 0.75),   (NP -> DET JJ NNS, 0.125) $\}$
       (NP-OBJ -> DET JJ NNS, 0.25) $\}$

---

[5] In the example grammars in this and the following section, preterminals (NNS, DET, NN, etc.) are used in place of terminals (words) for brevity. Preterminals are capitalised for consistency with later examples.

One way of determining the probability of the new rule NP -> NNS is to sum the probabilities of the old rules and renormalise by the number of nonterminals that are being merged[6]. In the above example this means e.g. p(NP -> NNS) = $(0.5 + 0.75)/2 = 0.625$[7].

An alternative would be to reestimate the new grammar on some new corpus, but this is not appropriate in the current context: merge operations are used in a search process (see below), and it would be expensive to reestimate each new candidate grammar derived by a merge. It is better to use any available training data to estimate the original grammar's probabilities, then the probabilities of all derived grammars can simply be calculated as described above.

Nonterminal splitting: Deriving a new PCFG from an old one by splitting nonterminals in the old PCFG is not quite the exact reverse of deriving a new PCFG by merging nonterminals. The difference lies in determining probabilities for new rules. Consider the following grammars G and G':

$G = (W, N, N_S, R),$	$G' = (W, N', N_S, R'),$
$W = \{$ NNS, DET, NN, VBD, JJ $\}$	$W = \{$ NNS, DET, NN, VBD, JJ $\}$
$N = \{$ S, NP, VP $\}$	$N' = \{$ S, NP-SUBJ, VP, NP-OBJ $\}$
$N_S = $ S	$N_S = $ S
$R = \{$ (S -> NP VP, 1),	$R' = \{$ (S -> NP-SUBJ VP, ?),
(NP -> NNS, 0.625),	(S -> NP-OBJ VP, ?),
(NP -> DET NN, 0.25),	(NP-SUBJ -> NNS, ?),
(VP -> VBD NP, 1),	(NP-SUBJ -> DET NN, ?),
(NP -> DET JJ NNS, 0.125) $\}$	(NP-SUBJ -> DET JJ NNS, ?)
	(VP -> VBD NP-SUBJ, ?),
	(VP -> VBD NP-OBJ, ?),
	(NP-OBJ -> NNS, ?),
	(NP-OBJ -> DET NN, ?),
	(NP-OBJ -> DET JJ NNS, ?) $\}$

To derive G' from G, the single nonterminal NP in G is split into two nonterminals NP-SUBJ and NP-OBJ in G'. This split results in several new rules. For example, for the old rule NP -> NNS in G, there now are two new rules NP-SUBJ -> NNS and NP-OBJ -> NNS in G'. One possibility for determining the new rule probabilities is to make pairs of split rules equally likely, i.e. for the current example, p(NP -> NNS) = p(NP-SUBJ -> NNS) = p(NP-OBJ -> NNS). However, then there would be no benefit at all from performing such a split: the resulting grammar would be larger, the most likely parses remain unchanged, and for each parse p under G that contains a nonterminal that is split, there would be at least two equally likely parses under G'.

The new probabilities cannot be calculated directly from G. The redistribution of the probability mass has to be motivated from a knowledge source

---

[6] Reestimating the probabilities on the training corpus would of course produce identical results.

[7] Renormalisation is necessary because the probabilities of all rules expanding the same nonterminal sum to one, therefore the probabilities of all rules expanding a new nonterminal resulting from merging n old nonterminals will sum to n.

outside of G. The reason why there is this difference between the merge and the split operation is that when performing a merge, information is removed from the grammar, whereas when performing a split, information is added.

One way to proceed is to estimate the new rule probabilities on the original corpus — provided that it contains in extractable form the information on the basis of which a split operation was performed. For the current example, a corpus in which objects and subjects are annotated could be used to estimate the probabilities of the rules in G', and might yield a rule set which is, with rules of zero probability removed, identical to that of the original grammar G in the example in Section 2.1.

2.2   Nonterminal Merge/Split GI Methods

PCFG learning by Partition Search belongs to a family of GI methods that infer CF grammars using the merge and split operations introduced in the last section. This family of GI methods can be characterised as follows.

The inference domain $\mathbf{L}$ is the context-free languages. Information I about a language $L \in \mathbf{L}$ comes in the form of elements of L with or without annotation indicating their correct derivation. The set of admissible languages $\mathbf{L_I}$ for each information set I is the subset of $\mathbf{L}$ containing all and only languages for which grammars can be derived from the canonical grammar for I by a combination of merge and/or split operations.

What is needed for a full specification of a GI method is restrictions (if any) on the nature of I, a definition of the canonical grammar for I, and a method for selecting a final inferred grammar from $\mathbf{L_I}$. An example of a canonical grammar is one that has a production $n \rightarrow t_1 t_2 \ldots t_m$ for each string $t_1 t_2 \ldots t_m$ in I. Examples of selection methods are random selection and search through the set of admissible grammars guided by some objective function.

If no further restriction is placed on the kind of split operations that can be performed, the set of admissible languages is infinite. Furthermore, in the case of PCFGs, split operations are expensive because they require the reestimation of rule probabilities from a training corpus. Partition Search PCFG Learning avoids both of these problems.

3   PCFG Learning by Partition Search

PCFG Learning by Partition Search has the characteristics of all nonterminal split/merge GI methods with the following additions. I is a set of elements from some CF language, annotated with a correct derivation. Annotation is either labelled or unlabelled, e.g. for the sentence *the cat sat on the mat*[8], a labelled annotation would be *(S (NP (DET the) (N cat)) (VP (VB sat) (PP (PRP on) (NP (DET the) (N mat)))))*, whereas the unlabelled equivalent would be *(((the) (cat)) ((sat) ((on) ((the) (mat)))))*.

---

[8] The convention for NL grammars is to insert spaces between the terminals in a derived string of terminals.

The canonical grammar is constructed by converting each bracket pair in I into a production rule[9]. The set of productions for the annotated example above would be { $S \rightarrow NP\ VP$, $NP \rightarrow DET\ N$, $VP \rightarrow VB\ PP$, $PP \rightarrow PRP\ NP$, $DET \rightarrow the$, $N \rightarrow cat$, $VB \rightarrow sat$, $PRP \rightarrow on$, $N \rightarrow mat$ }. For the unannotated equivalent it would be something like { $N1 \rightarrow N2\ N3$, $N2 \rightarrow N4\ N5$, $N3 \rightarrow N6\ N7$, $N7 \rightarrow N8\ N9$, $N9 \rightarrow N4\ N10$, $N4 \rightarrow the$, $N5 \rightarrow cat$, $N6 \rightarrow sat$, $N8 \rightarrow on$, $N10 \rightarrow mat$ }. The probabilities are derived from the production frequencies in I.

A maximally split grammar (Max Grammar) is derived from the canonical grammar by a set of split operations. Then, the set of admissible languages $\mathbf{L_I}$ is defined as the (finite) set of languages for which grammars can be derived from the Max Grammar by PCFG partitioning (equivalent to a set of merges, for definition see below). The final inferred grammar is determined by some search mechanism guided by an objective function evaluating members of $\mathbf{L_I}$.

In the current implementation, a variant of beam search is used, and the objective function evaluates grammars in terms of their size and performance on a given parsing task. In the experiments carried out so far, the data used for I is fully annotated (labelled) English text corpora. Maximally split grammars were defined on the basis of additional information available from the corpora.

The remainder of this section describes Partition Search PCFG Learning in more detail. First, the merge operation that was informally introduced in Section 2.1 is generalised and defined formally. Next, search space, search task and objective function are discussed, and finally, the whole algorithm is presented.

3.1   PCFG Partitioning

Any possible combination of nonterminal merges can be represented by a partition of the set of nonterminals.

Definition 2. *Set Partition*

A partition of a nonempty set A is a subset Π of 2^A such that $\emptyset$ is not an element of Π and each element of A is in one and only one set in Π.

The partition of A where all elements are singleton sets is called the trivial partition of A.

For the example presented in Section 2.1 above, the partition of the nonterminal set N in G that corresponds to the nonterminal set N' in G' is { {S}, {NP-SBJ, NP-OBJ}, {VP} }. The original grammar G together with a partition of its nonterminal set fully specifies the new grammar G': the new rules and probabilities, and the entire new grammar G' can be derived from the partition together with the original grammar G. The process of obtaining a new grammar

---

[9] I have also used existing grammars (manually constructed, or by some other method) in place of the canonical grammars.

G', given a grammar G and a partition of the nonterminal set N of G, will be called PCFG Partitioning[10].

In the examples in Section 2.1, a notational convention was tacitly adopted which is also used in the following definition of PCFG Partitioning. As a result of merging, NP-SUBJ and NP-OBJ become a single new nonterminal. This new nonterminal was represented above by the set of merged nonterminals {NP-SBJ, NP-OBJ} (in the partition), as well as by a new symbol string NP (in the definition of G'). The two representations are treated as interchangeable: the new nonterminal is represented either as a set or a nonterminal symbol[11].

Definition 3. *PCFG Partitioning*
  Given a PCFG *$G = (W, N, N_S, R)$ and a partition Π_N of the set of nonterminals N, the* PCFG *derived by partitioning G with Π_N is $G' = (W, \Pi_N, N_S, R')$, where:*

$$R' = \Big\{ (a_1 \rightarrow a_2 \ldots a_n,\ p) \ \Big|$$
$$\{(b_1^1 \rightarrow b_2^1 \ldots b_n^1,\ p^1),\ \ldots (b_1^m \rightarrow b_2^m \ldots b_n^m,\ p^m)\} \in \Omega,$$
$$a_1 \in \Pi^N, b_i^j \in a_1,$$
$$\forall i, 2 \leq i \leq n \ \big(\ \text{either } a_i = b_i^j \in W,\ \text{or } a_i \in \Pi^N, b_i^j \in a_i \ \big),$$
$$p = \big(\textstyle\sum_{j=1}^m p^j\big)/|a_1| \ \Big\}, \ and$$

Ω *is a partition of R such that each $O \in \Omega$ contains all and only elements from R $(b_1^1 \rightarrow b_2^1 \ldots b_n^1,\ p^1),\ \ldots (b_1^m \rightarrow b_2^m \ldots b_n^m,\ p^m)$ for which the following holds: $\forall i, 1 \leq i \leq n$*
  $\big(\ \text{either } b_i^1 = b_i^2 = \ldots b_i^m \in W,\ \text{or } \{b_i^1, b_i^2, \ldots b_i^m\} \subseteq P,\ P \in \Pi_N \ \big)$.

The definition of PCFG Partitioning can be paraphrased as follows. Given a PCFG $G = (W, N, N_S, R)$ and a partition Π_N of the set of nonterminals N, the PCFG derived from G by Π_N is $G' = (W, \Pi_N, N_S, R')$. That is, the set of terminals remains the same, and the new set of nonterminals is just the partition Π_N. Ω is the partition of R in which all production rules are grouped together that become identical as a result of the nonterminal merges specified by Π_N. Then, the new set of probabilistic rules R' contains one element $(a_1 \rightarrow a_2 \ldots a_n, p)$ for each element $\{(b_1^1 \rightarrow b_2^1 \ldots b_n^1, p^1), \ldots (b_1^m \rightarrow b_2^m \ldots b_n^m, p^m)\}$ of Ω, such that the following holds between them: a_1 is a nonterminal from Π^N and contains all the b_1^j; for the other a_i, either a_i is a nonterminal and contains all the b_i^j, or it is a terminal and is identical to b_i^j. The new rule probability p is the sum of all probabilities $p^j, 1 \leq j \leq m$ renormalised by the size of the set a_1.

The new grammar G' derived from an old grammar G by merging nonterminals in G is a generalisation of G: the language of G', or $L(G')$, is a superset of the language of G, or $L(G)$. For any sentence $s \in L(G)$, the parses assigned to s

---

[10] The concept of context-free grammar partitioning in this paper is not directly related to that in [7,13], and later publications by Weng et al. In these previous approaches, a non-probabilistic CFG's *set of rules* is partitioned into subsets of rules.

[11] The name assigned to the new nonterminal in the current implementation of PCFG Partitioning is the longest common prefix of the old nonterminals that are merged followed by an indexation tag (to distinguish otherwise identical names).

by G' form a superset of the set of parses assigned to s by G. The probabilities of parses for s can change, and so can the probability ranking of the parses, i.e. the most likely parse for s under G may differ from the most likely parse for s under G'. Finally, G' has the same number of rules as G or fewer.

3.2   Search Space

The number of merge operations that can be applied to a nonterminal set is finite, because after some finite number of merges there remains only one nonterminal. On the other hand, the number of split operations that can sensibly be applied to a nonterminal NT has a natural upper bound in the number of different terminal strings dominated by NT in a corpus of evidence. For example, when splitting the nonterminal NP into subjects and objects, there would be no point in creating more new nonterminals than the number of different subjects and objects found in the corpus. Given these bounds, there is a finite number of distinct grammars derivable from the original grammar by different combinations of merge and split operations. This forms the basic space of candidate solutions for Grammar Learning by Partition Search.

Imposing an upper limit on the number and kind of split operations permitted not only makes the search space finite but also makes it possible to directly derive the *maximally split nonterminal set* (Max Set). Once the Max Set has been defined, the single grammar corresponding to it — the *maximally split Grammar* (Max Grammar) — can be derived and retrained on the training corpus. The set of points in the search space corresponds to the set of partitions of the Max Set. Search for an optimal grammar can thus be carried out directly in the partition space of the Max Grammar.

The finite search space can be given hierarchical structure as shown in Figure 1 for an example of a simple base nonterminal set {NP, VP, PP}, and a corpus which contains three different NPs, three different VPs and two different PPs.

At the top of the graph is the Max Set. The sets at the next level down (level 7) are created by merging pairs of nonterminals in the Max Set, and so on for subsequent levels. At the bottom is the *maximally merged nonterminal set* (Min Set) consisting of a single nonterminal NT. The original nonterminal set ends up somewhere in between the top and bottom (at level 3 in this example). The numbers to the right of the graph indicate the size of the nonterminal set and (in brackets) the number of different partitions at a given level.

While this search space definition results in a finite search space and obviates the expensive split operation, the space will still be vast for all but trivial corpora. In Section 17 below, alternative ways for defining the Max Set are described that result in much smaller search spaces.

3.3   Search Task and Evaluation Function

The input to the Partition Search procedure consists of a canonical grammar G_0, a base training corpus C, and a task-specific training corpus D^T (C and

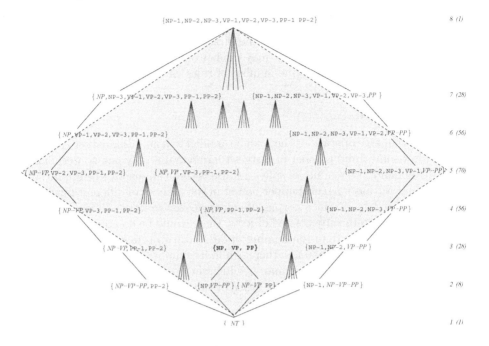

Fig. 1. Simple example of a partition search space.

D^T may be identical). G_0 and C are used to create the Max Grammar G. The **search task** can then be defined as follows:

> Given the maximally split PCFG $G = (W, N, N_S, R)$, a data set of sentences D, and a set of target parses D^T for D, find a partition Π_N of N that derives a grammar $G' = (W, \Pi_N, N_S, R')$, such that $|R'|$ is minimised, and $f(G', D, D^T)$ is maximised, where f scores the performance of G' on D as compared to D^T.

The size of the nonterminal set and hence of the grammar decreases from the top to the bottom of the search space. Therefore, if the partition space is searched top-down, grammar size is minimised automatically and does not need to be assessed explicitly.

In the current implementation, the **evaluation function** f simply calculates the F-Score achieved by a candidate grammar on D as compared to D^T. The F-Score is obtained by combining the standard evaluation metrics *Precision* and *Recall*, where Precision is the proportion of correct constituents that are identified, and Recall is the proportion identified constituents that are correct.

3.4   Search Algorithm

Since each point in the search space can be accessed directly by applying the corresponding nonterminal set partition to the Max Grammar, the search space can be searched in any direction by any search method using partitions to represent candidate grammars.

In the current version of the Partition Search algorithm (shown in pseudo-code representation in Procedure 1), a variant of beam search is used to search the partition space top down. A list of the n current best candidate partitions is maintained (initialised to the Max Set). For each of the n current best partitions a random subset of size b of its children in the hierarchy is generated and evaluated. From the union of current best partitions and the newly generated candidate partitions, the n best elements are selected and form the new current best set. This process is iterated until either no new partitions can be generated that are better than their parents, or the lowest level of the partition space is reached. In each iteration the size of the nonterminal set decreases by one.

The size of the search space grows exponentially with the size i of the Max Set. However, the complexity of the Partition Search algorithm is only $O(nbi)$, because only up to $n \times b$ partitions are evaluated in each of up to i iterations[12].

4 Building a Grammar for NP Extraction

This section describes experiments and results for an example application of Partition Search PCFG Learning to the task of building a grammar for noun phrase extraction (used in NLP applications such as information extraction) from a corpus of annotated text. Other applications and results are described in [2].

4.1 Experiment Set-Up

The objective was to start from a canonical grammar automatically derived from the Wall Street Journal Corpus (WSJC), to define a Max Grammar using information available in the same corpus, and then to find a new grammar by Partition Search that performs as well as possible on the task of NP identification.

Data: Sections 15–18 of WSJC were used for deriving the canonical grammar and as the base training corpus, and different randomly selected subsets of Section 1 from the same corpus were used as task-specific training corpora during search. Section 1 was also used as a testing set during the development of the Partition Search method, while Section 20 was used for final performance tests.

Parsing task: In *NP identification* the task is to identify in the input sentence all noun phrases[13], nested and otherwise, in the corresponding WSJC parse.

Evaluation: The Brill Tagger was used for POS tagging testing data, and achieved an average accuracy of 97.5%[14]. An existing parser[15] was used to obtain

---

[12] As before, n is the number of current best candidate solutions, b is the width of the beam, and i is the size of the Max Set.

[13] WSJC categories NP, NX, WHNP and NAC.

[14] The data was automatically POS tagged to make results comparable, in particular to those produced by the LCG Project [9] and for CoNLL Workshop shared tasks.

[15] LoPar [11] in its non-head-lexicalised mode. Available from http://www.ims.uni-st uttgart.de/projekte/gramotron/SOFTWARE/LoPar-en.html.

Procedure 1

PARTITION_SEARCH$\big((W, N, N_S, R), D, D^T, n, x, b\big)$

1: $Stop \leftarrow FALSE$
2: $P_{intermediate} \leftarrow$ INITIALISE(N)
3: EVALUATE$(P_{intermediate}, G, D, D^T, x)$
4: **while not** $Stop$ **do**
5:   $P_{current} \leftarrow$ SELECT$(P_{intermediate})$
6:   $P_{new} \leftarrow$ GENERATE$(P_{current}, b)$
7:   **if** $P_{new} = EMPTYLIST$ **then**
8:     $Stop \leftarrow TRUE$
9:   **else**
10:     $P_{intermediate} \leftarrow$ APPEND$(P_{current}, P_{new})$
11:     EVALUATE$(P_{intermediate}, G, D, D^T, x)$
12:   **end if**
13: **end while**
14: return $P_{current}$
15:
16: **Subprocedure** INITIALISE(N)
17: return set containing trivial partition of N
18:
19: **Subprocedure** SELECT$(P_{intermediate}, n)$
20: return n best elements from $P_{intermediate}$
21:
22: **Subprocedure** GENERATE$(P_{current}, b)$
23: $ReturnVal \leftarrow EMPTYLIST$
24: **for all** $p \in P_{current}$ **do**
25:   $List \leftarrow$ generate b random elements of $\big\{\Pi \mid \Pi$ is a partition of p and $|\Pi| = |p| - 1\big\}$
26:   $ReturnVal \leftarrow$ APPEND$(ReturnVal, List)$
27: **end for**
28: return $ReturnVal$
29:
30: **Subprocedure** EVALUATE$(P_{intermediate}, G, D, D^T, x)$
31: **for all** $p \in P_{intermediate}$ **do**
32:   $G' \leftarrow$ partition grammar G with p
33:   $D^A \leftarrow$ parse data D with G'
34:   score of p is F-Score of D^A against D^T
35: **end for**

Viterbi parses. If the parser failed to find a complete parse for a sentence, a simple grammar extension method was used to obtain partial parses instead (based on Schmid and Schulte im Walde [10, p. 728]). The `evalb` program by Sekine and Collins[16] was used to obtain Precision and Recall figures on parses.

Canonical grammar derivation: A simple treebank grammar[17] was derived from Sections 15–18 of the WSJC by converting brackets and their imme-

---

[16] http://cs.nyu.edu/cs/projects/proteus/evalb/.
[17] The term was coined by Charniak [4].

Max Grammar	Result type	Iter.	Eval.	F-Score (subset)	Grammar		F-Score	
					Rules	NTs	S 01	S 20
BARE	Max Grammar result	—	—	—	10,118	147	79.29	78.996
	Average	111.4	2,629	87.83	8,655	37.6	79.10	78.14
	Best size	113	2,679	86.14	8,374	36	78.90	78.06
	Best F-score S 01	114	2,694	90.25	8,541	41	79.51	78.16
	Best F-score S 20	114	2,667	86.88	8,627	35	79.08	78.29
PN	Max Grammar result	—	—	—	16,480	970	82.01	81.31
	Average	852.6	21,051	91.21	13,202.8	119.4	81.41	80.33
	Best size	909	22,474	91.88	12,513	63	80.98	80.22
	Best F-scores	658	16,286	89.57	15,305	314	**82.05**	**80.89**

Table 1. Partition Search results for NP identification task.

diate constituents into production rules and calculating their probabilities from their frequencies by Maximum Likelihood Estimation.

Parameters: All results were averaged over 5 runs differing only in random selection of the training data set. The algorithm parameters were training data set size $x = 50$, beam width $b = 5$, and size of current best set $n = 5$.

Max Grammar definition: Two different approaches to defining the Max Grammar were used. In the first, the canonical grammar BARE itself was used as the Max Grammar. This results in a very restrictive search space definition and amounts to optimising the canonical grammar in terms of size and performance on a given task without adding any information to it.

In the second approach, Local Structural Context [1] was used for defining the Max Grammar, resulting in grammar PN. Using Local Structural Context (LSC) means weakening the independence assumptions inherent in PCFGs by making the rules' expansion probabilities dependent on part of their immediate context. The LSC that was used here was parent phrase categories, where the parent of a phrase is the phrase that immediately contains it[18]. Thus, in the PN grammar, each nonterminal has a suffix indicating one of its possible parent phrase categories. For example, the two main parent phrase categories of the nonterminal NP (noun phrase) are S (sentence) and VP (verb phrase). It is the equivalent of making rule probabilities for NP productions dependent on whether the noun phrase is immediately contained in a sentence or in a verb phrase (this roughly corresponds to the subject/object distinction and probabilities can vary greatly between the two)[19].

4.2 NP Identification

Table 1 shows the complete set of results for Partition Search and the NP identification task. The first column shows the Max Grammar used in a given batch

---

[18] Several previous investigations have demonstrated improvement in parsing results due to the inclusion of parent phrase category information [3,6,12].

[19] More detail on this is given in [2].

of experiments. The second column indicates the type of result, where the Max Grammar result is grammar size, performance and F-Scores of the Max Grammar itself, and the remaining results are the average and single best results for size and F-Scores achieved by Partition Search. The third and fourth columns show the number of iterations and evaluations carried out during search. Columns 5–9 show details of the final solution grammars: column 5 shows the evaluation score on the training data, column 6 the number of rules, column 7 the number of nonterminals, and columns 8 and 9 the overall F-Score on Sections 1 and 20 respectively.

The relevant comparison is between the canonical grammar *BARE* and the best grammars learned by Partition Search. The best result (boldface) was an F-Score of 82.05% for Section 1 (the result for the canonical grammar was 79.29%), although it was accompanied by an increase in the number of rules from 10,118 to 15,305. This result improves grammar *BARE* by 3.48%.

The existing results cited for comparison below use Section 20 of the WSJC as a testing set. For NP identification, the canonical grammar *BARE* achieves an F-Score of 78.996 on this section, and Partition Search improves this to 80.89.

The following table shows how these results compare with existing results, all of which are reported by Nerbonne et al. [9, p. 103].

	NP identification
Chunk Tag Baseline	67.56
Grammar *BARE* (S 20)	78.996
Current best nonlexicalised	80.15
Best S 20 PS result (PN)	**80.89**
Current best lexicalised	83.79

The chunk tag baseline F-Score is obtained by tagging each POS tag in a sentence with its most frequent chunk tag, which is a standard baseline for tasks like this one[20]. The best lexicalised result was achieved with a cascade of memory-based learners. The nonlexicalised result was for a treebank grammar with LSC. The best Partition Search result for this task lags behind the best lexicalised result, which is not surprising as the improvements in parsing due to lexicalisation are well-known.

5   Conclusions

This paper described Partition Search PCFG Learning, a grammatical inference method for building, adapting and optimising grammars for natural languages, also providing theoretical background and a characterisation of the family of GI methods that Partition Search PCFG Learning belongs to. An example application was described where Partition Search PCFG Learning was successfully applied to the task of building a grammar for noun phrase extraction from a corpus of annotated English text.

---

[20] Chunk tags may correspond e.g. to the beginning/end/inside/outside of an NP.

Partition Search PCFG Learning has a wide range of possible applications, to grammar adaptation and optimisation as well as grammar building. Future research will look at adding lexicalisation to grammars built from annotated corpora, and parameter optimisation for beam search and training data set size. A related project will look at building grammars from unlabelled annotations, where the set of nonterminals (word and phrase categories) also needs to be inferred.

6   Acknowledgements

The research reported in this paper was in part funded under the European Union's TMR programme (Grant No. ERBFMRXCT980237).

References

1. A. Belz. 2001. Optimising corpus-derived probabilistic grammars. In *Proceedings of Corpus Linguistics 2001*, pages 46–57.
2. A. Belz. 2002. Learning Grammars for Different Parsing Tasks by Partition Search. To appear in *Proceedings of COLING 2002*.
3. E. Charniak and G. Carroll. 1994. Context-sensitive statistics for improved grammatical language models. Technical Report CS-94-07, Department of Computer Science, Brown University.
4. E. Charniak. 1996. Tree-bank grammars. Technical Report CS-96-02, Department of Computer Science, Brown University.
5. , E. M. Gold. 1967. Language Identification in the Limit. *Information and Control*, 10:447–474.
6. M. Johnson. 1998. PCFG models of linguistic tree representations. *Computational Linguistics*, 24(4):613–632.
7. A. J. Korenjak. 1969. A practical method for constructing LR(k) processors. *Communications of the ACM*, 12(11).
8. Po Chui Luk, Helen Meng, and Fuliang Weng. 2000. Grammar partitioning and parser composition for natural langugage understanding. In *Proceedings of ICSLP 2000*.
9. J. Nerbonne, A. Belz, N. Cancedda, H. Déjean, J. Hammerton, R. Koeling, S. Konstantopoulos, M. Osborne, F. Thollard, and E. Tjong Kim Sang. 2001. Learning computational grammars. In *Proceedings of CoNLL 2001*, pages 97–104.
10. H. Schmid and S. Schulte Im Walde. 2000. Robust German noun chunking with a probabilistic context-free grammar. In *Proceedings of COLING 2000*, pages 726–732.
11. H. Schmid. 2000. LoPar: Design and implementation. Bericht des Sonderforschungsbereiches "Sprachtheoretische Grundlagen für die Computerlinguistik" 149, Institute for Computational Linguistics, University of Stuttgart.
12. J. Luis Verdú-Mas, J. Calera-Rubio, and R. C. Carrasco. 2000. A comparison of PCFG models. In *Proceedings of CoNLL-2000 and LLL-2000*, pages 123–125.
13. F. L. Weng and A. Stolcke. 1995. Partitioning grammars and composing parsers. In *Proceedings of the 4th International Workshop on Parsing Technologies*.
14. J. G. Wolff. 1982. Language Acquisition, Data Compression and Generalization. In *Language and Communication*, 2(1):57–89.

Inferring Subclasses of Regular Languages Faster Using *RPNI* and Forbidden Configurations*

Antonio Cano, José Ruiz, and Pedro García

Depto. de Sistemas Informáticos y Computación.
Universidad Politécnica de Valencia. Valencia (Spain).
{acano,jruiz,pgarcia}@dsic.upv.es

Abstract. Many varieties of regular languages have characterizations in terms of forbidden-patterns of their accepting finite automata. The use of patterns while inferring languages belonging to those families through the *RPNI*-Lang algorithm help to avoid overgeneralization in the same way as negative samples do. The aim of this paper is to describe and prove the convergence of a modification of the *RPNI*-Lang algorithm that we call *FCRPNI*. Preliminary experiments done seem to show that the convergence when we use *FCRPNI* for some subfamilies of regular languages is achieved faster than when we use just the *RPNI* algorithm.

Keywords: Variety of languages, grammatical inference, forbidden configurations.

1 Introduction

Finite automata identification from positive and negative samples is a solved problem in automata theory. If we exclude the general enumeration algorithm there are two constructive algorithms that identify any deterministic finite automaton in deterministic polynomial time.

The first one (*TBG*) is due to Trakhtenbrot and Barzdin [21] by one hand and Gold [10] by the other and the second is due to Oncina and García (*RPNI*) [16] and to Lang [14]. This later algorithm behaves better than *TBG* does [7] as it makes better use of the information contained in the data and thus the convergence is achieved more rapidly.

Even so, the convergence is still slow, which restricts the use of this algorithm in real learning tasks. Several approaches have been proposed aiming to overcome this difficulty. If we exclude the probabilistic approaches [20], [3] and we remain in the classical model of identification in the limit, most of the proposals consist in the modification of *RPNI*-Lang algorithm by means of introducing heuristics that modify the order of merging states from the prefix tree acceptor [11], [15], [5].

The theoretical interest of those approaches is somehow relative as they usually do not guarantee the identification in the limit and then the inferred languages can not be characterized.

---

* Work partially supported by the Spanish CICYT under contract TIC2000-1153

P. Adriaans, H. Fernau, and M. van Zaanen (Eds.): ICGI 2002, LNAI 2484, pp. 28–36, 2002.

The situation today with respect to the inference from positive and negative samples is similar to the situation existing with the inference from only positive samples in the 80's. The distinction between heuristic and characterizable methods [1] opened new possibilities of research [2], [8], [18] etc. Angluin's proposal can be summarized as follows: as the family of regular languages is not identifiable with the use of only positive samples, let us find subclasses which are identifiable in this way and let us propose algorithms for them.

Coming back to inference from complete presentation we can postulate the following question: if we restrict ourselves to the inference of subclasses of regular languages, can we speed up the convergence without dropping the requisite of identification? The starting point of our proposal is to answer positively to this question, it seems that if we restrict the searching space, the identification process will need less information to converge.

Research in language theory has been fruitful in the discovery of subclasses of the regular languages family. The concept of variety of regular languages (also known as pseudovariety), that is, a class of regular languages closed under boolean operations, inverse morphisms and quotients, and its one to one correspondence with the algebraic concept of pseudovariety of semigroups (monoids) [6] can be useful in grammatical inference.

There exist many varieties of languages which are decidable, meaning that given a DFA that recognizes a language, its membership to a certain variety can be decided. Among the decidable varieties we have the well known families of finite and cofinite languages, definite, reverse definite and generalized definite languages, locally testable and piecewise testable languages, star free languages, (see [6] or [17]) etc. Note that neither of those families are identifiable from only positive samples. Whithout considering now facts about the complexity of the algorithms for each particular situation, the decidability of those families permit a simple modification of the $RPNI$-Lang algorithm: each time that this algorithm tries a merge, besides the usual considerations we have to make sure that the resulting automaton (the language) can still belong to the variety to which we have restricted the inference.

The work we present here wants to be the beginning of a research in order to study the influence that restrictions in the learning domain may have in regular language inference from positive and negative data. We have paid no attention to to the time complexity of the proposed method. It is obvious that this complexity will depend on the variety under study and, in fact, there will be varieties for which this method could not be applied for complexity reasons. We describe the method and prove it converges. The experimental results are very limited and they are restricted to two examples of varieties, the families of star-free and piecewise testable languages.

2   Definitions and Notation

In this section we will describe some facts about semigroups and formal languages in order to make the notation understandable to the reader. For further details about the definitions, the reader is referred to [12] (formal languages) and to [6] and [17] (varieties of finite semigroups).

2.1   Automata, Languages, and Semigroups

Throughout this paper Σ will denote a finite alphabet and Σ^* will be the free monoid generated by Σ with concatenation as the internal law and λ as neutral element. A *language* L over Σ is a subset of Σ^*. The elements of L are called *words*. Given $x \in \Sigma^*$, if $x = uv$ with $u, v \in \Sigma^*$, then u (resp. v) is called *prefix* (resp. *suffix*) of x.

A deterministic finite automaton (DFA) is a quintuple $A = (Q, \Sigma, \cdot, q_0, F)$ where Q is a finite set of states, Σ is a finite alphabet, $q_0 \in Q$ is the initial state, $F \subseteq Q$ is the set of final states and $\cdot$ is a partial function that maps $Q \times \Sigma$ in Q, which can be easily extended to words. A word x is accepted by an automaton A if $q_0 \cdot x \in F$. The set of words accepted by A is denoted by $L(A)$.

Given an automaton A, $\forall a \in \Sigma$, we can define the function $a^A : Q \to Q$ as $qa^A = q \cdot a$, $\forall q \in Q$. For $x \in \Sigma^*$, the function $x^A : Q \to Q$ is defined inductively: λ^A is the identity on Q and $(xa)^A = x^A a^A$, $\forall a \in \Sigma$. Clearly, $\forall x, y \in \Sigma^*$, $(xy)^A = (x)^A (y)^A$. The set $\{a^A : a \in \Sigma\}$ is denoted by M_A. The set of functions $\{x^A : x \in \Sigma^+\}$ is a finite semigroup under the operation of composition of functions, and is denoted as S_A and called *semigroup of* A.

A Moore machine is a 6-tuple $M = (Q, \Sigma, \Gamma, \cdot, q_0, \Phi)$, where Σ (resp. Γ) is the input (resp. output) alphabet, $\cdot$ is a partial function that maps $Q \times \Sigma$ in Q and Φ is a function that maps Q in Γ called *output function*. The behavior of M is given by the partial function $t_M : \Sigma^* \to \Gamma$ defined as $t_M(x) = \Phi(q_0 \cdot x)$ for every $x \in \Sigma^*$ such that $q_0 \cdot x$ is defined.

Given two finite sets of words D_+ and D_-, we define the (D_+, D_-)-*prefix Moore machine* $(PTM(D_+, D_-))$ as the Moore machine having $\Gamma = \{0, 1, \uparrow\}$, $Q = \Pr(D_+ \cup D_-)$, $q_0 = \lambda$ and $u \cdot a = ua$ if $u, ua \in Q$ and $a \in \Sigma$. For every state u, the value of the output function associated to u is 1, 0 or $\uparrow$ (undefined) depending whether u belongs to D_+, to D_- or to the complementary set of $D_+ \cup D_-$.

A Moore machine $M = (Q, \Sigma, \{0, 1, \uparrow\}, \delta, q_0, \Phi)$ is *consistent* with (D_+, D_-) if $\forall x \in D_+$ we have $\Phi(q_0 \cdot x) = 1$ and $\forall x \in D_-$ we have $\Phi(q_0 \cdot x) = 0$.

2.2   Varieties of Finite Semigroups and Languages

A *finite semigroup* (resp. *monoid*) is a couple formed from a finite set and an internal associative operation (resp. that has a neutral element).

For every $L \subseteq \Sigma^*$, the congruence $\sim_L$ defined as $x \sim_L y \Leftrightarrow (\forall u, v \in \Sigma^*, uxv \in L \Leftrightarrow uyv \in L)$, is called the *syntactic congruence* of L and it is the coarsest congruence that saturates L. $\Sigma^* / \sim_L$ is called the *syntactic monoid of* L and is denoted as $S(L)$. The morphism $\varphi : \Sigma^* \to S(L)$, that maps each word to its equivalence class modulo $\sim_L$ is called the *syntactic morphism* of L.

A *variety of finite monoids* (also denoted as *pseudovariety*) is a class of finite monoids closed under morphic images, submonoids and finite direct products.

A *variety of recognizable languages* is a class of languages closed under finite union and intersection, complement, inverse morphisms and right and left quotients. Eilenberg [6] proved that varieties of finite monoids and varieties of languages are in one-to-one correspondence. If **V** is a variety of semigroups, we denote as $\mathcal{L}_V(\Sigma^*)$ the variety of languages over Σ whose syntactic semigroups lie in **V**.

Some instances of this correspondence that will be used throughout this paper are the relations between:

- The variety of locally testable languages and the variety of locally idempotent and commutative semigroups.
- The variety of piecewise testable languages and the variety of J-trivial semigroups.
- The variety of star-free languages and the variety of aperiodic semigroups.

2.3   Forbidden Configurations

Given an automaton $A = (Q, \Sigma, \cdot, q_0, F)$, the set of all paths in A defines an infinite labelled graph $G(A)$ where the set of vertices is Q and the set of edges is $\{(q, w, q \cdot w) : q \in Q, w \in \Sigma^+\}$. A labelled subgraph $\mathbb{P}$ of $G(A)$ is said to be a configuration, or a pattern, present in A.

The forbidden-pattern characterizations have been developed in the study of the relations between logic and formal languages. They are results of the following type: "A language L belongs to a class $\mathcal{C}$ if and only if the accepting finite automaton does not have subgraph $\mathbb{P}$ in its transition graph". Usually, forbidden-pattern characterizations imply the decidability of the characterized class, since we only have to test whether the forbidden-pattern occurs in an automaton.

For many varieties of regular languages the forbidden-pattern characterization is well known, but for others the question remains open, for example it can be shown that the semigroup of a (minimal) deterministic automaton A is idempotent if and only if there exist no configuration of A of the form depicted in figure 1, where $x \in \Sigma^+$ and $p \neq q$.

Fig. 1. Forbidden configuration for an automaton whose semigroup is idempotent

Forbidden-pattern characterization for several varieties of languages can be found in [4], [9] and [19].

3   A Description of the *FCRPNI* Algorithm

We suppose that the reader is familiar with $RPNI$-Lang algorithm [16], [14]. The version we use presents $DFAs$ as Moore machines with output belonging to the set $\{0, 1, \uparrow\}$. Any word x such that $\Phi(q_0 \cdot x) = 0$ (resp. 1) (resp.$\uparrow$) is considered negative (resp. positive) (resp. not defined). The only changes that our algorithm makes with respect to $RPNI$-Lang algorithm is that before we definitively merge two states, we test if the resulting automaton can still belong to the considered variety. This is done by looking for possible forbidden configurations in the stable part of the automaton. In the sequel, the modification we propose will be denoted as $FCRPNI$ (Forbidden Patterns $RPNI$).

Merging two states in $RPNI$-Lang algorithm possibly makes some other states to be merged in order to guarantee the determinism of the automaton. Then this automaton is tested for consistency with the data (a state can not be positive and negative) and if it is not consistent we have to undo the merging.

Besides that test, $FCRPNI$ has to establish that the current automaton can still belong to the variety to be learned. This is done by testing whether the forbidden-patterns occur in the consolidated part of the automaton.

The following example illustrates the diferences between $RPNI$-Lang and $FCRPNI$ algorithms, we restrict ourselves to the variety of star-free languages. We recall that a language is star-free if and only if the minimal automaton that recognizes it is permutation-free[1].

Example 1. Let $L = aa^*$ (which is star-free) and let $D_+ = \{a, aaa\}$ and $D_- = \{\lambda\}$. The prefix tree acceptor is represented in Figure 2

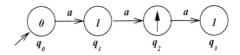

Fig. 2. Prefix Moore machine for the sample $D_+ = \{a, aaa\}$ and $D_- = \{\lambda\}$.

$RPNI$-Lang tries to merge q_0 and q_1 but the consistency test fails. In the following step it tries to merge q_0 and q_2 which implies the merging of q_1 and q_3. The result is depicted in Figure 3.

As every state in the prefix Moore machine has been considered, the algorithm finishes. We see that the input was not enough to learn aa^*.

$FCRPNI$ with the restriction to star-free languages procceds in the same way but as the automaton depicted in Figure 3 fails in the test of forbidden patterns for star-free languages, it can not merge states q_0 and q_2. The following step is to try to merge q_1 and q_2 which implies the merging of q_1 and q_3. The final result is the automaton represented in figure 4.

---

[1] An automaton has a permutation if there exists a subset $P \subseteq Q$ and a word x such that $P \cdot x = P$, where $P \cdot x = \cup_{p \in P} p \cdot x$

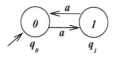

Fig. 3. DFA output by $RPNI$ algorithm on input of $D_+ = \{a, aaa\}$ and $D_- = \{\lambda\}$.

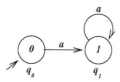

Fig. 4. DFA output by $FCRPNI$ algorithm on input of $D_+ = \{a, aaa\}$ and $D_- = \{\lambda\}$.

3.1   Convergence of $FCRPNI$ Algorithm

Fact. Let $L \in \mathcal{L}_V(\Sigma^*)$ be the target language and let $D_+ \cup D_-$ a complete sample for the inference of language L using $RPNI$-Lang algorithm. At every step this algorithm outputs a finite automaton with no forbidden configurations as those forbidden patterns may only appear in consolidated part of the automaton and that subautomaton remains stable during the rest of the process.

Proposition 1. $FCRPNI$ algorithm identifies any variety $\mathcal{L}_V(\Sigma^*)$ from a complete presentation in the limit.

Proof. Let $L \in \mathcal{L}_V(\Sigma^*)$ be the target language. If the samples used for inference contain a characteristic sample of L for the $RPNI$-Lang algorithm, no forbidden configuration can appear in the stable part of the automaton during the process of inference, and $FCRPNI$ algorithm behaves in the same way as $RPNI$-Lang algorithm does and thus, it identifies the language L.

Proposition 2. Let $L \in \mathcal{L}_V(\Sigma^*)$ be the target language and let $D_+ \cup D_-$ an arbitrary sample such that when it is used as input for the $RPNI$-Lang algorithm, it outputs the canonical acceptor for L. Then $FCRPNI$ algorithm outputs the same automaton.

Proof. It is obvious that if $RPNI$-Lang algorithm enters in a forbidden configuration it will not identify language L.

Propositions 2 and 3 show in theory that if we restrict the identification to varieties of regular languages, $FCRPNI$ algorithm works somehow better than $RPNI$-Lang does. It is clear that there are situations in which the former converges whereas the later does not (see example 1). The cost is that we have to check for forbidden configurations, so only a complete set of experiments will allow us to quantify the differences.

4   Experimental Results

We have done some small experiments in order to compare the behavior of $RPNI$ and $FCRPNI$ for two varieties of formal languages, the variety of piecewise testable languages and the variety of star-free languages.

Description of the experiments:

- We work with minimal automata having 5 states, the alphabet is $\Sigma = \{a, b\}$. Each of them recognizes either a piecewise testable language or a star-free one. We obtain them beginning with larger automata, we then minimize them and discard the automata which do not have the required size. Afterwards we calculate the transformation semigroup of each automaton and discard the ones that does not belong to the required class.
- For the learning process we use randomly generated strings of length less than or equal to 10 over Σ. The number of them is shown in the tables that describe the results of the experiments.
- The comparison of the obtained automata is done using all the words of length less than or equal to 15 not used in the learning process.
- We have done 200 experiments for each different types of languages.

Table 1 (resp. Table 2) shows the mean of the error rate (percentage of words not correctly classified) in terms of the number of words used in the learning process when $RPNI$-Lang and $FCRPNI$ are used for inference of piecewise testable (resp. star-free) languages.

Number of samples used for inference	20	40	60	80	100
error rate of $RPNI$-Lang	12,12	3,42	2,00	0,93	0,77
error rate of $FCRPNI$	9,73	2,57	0,62	0,26	0,11

Table 1. Mean of the error rate when of $RPNI$ and $FCRPNI$ are used for the inference of piecewise testable languages in terms of the number of words used in the learning process

Number of samples used for inference	20	40	60	80	100
error rate of $RPNI$-Lang	8,10	1,63	0,75	0,28	0,24
error rate of $FCRPNI$	7,11	1,23	0,38	0,13	0,12

Table 2. Mean of the error rate when of $RPNI$ and $FCRPNI$ are used for the inference of star-free languages in terms of the number of words used in the learning process

5 Conclusions and Future Work

We have described $FCRPNI$, a modification of $RPNI$-Lang algorithm aiming to show how the restriction of the learning domain to certain well characterized subclasses of the family regular languages affects to the convergence.

We have proved that if $RPNI$-Lang algorithm has been given enough samples to converge, so does $FCRPNI$. Then, this later algorithm converges faster than the former one at the cost of:

- Restrict the domain of the inference process.
- The additional cost of having to do the forbidden-pattern tests.

We have done some preliminary experiments for two varieties of languages, the aperiodic and the piecewise testable. Although the error rates for $FCRPNI$ are better in both cases, as the size of the automata we have used is very small, we can not be conclusive about how much better they are.

As future work we should make efficient algorithms for some of the varieties for which it is possible and we should make a complete experimentation to measure how both algorithms behave.

References

1. Angluin, D. *Inductive Inference of Formal Languages from Positive Data*. Inform and Control, pp. 117-135 (1980).
2. Angluin, D. *Inference of Reversible Languages*. Journal of the ACM, Vol 29-3. pp. 741-765 (1982).
3. Carrasco, R. and Oncina, J. *Learning Stochastic Regular Grammars by means of a State Merging Method*. In Grammatical Inference and Applications. R. Carrasco and J. Oncina (Eds.). LNAI 862. Springer-Verlag, pp. 139-152 (1994).
4. Cohen, J. Perrin D. and Pin J-E. *On the expressive power of temporal logic*. Journal of computer and System Sciences 46, pp 271-294 (1993).
5. Coste, F. and Nicolas J. *How considering Incompatible State Mergings May Reduce the DFA induction Search Tree*. In Grammatical Inference. V. Honavar and G. Slutzki (Eds.) LNAI 1433. Springer-Verlag, pp 199-210 (1998).
6. Eilenberg, S. Automata, Languages and Machines, Vol A and B (Academic Press, 1976)
7. García, P. Cano, A. and Ruiz, J. *A comparative study of two algorithms for automata identification*. In Grammatical Inference: Algorithms and Applications. A.L. Oliveira (Ed.) LNAI 189. Springer-Verlag, pp. 115-126 (2000).
8. García P. and Vidal E. *Inference of k-Testable languages in the Stric Sense and Applications to Syntactic Pattern Recognition*. IEEE Transactions on Pattern Analysis and Machine Intelligence 12/9, pp 920-925 (1990).
9. Glaβer, C. *Forbidden-Patterns and Word Extensions for Concatenation Hierarchies*. Ph dissertation, Würzburg University, Germany, 2001.
10. Gold , M. *Complexity of Automaton Identification from Given Data*. Information and Control 37, pp 302-320 (1978).
11. de la Higuera, C. Oncina, J. and Vidal, E. *Data dependant vs data independant algorithms*. In Grammatical Inference: Learning Syntax from Sentences. L. Miclet and C. de la Higuera (Eds.). LNAI 1147. Springer-Verlag, pp. 313-325 (1996).

12. Hopcroft, J. and Ullman, J. *Introduction to Automata Theory, Languages and Computation.* Addison-Wesley (1979).
13. Juillé , H. and Pollack J. *A Stochastic Search Approach to Grammar Induction.* In Grammatical Inference. V. Honavar and G. Slutzki (Eds.) LNAI 1433. Springer-Verlag, pp 126-137 (1998).
14. Lang , K.J. *Random DFA's can be Approximately Learned from Sparse Uniform Examples.* In Proceedings of the Fifth Annual ACM Workshop on Computational Learning Theory, pp 45-52. (1992).
15. Lang , K.J., Pearlmutter B.A. and Price R.A. *Results on the Abbadingo One DFA Learning Competition and a New Evidence-Driven State Merging Algorithm.* In Grammatical Inference. V. Honavar and G. Slutzki (Eds.) LNAI 1433. Springer-Verlag, pp 1-12 (1998).
16. Oncina, J. and García, P. *Inferring Regular Languages in Polynomial Updated Time.* In Pattern Recognition and Image Analysys. Pérez de la Blanca, Sanfeliú and Vidal (Eds.) World Scientific. (1992).
17. Pin, J. *Varieties of formal languages.* Plenum. (1986).
18. Ruiz, J. and García, P. *Learning k-piecewise testable languages from positive data.* In Grammatical Inference: Learning Syntax from Sentences. L. Miclet and C. de la Higuera (Eds.). LNAI 1147. Springer-Verlag, pp. 203-210 (1996).
19. Schmitz, H. *The Forbidden-Pattern approach to Concatenation Hierarchies.* Ph dissertation, Würzburg University, Germany, 2001.
20. Stolcke, A. and Omohundro, S. *Inducing Probabilistic Grammars by Bayesian Model Merging.* In Grammatical Inference and Applications. R. Carrasco and J. Oncina (Eds.). LNAI 862. Springer-Verlag, pp. 106-118 (1994).
21. Trakhtenbrot B. and Barzdin Ya. *Finite Automata: Behavior and Synthesis.* North Holland Publishing Company. (1973).
22. Vidal, E. and Llorens, S. *Using Knowledge to improve N-Gram Language Modelling through the MGGI Methodology.* In Grammatical Inference: Learning Syntax from Sentences. L. Miclet and C. de la Higuera (Eds.). LNAI 1147. Springer-Verlag, pp. 179-190 (1996).

Beyond EDSM

Orlando Cicchello and Stefan C. Kremer*

Guelph Natural Computation Group
Dept. of Computing and Information Science
University of Guelph
Guelph, ON   N1G 2W1
CANADA
{ocicchel,skremer}@uoguelph.ca

Abstract. In this paper, we analyze the effectiveness of a leading finite state automaton (FSA) induction algorithm, windowed evidence driven state merging (W-EDSM). W-EDSM generates small automata that correctly label a given set of positive and a given set of negative example strings defined by a regular (Type 3) language. In particular, W-EDSM builds a prefix tree for the exemplars which is then collapsed into a FSA. This is done by selecting nodes to merge based on a simple heuristic until no more merges are possible. Our experimental results show that the heuristic used works well for later merges, but not very well for early merges. Based on this observation, we are able to make a small modification to W-EDSM which improves the performance of the algorithm by 27% and suggest other avenues for futher enhancement.

1   Introdrtion

In this paper, we are interested in inducing a finite state automaton that accepts a regular (Type 3) language [1] given a finite number of positive and negative example strings drawn from that language. The finite number of exemplars differentiates this problem from Gold's language identification in the limit [2]. In fact, our problem never has a single correct solution since no finite set of exemplars can uniquely identify any one particular automaton. In order to resolve this, we require an inductive bias to allow us to select the most probably correct automaton.

Without domain specific knowledge, we must rely on Occam's razor [3], which favours the simplest or smallest solution to a given problem. In the context of automaton induction, we define this to mean the automaton with the smallest number of states. Thus, our original problem can be redefined formally as:

Given an alphabet Σ, a set of positive examples S_+, and a set of negative examples S_- for some unknown language L, such that $S_+ \subset L \subset \Sigma^*$ and $S_- \subset L' \subset \Sigma^*$, construct a FSA ($A$) with the least number of states possible such that the automaton accepts S_+ and rejects S_-.

---

* To whom correspondence should be addressed.

P. Adriaans, H. Fernau, and M. van Zaanen (Eds.): ICGI 2002, LNAI 2484, pp. 37–48, 2002.
© Springer-Verlag Berlin Heidelberg 2002

Only Type 3 languages are considered for the above problem since the languages that they generate are precisely the sets accepted by finite state automata [1].

To simplify matters, the problem domain is further restricted to only consist of Type 3 languages on the alphabet $\Sigma = \{0, 1\}$, though there is no reason why other alphabets could not be used.

A target FSA representing such grammars is a quintuple $A = \{Q, \Sigma, \delta, s, F\}$ where Q is a finite non-empty set of states, $\delta : Q \times \Sigma \rightarrow Q$ is the transition function, $s \in Q$ is the start state, and F is the set of the final states or accepting states. It is now easy to construct an automaton that accepts S_+ and rejects S_-, by creating an Augmented Prefix Tree Acceptor (APTA). This is done by starting with an automaton with a single start node and then adding or following the transitions for each string in turn adding nodes as necessary. When a string terminates, the final state is labelled *accepting* or *rejecting* depending on whether the string was legal or illegal. This will result in a tree with some unlabelled state nodes and many missing transitions (particularly at the leaves of the tree).

As an example, consider sets $S_+ = \{1, 110, 01, 001\}$ and $S_- = \{00, 10, 000\}$. The APTA with respect to S_+ and S_- is illustrated in Figure 1. Each node within the APTA is assigned one of three labels. All paths that start from the root of the tree and end on a node with an accepting label, a rejecting label, or an unknown label represent elements of S_+, S_-, and $S_{tot}/(S_+ \cup S_-)$, respectively. S_{tot} is the set of all prefixes of strings in $S_+ \cup S_-$ but not themselves in $S_+ \cup S_-$.

It is then possible to assign any labels to the remaining unlabelled nodes, and insert transitions to any state for the missing transitions to create a finite state automaton which labels all positive and negative example strings correctly. While this automaton could then be minimized with Moore's algorithm, each arbitrary assignment of labels and transitions will yield a different minimized automaton. Unfortunately, searching over all possible state labellings and missing transition assignments for the minimal resulting automaton is an exponential algorithm.

Instead, we must directly reduce the prefix tree acceptor. The problem of inferring unknown FSA from example sets S_+ and S_- can then be reduced to simply contracting the APTA by merging nodes to directly obtain the target FSA. In other words, a FSA can be obtained by selecting the appropriate order for merging pairs of equivalent nodes within the APTA. To clarify what is implied by equivalent nodes the following definition has been included.

Two nodes q_i and q_j in the APTA are considered not equivalent if and only if:

1. $(q_i \in F_+$ and $q_j \in F_-)$ or $(q_i \in F_-$ and $q_j \in F_+)$, or
2. $\exists s \in \Sigma$ if $\delta(q_i, s)$ not equivalent to $\delta(q_j, s)$

Such constraints maintain the property of determinism for the hypothesis FSA. For instance, this guarantees that each state within the hypothesis will have at most, one transition defined for each element of Σ and that the hypothesis FSA is consistent with S_+ and S_-.

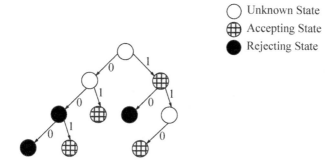

Fig. 1. An incompletely labelled APTA of depth 3, representing sets $S_+ = \{1, 110, 01, 001\}$ and $S_- = \{00, 10, 000\}$. Note that the label associated with an example string of length 0 is the label assigned to the root node. Hence, in this example, it is unknown whether a string of length zero is accepted or rejected by the unknown target FSA.

2   History

An algorithm initially designed for dealing with completely labelled data sets was proposed several years ago by Trakhtenbrot and Barzdin [4]. The algorithm is guaranteed to produce a Moore-Minimized FSA, in polynomial time, for any language for which it obtains the complete data set. A slight modification to the algorithm, first introduced by [5], resulted in an algorithm (Traxbar) that can deal with incomplete data sets as well as complete data sets. Of course, this has had a great impact on the rule induction community since languages of infinite size become learnable. In fact, [5] has shown empirically that the average case is tractable. In other words, randomly generated FSA can be approximately learned[1] from sparse uniform examples within polynomial time. In addition to rekindling interest in the area of rule induction, this has also lead to new algorithms for a specific class of problems.

In 1997 Kevin J. Lang and Barak A. Pearlmutter held a FSA learning competition. The competition presented the challenge of predicting, with 99% accuracy, the labels which an unseen FSA would assign to test data given training data consisting of positive and negative examples. As described by [6], there were 3 main goals of the competition. The first of which was to promote the development of new and better algorithms. The second goal of the competition was to present to the machine learning community, problems which lie beyond proven bounds with respect to sparseness of the training data and to collect data regarding the performance of various algorithms on such problems. Finally, the third

---

[1] FSA where considered approximately learned when 99% or greater of the test data, t_e, was correctly classified. Here, t_e was defined as the set of all strings of a given length not including the training data $(S_+ \cup S_-)$.

main goal of the competition was to provide a consistent means of comparing the effectiveness of new and existing algorithms for learning FSA.

The competition consisted of 16 problems in total, 4 of which where for practice and had been previously solved by the Traxbar algorithm and the remaining 12 which where the official challenge problems. It was organized along two dimensions (Table 1): the density of the training set and the target FSA size. Problems with a sparse density are more difficult because there will be a larger number of unlabelled nodes and missing transitions in the APTA. This results in a larger number of free parameters for the minimization problem. Similarly larger FSA also make the problem more difficult, since there are more states that need to be merged.

Table 1. The two-dimensional problem grid for the *Abbadingo* competition. The first number indicates the number of strings in the training set, while the second number is the number of states in the (otherwise) unknown target automaton.

		training set coverage			
		dense			sparse
target	small	4456, 61	3478, 63	2499, 68	1521, 65
FSA		13894, 119	10723, 138	7553, 130	4382, 125
size		36992, 247	28413, 247	19834, 262	11255, 267
	large	115000, 498	87500, 499	60000, 506	32500, 519

There were two winners of the *Abbadingo One Learning Competition*: Rodney Price, for solving the 60,000-string, 506-state problem; and, Hugues Juillé for solving the 1521-string, 65 state problem. Price was able to win the *Abbadingo One Learning Competition* by using an evidence driven state merging (EDSM) algorithm which is the basis for the analysis contained in this paper. Essentially, Price realized that an effective way of choosing which pair of nodes to merge next within the APTA would simply involve selecting the pair of nodes whose subtrees share the most similar labels. A post-competition version of the EDSM algorithm as described by [6] is included below:

1. Evaluate all possible pairings of nodes within the APTA.
2. Merge the pair of nodes which has the highest calculated score.
3. Repeat the steps above until no other nodes within the APTA can be merged.

3   EDSM Is Not Perfect

The general idea of the EDSM approach to merge pair selection is to avoid bad merges by selecting the pair of nodes within the APTA which has the highest correctness heuristic [6]. Unfortunately, the difficulty of detecting bad merge choices increases as the density of the training data decreases, since the number of labelled nodes decreases within the APTA as the training data becomes more sparse. Thus, the idea of selecting merge pairs based on the highest score proves less effective.

Unlike the Traxbar algorithm introduced earlier, the EDSM approach for FSA learning relies on the training data to select it's merge order. The order in which nodes are merged is directly dependant on the number of matched labels within the subtrees rooted at each node. By contrast, the Traxbar algorithm attempts to merge nodes in a predefined (breadth-first) order with no regard to the evidence available in the training data. Different merge orders result in a trade-off of accuracy for simplicity and fast performance. Performance is the biggest disadvantage to the EDSM approach in that it is not very practical for large problems. Considering every potential merge pair at each stage of the inference process is computationally expensive and very time consuming.

It is conjectured that a tight upper bound on the running time for the EDSM approach is closer to m^3n than to m^4n, where m is the number of nodes in the APTA and n is the number of nodes in the final hypothesis [6]. To improve the running time of the EDSM algorithm, Lang et al. suggest only considering those nodes that lie within a fixed sized window from the root node of the APTA for merging. The idea is incorporated in the following pseudocode.

1. In breadth first order, create a window of nodes starting from the root of the APTA. The recommended size of the window is twice the size of the target FSA.
2. Evaluate all possible merge pairs within the window. Ties are broken randomly.
3. Merge the pair of nodes which has the highest calculated score.
4. If the merge reduces the size of the window, in breadth first order, include the number of nodes needed to regain a window of size twice the target FSA.
5. If a merge is not possible within the given window, increase the size of the window by a factor of 2.
6. Terminate when no merges are possible.

As should be expected, the running time of the windowed EDSM algorithm (W-EDSM) is better than its full-width counterpart. The improvement in the running time is due to the reduction of the search space at each merge step of the algorithm. Of course, this can hurt the performance of the algorithm in that relatively rare, high-scoring merges involving deep nodes may be excluded from the window [6]. This of course, presents the task of selecting the correct set of nodes to be included within the window. Similar to Traxbar, nodes are included within the window based on a breadth-first order. Unfortunately, this selection process does not include nodes based on the evidence within the training data, hence, limiting the success of the algorithm to problems that favour windows which grow in breadth-first order. Another disadvantage with W-EDSM is that the recommended window size is dependant upon the size of the target FSA. If the size of the target FSA is not known then this could be a problem.

By contrast, the inference engine used by Hugues Juillé is vastly different from the algorithms discussed thus far. The algorithm is based on a Self-Adaptive

Greedy Estimate search procedure (SAGE). Each iteration of the search procedure is composed of two phases, a *construction phase* and a *competition phase*.

It is in the *construction phase* where the list of alternatives or merge choices is determined. All the alternatives in the list have the same depth within the search tree. Each member of a population of processing elements is then assigned one alternative from the list. Each processing element then scores its assigned alternative by randomly choosing a path down the search tree until a leaf node is reached or a valid solution is encountered. Next, the *competition phase* kicks in.

The scores assigned to each alternative in the search tree is then used to guide the search. The meta-level heuristic determines whether to continue with the next level of search. If so, each processing element is randomly assigned one of the children of it's assigned alternative. The search ends when no new node can be expanded upon.

The idea of using a tree to represent the search space is very practical. For instance, each node within the search tree, excluding the root and leaf nodes, represents a partial solution to the problem. The root node represents the APTA and all transitions leading from the root are valid merge choices. Transitions signify commitments or decisions of what nodes to merge next within the APTA. Continuing to select transitions within the search tree at each merge level will eventually lead to a leaf node. Once a leaf node has been reached no other merge choices are available and a solution to the problem is obtained. Therefore, the inference engines used for FSA learning are essentially searching for the path that leads from the root of the search tree to the leaf node that represents the target FSA.

Juillé and Pollack are the first to use random sampling techniques on search trees as a heuristic to control the search [7]. Others such as [8], [9], and [10] have tried to implement more intelligent search methods. For instance, by refining the search space, more time can be spent exploring regions of the search tree that are expected to contain as a leaf the target FSA. This results in a more efficient search and avoids exhaustively searching unfruitful regions of the search tree. Unfortunately, pruning the search tree comes at a cost and as a result requires intensive search and book keeping at each merge level. Also, determining an incorrect move is not a trivial task and tends to require additional search.

4   Analysis of W-EDSM

From the results obtained by the *Abbadingo One Learning Competition*, the correct heuristic for choosing merge pairs proved to be that which assigns scores to node pairs based on the number of matched labels within their respective subtrees. We begin our analysis of the W-EDSM algorithm by evaluating this best-match heuristic. In particular, we would like to know how effective the heuristic is and under what conditions the heuristic successfully guides us to a good solution and when it is less reliable. This knowledge will give us some ideas about where we might concentrate our search for superior solutions than those already found.

We proceed by posing the question, *how well does the heuristic do at selecting a pair of nodes to merge, compared to a random guess?* We have answered this question by comparing the performance of the W-EDSM algorithm on randomly generated *Abbadingo-Style* problems to the performance of a slightly modified W-EDSM (MW-EDSM). Thus, MW-EDSM makes a single random selection of a merge-pair from the lowest ranked 2500 pairs in the breadth-first window, instead of selecting one of the nodes tied for the highest score. With the exception of this single random step, the modified algorithm proceeds just as W-EDSM does. By varying the depth of the single random move in the collapsing process, we can compare the effectiveness of the best-match heuristic to a random selection.

In order to evaluate the performance in a statistically significant way, we performed 2500 simulations of both the W-EDSM and the MW-EDSM algorithms for each of 50 randomly generated target FSA. Also, rather than randomly selecting one of the 2500 possible moves in the MW-EDSM algorithm, we explicitly sampled each one in turn to explicitly compute the statistically expected value. Thus, for a specific level within the search tree, MW-EDSM chooses not the highest scoring merge pair but the lowest then proceeds as would W-EDSM for the rest of the inference process. On the second attempt at the same problem MW-EDSM would choose the second lowest scoring merge pair and so on. Both W-EDSM and MW-EDSM had 2500 attempts at each of the problems (recall that there is a random element in W-EDSM as well, in the form of tie-breaking). The window size chosen for each attempt was $2(m+1)$ where m was the number of states for the corresponding target FSA.

There were 50 target FSA used in the experiments, each had from 57 to 75 states. The mean FSA size was 65.00 states with a standard deviation of 4.36 states. In a fashion analogous to that used in the *Abbadingo competition*, they were generated by first creating a random digraph with $(5/4)n$ states where $n = 65$. Each state was assigned a 0 and 1 outgoing edge and a label of either accept or reject with equal probability. The start state (s) was chosen uniformly from the complete set of states. Any state which was not reachable from s was discarded. Finally, the Moore minimization algorithm was applied to the FSA. If the resulting FSA did not have depth equal to $\lfloor (2log_2n) - 2 \rfloor$, it was discarded and the procedure was repeated.

All binary strings up to length 15 were then classified according to each of the 50 target FSA. Their respective training and testing sets were then uniformly drawn without replacement from the labelled binary strings. The training data for each of the 50 target FSA consisted of 1521 example strings. Note, this is consistent with the density level and target size of one of the two most difficult solvable problems of the *Abbadingo One Learning Competition*.

Random merges were performed for only the first 5 levels of the search tree by MW-EDSM for these experiments. The idea behind the search was to try to determine which level or levels within the search tree are most critical and how fatal an incorrect merge can be. Some early investigations had suggested to us that the first moves were most important.

5   Results

Our results are presented in Figure 2. This graph shows the performance of the modified W-EDSM technique (which makes one random move) in comparison to the W-EDSM. The centre of each bar represents the mean of the best automaton size for a given problem obtained with the algorithm, while the upper and lower ends of each bar represent the mean-best automaton size ± 1 standard deviation. The middle (top, bottom) dashed horizontal line, shows the mean (mean plus one standard deviation, mean minus one standard deviation) performance of the best automaton for a given problem the W-EDSM algorithm for comparison.

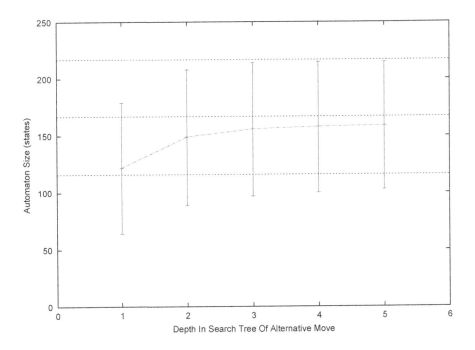

Fig. 2. Comparison between W-EDSM and MW-EDSM with random move at different depths. Bars represent the mean best automaton size ± 1 standard deviation for MW-EDSM, while dotted lines show the mean best automaton size ± 1 standard deviation for W-EDSM.

Table 2 shows the percentage improvement of MW-EDSM over W-EDSM realized on the first few steps. It is computed as

$$\frac{|Q_{\text{W-EDSM}}| - |Q_{\text{MW-EDSM}}|}{|Q_{\text{W-EDSM}}|} * 100\%, \tag{1}$$

where $|Q_{\text{W-EDSM}}|$ and $|Q_{\text{MW-EDSM}}|$ represent the final average automaton sizes of the W-EDSM and MW-EDSM algorithms respectively. Note that if random moves are simply made on the first step of the W-EDSM algorithm, the average best automaton size is reduced from 167 to 122 states—an improvement of 27%.

Table 2. Average best automaton size reduction.

Random Move Depth	1	2	3	4	5
Size Reduction	27%	11%	7%	5%	5%

6   Implications and Conclusion

This experiment has shown that while the W-EDSM algorithm's best-match heuristic may be very effective at finding a route to a small automaton in general, it does not do very well on the first few steps. From this we can draw the following conclusions:

- there is certainly room for a better heuristic for selecting early merges,
- if an iterative refinement approach to finding a smaller automaton is applied, it should modify the earliest moves in search of a better solution, and
- a 27% performance improvement over W-EDSM can be realized by searching for a first merge in the last 2500 merge pairs in the breadth-first-window.

Clearly, this work represents a very preliminary foray into the analysis of the W-EDSM algorithm and its merge-pair selection heuristic. Future work will focus on developing iterative refinement algorithms to find smaller automata and developing new heuristics to better select merges in the very early states of the problem without the need for search.

7   Acknowledgements

Prof. Kremer's work was supported by grants from the National Science and Engineering Research Council (NSERC), the Canada Foundation for Innovation (CFI), the Ontario Innovation Trust (OIT), and the Ontartio Research and Development Challenge Fund (ORDCF). The simulations were performed on the SHARCNET high performance computing consortiums hardware (which is funded by CFI, OIT and ORDCF).

A Appendix

The following tables list the minimum size FSA obtained by both W-EDSM and MW-EDSM for each of the 50 problems. Also included within the tables under each problem number is the actual size of the target FSA. Each column represents 1 of the 50 problems and each row contains either the result of W-EDSM (-) or MW-EDSM for 1 of the 5 possible levels within the search tree. It should be noted that the size of the hypothesis FSA obtained for several of the 50 problems are actually smaller than the target FSA. This is perfectly valid since the inference engines do not have access to the testing data and therefore, try to infer the smallest FSA possible that is consistent with the training examples and are most likely to correctly label the unseen example strings.

Table 3. The minimum size FSA obtained by W-EDSM and MW-EDSM for problems 1 to 10.

	1/61	2/64	3/69	4/68	5/71	6/70	7/73	8/64	9/64	10/67
-	203	201	205	187	200	184	203	88	204	72
1	63	91	75	66	201	139	203	89	200	72
2	204	169	75	189	201	152	202	89	205	65
3	202	192	203	190	200	169	200	90	204	65
4	185	202	206	187	200	185	202	90	204	65
5	181	203	207	187	201	184	202	90	202	64

Table 4. The minimum size FSA obtained by W-EDSM and MW-EDSM for problems 11 to 20.

	11/61	12/66	13/75	14/61	15/70	16/64	17/57	18/65	19/73	20/64
-	161	204	204	203	157	206	204	167	204	168
1	81	185	199	85	69	206	76	132	205	68
2	160	204	203	90	69	204	206	113	205	68
3	163	203	203	188	69	205	205	120	204	68
4	157	205	204	198	70	202	203	114	205	68
5	165	203	204	204	135	206	204	112	203	63

References

1. J. E. Hopcroft and J. D. Ullman, *Formal Languages And Their Relation to Automata*. Reading, Mass.: Addison-Wesley, 1969.

Table 5. The minimum size FSA obtained by W-EDSM and MW-EDSM for problems 21 to 30.

	21/57	22/67	23/65	24/70	25/72	26/72	27/63	28/74	29/66	30/63
-	194	193	179	204	209	207	202	204	122	193
1	64	96	177	137	88	207	203	205	84	130
2	193	192	179	204	208	204	203	204	93	191
3	193	191	178	204	207	205	205	201	84	192
4	193	188	178	202	207	207	205	204	90	191
5	193	189	177	205	208	204	203	206	99	191

Table 6. The minimum size FSA obtained by W-EDSM and MW-EDSM for problems 31 to 40.

	31/67	32/61	33/66	34/69	35/61	36/67	37/58	38/68	39/64	40/63
-	207	78	60	207	98	78	195	67	76	195
1	203	80	60	205	87	78	58	67	63	79
2	205	80	60	204	74	78	58	67	63	80
3	210	78	60	207	74	78	58	67	63	188
4	208	80	60	205	61	78	147	67	63	194
5	209	80	60	207	61	78	135	67	63	194

Table 7. The minimum size FSA obtained by W-EDSM and MW-EDSM for problems 41 to 50.

	41/62	42/66	43/61	44/60	45/69	46/68	47/63	48/71	49/67	50/62
-	107	63	199	200	92	199	197	201	134	195
1	62	63	63	132	92	165	197	201	96	195
2	62	63	199	199	89	201	198	201	137	191
3	62	63	198	199	87	200	197	200	135	194
4	62	63	199	202	86	197	197	201	135	196
5	62	63	198	200	90	198	197	201	138	195

2. E. Gold, "Complexity of automaton identification from given data," *Information and Control*, vol. 37, pp. 302–320, 1978.
3. A. Blumer, A. Ehrenfeucht, D. Haussler, and M. K. Warmuth, "Occam's razor," *Information Processing Letters*, vol. 24, pp. 377–380, 1987.
4. B. A. Trakhtenbrot and Y. M. Barzdin, *Finite Automata*. Amsterdam: North-Holland, 1973.
5. K. J. Lang, "Random DFA's can be approximately learned from sparse uniform examples," in *Proceedings of the Fifth ACM Workshop on Computational Learning Theory*, (New York, N.Y.), pp. 45–52, ACM, 1992.
6. K. J. Lang, B. A. Pearlmutter, and R. A. Price, "Results of the Abbadingo one DFA learning competition and a new evidence-driven state merging algorithm," in *Proc. 4th International Colloquium on Grammatical Inference - ICGI '98*, vol. 1433, pp. 1–12, Springer-Verlag, 1998.
7. H. Juille and J. B. Pollack, "A sampling-based heuristic for tree search applied to grammar induction," in *Proceedings of the Fifteenth National Conference on Artificial Intelligence (AAAI-98) Tenth Conference on Innovative Applications of Artificial Intelligence (IAAI-98)*, (Madison, Wisconsin, USA), AAAI Press Books, 26-30 1998.
8. K. Lang, "Evidence-driven state merging with search," 1998.
9. A. L. Oliveira and J. P. M. Silva, "Efficient search techniques for the inference of minimum size finite automata," in *String Processing and Information Retrieval*, pp. 81–89, 1998.
10. J. M. Pena and A. L. Oliveira, "A new algorithm for the reduction of incompletely specified finite state machines," in *Proc. of the ACM/IEEE International Conference on Computer Aided Design*, (San Jose), pp. 482–489, IEEE Computer Society Press, 1998.

Consistent Identification in the Limit of Rigid Grammars from Strings Is NP-hard

Christophe Costa Florêncio

UiL OTS (Utrecht University)
Trans 10, 3512 JK Utrecht, Netherlands
costa@let.uu.nl

Abstract. In [Bus87] and [BP90] some 'discovery procedures' for classical categorial grammars were defined. These procedures take a set of structures (strings labeled with derivational information) as input and yield a set of hypotheses in the form of grammars.
In [Kan98] learning functions based on these discovery procedures were studied, and it was shown that some of the classes associated with these functions can be identified in the limit (i.e. are learnable) from strings, by a computable function. The time complexity of these functions however was still left an open question.
In this paper we will show that the learning functions for these learnable classes are all NP-hard.

1 Identification in the Limit

In [Gol67] the notion *identification in the limit* was introduced. In this model a learning function sees an infinite sequence with the target language as range, called a *text*, and hypothesizes a grammar for the target language at each time-step. A *class* of languages is called *learnable* if and only if there exists a learning function that, after a finite number of presentations, guesses the right language on every text for every language from that class and does not deviate from this hypothesis.

Research within this framework is known as *formal learning theory*. Only those aspects of formal learning theory that are relevant to our result will be discussed, see [JORS99] for a comprehensive overview of the field.

Many different variants of the paradigm have been studied, amongst them the learning of *indexed families of computable languages*, i.e. learning in the presence of a uniform decision procedure for languages in the class (see [Ang80]). This is a natural assumption when studying grammar induction, and we will assume it in the remainder of this paper.

Let the set Ω denote the hypothesis space, which can be any class of finitary objects. Members of Ω are called *grammars*. The set $\mathbf{S}$ denotes the sample space, a recursive subset of Σ^* for some fixed finite alphabet Σ. Elements of $\mathbf{S}$ are called *sentences*, subsets of $\mathbf{S}$ are called *languages*.

The *naming function* L maps elements of Ω to subsets of $\mathbf{S}$. If G is a grammar in Ω, then $\mathrm{L}(G)$ is called the *language generated by (associated with)* G. The

P. Adriaans, H. Fernau, and M. van Zaanen (Eds.): ICGI 2002, LNAI 2484, pp. 49–62, 2002.
© Springer-Verlag Berlin Heidelberg 2002

question whether a sentence belongs to a language generated by a grammar is called the *universal membership problem*. A triple $\langle \Omega, \mathbf{S}, \mathrm{L} \rangle$ satisfying the above conditions is called a *grammar system*. A class of grammars is denoted $\mathcal{G}$, a class of languages is denoted $\mathcal{L}$.

I will adopt notation from [Kan98] and let $\mathcal{FL}$ denote a class of *structure languages*, to be defined in Section 3. The corresponding naming function is $\mathrm{FL}(G)$. Learning functions are written as φ, their input sequences as σ or τ.

1.1   Constraints on Learning Functions

The behaviour of learning functions can be constrained in a number of ways, such a constraint is *restrictive* if it restricts the space of learnable classes. Only some important constraints relevant to this discussion will be defined here:

Definition 1. *Consistent Learning(See [Ang80])*
A learning function φ is consistent *on $\mathcal{G}$ if for any $L \in \mathrm{L}(\mathcal{G})$ and for any finite sequence $\langle s_0, \ldots, s_i \rangle$ of elements of L, either $\varphi(\langle s_0, \ldots, s_i \rangle)$ is undefined or $\{s_0, \ldots, s_i\} \subseteq \mathrm{L}(\varphi(\langle s_0, \ldots, s_i \rangle))$.*

Informally, consistency requires that the learning function explains all the data it sees with its conjecture.[1]

Definition 2. *Prudent Learning(See [Ful90])*
A learning function φ learns $\mathcal{G}$ prudently *if φ learns $\mathcal{G}$ and* content$(\varphi) \subseteq \mathcal{G}$.

Prudent learners only hypothesize grammars that are in their class.

Definition 3. *Responsive Learning(See [Ful90])*
A learning function φ is responsive *on $\mathcal{G}$ if for any $L \in \mathrm{L}(\mathcal{G})$ and for any finite sequence $\langle s_0, \ldots, s_i \rangle$ of elements of L ($\{s_0, \ldots, s_i\} \subseteq L$), $\varphi(\langle s_0, \ldots, s_i \rangle)$ is defined.*

A responsive learning function is always defined, as long as the text is consistent with a language from its class.

Given the assumptions mentioned earlier, none of these constraints are restrictive.

1.2   Time Complexity of Learning Functions

In formal learning theory there are no a priori constraints on the computational resources required by the learning function. It turns out that giving a usable definition of the complexity of learning functions is not exactly easy. In [CF00] different proposals are briefly discussed. For a thorough overview see Chapter 12 of [JORS99].

---

[1] The literature offers many different notions of consistency: in [WZ95] some stronger forms of consistent function learning are defined, in [B̄74] a definition of class consistency can be found.

Let the complexity of the update-time of some (computable) learning function φ be defined as the number of computing steps it takes to learn a language, with respect to $|\sigma|$, the size of the input sequence. In [Pit89] it was first noted that requiring the function to run in a time polynomial with respect to $|\sigma|$ does not constitute a significant constraint, since one can always define a learning function φ' that combines φ with a clock so that its amount of computing time is bounded by a polynomial over $|\sigma|$. Obviously, φ' learns the same class as φ, and it does so in polynomial update-time[2].

The problem here is that without additional constraints on φ the 'burden of computation' can be shifted from the number of computations the function needs to perform to the amount of input data considered by the function[3]. Requiring the function to be consistent already constitutes a significant constraint when used in combination with a complexity restriction (see [B̄74]). See [Ste98] for a discussion of consistent polynomial-time identification.

I will apply only the restrictions of consistency and polynomial update-time, since this seems to be the weakest combination of constraints that is not trivial and has an intuitive relation with standard notions of computational complexity. This definition has drawbacks too: not all learnable classes can be learned by a learning function that is consistent on its class, so even this complexity measure cannot be generally applied. There is also no guarantee that for a class that is learnable by a function consistent on that class characteristic samples (i.e. samples that justify convergence to the right grammar) can be given that are uniformly of a size polynomial in the size of their associated grammar.

2 Classical Categorial Grammar and Structure Languages

The classes defined in [Bus87, BP90] are based on a formalism for (ϵ-free) context-free languages called classical categorial grammar (CCG). In this section the relevant concepts of CCG will be defined. I will adopt notation from [Kan98].

In CCG each symbol in the alphabet Σ gets assigned a finite number of *types*. Types are constructed from *primitive types* by the operators $\backslash$ and $/$. We let Pr denote the (countably infinite) set of primitive types. The set of types Tp is defined as the smallest set satisfying:

1. $\text{Pr} \subseteq Tp$,
2. if $A \in Tp$ and $B \in Tp$, then $A \backslash B \in Tp$.
3. if $A \in Tp$ and $B \in Tp$, then $B / A \in Tp$.

One member t of Pr is called the *distinguished type*. In CCG there are only two modes of type combination, *backward application*, $A, A \backslash B \Rightarrow B$, and *forward*

---

[2] To be more precise: in [DS86] it was shown that any unbounded monotone increasing update boundary is not by itself restrictive.

[3] Similar issues seem to be important in the field of *computational learning theory* (see [KV94] for an introduction). The notion *sample complexity* from this field seems closely related to the notions of text- and data-efficiency. There also exists a parallel with our notion of (polynomial) update-time.

application, $B/A, A \Rightarrow B$. In both cases, type A is an *argument*, the complex type is a *functor*. *Grammars* consist of type assignments to symbols, i.e. $\texttt{symbol} \mapsto T$, where $\texttt{symbol} \in \Sigma$, and $T \in \text{Tp}$.

Definition 4. *A derivation of B from $A_1, \ldots, A_n$ is a binary branching tree that encodes a proof of $A_1, \ldots, A_n \Rightarrow B$.*

Through the notion of derivation the association between grammar and language is defined. All structures contained in some given structure language correspond to a derivation of type t based solely on the type assignments contained in a given grammar. The *string language* associated with G consists of the strings corresponding to all the structures in its structure language, where the string corresponding to some derivation consists just of the leaves of that derivation.

The class of all categorial grammars is denoted CatG, the grammar system under discussion is $\langle \text{CatG}, \Sigma^{\text{F}}, \text{FL} \rangle$. The symbol FL is an abbreviation of functor-argument language, which is a structure language for CCG. Structures are of the form $\texttt{symbol}$, $\texttt{fa(s1,s2)}$ or $\texttt{ba(s1,s2)}$, where $\texttt{symbol} \in \text{Pr}$, $\texttt{fa}$ stands for forward application, $\texttt{ba}$ for backward application and $\texttt{s1}$ and $\texttt{s2}$ are also structures.

All learning functions in [Kan98] are based on the function GF. This function receives a sample of structures D as input and yields a set of assignments (i.e. a grammar) called the *general form* as output. It is a homomorphism and runs in linear time. It assigns t to each root node, assigns distinct variables to the argument nodes, and computes types for the functor nodes: if $\texttt{s1} \mapsto A$, given $\texttt{ba(s1,s2)} \Rightarrow B$, $\texttt{s2} \mapsto A \backslash B$. If $\texttt{s1} \mapsto A$, given $\texttt{fa(s2,s1)} \Rightarrow B$, $\texttt{s2} \mapsto B/A$. When learning from strings the structure language is not available to the learner, but given a set of strings there exist only finitely many possible sets of structures for the classes under discussion.

Categorial types can be treated as terms, so natural definitions of substitution and unification apply. A substitution over a grammar is just a substitution over all of the types contained in its assignments. We state without proof that $\text{FL}(G) \subseteq \text{FL}(\Theta[G])$, see [Kan98] for details.

3   The Classes of Grammars

We define the relevant classes as follows:

Rigid Grammars: A *rigid grammar* is a partial function from Σ to Tp. It assigns either zero or one type to each symbol in the alphabet.

We write $\mathcal{G}_{\text{rigid}}$ to denote the class of rigid grammars over Σ. The class $\{\text{L}(G) \mid G \in \mathcal{G}_{\text{rigid}}\}$ is denoted $\mathcal{L}_{\text{rigid}}$.

This class is learnable with polynomial update-time, by simply unifying all types assigned to the same symbol in the general form. The other classes defined in [Bus87, BP90] are generalizations of this class.

k-Valued Grammars: A *k-valued* grammar is a partial function from Σ to Tp. It assigns at most k types to each symbol in the alphabet.

We write $\mathcal{G}_{k\text{-valued}}$ to denote the class of k-valued grammars over Σ. The class $\{L(G) \mid G \in \mathcal{G}_{k\text{-valued}}\}$ is denoted $\mathcal{L}_{k\text{-valued}}$.

Note that in the special case $k = 1$, $\mathcal{G}_{k\text{-valued}}$ is equivalent to $\mathcal{G}_{\text{rigid}}$.

The learning function φ_{VG_k}[4] learns $\mathcal{G}_{k\text{-valued}}$ from structures.

4   The Complexity of Learning Rigid Grammars

The learnability of classes from [Bus87, BP90] from both structures and strings has been studied in [Kan98], complexity results for learning from structures by means of a consistent learning function can be found in [CF00], [CF01]. We now turn to learning from *strings*, which is far more difficult to analyze than learning from structures.

Note that learning from structures and from strings are two logically independent paradigms. One may be tempted to think that learning from structures is the easier task of the two, since structures contain more information than strings. However, the identification criterion is stricter in the case of learning from structures: to succeed the learning function must find a grammar that not only generates the same sentences as the target grammar, but also generates them *in exactly the same way*. In linguistic terms: the conjectured grammar must ultimately have the same *strong generative capacity* as the target grammar.

In order to prove NP-hardness of an algorithmic problem L, it suffices to show that there exists a polynomial-time reduction from an NP-complete problem L' to L. In this case this will be the decision version of vertex-cover problem, a well-known NP-hard problem from the field of operations research.

The following is a corollary from [CF00]:

Lemma 1. *For every consistent learning function φ learning a subclass of* CatG *and every sequence σ for a language from that subclass there exists a substitution Θ such that $\Theta[\text{GF}(\sigma)] \subseteq \varphi(\sigma)$, if $\varphi(\sigma)$ is defined.*

Even though this lemma is restricted to structure languages[5], it can also be used for dealing with string languages in special cases. Consider the following lemma that details a sample such that there is only one derivation consistent with each string, and the resulting type assignments only contain a constant as primitive type.

Lemma 2.   *Let $D = \{\texttt{t}, \texttt{te}, \texttt{jt}, \texttt{en}, \texttt{xee}, \texttt{kj}, \texttt{tjy}, \texttt{uyt}, \texttt{up}, \texttt{jhyt}, \texttt{jhp}, \texttt{kgu}, \texttt{gut},$ $\texttt{jijht}, \texttt{tjijhy}, \texttt{nb}, \texttt{ekz}, \texttt{cnn}, \texttt{tcn}, \texttt{zq}, \texttt{rz}, \texttt{onq}, \texttt{ron}, \texttt{ttf}, \texttt{nl}, \texttt{kmb}, \texttt{tmdb}, \texttt{stt}\}$. Then,*

---

[4] With this function, and the functions defined for the other classes, we will denote arbitrary learning functions that learn these classes, not necessarily the particular functions defined in [Kan98].

[5] There is a unique (up to alphabetic variation) general form for every sequence of structures. Since strings may be assigned multiple structures a GF-like function for classes of string languages will in general yield multiple general forms.

for any responsive and prudent φ that learns rigid grammars consistently, $G = \varphi(D)$:

$$
G : \begin{array}{ll}
\mathtt{t} \mapsto t & \mathtt{i} \mapsto ((t/t)\backslash(t/t))/((t/t)/((t/t)\backslash(t\backslash t))) \\
\mathtt{e} \mapsto t\backslash t & \mathtt{b} \mapsto A\backslash t \\
\mathtt{j} \mapsto t/t & \mathtt{z} \mapsto B\backslash A \\
\mathtt{n} \mapsto A & \mathtt{c} \mapsto (t\backslash t)/A \\
\mathtt{x} \mapsto (t/(t\backslash t))/(t\backslash t) & \mathtt{q} \mapsto (B\backslash A)\backslash t \\
\mathtt{k} \mapsto B & \mathtt{r} \mapsto t/(B\backslash A) \\
\mathtt{y} \mapsto (t/t)\backslash(t\backslash t) & \mathtt{o} \mapsto B\backslash(A/A) \\
\mathtt{u} \mapsto (t/t)/((t/t)\backslash(t\backslash t)) & \mathtt{f} \mapsto t\backslash(t\backslash t) \\
\mathtt{p} \mapsto ((t/t)/((t/t)\backslash(t\backslash t)))\backslash t & \mathtt{l} \mapsto A\backslash t \\
\mathtt{h} \mapsto (t/t)\backslash((t/t)/((t/t)\backslash(t\backslash t))) & \mathtt{m} \mapsto B\backslash A \\
\mathtt{g} \mapsto (t/t)/((t/t)/((t/t)\backslash(t\backslash t))) & \mathtt{d} \mapsto (B\backslash A)\backslash(t\backslash A) \\
\mathtt{s} \mapsto (t/t)/t &
\end{array}
$$

For ease of reading B and A are written as shorthand for $t/(t/t)$ and $(t\backslash t)\backslash t$, respectively.

Proof. Let σ be the sequence $\langle \mathtt{t}, \mathtt{te}, \mathtt{jt}, \mathtt{en}, \mathtt{xee}, \mathtt{kj}, \mathtt{tjy} \rangle$. It is obvious that φ's conjecture G has to include $\{\mathtt{t} \mapsto t, \mathtt{e} \mapsto t\backslash t, \mathtt{j} \mapsto t/t\}$. The assignments to $\mathtt{n}$, $\mathtt{x}$, $\mathtt{k}$ and $\mathtt{y}$ follow directly from these and the given strings.

Let σ' be the sequence $\langle \mathtt{uyt}, \mathtt{up} \rangle$. The first string from this sequence corresponds to the sequent $U, (t/t)\backslash(t\backslash t), t \Rightarrow t$, so $\mathtt{u} \mapsto (t/t)/((t/t)\backslash(t\backslash t))$. Now consider the second string. It corresponds to the sequent $(t/t)/((t/t)\backslash(t\backslash t)), P \Rightarrow t$, so $\mathtt{p} \mapsto ((t/t)/((t/t)\backslash(t\backslash t)))\backslash t$.

Let σ'' be the sequence $\langle \mathtt{jhyt}, \mathtt{jhp} \rangle$. The first string from this sequence corresponds to the sequent $t/t, H, (t/t)\backslash(t\backslash t), t \Rightarrow t$, so the type H can be $(t/t)\backslash((t/t)/((t/t)\backslash(t\backslash t)))$, $((t/t)\backslash(t/t))/((t/t)\backslash(t\backslash t))$, $(((t\backslash t)\backslash t)/t)/((t/t)\backslash(t\backslash t))$, or $(t/t)/((t/t)\backslash(t\backslash t))$.

Now consider the second string. Given the possible assignments to the symbols it contains, it has to correspond to the sequent $t/t, H, ((t/t)/((t/t)\backslash(t\backslash t)))\backslash t \Rightarrow t$. Trying the four possible assignments to $\mathtt{h}$ will show that only the first, $(t/t)\backslash((t/t)/((t/t)\backslash(t\backslash t)))$ is possible.

Let σ''' be the sequence $\langle \mathtt{kgu}, \mathtt{gut} \rangle$. The first string from this sequence corresponds to the sequent $t/(t/t), G, (t/t)/((t/t)\backslash(t\backslash t)) \Rightarrow t$, so the type G can be $(t/t)/((t/t)/((t/t)\backslash(t\backslash t)))$, $((t/(t/t))\backslash t)/((t/t)/((t/t)\backslash(t\backslash t)))$, or $(t/(t/t))\backslash(t/((t/t)/((t/t)\backslash(t\backslash t))))$. Now consider the second string. Given the possible assignments to the symbols it contains, it has to correspond to the sequent $G, (t/t)/((t/t)\backslash(t\backslash t)), t \Rightarrow t$. Only the first type, $(t/t)/((t/t)/((t/t)\backslash(t\backslash t)))$, is possible.

Let σ'''' be the sequence $\langle \mathtt{jiut}, \mathtt{tjiuy} \rangle$. The first string from this sequence corresponds to the sequent $t/t, I, (t/t)/((t/t)\backslash(t\backslash t)), t \Rightarrow t$, so the type I can be $((t/t)\backslash(t/t))/((t/t)/((t/t)\backslash(t\backslash t)))$, $(((t/t)\backslash t)/t)/((t/t)/((t/t)\backslash(t\backslash t)))$, or $(t/t)/((t/t)/((t/t)\backslash(t\backslash t)))$. Now consider the second string. Given the possible assignments to the symbols it contains, it has to correspond to the sequent
$$t, t/t, I, (t/t)/((t/t)\backslash(t\backslash t)), (t/t)\backslash(t\backslash t) \Rightarrow t.$$

Only the first type, $((t/t)\backslash(t/t))/((t/t)/((t/t)\backslash(t\backslash t)))$, is possible.

From the presence of string **nb** the assignment $\mathsf{b} \mapsto ((t\backslash t)\backslash t)\backslash t$ immediately follows. The string **ekz** corresponds to sequent $t\backslash t, t/(t/t), Z \Rightarrow t$, from which follows immediately that $\mathsf{z} \mapsto (t/(t/t))\backslash((t\backslash t)\backslash t)$. The string **cnn** corresponds to the sequent $C, (t\backslash t)\backslash t, (t\backslash t)\backslash t \Rightarrow t$. There are two types possible for C, $(t\backslash t)/((t\backslash t)\backslash t)$ and $(t/((t\backslash t)\backslash t))/((t\backslash t)\backslash t)$. The string **tcn** corresponds to the sequent $t, C, (t\backslash t)\backslash t \Rightarrow t$. Only the first type applies here, so $\mathsf{c} \mapsto (t\backslash t)/((t\backslash t)\backslash t)$.

The string **zq** immediately implies $\mathsf{q} \mapsto ((t/(t/t))\backslash((t\backslash t)\backslash t))\backslash t$. The string **rz** immediately implies $\mathsf{r} \mapsto t/((t/(t/t))\backslash((t\backslash t)\backslash t))$. The string **onq** corresponds to the sequent $t/(t/t), O, (t\backslash t)\backslash t, ((t\backslash t)\backslash t)\backslash t \Rightarrow t$. This implies that O is either $(t/(t/t))\backslash((t\backslash t)\backslash t)/((t\backslash t)\backslash t)$ or $(t/((t/(t/t))\backslash((t\backslash t)\backslash t)\backslash t))/((t\backslash t)\backslash t)$. The string **ron** corresponds to the sequent $t/(t/(t/t))\backslash((t\backslash t)\backslash t), O, (t\backslash t)\backslash t \Rightarrow t$. Only the first possibility for O works here, so $\mathsf{o} \mapsto (t/(t/t))\backslash((t\backslash t)\backslash t)/((t\backslash t)\backslash t)$.

By Lemma 1, $\Theta[\mathrm{GF}(\sigma)] \subseteq \varphi(\sigma)$, if $\varphi(\sigma)$ is defined. Since $\mathrm{GF}(D)$ only contains ground types for this sample, Θ must be the empty substitution, so any consistent hypothesis should contain $\mathrm{GF}(D)$. This also shows that the order of presentation of D is irrelevant.

Since φ is restricted to the class of rigid grammars no other types can be assigned to the symbols occurring in G. □

Lemma 3. *Let p and q be two propositions, and f be the function that maps true to type t/t, and false to type $(t/t)/((t/t)\backslash(t\backslash t))$. Then $p \vee q$ if and only if*[6]

$$(t/t)/t, t, (t/t)/((t/t)/((t/t)\backslash(t\backslash t))), \underline{f(p)}, (t/t)\backslash((t/t)/((t/t)\backslash(t\backslash t))),$$
$$((t/t)\backslash(t/t))/((t/t)/((t/t)\backslash(t\backslash t))), \underline{f(q)}, (t/t)\backslash((t/t)/((t/t)\backslash(t\backslash t))), t \Rightarrow t.$$

Proof. The truth table for $\vee$ shows that $p \vee q$ is false if and only if both p and q are false, and is true otherwise. Simply checking the four possible combinations for the categorial derivation yields:

1. Both p and q true implies $p \vee q$ true, so t should be derived:

$$(t/t)/t, t, (t/t)/((t/t)/((t/t)\backslash(t\backslash t))), \underline{t/t}, (t/t)\backslash((t/t)/((t/t)\backslash(t\backslash t))),$$
$$((t/t)\backslash(t/t))/((t/t)/((t/t)\backslash(t\backslash t))), \underline{t/t}, (t/t)\backslash((t/t)/((t/t)\backslash(t\backslash t))), t \Rightarrow t$$
$$(t/t)/t, t, (t/t)/((t/t)/((t/t)\backslash(t\backslash t))), \underline{(t/t)/((t/t)\backslash(t\backslash t))},$$
$$((t/t)\backslash(t/t))/((t/t)/((t/t)\backslash(t\backslash t))), t/t, (t/t)\backslash((t/t)/((t/t)\backslash(t\backslash t))), t \Rightarrow t$$
$$(t/t)/t, t, t/t, ((t/t)\backslash(t/t))/((t/t)/((t/t)\backslash(t\backslash t))), t/t,$$
$$(t/t)\backslash((t/t)/((t/t)\backslash(t\backslash t))), t \Rightarrow t$$
$$(t/t)/t, t, t/t, ((t/t)\backslash(t/t))/((t/t)/((t/t)\backslash(t\backslash t))), (t/t)/((t/t)\backslash(t\backslash t)), t \Rightarrow t$$
$$(t/t)/t, t, t/t, (t/t)\backslash(t/t), t \Rightarrow t$$
$$(t/t)/t, t, t, t/t, t \Rightarrow t$$
$$(t/t)/t, t, t, t \Rightarrow t$$
$$t/t, t \Rightarrow t.$$

---

[6] For ease of reading the types corresponding to $f(p)$ and $f(q)$ have been underlined in the derivations.

2. Proposition p true, q false implies $p \vee q$ true, so t should be derived:

$$(t/t)/t, t, (t/t)/((t/t)/((t/t)\backslash(t\backslash t))), \underline{t/t}, (t/t)\backslash((t/t)/((t/t)\backslash(t\backslash t))),$$
$$((t/t)\backslash(t\backslash t))/((t/t)/((t/t)\backslash(t\backslash t))), \underline{(t/t)/((t/t)\backslash(t\backslash t))},$$
$$(t/t)\backslash((t/t)/((t/t)\backslash(t\backslash t))), t \Rightarrow t$$
$$(t/t)/t, t, (t/t)/((t/t)/((t/t)\backslash(t\backslash t))), (t/t)/((t/t)\backslash(t\backslash t)),$$
$$((t/t)\backslash(t\backslash t))/((t/t)/((t/t)\backslash(t\backslash t))), (t/t)/((t/t)\backslash(t\backslash t)),$$
$$(t/t)\backslash((t/t)/((t/t)\backslash(t\backslash t))), t \Rightarrow t$$
$$(t/t)/t, t, (t/t)/((t/t)/((t/t)\backslash(t\backslash t))), (t/t)/((t/t)\backslash(t\backslash t)), ((t/t)\backslash(t\backslash t)),$$
$$(t/t)\backslash((t/t)/((t/t)\backslash(t\backslash t))), t \Rightarrow t$$
$$(t/t)/t, t, (t/t)/((t/t)/((t/t)\backslash(t\backslash t))), t/t, (t/t)\backslash((t/t)/((t/t)\backslash(t\backslash t))), t \Rightarrow t$$
$$(t/t)/t, t, (t/t)/((t/t)/((t/t)\backslash(t\backslash t))), (t/t)/((t/t)\backslash(t\backslash t)), t \Rightarrow t$$
$$(t/t)/t, t, t/t, t \Rightarrow t$$
$$(t/t)/t, t, t \Rightarrow t$$
$$t/t, t \Rightarrow t.$$

3. Proposition p false, q true implies $p \vee q$ true, so t should be derived:

$$(t/t)/t, t, (t/t)/((t/t)/((t/t)\backslash(t\backslash t))), \underline{(t/t)/((t/t)\backslash(t\backslash t))},$$
$$(t/t)\backslash((t/t)/((t/t)\backslash(t\backslash t))), ((t/t)\backslash(t\backslash t))/((t/t)/((t/t)\backslash(t\backslash t))), \underline{t/t},$$
$$(t/t)\backslash((t/t)/((t/t)\backslash(t\backslash t))), t \Rightarrow t$$
$$(t/t)/t, t, (t/t)/((t/t)/((t/t)\backslash(t\backslash t))), (t/t)/((t/t)\backslash(t\backslash t)),$$
$$(t/t)\backslash((t/t)/((t/t)\backslash(t\backslash t))), ((t/t)\backslash(t\backslash t))/((t/t)/((t/t)\backslash(t\backslash t))),$$
$$(t/t)/((t/t)\backslash(t\backslash t)), t \Rightarrow t$$
$$(t/t)/t, t, (t/t)/((t/t)/((t/t)\backslash(t\backslash t))), (t/t)/((t/t)\backslash(t\backslash t)),$$
$$(t/t)\backslash((t/t)/((t/t)\backslash(t\backslash t))), (t/t)\backslash(t\backslash t), t \Rightarrow t$$
$$(t/t)/t, t, t/t, (t/t)\backslash((t/t)/((t/t)\backslash(t\backslash t))), (t/t)\backslash(t\backslash t), t \Rightarrow t$$
$$(t/t)/t, t, (t/t)/((t/t)\backslash(t\backslash t)), (t/t)\backslash(t\backslash t), t \Rightarrow t$$
$$(t/t)/t, t, t/t, t \Rightarrow t$$
$$(t/t)/t, t, t \Rightarrow t$$
$$t/t, t \Rightarrow t.$$

4. Both propositions false implies $p \vee q$ false, so t should not be derivable:

$$(t/t)/t, t, (t/t)/((t/t)/((t/t)\backslash(t\backslash t))), \underline{(t/t)/((t/t)\backslash(t\backslash t))},$$
$$(t/t)\backslash((t/t)/((t/t)\backslash(t\backslash t))), ((t/t)\backslash(t\backslash t))/((t/t)/((t/t)\backslash(t\backslash t))),$$
$$\underline{(t/t)/((t/t)\backslash(t\backslash t))}, (t/t)\backslash((t/t)/((t/t)\backslash(t\backslash t))), t \not\Rightarrow t$$

Consider the second to last type in the sequent. Since it selects for $(t/t)\backslash(t\backslash t)$ to the right and there is only t to the right of it, a type to the left of it must have $X/((t/t)\backslash((t/t)/((t/t)\backslash(t\backslash t))))$ or $X/(t/t)/((t/t)\backslash(t\backslash t))$ as its range (here X is an arbitrary type). There is no candidate for the former, there are two for the latter: the third and the sixth type in the sequent. We proceed by case analysis:

(a) For the third type, $(t/t)/((t/t)/((t/t)\backslash(t\backslash t)))$ to combine with $(t/t)/((t/t)\backslash(t\backslash t)))$, the sequent between the third and eighth type must derive t/t. Thus it needs to be shown that

$$(t/t)/((t/t)\backslash(t\backslash t)), (t/t)\backslash((t/t)/((t/t)\backslash(t\backslash t))),$$
$$((t/t)\backslash(t\backslash t))/((t/t)/((t/t)\backslash(t\backslash t))), (t/t)/((t/t)\backslash(t\backslash t)) \not\Rightarrow t/t$$

There is only one possible application step, which yields:
$$(t/t)/((t/t)\backslash(t\backslash t)), (t/t)\backslash((t/t)/((t/t)\backslash(t\backslash t))), (t/t)\backslash(t\backslash t) \not\Rightarrow t/t$$
This sequent cannot be further reduced, so t/t indeed cannot be derived.

(b) For the sixth type, $((t/t)\backslash(t\backslash t))/((t/t)/((t/t)\backslash(t\backslash t)))$ to combine with $(t/t)\backslash((t/t)/((t/t)\backslash(t\backslash t)))$, the sequent between them must derive t/t. Since this sequent consists just of the type $(t/t)/((t/t)\backslash(t\backslash t))$, t/t cannot be derived.

$\square$

The type assignments obtained from D will be used in the other lemmas in this paper.

The following lemma details a sample that will result in the possibility of choice for φ between two possible type assignments for a given symbol.

Lemma 4. *Let D be as defined in Lemma 2. For a given constant v, let sample*
$$D' = D + \bigcup_{i=1}^{v} \{v_i ab, tc v_i a\}.$$
Let $G = \varphi(D')$. Then, for every $1 \le i \le v$, symbol v_i is assigned either $t/(t/t)$ or $((t\backslash t)\backslash t)/((t/(t/t))\backslash((t\backslash t)\backslash t))$ in G.

Proof. For every string $v_i ab$ there are three possible corresponding sequents:

$$
\begin{array}{lll}
1\ B, & B\backslash A, A\backslash t \Rightarrow t \\
2\ A/(B\backslash A), & B\backslash A, A\backslash t \Rightarrow t \\
3\ (t/(A\backslash t))/(B\backslash A), & B\backslash A, A\backslash t \Rightarrow t
\end{array}
$$

For every string $tc v_i a$ there are two possible corresponding sequents. The third option is out by the following table:

$$
\begin{array}{lll}
1\ t, (t\backslash t)/A, B, & B\backslash A \Rightarrow t \\
2\ t, (t\backslash t)/A, A/(B\backslash A), & B\backslash A \Rightarrow t \\
3\ t, (t\backslash t)/A, (t/(A\backslash t))/(B\backslash A), & B\backslash A \Rightarrow t
\end{array}
$$

Thus, for every $1 \le i \le v$, symbol v_i is assigned either $t/(t/t)$ or $((t\backslash t)\backslash t)/((t/(t/t))\backslash((t\backslash t)\backslash t))$ in $\varphi(D')$.

$\square$

The following lemma shows how one can construct a sample that places a bound on the number of symbols that are assigned a particular type.

Lemma 5. *Let D' be as in Lemma 4, and let $D'' = D' + \{\underbrace{z \ldots z}_{c\ times} w, \underbrace{ov_1 z \ldots ov_t z}_{t\ times} w\}$, for some given constants c and t, $c \ge t$.*

Let $C = \{i \mid 1 \le i \le t, v_i \mapsto A \in \varphi(D'')\}$ and $N = \{i \mid 1 \le i \le t, v_i \mapsto A/(B\backslash A) \in \varphi(D'')\}$. Then $|C| = c - t$ and $|V| = 2t - c$.

Proof. The string $\underbrace{\mathtt{z}\ldots\mathtt{z}}_{c\ \text{times}}\mathtt{w}$ implies $\mathtt{w} \mapsto \underbrace{(t/(t/t))\backslash((t\backslash t)\backslash t)\backslash(\ldots \backslash t)\ldots)}_{c\ \text{times}}$.

Finally, consider string $\underbrace{\mathtt{ov_1 z}\ldots\ \mathtt{ov_t z}}_{t\ \text{times}}$. Each substring $\mathtt{ov_x z}$ implies the an-

tecedent $(B\backslash A)/A, \frac{A}{A/(B\backslash A)}, B\backslash A$, which reduces to $(B\backslash A)/A, (B\backslash A)/A$ or $(B\backslash A)/A$, depending on the second type being A or $A/(B\backslash A)$, respectively. Since the type assigned to $\mathtt{w}$ selects for c types of the form $A/(B\backslash A)$ to the left, the number of distinct symbols $\mathtt{v}_x$ that are assigned A plus twice the number of distinct symbols $\mathtt{v}_x$ that are assigned $A/(B\backslash A)$ has to be c. Since there are t distinct symbols $\mathtt{v}_x$ and $t > c$, the former number of symbols is $c - t$ and the latter $2t - c$. □

The following lemma presents a method for creating a specific relation between the types assigned to two distinct symbols.

Lemma 6. *Let* $B = t/(t/t)$ *and* $A = (t\backslash t)\backslash t$. *Let* D'' *be as in Lemma 5, and*
$D''' =$

$$D'' + \{\mathtt{r_1 jtf}, \ldots, \mathtt{r_v jtf}, \mathtt{r}_{f(1)}\mathtt{w_1 y}, \ldots, \mathtt{r}_{f(v)}\mathtt{w_v y}, \mathtt{teer_1 ov_1 zdf}, \ldots, \mathtt{teer_v ov_v zdf}\},$$

where f *is a function with domain* $[1\ldots v]$ *and range* $[1\ldots w]$ *for some* $v, w \in \mathbb{N}$. *Then* $\mathtt{w}_i$ *is assigned* t/t *iff* $\mathtt{v}_i$ *is assigned* A, *and* $\mathtt{w}_i$ *is assigned* $(t/t)/((t/t)\backslash(t\backslash t))$ *iff* $\mathtt{v}_i$ *is assigned* $A/(B\backslash A)$.

Proof. Let D'' be as in Lemma 5. Every string $\mathtt{r}_i\mathtt{jtf}$ corresponding to sequent $R_i, t/t, t, t\backslash(t\backslash t) \Rightarrow t$ implies the assignment of either $t, t/(t/t), (t/(t\backslash t))/(t/t)$, or $((t/(t\backslash(t\backslash t))/t)/(t/t)$ to $\mathtt{r}_i$.

Let p_i be a true proposition. Then the string $\mathtt{r}_{f(i)}\mathtt{w}_i\mathtt{y}$ corresponding to sequent $R_{f(i)}, f(p_i), (t/t)\backslash(t\backslash t) \Rightarrow t$ implies that $\mathtt{r}_{f(i)}$ gets assigned t or $t/(t/t)$, depending on whether $\mathtt{w}_i$ is assigned t/t or $(t/t)/((t/t)\backslash(t\backslash t))$, respectively. Other type assignments are excluded by the string $\mathtt{r}_i\mathtt{jtf}$.

The string $\mathtt{teer}_i\mathtt{ov}_i\mathtt{zdf}$ corresponding to the sequent
$t, t\backslash t, t\backslash t, \frac{t}{B}, (B\backslash A)/A, \frac{A}{A/(B\backslash A)}, B\backslash A, (B\backslash A)\backslash(t\backslash A), t\backslash(t\backslash t) \Rightarrow t$ which reduces to
$t, t\backslash t, t\backslash t, \frac{t}{B}, \frac{B\backslash A}{B\backslash A, B\backslash A}, (B\backslash A)\backslash(t\backslash A), t\backslash(t\backslash t) \Rightarrow t$ then implies that $\mathtt{r}_i$ is assigned t iff $\mathtt{v}_i$ is assigned A, and $\mathtt{r}_i$ is assigned $t/(t/t)$ iff $\mathtt{v}_i$ is assigned $A/(B\backslash A)$. Thus $\mathtt{w}_i$ is assigned t/t iff $\mathtt{v}_i$ is assigned A, and $\mathtt{w}_i$ is assigned $(t/t)/((t/t)\backslash(t\backslash t))$ iff $\mathtt{v}_i$ is assigned $A/(B\backslash A)$. □

With the preliminaries taken care of we can now turn to the complexity result itself. In order to prove NP-hardness of an algorithmic problem L, it suffices to show that there exists a polynomial-time reduction from an NP-complete problem L' to L. We will present such a reduction using the vertex-cover problem, a well-known NP-hard problem from the field of operations research.

Definition 5. *Let* $G = (V, E)$ *be an undirected graph, where* V *is a set of vertices and* E *is a set of edges, represented as tuples of vertices. A vertex cover of* G *is a subset* $V' \subseteq V$ *such that if* $(u, v) \in E$, *then* $u \in V'$ *or* $v \in V'$ *(or both).*

That is, each vertex 'covers' its incident edges, and a vertex cover for G is a set of vertices that covers all the edges in E. The size *of a vertex cover is the number of vertices in it.*

The vertex-cover problem *is the problem of finding a vertex cover of minimum size (called an* optimal vertex cover*) in a given graph.*

The vertex cover problem can be restated as a decision problem*: does a vertex cover of given size k exist for some given graph?*

Proposition 1. *The decision problem related to the vertex-cover problem is* NP-*complete. The vertex-cover problem is* NP-*hard.*

This decision problem has been called one of the 'six basic NP-complete problems' by Garey and Johnson ([GJ79], Chapter 3).

Theorem 1. *Learning the class* $\mathcal{G}_{1-\text{valued}}$ *from strings by means of a function* φ *that is responsive and consistent on its class and learns its class prudently, is* NP-*hard in the size of the alphabet.*

Proof. Let $G = (V, E)$ be a graph as in Definition 5, let $v = |V|$, let $e = |E|$, and let *size* be the desired size of the vertex-cover. Let D be as defined in Lemma 2 (which provides a sample containing the type assignments needed in the other lemmas).

A graph is coded in the following way: let D' be the sample consisting of all strings $\{v_i \text{ab}, \text{tcv}_i \text{a}\}, 1 \leq i \leq v$ as in Lemma 4. Each v_i is intended to represent the vertex $i \in V$. This sample provides the learning function with a choice for in- or exclusion in the cover.

Lemma 5 provides means for stating the desired size for the cover, just let $t = v$ and $c = v + size$.

Lemma 6 ties Lemmas 5 and 4 together, with the symbols $r_1, \ldots, r_v$ acting as 'intermediaries' between the symbols $v_1, \ldots, v_v$ and symbols $w_1, \ldots, w_{2e}$. The function f should reflect the structure of G, i.e. for every edge $i = (x, y) \in E$, $f(2i - 1) = x$ and $f(2i) = y$. Thus every v_i represents a vertex in V and every w_j a *connection* of a vertex to an edge.

The coding defined in Lemma 3 can be used to enforce the constraint that at least one of the vertices incident on an edge is included in the cover. Let $D'' = \bigcup_{i=1}^{e} \{\text{stgw}_{2i-1} \text{hiw}_{2i} \text{ht}\}$ for every edge $i \in E$.

Let $V' = \bigcup \{i | v_i \mapsto (t \backslash t) \backslash t \in RG, 1 \leq i \leq v\}$, where RG is any rigid grammar consistent with $D''' = D + D' + D''$. By Lemma 5 there can only be *size* such type assignments in RG. By Lemma 3 at least one of the two symbols representing a vertex incident on a given edge is assigned t/t in RG, and thus, by Lemma 6, the symbol representing the corresponding vertex is assigned $(t \backslash t) \backslash t$. By Lemma 4 the learning function is free to assign any symbol v_i this type. Since we are assuming prudence $\varphi(D''')$ has to be a rigid grammar, and since we are assuming responsiveness $\varphi(D''')$ has to be defined if it exists. Therefore V' is a vertex cover for graph G of size *size*, if it exists. Since D''' can be constructed in polynomial time (relative to v and e) and V' can be constructed in polynomial time given

RG^7, learning the class $\mathcal{G}_{1-\text{valued}}$ from strings by means of a function φ that is responsive and consistent on its class and learns its class prudently, is NP-hard in the size of the alphabet[8].   □

Note that this theorem does not imply that superclasses of this class are not learnable by a consistent function with polynomial update time. This may seem surprising since it can perform the same task as a learning function for rigid grammars, but it corresponds to dropping the prudency constraint: such a function could, before convergence, conjecture languages outside the class of rigid grammars and would thus not be forced to exhibit the behaviour needed for this proof. However, it is possible to extend this proof for some superclasses.

The same holds for subclasses: there may or may not be a polynomial algorithm for producing consistent hypotheses that are in a given subclass. There are at least some trivial subclasses for which such an algorithm exists.

Theorem 2. *Learning the class* $\mathcal{G}_{k-\text{valued}}, k \geq 1$ *from strings by means of a function* φ *that is responsive and consistent on its class and learns its class prudently, is* NP*-hard in the size of the alphabet.*

Proof. The proof of Lemma 2 demonstrates that it is quite easy to produce strings that yield type-assignments that are not pairwise unifiable. Doing this $k-1$ times for each symbol in a given alphabet, combined with the other strings mentioned in the lemmas, yields a proof of NP-hardness for $\mathcal{G}_{k\text{-valued}}$.   □

Our complexity result leaves open the question of an upper bound. This can be obtained using the Catalan numbers $C_n = \frac{1}{n+1}\binom{2n}{n}$, which yields the number of binary trees with $n+1$ leaves (see [Sta98]). Since these trees have n internal nodes and every one of these can be labeled as forward or backward application, $2^{l-1}C_{l-1}$ gives the number of possible categorial derivations for a string of length l. Thus a naive algorithm that simply checks all combinations of these derivations for a sample D containing d sentences has to go through $\prod_{i=1}^{d} 2^{|s_i|-1} \cdot C_{|s_i|-1}$ grammars.

5   Conclusions and Further Research

It has been shown that learning any of the classes $\mathcal{G}_{k-\text{valued}}$, $k \geq 1$, from strings by means of a function φ that is responsive and consistent on its class and learns its class prudently, is NP-hard in the size of the alphabet. Note that this is a weaker result than NP-hardness in the size of the sample would be, it is an open question whether there exists a proof with an alphabet of some constant size.

---

[7] Since RG can contain an arbitrary number of type assignments if Σ is not given this is not totally accurate, but in the case that the construction of V' is not bounded by some polynomial because $|RG|$ is not, the construction of RG from D''' obviously cannot be performed in polynomial time either, and in that case φ is not even in NP.

[8] The procedure requires v distinct symbols v and $2e$ distinct symbols w in Σ.

A similar result for learning the class of pattern languages PAT[9] consistently from informant[10] can be found in [WZ94]. It differs from ours in that it crucially depends on the membership test for PAT being NP-complete, whereas membership for (subclasses of) CCG languages can be decided in polynomial time.

Previous complexity results for the classes discussed in [Kan98] only hold for learning from structures. In [CF00] it was shown that learning any of the classes $\mathcal{G}_{\text{least-valued}}$, $\mathcal{G}_{\text{least-card}}$, and $\mathcal{G}_{\text{minimal}}$ from structures by means of a learning function that is consistent on its class is NP-hard in the size of the sample. In [CF01] it was shown that learning any of (the maximal unidirectional subclasses of) the classes $\mathcal{G}_{k\text{-valued}}$, $k \geq 2$ from structures by means of a learning function that is consistent on its class is NP-hard in the size of the alphabet.

It is a well-known fact that learning functions for any learnable class without consistency- and monotonicity constraints (see e.g. [ZL95]) can be transformed to trivial learning functions that have polynomial update-time (see Subsection 1.2). It is an open question whether there exist 'intelligent' inconsistent learning functions that have polynomial update-time for the classes under discussion. In [LW91] an example of such a function can be found that learns PAT ([Ang79]).

A final remark, note that the proof of Theorem 1 relies on a subclass of languages that can all be identified with sequences that have a length polynomial in the size of their associated grammars. This is not necessarily true for all languages in the class, so data-complexity issues may make the complexity of learning these classes in practice even worse than Theorem 1 suggests.

References

[Ang79]   Dana Angluin. Finding common patterns to a set of strings. In *Proceedings of the 11th Annual Symposium on Theory of Computing*, pages 130–141, 1979.

[Ang80]   Dana Angluin. Inductive inference of formal languages from positive data. *Information and Control*, 45:117–135, 1980.

[B̄74]   Janis Bārzdiņš. Inductive inference of automata, functions and programs. In *Proceedings International Congress of Math.*, pages 455–460, Vancouver, 1974.

[BP90]   Wojciech Buszkowski and Gerald Penn. Categorial grammars determined from linguistic data by unification. *Studia Logica*, 49:431–454, 1990.

[Bus87]   Wojciech Buszkowski. Discovery procedures for categorial grammars. In E. Klein and J. van Benthem, editors, *Categories, Polymorphism and Unification*. University of Amsterdam, 1987.

[CF00]   Christophe Costa Florêncio. On the complexity of consistent identification of some classes of structure languages. In Arlindo L. Oliveira, editor, *Grammatical Inference: Algorithms and Applications*, volume 1891 of *Lecture Notes in Artificial Intelligence*, pages 89–102. Springer-Verlag, 2000.

---

[9] Note that PAT is also an indexed family.

[10] This result was conjectured to remain valid for learning from strings.

[CF01]   Christophe Costa Florêncio. Consistent Identification in the Limit of the Class k-valued is NP-hard. In Philippe de Groote, Glyn Morrill, and Christian Retoré, editors, *LACL*, volume 2099 of *Lecture Notes in Computer Science*, pages 125–138. Springer, 2001.

[DS86]   Robert P. Daley and Carl H. Smith. On the complexity of inductive inference. *Information and Control*, 69:12–40, 1986.

[Ful90]   Mark Fulk. Prudence and other conditions on formal language learning. *Information and Computation*, 85:1–11, 1990.

[GJ79]   Michael R. Garey and David S. Johnson, editors. *Computers and Intractability. A Guide to the Theory of NP-completeness*. Freeman, New York, 1979.

[Gol67]   E. Mark Gold. Language identification in the limit. *Information and Control*, 10:447–474, 1967.

[JORS99]   Sanjay Jain, Daniel Osherson, James Royer, and Arun Sharma. *Systems that Learn: An Introduction to Learning Theory*. The MIT Press, Cambridge, MA., second edition, 1999.

[Kan98]   Makoto Kanazawa. *Learnable Classes of Categorial Grammars*. CSLI Publications, Stanford University, 1998.

[KV94]   Michael J. Kearns and Umesh V. Vazirani. *An Introduction to Computational Learning Theory*. Cambridge, Mass.: MIT Press, 1994.

[LW91]   Steffen Lange and Rolf Wiehagen. Polynomial time inference of arbitrary pattern languages. *New Generation Computing*, 8:361–370, 1991.

[Pit89]   Leonard Pitt. Inductive inference, DFAs, and computational complexity. In K. P. Jantke, editor, *Proceedings of International Workshop on Analogical and Inductive Inference*, number 397 in Lecture Notes in Computer Science, pages 18–44, 1989.

[Sta98]   Richard P. Stanley. Excercises on Catalan and Related Numbers. `http://www-math.mit.edu/~rstan/ec/catalan.ps.gz`, June 23rd 1998. Excerpted from [Sta99].

[Sta99]   Richard P. Stanley. *Enumerative Combinatorics*, volume 2. Cambridge University Press, 1999.

[Ste98]   Werner Stein. Consistent polynominal identification in the limit. In *Algorithmic Learning Theory (ALT)*, volume 1501 of *Lecture Notes in Computer Science*, pages 424–438, Berlin, 1998. Springer-Verlag.

[WZ94]   Rolf Wiehagen and Thomas Zeugmann. Ignoring data may be the only way to learn efficiently. *Journal of Experimental and Theoretical Artificial Intelligence*, 6:131–144, 1994.

[WZ95]   Rolf Wiehagen and Thomas Zeugmann. Learning and consistency. In K. P. Jantke and S. Lange, editors, *Algorithmic Learning for Knowledge-Based Systems*, number 961 in Lecture Notes in Artificial Intelligence, pages 1–24. Springer-Verlag, 1995.

[ZL95]   Thomas Zeugmann and Steffen Lange. A guided tour across the boundaries of learning recursive languages. In K. P. Jantke and S. Lange, editors, *Algorithmic Learning for Knowledge-Based Systems - GOSLER Final Report*, number 961 in Lecture Notes in Computer Science, pages 190–258. Springer-Verlag, 1995.

Some Classes of Regular Languages Identifiable in the Limit from Positive Data

François Denis[1], Aurélien Lemay[2], and Alain Terlutte[2]

[1] Équipe BDAA, LIF, UMR 6166 CNRS,
CMI, Université de Provence, 39, rue F. Joliot Curie
13453 Marseille cedex 13, France
fdenis@cmi.univ-mrs.fr
[2] Équipe Grappa, Université de Lille 3
59653 Villeneuve d'Ascq cedex, France
{lemay,terlutte}@lifl.fr

Abstract. Angluin defined in [Ang82] the classes of k-reversible regular languages and showed that these classes are identifiable in the limit from positive data. We introduced in [DLT01b] a class of automata based on properties of residual languages (RFSA) and showed in [DLT00] and [DLT01a] that this class could be interesting for grammatical inference purpose. Here, we study properties of 0-reversible languages that can be expressed as properties of their residual languages and that are useful for identification from positive data. This leads us to define classes of languages which strictly contain the class of 0-reversible languages and are identifiable in the limit from positive data.

Key Words: grammatical inference, regular languages, identifiability in the limit from positive data.

1 Introduction

When Gold introduced his model of identification in the limit in [Gol67], his ultimate goal was to explain the learning process of the natural language. In the same paper, he observed that, according to works of psycho-linguists, children learn their own language from syntaxically correct sentences but none of the language classes defined by Chomsky to model natural language is identifiable in the limit from positive data only. He suggested several hypothesis to overcome this difficulty: 1. "The class of possible natural languages is much smaller than one would expect from our present models of syntax." 2. "The child receives negative instances by being corrected in a way we do not recognize." 3. "There is an a priori restriction on the class of texts which can occur, such as restriction on the order of text presentation". A lot of works already explored these paths.

Angluin defined in [Ang82] non trivial classes of regular languages identifiable in the limit from positive data: the classes of k-*reversible* languages. The identification algorithm she defined has next been adapted and used in several richer

P. Adriaans, H. Fernau, and M. van Zaanen (Eds.): ICGI 2002, LNAI 2484, pp. 63–76, 2002.
© Springer-Verlag Berlin Heidelberg 2002

context to learn some classes of *context-free grammars* [Sak92] or to learn some classes of *categorial grammars* [Kan98]. Note that this goes against the idea that regular languages are not expressive enough to be of some interest. The seminal paper from Angluin has been followed by a long list of works which introduced new classes of regular languages learnable from positive examples only (*locally testable languages* in [KY94], *terminal distinguishable languages* in [Fer00a], see also [HKY98], [Fer00b]) and which show that the first path mentioned above can be successful. This paper is following these leads, and presents some new classes of regular languages identifiable in the limit from positive data only.

We introduced in [DLT01b] a new class of automata, *residual finite state automata* (RFSA). Every regular language is recognized by a minimal size canonical RFSA and the study of RFSA leads to a natural categorization of residual languages: they can be *prime* or *composite*. We studied in [DLT00] and [DLT01a] applications of RFSA in grammatical inference. We present here a similar study for inference of regular languages from positive examples. More precisely, we study properties of 0-reversible languages that can be expressed as properties of their residual languages and that are useful for identification from positive data.

0-reversible languages can be defined as regular languages with disjoint residual languages. Thus, it is natural to consider the class of regular languages whose *prime* residual languages are disjoint. Unfortunately, we show that this class is not identifiable from positive data. As all residual languages of 0-reversible languages are prime, they trivially verify several other properties that we study. This leads us to define three new classes of languages strictly containing the class of 0-reversible languages and identifiable in the limit from positive data.

We recall some definitions and results on language theory and the model of identification in the limit from positive data in Section 2. We define the classes of languages that we study in Section 3. We show relations between these classes in Section 4. We present some results of non identifiability in Section 5. And we finally prove that three of the classes defined here are identifiable in the limit using positive data. We present some comments in the last section.

2   Preliminaries

2.1   Languages and Automata

We present here classical results on regular languages. The reader can refer to [Yu97] for general results and to [DLT01b] for results concerning RFSA. Let Σ be a finite alphabet and let Σ^* be the set of words built on Σ. We denote by ε the empty word. We assume that words of Σ^* are ordered the following way: $u < v$ iff $[|u| < |v|$ or $(|u| = |v|$ and u is before v in the lexicographic order$)]$. A language is a subset of Σ^*. A *class of languages* is a set of languages. A positive sample S of a language L is a finite subset of L. We denote by $|S|$ the cardinal of S. A *positive presentation* of L is an infinite sequence of elements of L containing every element of L. If u is a word of Σ^*, we note $Pref(u) = \{u' \in \Sigma^* | \exists v \in \Sigma^*$ s. t. $u'v = u\}$; if L is a language, we also note $Pref(L) = \bigcup_{u \in L} Pref(u)$.

A language L is *prefixial* iff $\forall u \in L$, $Pref(u) \subseteq L$. A *non deterministic finite automata* (NFA) is a quintuple $A = \langle \Sigma, Q, Q_0, F, \delta \rangle$ where Q is a finite set of states, $Q_0 \subseteq Q$ is the set of initial state , $F \subseteq Q$ is the set of final states and δ is a set of transitions included in $Q \times \Sigma \times Q$. We also denote by δ the extended function defined from $Q \times \Sigma^*$ to 2^Q such that $\delta(q, \varepsilon) = \{q\}$ and $\forall u \in \Sigma^*$ and $\forall x \in \Sigma$, $\delta(q, ux) = \{q'' \in Q \mid \exists q' \in \delta(q, u) \text{ and } q'' \in \delta(q', x)\}$. We denote by $\tilde{A} = \langle \Sigma, Q, F, Q_0, \tilde{\delta} \rangle$ the *reversal* of A where $\tilde{\delta} = \{(q, x, q') \mid (q', x, q) \in \delta\}$. A language L is *regular* if there exists a NFA $A = \langle \Sigma, Q, Q_0, F, \delta \rangle$ such that $L = \{u \in \Sigma^* \mid \delta(Q_0, u) \cap F \neq \emptyset\}$. We denote by REG the set of regular languages. Let $A = \langle \Sigma, Q, Q_0, F, \delta \rangle$ be a NFA and q a state of Q, we define the language $L_q = \{u \in \Sigma^* \mid \delta(q, u) \cap F \neq \emptyset\}$. An automaton is *deterministic* (DFA) if $Q_0 = \{q_0\}$ and if for any state q and for any letter x, $|\delta(q, x)| \leq 1$. Every regular language is recognized by an unique minimal DFA. Let S be a positive sample, the *prefix tree* of S is the automaton $A = \langle \Sigma, Q, Q_0, F, \delta \rangle$ where $Q = Pref(S)$, $Q_0 = \varepsilon$, $F = S$, $\delta = \{(u, x, v) \mid v = ux\}$.

Let L be a regular language and let u be a word of Σ^*, $u^{-1}L = \{v \in \Sigma^* \mid uv \in L\}$ is the *residual* language of L with respect to u. According to the Myhill-Nerode theorem, a language is regular iff the set of its residual languages is finite. Let $A = \langle \Sigma, Q, q_0, F, \delta \rangle$ be the minimal DFA recognizing L, $u^{-1}L \rightarrow \delta(q_0, u)$ is a bijection from the set of residual languages of L to Q. A residual language is *composite* if it is union of other residual languages of L, i.e. if $u^{-1}L = \bigcup_i \{u_i^{-1}L \mid u_i^{-1}L \subsetneq u^{-1}L\}$, a residual language is *prime* if it is not composite. Let $A = \langle \Sigma, Q, q_0, F, \delta \rangle$ be a NFA recognizing L, A is a RFSA (Residual Finite State Automaton) if $\forall q \in Q$, $\exists u \in \Sigma^*$ such that $L_q = u^{-1}L$. It is proved in [DLT01b] that we can associate to every regular language L a canonical RFSA whose set of states Q is the set of prime residual languages of L , $Q_0 = \{R \in Q \mid R \subseteq L\}$, $F = \{R \in Q \mid \varepsilon \in R\}$, and $\delta = \{(R_1, x, R_2) \mid R_2 \subseteq x^{-1}R_1\}$. This canonical RFSA is minimal with respect to the number of states. Let R be a residual language of a language L defined on Σ^*, $u \in \Sigma^*$ is a *characteristic word* of R if $R = u^{-1}L$. The set of smallest characteristic words of residual languages is a prefixial set. We denote by P_L the set of smallest characteristic words of *prime residual languages* of L. A regular language is 0-reversible if the reversal of a DFA recognizing it is deterministic (see [Ang82]). In this case the reversal of its minimal DFA is also deterministic. Also, an automaton $A = \langle \Sigma, Q, Q_0, F, \delta \rangle$ is *k-reversible* if it is deterministic, and if for every state $q \in Q$ and for every word $u \in \Sigma$ with $|u| \geq k$, $|\tilde{\delta}(q, u)| \leq 1$.

2.2   Identifiability in the Limit

This paper is about learnability of languages in the model of identification in the limit of Gold ([Gol67], [Ang80]). We sum up here some classical definitions.

Let S be a positive presentation of a language, we denote by S_t the first t elements of S. Let M be an algorithm that takes as input a finite set of words and that outputs a representation of a language (an automaton for example). M identifies in the limit a class of languages $\mathcal{L}$ from positive data if for all language L of $\mathcal{L}$ and for every positive presentation of L, there exists an index T from which $M(S_t)$ is always a representation of L. A class of languages is identifiable in the limit from positive data if there exists an algorithm M that identifies it in the limit. [Ang82] proves that the class of k-reversible languages is identifiable in the limit when k is given. The following lemma is often useful to show that a class of language is identifiable in the limit from positive data.

Lemma 1. *A class of language $\mathcal{L}$ is identifiable in the limit from positive data if there exists an algorithm M that takes as input a set of words and outputs the representation of a language, and if we can associate with each language L of $\mathcal{L}$ a characteristic positive sample $S(L)$ such that, for every sample $S \subseteq L$ with $S(L) \subseteq S$, $M(S)$ is a representation of L.*

Gold also proved that a class of languages that contains all of the finite languages and at least one infinite language cannot be identified in the limit from positive data. As a consequence, the class of regular languages is not identifiable in the limit from positive data. In this paper, we use the following extension of Gold's result (see [BB75] and [Kan98]):

Lemma 2. *If a class of languages $\mathcal{L}$ contains an infinite sequence $(L_n)_{n \in \mathbb{N}}$ of languages such that $\forall n, L_n \subsetneq L_{n+1}$ and $\cup_{n \in \mathbb{N}} L_n \in \mathcal{L}$, then $\mathcal{L}$ is not identifiable in the limit from positive data.*

We also use the following stronger result from [Kap91]:

Lemma 3. *If a class of languages $\mathcal{L}$ contains an infinite sequence $(L_n)_{n \in \mathbb{N}}$ such that there exists an infinite sequence $(S_n)_{n \in \mathbb{N}}$ with $\forall n, S_n \subsetneq S_{n+1}$, $S_n \subseteq L_n$ and $\cup_{n \in \mathbb{N}} S_n \in \mathcal{L}$, then $\mathcal{L}$ is not identifiable in the limit from positive data.*

3   Definitions

The family of *k-reversible* languages is one of the largest class of regular languages known to be identifiable in the limit using positive data. We study here properties of *k-reversibles* languages that allows this identification process. We first observe that a regular language is 0-*reversible* if and only if all its residual languages are disjoint ([Ang82]). Therefore, it is natural to extend the definition of 0-reversible to regular language which have *disjoint prime* residual languages.

Definition 1. *A regular language has* disjoint prime *residual languages if any two distinct prime residual languages are disjoint.*

We obtain a characterization of these languages similar to the definition of 0-reversible languages.

Property 1 *A regular language has disjoint prime residual languages if and only if there exists a RFSA A that recognizes it and such that the reversal of A is deterministic.*

It would have been nice to observe that regular languages with disjoint prime residual languages are identifiable in the limit from positive data, but unfortunately we prove in Section 4 that it is not the case. We introduce two complementary notions.

The set of the smallest characterizing words of the residual languages of a regular language is prefixial. However, this property does not hold when we consider only prime residual languages. For example, the prime residual languages of $L = 0^* + 1^*$ are $0^{-1}L = 0^*$ and $1^{-1}L = 1^*$, so $P_L = \{0, 1\}$. Therefore, we can consider regular languages such that P_L is a prefixial set.

Definition 2. *A regular language L has* prefixial prime *residual languages if P_L is prefixial.*

A residual language can be composed by prime residual languages having longer smallest characteristic words. The following notion defines languages such that every composite residual language contains a prime residual language which precedes it in the prefix tree.

Definition 3. *A regular language L has* foreseeable composite *residual languages if, for every composite residual language R of L and for every word u such that $R = u^{-1}L$, there exists a prime residual language $v^{-1}L$ such that $v < u$ and $v^{-1}L \subset R$.*

For example, the language $L = 0^* + 1$ is not a regular language with foreseeable composite residual languages as $\varepsilon^{-1}L$ is the union of $0^{-1}L$ and $1^{-1}L$ and $0 > \varepsilon$ and $1 > \varepsilon$. Note that if L is a non empty regular language with foreseeable composite residual languages, then $\varepsilon^{-1}L$ is a prime residual language.

Property 2 *The class of regular languages with prefixial disjoint prime residual languages and with foreseeable composite residual languages strictly contains the class of 0-reversible languages.*

Proof.
    All residual languages of a 0-reversible language L are prime and disjoint. As there are no composite residual languages, L is trivially with foreseeable composite residual languages, and P_L is prefixial. On the other hand, the language $L = 0^*\Sigma = 0^+ + 0^*1$ has two prime residual languages: $\varepsilon^{-1}L = 0^+ + 0^*1$ and $1^{-1}L = \{\varepsilon\}$. $0^{-1}L = 0^* + 0^*1 = \varepsilon^{-1}L \cup 1^{-1}L$ is composite. So L has disjoint prefixial prime residual languages and foreseeable composite residual languages although L is not 0-reversible.   □

One can observe that no inclusion relations hold between the three classes of languages deefined above: the language $0^*11 + 1^*00$ has disjoint prime residual languages but neither with prefixial prime residual languages nor with foreseeable composite residual languages; the language $\{00, 100, 01, 111\}$ has prefixial prime residual languages but neither with disjoint prime residual languages nor with foreseeable composite residual languages; the language $0^+1^* + 1$ is with foreseeable composite residual languages but neither with disjoint prime residual languages nor with prefixial prime residual languages.

Also, none of these classes contains the intersection of the two others: the language 0^+1^* has prime residual languages and foreseeable composite residual languages but not with prefixial prime residual languages; $\varepsilon + 01^*$ is a language with prefixial prime residual languages and with foreseeable composite residual languages but not with disjoint prime residual languages; $\{00, 01, 110, 1011\}$ is a language with prefixial disjoint prime residual languages but not with foreseeable composite residual languages.

4   Non Identifiability

None of the properties defined in the previous section is sufficient by itself to define a class of languages identifiable in the limit from positive data.

Proposition 1. *Regular languages with disjoint prime residual languages are not identifiable in the limit from positive data.*

Proof.
   Let $\Sigma = \{0, 1\}$. We associate to every integer $n > 1$, the automaton $A^n = \langle Q^n, Q_0^n, F^n, \delta^n, \Sigma \rangle$ defined by:

- $Q^1 = Q_0^1 = \{1, 2, 3\}$, $F^1 = \{1\}$, $\delta^1 = \{(2, 0, 1), (3, 1, 1), (2, 1, 2), (3, 0, 3)\}$
- $Q^n = Q_0^n = \{1, \ldots, 2^{n+1} - 1\}$,
- $F^n = \{1\}$,
- $\delta^n = \{(i + 1, x, j + 1) \mid (i, x, j) \in \delta^{n-1}$ and $(i, x, j) \neq (2^n - 1, 0, 2^n - 1)\}$
    $\cup \{(i + 2^n, x, j + 2^n) \mid (i, x, j) \in \delta^{n-1}$ et $(i, x, j) \neq (n, 1, n)\}$
    $\cup \{(2, 0, 1), (2^n + 1, 1, 1), (2, 1, 2^n + n), (2^n + 1, 0, 2^n)\}$

   Figure 1 shows A^1 and A^2. We prove the following points:

- A^n is a RFSA. Indeed, states $n+1$ and $2^{n+1}-1$ are characterized respectively with 1^{n+1} and 0^{n+1}, and for every other state q, there exists a word u such that either $\delta(n + 1, u) = \{q\}$, or $\delta(2^{n+1} - 1, u) = \{q\}$; the state q is then characterized either by $1^{n+1}u$ or by $0^{n+1}u$,
- The reversal of A^n is deterministic,
- Let L_n be the language recognized by A^n. According to Property 1, L_n has disjoint prime residual languages,
- $\forall n, \Sigma^{\leq n} \subsetneq L_n$.
- $\Sigma^* = \bigcup_{n \in \mathbb{N}} L_n$ is a language with disjoint prime residual languages.

   Lemma 3 terminates the proof.   □

Proposition 2.

- *The class of regular languages with prefixial prime residual languages are not identifiable in the limit from positive data.*

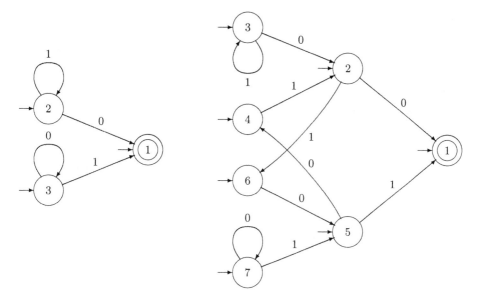

Fig. 1. Automata A^1 and A^2. The sequence of automata A^n illustrates the fact that the class of languages with disjoint prime residual languages are not identifiable in the limit from positive data.

- *The class of regular languages with foreseeable composite residual languages are not identifiable in the limit from positive data.*
- *The class of regular languages with prefixial prime residual languages and with foreseeable composite residual languages are not identifiable in the limit from positive data,*

Proof. These three classes contain the language 0^* and all languages $\{0^{\leq n} \mid n \in \mathbb{N}\}$. We can conclude using Lemma 2. □

5   Identifiability

We now prove that the following classes are identifiable in the limit from positive data: regular languages with prefixial disjoint prime residual languages, regular language with disjoint prime residual language and with foreseeable composite residual languages, and regular languages with disjoint prefixial prime residual languages and with foreseeable composite residual languages. Although the last result is obvious regarding to the two others, we will prove that the identification process is much more efficient in this case. For each of these classes, we define a notion of characteristic sample and an identification algorithm satisfying conditions of Lemma 1.

We first define a procedure that builds an automaton from sets of words.

Definition 4. *Let S and P be two sets of words of Σ^* such that $P \subseteq Pref(S)$. We define $A_{(S,P)} = \langle \Sigma, Q, Q_0, F, \delta \rangle$ such that $Q = P$, $Q_0 = \{u \in P \mid u^{-1}S \cap S \neq \emptyset\}$, $F = \{u \in P \mid u \in S\}$, δ contains all transitions (u, x, v) where $u, v \in P$, $ux \in Pref(S)$ and $(ux)^{-1}S \cap v^{-1}S \neq \emptyset$.*

We note that one can build $A_{(S,P)}$ in time $\mathcal{O}(n^4 \times |\Sigma|)$ where n is the sum of lengths of words of S.

Example 1 *Let $S = \{01, 1\}$ and $P = \{\varepsilon, 1\}$. Then $Q_0 = \{\varepsilon\}$ and $F = \{1\}$. We indicate the the relevant intersections and the automaton $A_{(S,P)}$:*

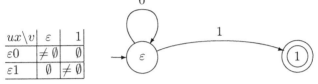

$ux\backslash v$	ε	1
$\varepsilon 0$	$\neq \emptyset$	$\emptyset$
$\varepsilon 1$	$\emptyset$	$\neq \emptyset$

Definition 5. *Let $\bar{u}_L$ be the smallest word of $u^{-1}L$. $S_{RFSA}(L)$ is the smallest set such that:*

- *$\forall u \in P_L$, if $u^{-1}L \subseteq L$ then $\bar{u}_L \in S_{RFSA}(L)$,*
- *$\forall u \in P_L$, $u\bar{u}_L \in S_{RFSA}(L)$,*
- *$\forall u, v \in P_L, \forall x \in \Sigma$, if $v^{-1}L \subseteq (ux)^{-1}L$, then $ux\bar{v}_L \in S_{RFSA}(L)$.*

Example 2 *The language $0^*\Sigma$ has two prime residual languages ($\varepsilon^{-1}L$ and $1^{-1}L$) and $P_L = \{\varepsilon, 1\}$.*
The smallest word of $\varepsilon^{-1}L$ is 0, so $\varepsilon 0 \in S_{RFSA}(L)$; the smallest word of $1^{-1}L$ is ε, so $1\varepsilon \in S_{RFSA}(L)$.

Following intersections can be observed:

$v\backslash ux$	$\varepsilon 0$	$\varepsilon 1$	10	11
ε	0	$\emptyset$	$\emptyset$	$\emptyset$
1	ε	ε	$\emptyset$	$\emptyset$

Therefore, $S_{RFSA}(L)$ contains $\varepsilon 00$, $\varepsilon 0\varepsilon$ and $\varepsilon 1\varepsilon$. So $S_{RFSA}(L) = \{0, 1, 00\}$.

The size of $S_{RFSA}(L)$, i.e. the sum of the lengths of its words, is bounded above by $6N_Q{}^3 * |\Sigma|$ where N_Q is the number of residual languages of L. When L has prefixial prime residual languages, the size of $S_{RFSA}(L)$ is bounded above by $6N_P{}^3 * |\Sigma|$ where N_P is the number of prime residual languages of L.

Proposition 3. *If L has disjoint prime residual languages, and if S and P are such that: $S \subseteq L$, $S_{RFSA}(L) \subseteq S$ and $P = P_L$, then $A_{(S,P)}$ is the canonical RFSA of L.*

Proof.
We first observe that $u^{-1}L \subseteq v^{-1}L \Leftrightarrow u^{-1}L \cap v^{-1}L \neq \emptyset$ if $u^{-1}L$ is prime (because prime residual languages are disjoint), and the choice of S and P is such that:

- $\forall u \in P,\ u^{-1}L \subseteq L \Leftrightarrow u^{-1}S \cap S \neq \emptyset$ and
- $\forall x \in \Sigma,\ \forall u,\ v \in P,\ v^{-1}L \subseteq (ux)^{-1}L \Leftrightarrow v^{-1}S \cap (ux)^{-1}S \neq \emptyset$

To build $A_{(S,P)}$ is then equivalent to build the canonical RFSA of L.   □

Example 3 *(continuation)*
For $L = 0^*\Sigma$, we have $S_{RFSA}(L) = \{0, 1, 00\}$. If $S = S_{RFSA}(L)$ and $P = P_L = \{\varepsilon, 1\}$, then $Q_0 = \{\varepsilon\}$ and $F = \{1\}$. From the following intersections, we compute $A_{(S,P)}$

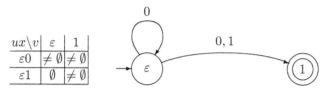

$ux\backslash v$	ε	1
$\varepsilon 0$	$\neq \emptyset$	$\neq \emptyset$
$\varepsilon 1$	$\emptyset$	$\neq \emptyset$

In the three identification algorithms we will present, we enumerate states of the prefix tree using the lexicographic order with increasing length. The purpose is to find the set P_L to build the canonical RFSA $A_{(S,P_L)}$.

The first identification algorithm operates in three steps. As a first step, it limits the size of interesting prefixes, then it suppresses prefixes that has the same behavior as a shorter prefix, and then it suppresses characteristic words of composite residual languages.

Proposition 4. *Regular languages with prefixial disjoint prime residual languages are identifiable in the limit from positive data.*

Proof.
Let L be a regular language with disjoint prefixial prime residual languages. Let $A = \langle Q, \Sigma, q_0, F, \delta \rangle$ be the minimal DFA that recognizes it. Let N_Q be the number of states of this DFA. We note that for every word $u \in L$ such that $|u| \geq N_Q$, there exists a prefix $u_1 u_2$ of u with $|u_2| > 0$ such that $\delta(Q_0, u_1) = \delta(Q_0, u_1 u_2)$, so $u_1^{-1}L = (u_1 u_2)^{-1}L$. The characteristic sample $S_{car}(L)$ is defined the following way:

- $S_1 = \{uw \mid u \in \Sigma^{N_Q} \cap Pref(L)$ and w is the smallest word of $u^{-1}L\}$
- $S_2 = \Sigma^{\leq N_Q} \cap Pref(L)$,
- $S_3 = \{uw \mid u \in S_2,\ \exists v \in S_2,\ v \neq u$ and w is the smallest word of $u^{-1}L \cap v^{-1}L\}$,
- $S_{car}(L) = (\Sigma^{\leq N_Q} \cap L) \cup S_1 \cup S_3 \cup S_{AFER}(L)$.

We define the following identification algorithm:

Algorithm $PDPA$

Let S_t be the current sample.

- Consider the smallest integer $N > 0$ such that for every word $u \in Pref(S_t) \cap \Sigma^N$, there exists a prefix $u_1 u_2$ of u such that $|u_2| > 0$ and $u_1^{-1}S_t \cap (u_1 u_2)^{-1}S_t \neq \emptyset$. We define $T_1 = Pref(S_t) \cap \Sigma^{\leq N}$.
  If such a N does not exist, stop and output the prefix tree of S_t.

- T_2 is built from T_1 without words u' such that there exists $u < u'$, with $u^{-1}S_t \cap u'^{-1}S_t \neq \emptyset$ and $\forall v \in T_1$, $u^{-1}S_t \cap v^{-1}S_t \neq \emptyset \Leftrightarrow u'^{-1}S_t \cap v^{-1}S_t \neq \emptyset$
- T_3 is T_2 without states u that verifies Property (P)
  (P): *there exist v_1 and v_2 in T_2 such that* $u^{-1}S_t \cap v_1^{-1}S_t \neq \emptyset$
  $$u^{-1}S_t \cap v_2^{-1}S_t \neq \emptyset$$
  $$v_1^{-1}S_t \cap v_2^{-1}S_t = \emptyset$$
- Building of $A_{(S_t,T_3)}$. If $A_{(S_t,T_3)}$ is consistant with S_t, then output $A_{(S_t,T_3)}$ otherwise output the prefix tree of S_t.

There exists an index T such that $S_{car}(L) \subseteq S_{t \geq T}$. We then prove from the following points that the algorithm outputs the canonical RFSA of L.

- We first prove that $N \leq N_Q$. If $S_{car}(L) \subseteq S_t$ then $S_1 \subseteq S_t$. As a consequence $\forall u \in \Sigma^{N_Q} \cap Pref(S_t) = \Sigma^{N_Q} \cap Pref(L)$, there exists a prefix $u_1 u_2$ of u such that $|u_2| > 0$ and $u_1^{-1}L \cap (u_1 u_2)^{-1}L \neq \emptyset$. As $|u_1 u_2| \leq |u| \leq N_Q$, then u_1 and $u_1 u_2 \in S_2$, from the construction of S_3, $\exists w$ such that $u_1 w \in S_t$ and $u_1 u_2 w \in S_t$, so $u_1^{-1}S_t \cap (u_1 u_2)^{-1}S_t \neq \emptyset$. So $N \leq N_Q$.
- $P_L \subseteq Pref(S_t)$ because $S_{AFER}(L) \subseteq S_{car}(L) \subseteq S_t$.
- $T_1 = S_2 \cap \Sigma^{\leq N}$. Indeed, as $N \leq N_Q$ and $S_{car}(L) \subseteq S_t$, $T_1 = Pref(S_t) \cap \Sigma^{\leq N} \subseteq Pref(L) \cap \Sigma^{\leq N} = S_2 \cap \Sigma^{\leq N} \subseteq Pref(S_t) \cap \Sigma^{\leq N} = T_1$.
- $P_L \subseteq T_1$. Let us assume that there exist $u \in P_L$ and $u \notin T_1$. From the definition of T_1, this implies that $|u| > N$. From the definition of N, there exists a prefix $u_1 u_2 \in Pref(u)$ with $|u_1 u_2| \leq N$, $|u_2| > 0$ and $u_1^{-1}S_t \cap (u_1 u_2)^{-1}S_t \neq \emptyset$. As prime residual languages are prefixial, $u \in P_L$ implies that $u_1 \in P_L$ and $u_1 u_2 \in P_L$. As prime residual languages are disjoint, $u_1^{-1}S_t \cap (u_1 u_2)^{-1}S_t \neq \emptyset$ implies that $u_1^{-1}L = (u_1 u_2)^{-1}L$. In this case, $u_1 u_2$ is not the smallest characteristic word of $(u_1 u_2)^{-1}L$ and so $u_1 u_2 \notin P_L$, which is contradictory.
- Let $u \in T_2 \cap P_L$. We prove that for every u' such that $u'^{-1}L = u^{-1}L$ and $u' > u$, $u' \notin T_2$. Let $u' \in T_1$ be such that $u'^{-1}L = u^{-1}L$. Then $u'^{-1}L \cap u^{-1}L \neq \emptyset$ and $\forall v \in T_1$, $u^{-1}L \cap v^{-1}L \neq \emptyset \Leftrightarrow u'^{-1}L \cap v^{-1}L \neq \emptyset$. As $T_1 = S_2 \cap \Sigma^{\leq N}$, from the definition of S_3:
  • $u'^{-1}L \cap u^{-1}L \neq \emptyset$ implies that there exists $w \in u'^{-1}L \cap u^{-1}L$ such that $uw \in S_3 \subseteq S_t$ and $u'w \in S_3$. So $u'^{-1}S_t \cap u^{-1}S_t \neq \emptyset$.
  • $\forall v \in T_1$, $u^{-1}L \cap v^{-1}L \neq \emptyset$ implies that there exists $w \in u^{-1}L \cap v^{-1}L$ such that $uw \in S_3 \subseteq S_t$ and $vw \in S_3$ which implies that $u^{-1}S_t \cap v^{-1}S_t \neq \emptyset$.
  • Also, $\forall v \in T_1$, $u'^{-1}L \cap v^{-1}L \neq \emptyset$ implies that there exists $w \in u'^{-1}L \cap v^{-1}L$ such that $u'w \in S_3 \subseteq S_t$ and $vw \in S_3$ which implies that $u'^{-1}S_t \cap v^{-1}S_t \neq \emptyset$.
  • Trivially, $u^{-1}S_t \cap v^{-1}S_t \neq \emptyset$ implies that $u^{-1}L \cap v^{-1}L \neq \emptyset$ and $u'^{-1}S_t \cap v^{-1}S_t \neq \emptyset$ imply that $u'^{-1}L \cap v^{-1}L \neq \emptyset$.
  So $u'^{-1}S_t \cap u^{-1}S_t \neq \emptyset$ and $\forall v \in T_1$, $u^{-1}S_t \cap v^{-1}S_t \neq \emptyset \Leftrightarrow u'^{-1}S_t \cap v^{-1}S_t \neq \emptyset$. In this case u' is not in T_2.
- We prove that $P_L \subseteq T_2$.
  Let $u \in P_L$, then $u \in T_1$. Let us assume that $u \notin T_2$, then there exists $u'' \in T_2$ such that $u'' < u$, $u^{-1}S_t \cap u''^{-1}S_t \neq \emptyset$ and $\forall v \in T_1$, $u^{-1}S_t \cap v^{-1}S_t \neq \emptyset \Leftrightarrow u''^{-1}S_t \cap v^{-1}S_t \neq \emptyset$.

- If $u''^{-1}L$ is prime, then $u^{-1}L = u''^{-1}L$ (because prime residual languages are disjoint and $u^{-1}S_t \cap u''^{-1}S_t \neq \emptyset$). Then $u \notin P_L$, which is contradictory.
- If $u''^{-1}L$ is composite, then there exists a word $v \neq u$ and $v \in P_L \subseteq T_1$ such that $v^{-1}L \subsetneq u''^{-1}L$. As $T_1 = S_2 \cap \Sigma^{\leq N}$, from the definition of S_3, there exists w in $v^{-1}L$ such that $vw \in S_t$ and $u''w \in S_t$. So $v^{-1}S_t \cap u''^{-1}S_t \neq \emptyset$. But $v \neq u$ implies $v^{-1}S_t \cap u^{-1}S_t = \emptyset$. So $v^{-1}S_t \cap u''^{-1}S_t \neq \emptyset$ and $v^{-1}S_t \cap u^{-1}S_t = \emptyset$ which is contradictory with the initial guess.

So $u \in T_2$.

- We prove that $P_L = T_3$. Obviously, if $u^{-1}L$ is composite, u verifies (P).

  Let u verify Property (P). Let us assume that $u \in P_L$. If $v_1^{-1}L$ was prime, then $u^{-1}L = v_1^{-1}L$ and $v_1 > u$; we saw that in this case $v_1 \notin T_2$. Then $v_1^{-1}L$ is composite and $u^{-1}L \subset v_1^{-1}L$. The same way, $u^{-1}L \subset v_2^{-1}L$. As v_1 and $v_2 \in T_1 = S_2 \cap \Sigma^{\leq N}$ and $v_1^{-1}L \cap v_2^{-1}L \neq \emptyset$ (as they contain $u^{-1}L$), there exists a word $w \in v_1^{-1}L \cap v_2^{-1}L$ such that $v_1 w \in S_3 \subseteq S_t$ and $v_2 w \in S_3 \subseteq S_t$. Then $v_1^{-1}S_t \cap v_2^{-1}S_t \neq \emptyset$, which is contradictory with the Property (P).

  So, we take out words of T_2 corresponding to composite residual languages. As $P_L \subseteq T_2$, $P_L = T_3$.

- As $S_{AFER}(L)$ is included in $S_{car}(L)$, proposition 3 applies here and $A_{(S_t,T_3)}$ is the canonical RFSA of L.

$\square$

Proposition 5. *Regular languages with disjoint prime residual languages and with foreseeable composite residual languages are identifiable in the limit from positive data.*

Proof. Let L be a regular language with disjoint prime residual languages and with foreseeable composite residual languages. Let u_{max} be the greatest word of P_L. We define the following characteristic sample:

- $\forall u \leq u_{max}$
  - if $u^{-1}L$ is prime, then $uw \in S_1$, where w is the smallest word of $u^{-1}L$.
  - if $u^{-1}L$ is composite, for every v such that $v^{-1}L$ is prime and $v^{-1}L \subset u^{-1}L$, $uw \in S_1$, where w is the smallest word of $v^{-1}L$.
- $S_{car}(L) = S_1 \cup S_{RFSA}(L)$.

Let S_t be the current sample. We assume that words of $Pref(S_t)$ are numbered from $u_1 = \varepsilon$.

Algorithm $DPFCA$:

$i = 1$
$M = \emptyset$
found = false
while $i \leq |Pref(S_t)|$ and not found do
       if $\forall v \in M$, $v^{-1}S_t \cap u_i^{-1}S_t = \emptyset$ then add u_i to M
       if $A_{(S_t,M)}$ consistant with S_t then found = true else $i = i + 1$

done
if found $=$ true then output $A_{(S_t,M)}$ else output the prefix tree.

¿From some index, $S_{car}(L) \subseteq S_t$. We verify recursively on i that $\forall u_i \leq u_{max}$, $M \cap \{u \mid u \leq u_i\} = P_L \cap \{u \mid u \leq u_i\}$.

- We note that $\varepsilon \in P_L$. The property is true for $u_1 = \varepsilon$, because ε is added to M during the first iteration.
- Let us assume that the equality is true for u_{i-1}.
  - If $u_i \in P_L$, then $\forall v \in M \cap \{u \mid u < u_i\} = P_L \cap \{u \mid u < u_i\}$, $v^{-1}L \cap u_i^{-1}L = \emptyset$ because prime residual languages are disjoint and u_i is the smallest characterizing word of $u_i^{-1}L$; so $v^{-1}S_t \cap u_i^{-1}S_t = \emptyset$ and $u_i \in M$.
  - If $u_i \in M$, then
    * if $u_i^{-1}L$ is composite then $\exists v \in M \cap \{u \mid u < u_i\} = P_L \cap \{u \mid u < u_i\}$ such that $v^{-1}L \subset u_i^{-1}L$, because composite residual languages are foreseeable; from the definition of the characteristic sample, v and u_i being smaller than u_{max}, there exists $w \in v^{-1}L$ such that $vw \in S_{car}(L) \subseteq S_t$ and $u_iw \in S_{car}(L)$, which is contradictory with $u_i \in M$,
    * if $u_i^{-1}L$ is prime but if u_i is not the smallest characteristic word of $u_i^{-1}L$, then $\exists v \in M \cap \{u \mid u < u_i\}$ such that $v^{-1}L = u_i^{-1}L$; from the definition of the characteristic sample, v and u_i being smaller than u_{max}, there exists $w \in v^{-1}L = u_i^{-1}L$ such that $vw \in S_{car}(L) \subseteq S_t$ and $u_iw \in S_{car}(L)$, which is contradictory with $u_i \in M$,
    * So $u_i^{-1}L$ is prime and u_i is the smallest characteristic word of $u_i^{-1}L$; so $u_i \in P_L$.

When $S_{car}(L) \subseteq S_t$, the algorithm cannot stop on an index i such that $u_i < u_{max}$. Indeed, if $u_i < u_{max}$ then $M \subsetneq P_L$ because $u_{max} \notin M$ and $A_{(S_t,M)}$ is a sub-automaton of the canonical RFSA that does not contain the state u_{max}; there exists a word $u_{max}w \in S_t$ which is not recognized by $A_{(S_t,M)}$ because, in the canonical RFSA of a language with disjoint prime residual languages, a characteristic word of a prime residual language only reaches the state associated to its residual language. So $A_{(S_t,M)}$ is not consistant with S_t.

On the other hand, if $u_i = u_{max}$ then $A_{(S_t,M)} = A_{(S_t,P_L)}$. As $S_{AFER}(L) \subseteq S_t$, the proposition 3 can be applied and $A_{(S_t,M)}$ is the canonical RFSA of L which is consistant with S_t. □

We prove now that the conjunction of the previous properties defines a class of languages identifiable in the limit from positive data using a polynomial size sample.

Proposition 6. *Regular languages with prefixial disjoint prime residual languages and with foreseeable composite residual languages are identifiable efficiently in the limit from positive data and admit characteristic samples whose size is a polynomial of the size of their canonical RFSA.*

Proof. Let L be a language with prefixial disjoint prime residual languages and with foreseeable composite residual languages.

We choose $S_{RFSA}(L)$ as characteristic sample, $S_{car}(L) = S_{RFSA}(L)$.

Let S_t be the current sample. Words of $Pref(S_t)$ are numbered from $u_1 = \varepsilon$.

Algorithm $DPPFCA$:

$M = \emptyset$

For $i = 1$ to $|Pref(S_t)|$ do

    if $\forall u' \in Pref(u_i) \setminus \{u_i\}$, $u' \in M$ and if $\forall v \in M$, $v^{-1}S_t \cap u_i^{-1}S_t = \emptyset$ then add u_i to M

    done.

If $A_{(S_t,M)}$ is consistant with S_t then output $A_{(S_t,M)}$ else output the prefix tree.

The proof is similar to the proof of the previous proposition. We verify recursively on i that $\forall u_i \in Pref(S_t)$, $M \cap \{u \mid u \le u_i\} = P_L \cap \{u \mid u \le u_i\}$. During the proof, we verify the following additional properties: if $u_i \in P_L$, then $\forall u' \in Pref(u_i) \setminus \{u_i\}$, $u' \in P_L \cap \{u \mid u < u_i\} = M \cap \{u \mid u < u_i\}$, because prime residual languages are prefixial; on the opposite, let $u_i = u'x \in M$ then $u' \in M$, recursively $u' \in P_L$ and from the definition of the characteristic sample, $\forall v \in M$, $v^{-1}S_t \cap (u'x)^{-1}S_t = \emptyset$ implies $u_i \in P_L$.

Let u_{max} be the greatest word of P_L and u_m be the greatest word of $Pref(S_t)$. When $S_{car}(L) \subseteq S_t$, then $u_{max} \in Pref(S_t)$ and $M = M \cap \{u \mid u \le u_m\} = P_L \cap \{u \mid u \le u_m\} = P_L \cap \{u \mid u \le u_{max}\} = P_L$. To conclude, as $S_{AFER}(L)$ is included in S_t, the proposition 3 applies and $A_{(S_t,M)} = A_{(S_t,P_L)}$ is the canonical RFSA of L.

Let N_P be the number of prime residual languages. Let n be the size of the characteristic sample, i.e. the sum of lengths of words of S_t. The size n is bounded above by $6N_P{}^3 * |\Sigma|$. In other respects, time complexity of the algorithm $DPPFCA$ is bounded above by $\mathcal{O}(n^4 \times |\Sigma|)$. $\qquad\square$

Example 4 *If $S = \{0, 1, 00\}$, successive steps of the algorithm are: $M = \emptyset$; $u_1 = \varepsilon$ and $M = \{\varepsilon\}$; $u_2 = 0$ and as $0 \in \varepsilon^{-1}S \cap 0^{-1}S$, $M = \{\varepsilon\}$; $u_3 = 1$ and $M = \{\varepsilon, 1\}$; $u_4 = 00$ and as $0 \notin M$; $M = \{\varepsilon, 1\}$; the algorithm outputs $A_{(S,M)}$ which is the canonical RFSA of $0^*\Sigma$ (see example 2).*

6 Conclusion

We have shown that it is possible to extend the class of 0-reversible languages while keeping the property of being identifiable in the limit from positive data. We still have to quantify the importance of this extension: this is a work in progress. Two of the algorithms we proposed are strictly in the learning model proposed by Gold: They accomplish their identification task without trying to be efficient! The question to know whether these two classes can be identified efficiently is still open. On the other hand, the third class we defined can be identified using a polynomial size sample and an efficient algorithm. Some works have used the class of reversible languages to learn approximatively the class of regular languages [KY97]; it would be interesting to achieve a similar study using our algorithm. Finally, the extension of results from 0-reversible languages to k-reversible languages is simple, although not trivial: a language is k-reversible if its residual languages are k-disjoint, i.e. disjoint with lookahead k. We can define in a similar way the class of regular languages with k-disjoint prime residual languages and we think that results presented here can be extended in a natural way: this is a work in progress.

References

[Ang80]   D. Angluin. Inductive inference of formal languages from positive data. *Inform. Control*, 45(2):117–135, May 1980.

[Ang82]   D. Angluin. Inference of reversible languages. *J. ACM*, 1982.

[BB75]   M. Blum and L. Blum. Towards a mathematical theory of inductive inference. *Information and Control*, 28:125–155, 1975.

[DLT00]   F. Denis, A. Lemay, and A. Terlutte. Learning regular languages using non deterministic finite automata. In *ICGI'2000, 5th International Colloquium on Grammatical Inference*, volume 1891 of *LNAI*, pages 39–50. Springer Verlag, 2000.

[DLT01a] F. Denis, A. Lemay, and A. Terlutte. Learning regular languages using RFSA. In Springer-Verlag, editor, *Proceedings of the 12th International Conference on Algorithmic Learning Theory (ALT-01)*, 2001.

[DLT01b] F. Denis, A. Lemay, and A. Terlutte. Residual finite state automata. In *STACS 2001*, volume 2010 of *LNCS*, pages p. 144–157. Springer Verlag, 2001.

[Fer00a] H. Fernau. Learning of terminal distinguishable languages. In *Proc. AMAI 2000*, 2000.

[Fer00b] Henning Fernau. Identification of function distinguishable languages. In *11th International Conference on Algorithmic Learning Theory , ALT 2000*, volume 1968 of *LNAI*, pages 116–130. Springer, 2000.

[Gol67]   E.M. Gold. Language identification in the limit. *Inform. Control*, 10:447–474, 1967.

[HKY98]   T. Head, S. Kobayashi, and T. Yokomori. Locality, reversibility and beyond: Learning languages from positive data. In *ALT 98, 9th International Conference on Algorithmic Learning Theory*, volume 1501 of *LNAI*, pages 191–204. Springer-Verlag, 1998.

[Kan98]   M. Kanazawa. *Learnable Classes of Categorial Grammars*. The European Association for Logic, Language and Information. CLSI Publications, 1998.

[Kap91]   S. Kapur. *Computational Learning of Languages*. PhD thesis, Cornell University, 1991.

[KY94]   S. Kobayashi and T. Yokomori. Learning concatenations of locally testable languages from positive data. *LNCS*, 872:407–422, 1994.

[KY97]   Satoshi Kobayashi and Takashi Yokomori. Learning approximately regular languages with reversible languages. *Theoretical Computer Science*, 174(1–2):251–257, 15 March 1997. Note.

[Sak92]   Yasubumi Sakakibara. Efficient learning of context-free grammars from positive structural examples. *Information and Computation*, 1992.

[Yu97]   Sheng Yu. *Handbook of Formal Languages, Regular Languages*, volume 1, chapter 2, pages 41–110. Springer Verlag, 1997.

Learning Probabilistic Residual Finite State Automata

Yann Esposito[1], Aurélien Lemay[2], François Denis[1], and Pierre Dupont[3]

[1] LIF, UMR 6166, Université de Provence, Marseille, France.
`esposito@cmi.univ-mrs.fr, fdenis@cmi.univ-mrs.fr`
[2] GRAPPA-LIFL, Université de Lille, Lille, France.
`lemay@lifl.fr`
[3] INGI, University of Louvain, Louvain-la-Neuve, Belgium.
`pdupont@info.ucl.ac.be`

Abstract. We introduce a new class of probabilistic automata: Probabilistic Residual Finite State Automata. We show that this class can be characterized by a simple intrinsic property of the stochastic languages they generate (the set of residual languages is finitely generated by residuals) and that it admits canonical minimal forms. We prove that there are more languages generated by PRFA than by Probabilistic Deterministic Finite Automata (PDFA). We present a first inference algorithm using this representation and we show that stochastic languages represented by PRFA can be identified from a characteristic sample if words are provided with their probabilities of appearance in the target language.

Introduction

In the field of machine learning, most realistic situations deal with data provided by a stochastic source and probabilistic models, such as Hidden Markov Models (HMMs) or probabilistic automata (PA), become increasingly important. For example, speech recognition, computational biology and more generally, every field where statistical sequence analysis is needed, may use this kind of models. In this paper, we focus on Probabilistic Automata.

A probabilistic automata can be described by its structure (a Finite State Automata) and by a set of continuous parameters (probability to emit a given letter from a given state or to end the generation process). There exist several fairly good methods to adjust the continuous parameters of a given structure to a training set of examples. However the efficient building of the structure from given data is still an open problem. Hence most applications of HMMs or PA assume a fixed model structure, which is either chosen as general as possible (i.e. a complete graph) or *a priori* selected using domain knowledge.

Several learning algorithms, based on previous works in the field of grammatical inference, have been designed to output a deterministic structure (Probabilistic Deterministic Finite State Automata: PDFA) from training data ([CO94], [CO99], [TDdlH00]; see also [Ang88], [SO94] for early works) and several interesting theoretical and experimental results have been obtained. However, unlike

P. Adriaans, H. Fernau, and M. van Zaanen (Eds.): ICGI 2002, LNAI 2484, pp. 77–91, 2002.

to the case of non stochastic languages, DFA structures are not able to represent as many stochastic languages as non deterministic ones. Therefore using these algorithms to infer probabilistic automata structures introduces a strong, and possibly wrong, learning bias.

A new class of non deterministic automata, the Residual Finite State Automata (RFSA), has been introduced in [DLT01b]. RFSA have interesting properties from a language theory point of view, including the existence of a canonical minimal form which can offer a much smaller representation than an equivalent DFA ([DLT01a]). Several learning algorithms that output RFSA have been designed in [DLT00] and [DLT01a]. The present paper describes an extension to these works to deal with stochastic regular languages.

We introduce in Section 1 classical notions of probabilistic automata and stochastic languages. In Section 2 we explain how the definition of residual languages can be extended to stochastic languages, and we define a new class of probabilistic automata: Probabilistic Residual Finite State Automata (PRFA). We prove that this class has canonical minimal representations. In Section 3 we introduce an intrinsic characterization of stochastic languages represented by PDFA: a stochastic language can be represented by a PDFA if and only if the number of its residual languages is finite. We extend this characterization to languages represented by PRFA: a stochastic language can be represented by a PRFA if and only if the set of its residual languages is finitely generated. We prove in Section 4 that the class of languages represented by PRFA is more expressive than the one represented by PDFA. This results is promising as it means that algorithms that would identify stochastic languages represented by PRFA would be able to identify a larger class of languages than PDFA inference algorithms. Section 5 presents a preliminary result along this line: stochastic languages represented by PRFA can be identified from a characteristic sample if words are provided with their actual probabilities of appearance in the target language.

1   Probabilistic Automata and Stochastic Languages

Let Σ be a finite *alphabet* and let Σ^* be the set of finite words built on Σ. A language L is a subset of Σ^*. Let u be a word of Σ^*, the length of u is denoted by $|u|$, the empty word is denoted by ε. Σ^* is ordered in the usual way, i.e. $u \leq v$ if and only if $|u| < |v|$ or $|u| = |v|$ and u is before v in lexicographical order. Let u be a word of Σ^*, v is a *prefix* of u if there exists a word w such that $u = vw$. A language L is *prefixial* if for every word u of L, the set of prefixes of u is a subset of L. Let E be a set, $\mathcal{D}(E) = \left\{ (\alpha_e)_{e \in E} \in [0,1]^{\mathrm{Card}(E)} \mid \sum_{e \in E} \alpha_e = 1 \right\}$ denotes the set of distributions over E and $\mathcal{D}(\{1, \ldots, n\})$ is denoted by $\mathcal{D}(n)$.

A *stochastic language* L on Σ is a function from Σ^* to $[0,1]$ such that $\sum_{u \in \Sigma^*} L(u) = 1$. We note $p(w \mid L) = L(w)$, or simply $p(w)$ when there is no ambiguity. If W is a set of words, $p(W) = \sum_{w \in W} p(w)$. Let $SL(\Sigma)$ be the set of stochastic languages on Σ.

A *probabilistic finite state automaton (PFA)* is a quintuple $\langle \Sigma, Q, \varphi, \iota, \tau \rangle$ where Q is a finite set of states, $\varphi : Q \times \Sigma \times Q \to [0, 1]$ is the transition function, $\iota : Q \to [0, 1]$ is the probability for each state to be initial and $\tau : Q \to [0, 1]$ is the probability for each state to be terminal. A PFA need satisfy $\sum_{q \in Q} \iota(q) = 1$ and for each state q,

$$\tau(q) + \sum_{a \in \Sigma} \sum_{q' \in Q} \varphi(q, a, q') = 1. \tag{1}$$

Let φ also denote the extension of the transition function, defined on $Q \times \Sigma^* \times Q$ by $\varphi(q, wa, q') = \sum_{q'' \in Q} \varphi(q, w, q'') \varphi(q'', a, q')$ and $\varphi(q, \varepsilon, q') = 1$ if $q = q'$ and 0 otherwise.

We extend φ again on $Q \times 2^{\Sigma^*} \times Q$ by $\varphi(q, U, q') = \sum_{w \in U} \varphi(q, w, q')$.

The set of initial states is defined by $Q_I = \{q \in Q \mid \iota(q) > 0\}$, the set of reachable states is defined by $Q_{reach} = \{q \in Q \mid \exists q_I \in Q_I, \varphi(q_I, \Sigma^*, q) > 0\}$ and the set of terminal states is defined by $Q_T = \{q \in Q \mid \tau(q) > 0\}$. We only consider here PFA such that: $\forall q \in Q_{reach}, \exists q_T \in Q_T, \varphi(q, \Sigma^*, q_T) > 0$.

Let $A = \langle \Sigma, Q, \varphi, \iota, \tau \rangle$ be a PFA. Let p_A be the function defined on Σ^* by

$$p_A(u) = \sum_{q, q' \in Q \times Q} \iota(q) \varphi(q, u, q') \tau(q'). \tag{2}$$

It can be proved that p_A is a stochastic language on Σ which is called the stochastic language generated by A.

For every state q, we denote by A_q the PFA $A_q = \langle \Sigma, Q, \varphi, \iota_q, \tau \rangle$ where $\iota_q(q) = 1$. We denote $p_{A_q}(w)$ by $p_A(w|q)$.

A *probabilistic deterministic finite state automaton (PDFA)* is a PFA $A = \langle \Sigma, Q, \varphi, \iota, \tau \rangle$ with a single initial state and such that for any state q and for every letter a, there is at much one state q' such that $\varphi(q, a, q') > 0$.

The class of *stochastic regular languages* on Σ is denoted by $L_{PFA}(\Sigma)$. It consists of all stochastic languages generated by probabilistic finite automata. Also, the class of *stochastic deterministic regular languages* on Σ is denoted by $L_{PDFA}(\Sigma)$. It consists of all stochastic languages generated by probabilistic deterministic finite automata.

2   Probabilistic Residual Finite State Automata (PRFA)

We introduce in this section the class of probabilistic residual finite state automata (PRFA). This class extends the notion of RFSA defined in [DLT01b]. We extend the notion of residual language for stochastic languages and we define a class of probabilistic automata based on this new notion. We study its properties and prove that the class of PRFA also defines a new class of stochastic languages strictly including the class of stochastic deterministic regular languages. PRFA also have a canonical form, a property in common with RFSA and PDFA.

Let L be a language, and let u be a word. The *residual language* of L with respect to u is $u^{-1}L = \{v \mid uv \in L\}$. We extend this notion to the stochastic case as follows. Let L be a *stochastic* language, the *residual language* of L with respect to u, also denoted by $u^{-1}L$, associates to every word w the probability $p(w|u^{-1}L) = p(uw|L)/p(u\Sigma^*|L)$ if $p(u\Sigma^*|L) \neq 0$. If $p(u\Sigma^*|L) = 0$, $u^{-1}L$ is not defined. Let $L_{fr}(\Sigma)$ be the class of stochastic languages on Σ having a finite number of residual languages.

A RFSA recognizing a regular language L is an automaton whose states are associated with residual languages of L. We propose here a similar definition in the stochastic case.

Definition 1. *A PRFA is a PFA* $A = \langle \Sigma, Q, \varphi, \iota, \tau \rangle$ *such that every state defines a residual language. More formally*

$$\forall q \in Q, \exists u \in \Sigma^*, L_q = u^{-1}p_A. \tag{3}$$

The class of stochastic residual regular languages on the alphabet Σ is denoted by $L_{PRFA}(\Sigma)$. It consists of all stochastic languages generated by probabilistic residual finite automata on Σ. Figures 2 and 3.4 show two examples of PRFA.

Let L be a stochastic language on Σ, let U be a finite subset of Σ^* and let $w \in \Sigma^*$. We define the set of *linearly generated residual languages* of L associated with U:

$$LG_L(U) = \left\{ l \in SL(\Sigma) \mid \exists (\alpha_u)_{u \in U} \in \mathcal{D}(U), l = \sum_{u \in U} \alpha_u . u^{-1}L \right\} \tag{4}$$

and we define *the set of linear decompositions* of w associated with U in L:

$$Decomp_L(w, U) = \left\{ (\alpha_u)_{u \in U} \in \mathcal{D}(U) \mid w^{-1}L = \sum_{u \in U} \alpha_u . u^{-1}L \right\}. \tag{5}$$

Let U be a finite set of words. We say that U is a *finite residual generator of L* if every residual language of L belongs to $LG_L(U)$. U is short if and only if for all word u of U there is no smaller word v such that $v^{-1}L = u^{-1}L$. Let $L_{frg}(\Sigma)$ be the class of stochastic languages on Σ having a finite residual generator. Note that $L_{fr} \subseteq L_{frg}$.

We prove now that we can associate with every language L generated by a PRFA a unique minimal short residual generator, called the *base* $\mathcal{B}_L$ of L.

Remark 1. Let $A = \langle \Sigma, Q, \varphi, \iota, \tau \rangle$ be a PRFA generating a language L. We can observe that $\{ u \in \Sigma^* \mid \exists q \in Q, L_q = u^{-1}L \wedge \not\exists v < u, u^{-1}L = v^{-1}L \}$ is a finite short residual generator of L with the same cardinality as Q. Therefore finding a minimal residual generator of L gives us the possibility to construct a minimal PRFA generating L.

Theorem 1. *Base unicity*
   Every language L of L_{frg} has a unique minimal short residual generator denoted by $\mathcal{B}_L$.

Proof. Let $U = \{u_1, \ldots, u_l\}$ and $V = \{v_1, \ldots, v_m\}$ be two minimal short residual generators of L and suppose that $l \geq m$. We prove that $U = V$. From the definition of a residual generator, we can deduce that for all i in $\{1, \ldots, l\}$ there exists $\alpha_{i,j} \in \mathcal{D}(l)$ and for all j in $\{1, \ldots, m\}$ there exists $\beta_{j,k} \in \mathcal{D}(m)$ such that $u_i^{-1}L = \sum_{j=1}^{m} \alpha_{i,j} v_j^{-1}L$ and $v_j^{-1}L = \sum_{k=1}^{l} \beta_{j,k} u_k^{-1}L$. Therefore

$$u_i^{-1}L = \sum_{j=1}^{m} \alpha_{i,j} \left(\sum_{k=1}^{l} \beta_{j,k} u_k^{-1}L \right) = \sum_{k=1}^{l} \left(\sum_{j=1}^{m} \alpha_{i,j} \beta_{j,k} \right) u_k^{-1}L.$$

This implies that $\sum_{j=1}^{m} \alpha_{i,j} \beta_{j,k} = 1$ if $i = k$ and 0 otherwise. Indeed, if there exist $(\gamma_k)_{1 \leq k \leq l} \in \mathcal{D}(l)$ such that $u_i^{-1}L = \sum_{k=1}^{l} \gamma_k u_k^{-1}L$ with $\gamma_i \neq 1$ then

$$u_i^{-1}L = \gamma_i u_i^{-1}L + \sum_{k=1, k \neq i}^{l} \gamma_k u_k^{-1}L = \sum_{k=1, k \neq i}^{n} \frac{\gamma_k}{1 - \gamma_i} u_k^{-1}L.$$

Hence $U \setminus \{u_i\}$ would be a residual generator which contradicts the fact that U is a minimal residual generator.

Let j_0 be such that $\alpha_{i,j_0} \neq 0$. Thus for all $k \neq i$, $\alpha_{i,j_0}\beta_{j_0,k} = 0$. Hence $\beta_{j_0,k} = 0$ which implies that $\beta_{j_0,i} = 1$. As a consequence, $v_{j_0}^{-1}L = \sum_{k=1}^{l} \beta_{j_0,k} u_k^{-1}L = u_i^{-1}L$. Finally for all i there exists j such that $u_i^{-1}L = v_j^{-1}L$, that is $U = V$. $\square$

As we can associate with every language L of L_{frg} a base $\mathcal{B}_L$, we can build a minimal PRFA from $\mathcal{B}_L$ using the following definition. We call this automaton a minimal PRFA of L and we prove that it is a PRFA generating L and having the minimal number of states.

Definition 2. *Let L be a language of L_{frg}. For all word u, let $(\alpha_{u,v})_{v \in \mathcal{B}_L}$ be an element of $Decomp_L(u, \mathcal{B}_L)$ such that $u^{-1}L = \sum_{v \in \mathcal{B}_L} \alpha_{u,v} v^{-1}L$. A minimal PRFA of L is a PFA $A = \langle \Sigma, \mathcal{B}_L, \varphi, \iota, \tau \rangle$ such that*

$$\forall u \in \mathcal{B}_L, \iota(u) = \alpha_{\varepsilon,u},$$
$$\forall(u, u') \in \mathcal{B}_L, \forall a \in \Sigma, \varphi(u, a, u') = \alpha_{ua,u'} \cdot p(a\Sigma^*|u^{-1}L), \quad (6)$$
$$\forall u \in \mathcal{B}_L, \tau(u) = p(\varepsilon|u^{-1}L).$$

Theorem 2. *Let L be a language of L_{frg}, a minimal PRFA of L generates L and has the minimal number of states.*

Proof.
A is minimal:
    It is clear that a PRFA generating L must have at least as many states as words in the base of L, i.e. at least as many states as A.
A is a PRFA generating L:
    By construction we have for all u in $\mathcal{B}_L$, $p_A(\varepsilon|u) = p(\varepsilon|u^{-1}L)$.

Now suppose that for any word w such that $|w| \leq k$ and for all u in $\mathcal{B}_L$, we have $p_A(w|u) = p(w|u^{-1}L)$. Then considering the letter a

$$
\begin{aligned}
p_A(aw|u) &= \sum_{u' \in Q} \varphi(u, a, u') p_A(w|u') \\
&= \sum_{u' \in Q} \alpha_{ua,u'} p(a\Sigma^*|u^{-1}L) p_A(w|u') \\
&= \sum_{u' \in Q} \alpha_{ua,u'} p(a\Sigma^*|u^{-1}L) p(w|u'^{-1}L) \quad \text{(by the induction hypothesis)} \\
&= p(a\Sigma^*|u^{-1}L) p(w|ua^{-1}L) \quad\quad \text{(by } (ua)^{-1}L = \sum_{u' \in \mathcal{B}_L} \alpha_{ua,u'} u'^{-1}L) \\
&= p(aw|u^{-1}L).
\end{aligned}
$$

We proved that $\forall u \in \mathcal{B}_L, u^{-1}L = p_{A_u}$. Given that

$$
L = \varepsilon^{-1}L = \sum_{u \in \mathcal{B}_L} \alpha_{\varepsilon,u} u^{-1}L = \sum_{u \in \mathcal{B}_L} \alpha_{\varepsilon,u} p_{A_u} = \sum_{u \in \mathcal{B}_L} \iota(u) p_{A_u} = p_A
$$

A generates L. $\square$

One can observe that the above definition does not define a unique minimal PRFA, but a family of minimal PRFA. Every minimal PRFA is built on the base of the language, but probabilities on the transition depend on the choice of the values $\alpha_{u,v}$.

3   Characterization of Stochastic Languages

We propose here a characterization of stochastic languages represented by PDFA based on residual languages. We then prove that PRFA also have a similar characterization.

3.1   PDFA Generated Languages

The class of stochastic languages having a finite number of residual languages is equal to the class of stochastic languages generated by PDFA.

Theorem 3. $L_{fr} = L_{PDFA}$

Proof.
(1) Let $A = \langle \Sigma, Q, \varphi, \iota, \tau \rangle$ be a PDFA. For any state $q \in Q_{reach}$, we note u_q the smallest word such that $\varphi(q_0, u_q, q) > 0$ where $Q_I = \{q_0\}$. For any $w \in \Sigma^*$, if $w^{-1}L$ is defined, there exists a unique q such that $\varphi(q_0, w, q) > 0$ and therefore $w^{-1}L = u_q^{-1}L$.

(2) Let $L \in L_{fr}(\Sigma)$, let us construct a PDFA generating L. Let U be a minimal set of words such that for any word w such that $w^{-1}L$ is defined, there is a word u in U such that $w^{-1}L = u^{-1}L$.

For such words w, the word u of U such that $w^{-1}L = u^{-1}L$ is denoted by u_w. We construct $A = \langle \Sigma, U, \varphi, \iota, \tau \rangle$ with $\iota(u_\varepsilon) = 1$, $\tau(u) = p(\varepsilon|u^{-1}L)$ for all $u \in U$ and $\varphi(u, a, u') = p(a\Sigma^*|u^{-1}L)$ if $u' = u_{ua}$ and 0 otherwise, for all words u and u' of U and for every letter a.

In order to prove that $p_A = L$, it is sufficient to prove that $\forall w \in \Sigma^*$, $p_A(w\Sigma^*) = p(w\Sigma^*|L)$. By construction, for all word u in U:

$$p_A(\varepsilon\Sigma^*|u) = p(\varepsilon\Sigma^*|u^{-1}L) = 1 \text{ and } \forall a \in \Sigma, p_A(a\Sigma^*|u) = p(a\Sigma^*|u^{-1}L)$$

Let us assume that for every w in $\Sigma^{\leq k}$ and for every u in U, $p_A(w\Sigma^*|u) = p(w\Sigma^*|u^{-1}L)$. Let $w \in \Sigma^k$, $a \in \Sigma$ and $u \in U$, If $p(ua\Sigma^*|L) = 0$, we have $p_A(aw\Sigma^*|u) = p(aw\Sigma^*|u^{-1}L) = 0$ and otherwise let u' the unique word of U such that $\varphi(u, a, u') > 0$

$$
\begin{aligned}
p_A(aw\Sigma^*|u) &= \varphi(u, a, u')p_A(w\Sigma^*|u') \\
&= p_A(a\Sigma^*|u)p_A(w\Sigma^*|u') \\
&= p(a\Sigma^*|u^{-1}L)p(w\Sigma^*|u'^{-1}L) \text{ (by the induction hypothesis)} \\
&= p(aw\Sigma^*|u^{-1}L) \text{ since } (ua)^{-1}L = u'^{-1}.
\end{aligned}
$$

Then $\forall u \in U, p_{A_u} = u^{-1}L$. In particular, as $\iota(u_\varepsilon) = 1$, $p_A = p_{A_{u_\varepsilon}} = \varepsilon^{-1}L = L$. Therefore, A is a PDFA generating the language L. $\qquad\square$

We propose here a similar characterization for L_{PRFA}, also based on intrinsic properties of the associated languages.

3.2   PRFA Generated Languages

We prove that L_{PRFA} is the class of languages having finite residual generators; it includes languages which may have an infinite number of residual languages.

Theorem 4. $L_{frg} = L_{PRFA}$.

Proof. Let $A = \langle \Sigma, Q, \varphi, \iota, \tau \rangle$, we prove that $p_A \in L_{frg}(\Sigma)$. For all words w and u such that $p_A(u\Sigma^*) \neq 0$,

$$
\begin{aligned}
p_A(w|u^{-1}p_A) &= \left(\sum_{q \in Q} \sum_{q' \in Q_I} \iota(q')\varphi(q', u, q)p_A(w|q) \right) / p_A(u\Sigma^*) \\
&= \sum_{q \in Q} \alpha_q \cdot p_A(w|u_q^{-1}p_A)
\end{aligned}
$$

where u_q is the smallest word such that $(u_q)^{-1}p_A$ is the stochastic residual language generated by the state q, and $\alpha_q = \sum_{q' \in Q_I} \iota(q')\varphi(q', u, q)/p_A(u\Sigma^*)$. Verify that $\sum_{q \in Q} \alpha_q = 1$.

The converse is clear from Theorem 2. $\qquad\square$

4   Expressiveness of L_{PRFA}

In this section, we prove that the class of stochastic languages defined by PRFA is more expressive than the one defined by PDFA, although not as expressive as the one generated by general PFA.

Theorem 5.

$$L_{PDFA} \subsetneq L_{PRFA} \subsetneq L_{PFA}.$$

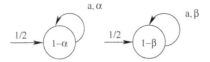

Fig. 1. A PFA generating a language not in L_{PRFA}

Proof. Inclusions are clear, we only have to show the strict inclusions.

(1) $L_{PRFA} \subsetneq L_{PFA}$

Let L be the language generated by the PFA described on Figure 1. As $\Sigma = \{a\}$, all residuals are $(a^n)^{-1}L$. We consider $\alpha = \beta^2$.

$$p(\varepsilon|(a^n)^{-1}L) = \frac{p(a^n|L)}{p(a^n\Sigma^*|L)} = \frac{\alpha^n(1-\alpha)+\beta^n(1-\beta)}{\alpha^n+\beta^n} = 1 - \frac{\alpha^{n+1}+\beta^{n+1}}{\alpha^n+\beta^n}$$

$$= 1 - \frac{\beta^{2(n+1)}+\beta^{n+1}}{\beta^{2n}+\beta^n} = 1 - \beta^2 - \frac{\beta-\beta^2}{\beta^n+1}$$

Hence $p(\varepsilon|(a^n)^{-1}L)$ is a strictly decreasing function (as $0 < \beta < 1$). Suppose that p_A has a finite residual generator U. Let $u_0 = a^{n_0} \in U$ such that for all u in U, $p(\varepsilon|u_0^{-1}L) \leq p(\varepsilon|u^{-1}L)$ and let $n > n_0$. Then there exists $(\alpha_u^n)_{u \in U} \in \mathcal{D}(\mathrm{Card}(U))$ such that

$$p(\varepsilon|(a^n)^{-1}L) = \sum_{u \in U} \alpha_u^n p(\varepsilon|u^{-1}L) \geq \sum_{u \in U} \alpha_u^n p(\varepsilon|u_0^{-1}L) = p(\varepsilon|u_0^{-1}L)$$

which is impossible since $p(\varepsilon|(a^n)^{-1}L)$ is strictly decreasing.

(2) $L_{PDFA} \subsetneq L_{PRFA}$

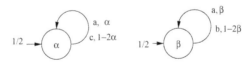

Fig. 2. A PRFA generating a language not in L_{PDFA}.

Let L be the language generated by the PRFA described on Figure 2. Let us consider the case when $\alpha = \beta^2$, then

$$p(a^m|L) = \frac{\alpha^{n+1} + \beta^{n+1}}{2} = \frac{\beta^{2n+2} + \beta^{n+1}}{2}$$

and

$$p(\varepsilon|(a^n)^{-1}L) = \frac{p(a^n|L)}{p(a^n\Sigma^*|L)} = \frac{\beta^{2(n+1)} + \beta^{n+1}}{\beta^{2n} + \beta^n} = \beta^2 + \frac{\beta - \beta^2}{\beta^n + 1}$$

as $p(\varepsilon|(a^n)^{-1}L)$ is a strictly increasing function ($0 < \beta < 1$), it is clear that the number of residual languages cannot be finite. Therefore it can not be generated by a PDFA. $\qquad\square$

5   PRFA Learning

We present in this section an algorithm that identifies stochastic languages. Unlike other learning algorithms, this algorithm takes as input words associated with their true probability to be a prefix in the target stochastic language. In this context, we prove that any target stochastic language L generated by a PRFA can be identified. We prove that the sample required for this identification task has a polynomial size as function of the size of the minimal prefix PRFA of L. As $L_{PDFA} \subsetneq L_{PRFA}$, the class of stochastic languages identified in this way strictly includes the class of stochastic languages identified by algorithms based on identification of PDFA. The use of an exact information on the probability of appearance of words is unrealistic. We will further extend our work to cases where probabilities are replaced by sample estimates.

5.1   Preliminary Definitions

Definition 3. *The* minimal prefix set *of a stochastic language L is the prefixial set composed of the words whose associated residual languages cannot be decomposed by residual generated by smaller words. More formally,*

$$Pm(L) = \{u \in L \mid p(u\Sigma^*|L) > 0 \wedge u^{-1}L \notin LG_L(\{v \in \Sigma^* \mid v < u\})\}. \quad (7)$$

Remark 2. For all word u, $LG_L(\{v \in \Sigma^* \mid v<u\})=LG_L(\{v \in Pm(L) \mid v<u\})$.

When L is a stochastic language generated by a PRFA, $Pm(L)$ is finite. This set will be the set of states of the PRFA output by our algorithm.

Definition 4. *The* kernel of L *contains $Pm(L)$ and some successors of elements of $Pm(L)$. More formally,*

$$K(L) = \{\varepsilon\} \cup \{wa \in \Sigma^* \mid p(wa\Sigma^*|L) > 0 \wedge w \in Pm(L) \wedge a \in \Sigma\}. \quad (8)$$

$K(L)$ contains the words which will be tested by the algorithm in order to know whether they are states of the output PRFA.

Remark 3. It can be easily be shown that $Pm(L)$ and $K(L)$ are prefixial sets, $\mathcal{B}_L \subseteq Pm(L) \subseteq K(L)$, and therefore $Pm(L)$ and $K(L)$ are finite residual generators of L.

Definition 5. *Prefix PRFA are PRFA based on a prefixial set of words and whose non deterministic transitions only occur on maximal words.*
    Let $A = \langle \Sigma, Q, \varphi, \iota, \tau \rangle$ be a PRFA. A is a prefix PRFA if

- *Q is a finite prefixial set of Σ^*,*
- *$\varphi(w, a, w') \neq 0 \Rightarrow w' = wa \vee (wa \notin Q \wedge w' < wa)$.*

Example 1. Automaton 4 in Figure 3 is an example of a minimal prefix PRFA. Its set of states is $Pm(L) = \{\varepsilon, a, b\}$, and $K(L) = \{\varepsilon, a, b, aa, ba\}$, where L is the generated language.

Proposition 1. *Every stochastic language L generated by a PRFA can be generated by a prefix PRFA whose set of states is $Pm(L)$. We call them minimal prefix PRFA of L.*

Proof. The proof is similar to the proof of Theorem 2.   □

Definition 6. *Let L be a stochastic language, a* rich sample *of L is a set S of couples $(u, p(u\Sigma^*|L)) \in \Sigma^* \times [0,1]$. Let $\pi_1(S)$ denote the set $\{u \in \Sigma^* \mid \exists (u, p) \in S\}$.*

Definition 7. *Let L be a stochastic language, v a word and U and W two finite sets of words such that: $\forall u \in U \cup \{v\}, u^{-1}L$ is defined. $E_L(v, U, W)$ is defined as the linear system composed of:*

1. *$0 \le \alpha_u \le 1$ for all $u \in U$,*
2. *$\sum_{u \in U} \alpha_u = 1$,*
3. *$p(w\Sigma^*|v^{-1}L) = \sum_{u \in U} \alpha_u p(w\Sigma^*|u^{-1}L)$ for every word w in W.*

Definition 8. *Linear systems associated with a rich sample.*
    Let L be a stochastic language, v a word and U a finite set of words. Let S be a rich sample of L such that: $\forall u \in U \cup \{v\}, u \in \pi_1(S)$ and $u^{-1}L$ is defined. Let $E_S(v, U) = E_L(v, U, W)$ where $W = \{w \in \Sigma^* | \forall u \in U \cup \{v\}, uw \in \pi_1(S)\}$. Note that $E_S(v, U)$ can be computed from S.
    The set of solutions of $E_S(v, U)$ is denoted by $sol(E_S(v, U))$.

We shall use this linear system to test whether a given stochastic residual language $v^{-1}L$ is in $LG_L(U)$.

Definition 9. *A* characteristic sample *of a stochastic language $L \in L_{frg}$ is a rich sample S such that*

$$K(L) \subseteq \pi_1(S) \text{ and } \forall v \in K(L), \text{ let } U_v = \{u \in Pm(L) \mid u < v\}$$
$$sol(E_S(v, U_v)) = Decomp_L(v, U_v).$$

Remark 4. Every rich sample containing a characteristic sample is characteristic.
    If S is a characteristic sample of L then for every v in $K(L)$, $sol(E_S(v, U_v)) \neq \emptyset$ is equivalent to $Decomp_L(v, U_v) \neq \emptyset$ which is equivalent to $v^{-1}L \in LG_L(U_v)$.

Lemma 1. *Every language L of L_{frg} has a finite characteristic sample containing $O(Card(Pm(L))^2 Card(\Sigma))$ elements.*

Proof. We note S_∞ the rich sample such that $\pi_1(S_\infty) = \Sigma^*$. It is clear that S_∞ is a characteristic sample. For every v in $K(L)$, solutions of $E_S(v, U_v)$ can be described as the intersection of an affine subspace of $\mathbb{R}^{\mathrm{Card}(U_v)}$ with $[0,1]^{\mathrm{Card}(U_v)}$. Hence there exists a finite set of equations (at most $\mathrm{Card}(U_v)+1$), and thus a finite set of words of Σ^*, providing the same solutions. The rich sample generated by these equations for every v in $K(L)$ is characteristic. Such a minimal rich sample contains at most $\mathrm{Card}(K(L)) \times (\mathrm{Card}(Pm\,(L)) + 1) = O\left(\mathrm{Card}(Pm\,(L))^2 \times \mathrm{Card}(\Sigma)\right)$ elements.   □

The learning algorithm described below outputs a minimal prefix PRFA of the target language when the input is a characteristic sample.

5.2   lmpPRFA **Algorithm**

lmpPRFA
input : a rich sample S
output : a prefix PRFA $A = \langle \Sigma, Q, \varphi, \iota, \tau \rangle$

begin
$\quad$ $Q \leftarrow \{\varepsilon\}$; $\iota(\varepsilon) \leftarrow 1$; $\forall a \in \Sigma, \varphi(\varepsilon, a, \varepsilon) \leftarrow 0$
$\quad$ $W \leftarrow \{a \in \Sigma \mid a \in \pi_1(S) \text{ and } p(a\Sigma^*) > 0\}$;
$\quad$ do while $W \neq \emptyset$
$\quad\quad$ $v \leftarrow \min W$; $W \leftarrow W - \{v\}$; Let $w \in \Sigma^*, a \in \Sigma$ s.t. $v = wa$;
$\quad\quad$ if $sol(E_S(v, Q)) = \emptyset$ then
$\quad\quad\quad$ $Q \leftarrow Q \cup \{v\}$; $\forall u \in Q, \forall x \in \Sigma, \varphi(v, x, u) \leftarrow 0$;
$\quad\quad\quad$ $W \leftarrow W \cup \{vx \in \pi_1(S) \mid x \in \Sigma \text{ and } p(vx\Sigma^*) > 0\}$;
$\quad\quad\quad$ $\varphi(w, a, v) \leftarrow p(wa\Sigma^*)/p(w\Sigma^*)$;
$\quad\quad$ else
$\quad\quad\quad$ let $(\alpha_u)_{u \in Q} \in sol(E_S(v, Q))$
$\quad\quad\quad$ for all $u \in Q$ do $\varphi(w, a, u) \leftarrow \alpha_u \times (p(wa\Sigma^*)/p(w\Sigma^*))$
$\quad\quad$ end if
$\quad$ end do
$\quad$ for all $q \in Q$ do $\tau(q) \leftarrow 1 - \varphi(q, \Sigma, Q)$;
end

Theorem 6. *Let $L \in L_{PRFA}$ and let S be a characteristic sample of L, then given input S, algorithm* lmpPRFA *outputs the minimal prefix PRFA in polynomial time as function of the size of S.*

Proof. **When the algorithm terminates, the set of states Q is $Pm\,(L)$**
$\quad$ Let $Q^{[i]}$ (resp. $v^{[i]}$) denote the set Q (the word v) obtained at iteration i just before the if. Considering $W \neq \emptyset$ at the beginning (else $p_A(\varepsilon) = 1$).
$\quad$ From the definition of $Pm\,(L)$, $Q^{[1]} = \{\varepsilon\} = \{u \in Pm\,(L) \mid u < v^{[1]}\}$.
$\quad$ Let us assume that $Q^{[k]} = \{u \in Pm\,(L) \mid u < v^{[k]}\}$. At step $k+1$ there are two possibilities:

1. If $sol(E_S(v, Q^{[k]})) \neq \emptyset$ then as $v^{-1}L \in LG_L(Q^{[k]})$, $v \notin Pm\,(L)$ and

$$Q^{[k+1]} = Q^{[k]} = \left\{u \in Pm\,(L) \mid u < v^{[k]}\right\} = \left\{u \in Pm\,(L) \mid u < v^{[k+1]}\right\}.$$

2. If $sol(E_S(v^{[k]}, Q^{[k]})) = \emptyset$ then as $(v^{[k]})^{-1}L \notin LG_L(Q^{[k]})$, $v \in Pm\,(L)$. It follows that $Q^{[k+1]} = Q^{[k]} \cup \{v^{[k]}\}$ and as the word v is increasing to each iteration

$$Q^{[k+1]} = \left\{u \in Pm\,(L) \mid u < v^{[k+1]}\right\}.$$

As a consequence $Q \subseteq Pm\,(L)$. We also have $Pm\,(L) \subseteq Q$. Indeed, if we assume that there exists w in $Pm\,(L)$ and not in Q then there exists a prefix x of w such that $Decomp_L(x, \{u \in Pm\,(L) \mid u < x\}) \neq \emptyset \Rightarrow x \notin Pm\,(L)$ and as $Pm\,(L)$ is a prefixial set this is contradictory. Consequently the output state set Q is $Pm\,(L)$.

The algorithm terminates
Let $W^{[i]}$ denote the set W obtained at iteration i. From the definition of the kernel of L

$$W^{[0]} = \{a \in \Sigma \mid a \in \pi_1(S) \text{ and } p(a\Sigma^*) > 0\} \subseteq K(L).$$

Assume that $W^{[k]} \subseteq K(L)$ then at step $k+1$ there are two possible cases:

1. If $sol(E_S(v, Q)) \neq \emptyset$ then $W^{[k+1]} = W^{[k]} - \{v\} \subseteq K(L)$
2. If $sol(E_S(v, Q)) = \emptyset$ then as $Decomp_L(v, Q) = \emptyset$, and $Q = \{u \in Pm\,(L) \mid u < v\}$ (see the first part of the proof), $v \in Pm\,(L)$ and for every letter a if $va \in \pi_1(S)$ and $p(va\Sigma^*) > 0$ then $va \in K(L)$. It follows

$$W^{[k+1]} = \left(W^{[k]} - \{v\}\right) \cup \{va \in \pi_1(S) \mid a \in \Sigma \text{ and } p(va\Sigma^*) > 0\} \subseteq K(L)$$

As at every step one element of W is removed and $K(L)$ is finite, the algorithm terminates.

The output automaton is a minimal prefix PRFA of L
By construction the automaton is a minimal prefix PRFA of L. Thus A generates L (see the proof of Proposition 1).

Complexity of the algorithm
There is $\mathrm{Card}(K(L))$ iterations of the main loop, and we operate a resolution of a linear system of maximal size $\mathrm{Card}(S) + \mathrm{Card}(Pm\,(L)) + 1$ (solvable in polynomial time), and $Pm\,(L) \subseteq K(L) \subseteq \pi_1(S)$. Hence the algorithm complexity is polynomial in the size of $\mathrm{Card}(S)$. $\qquad\square$

Example 2. We consider the target being automaton 4 at Figure 3. We construct a characteristic sample

$$S = \left\{(\varepsilon, 1), (a, \frac{1}{2}), (b, \frac{1}{2}), (aa, \frac{1}{2}), (ba, \frac{1}{6}), (aaa, \frac{1}{3}), (baa, \frac{1}{18}), (aaaa, \frac{7}{18}), (baaa, \frac{1}{54}).\right\}$$

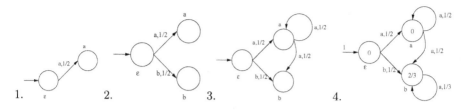

Fig. 3. An execution of algorithm lmpPRFA

First Step: The algorithm starts with $Q = \{\varepsilon\}$ and $W = \{a, b\}$. One considers adding the state a,

$$E_S(a, \{\varepsilon\}) = \begin{cases} \alpha_\varepsilon = 1 \\ p(a\Sigma^*|\varepsilon^{-1}L)\alpha_\varepsilon = p(a\Sigma^*|a^{-1}L) \\ \vdots \end{cases}$$

then $\alpha_\varepsilon = \frac{p(a\Sigma^*|a^{-1}L)}{p(a\Sigma^*|\varepsilon^{-1}L)} = \frac{p(aa\Sigma^*)/p(a\Sigma^*)}{p(a\Sigma^*)} = 2$. As this system has no solution, the state a is added (see Figure 3.1).

Step 2: $Q = \{\varepsilon, a\}$, $W = \{b, aa\}$
One considers adding the state b,

$$E_S(b, \{\varepsilon, a\}) = \begin{cases} \alpha_\varepsilon + \alpha_a = 1 \\ \frac{1}{2}\alpha_\varepsilon + 1\alpha_a = \frac{1}{3}(\text{obtained using } a) \\ \vdots \end{cases}$$

As this system has no solution in $[0, 1]^2$, the state b is added (see Figure 3.2).

Step 3: $Q = \{\varepsilon, a, b\}$, $W = \{aa, ba\}$
One considers adding the state aa,

$$E_S(aa, \{\varepsilon, a, b\}) = \begin{cases} \alpha_\varepsilon + \alpha_a + \alpha_b = 1 \\ \frac{1}{2}\alpha_\varepsilon + 1\alpha_a + \frac{1}{3}\alpha_b = \frac{2}{3}(\text{obtained using } a) \\ \frac{1}{2}\alpha_\varepsilon + \frac{2}{3}\alpha_a + \frac{1}{9}\alpha_b = \frac{7}{18}(\text{obtained using } aa) \end{cases}$$

wich is equivalent to $\alpha_\varepsilon = 0, \alpha_a = \frac{1}{2}, \alpha_b = \frac{1}{2}$. The state aa is not added and two transitions are added (see Figure 3.3).

Step 4: $Q = \{\varepsilon, a, b\}$, $W = \{ba\}$
One considers adding the state ba. The system $E_S(ba, \{\varepsilon, a, b\})$ is equivalent to $\alpha_\varepsilon = 0, \alpha_a = 0, \alpha_b = 1$. The state ba is not added and the target automaton is returned (see Figure 3.4).

Conclusion

Several grammatical inference algorithms can be described as looking for natural components of target languages, namely their residual languages. For example, in the deterministic framework, RPNI-like algorithm ([OG92], [LPP98]) try to identify the residual languages of the target language, while DELETE algorithms ([DLT00] and [DLT01a]) try to find inclusion relations between these languages. In the probabilistic framework, algorithms such as ALERGIA [CO94] or MDI [TDdlH00] also try to identify the residual languages of the target stochastic language. However these algorithms are restricted to the class L_{fr} of stochastic languages which have a finite number of residual languages.

We have defined the class L_{frg} of stochastic languages whose (possibly infinitely many) residual languages can be described by means of a linear expression of a finite subset of them. This class strictly includes the class L_{fr}.

A first learning algorithm for this class was proposed. It assumes the availability of a characteristic sample in which words are provided with their actual probabilities in the target language. Using similar techniques to those described in [CO99] and [TDdlH00], we believe that this algorithm can be adapted to infer correct structures from sample estimates. Work in progress aims at developing this adapted version and at evaluating this technique on real data.

References

[Ang88]   D. Angluin. Identifying languages from stochastic examples. Technical Report YALEU/DCS/RR-614, Yale University, New Haven, CT, 1988.

[CO94]   R.C. Carrasco and J. Oncina. Learning stochastic regular grammars by means of a state merging method. In *International Conference on Grammatical Inference*, pages 139–152, Heidelberg, September 1994. Springer-Verlag.

[CO99]   R. C. Carrasco and J. Oncina. Learning deterministic regular grammars from stochastic samples in polynomial time. *RAIRO (Theoretical Informatics and Applications)*, 33(1):1–20, 1999.

[DLT00]   F. Denis, A. Lemay, and A. Terlutte. Learning regular languages using non deterministic finite automata. In *ICGI'2000, 5th International Colloquium on Grammatical Inference*, volume 1891 of *Lecture Notes in Artificial Intelligence*, pages 39–50. Springer Verlag, 2000.

[DLT01a]   F. Denis, A. Lemay, and A. Terlutte. Learning regular languages using rfsa. In *ALT 2001*. Springer Verlag, 2001.

[DLT01b]   F. Denis, A. Lemay, and A. Terlutte. Residual finite state automata. In *18th Annual Symposium on Theoretical Aspects of Computer Science*, volume 2010 of *Lecture Notes in Computer Science*, pages 144–157, 2001.

[LPP98]   K. J. Lang, B. A. Pearlmutter, and R. A. Price. Results of the Abbadingo one DFA learning competition and a new evidence-driven state merging algorithm. In *Proc. 4th International Colloquium on Grammatical Inference - ICGI 98*, volume 1433 of *Lecture Notes in Artificial Intelligence*, pages 1–12. Springer-Verlag, 1998.

[OG92]   J. Oncina and P. Garcia. Inferring regular languages in polynomial update time. In *Pattern Recognition and Image Analysis*, pages 49–61, 1992.

[SO94]   A. Stolcke and S. Omohundro. Inducing probabilistic grammars by
            Bayesian model merging. *Lecture Notes in Computer Science*, 862:106–
            118, 1994.

[TDdlH00]   Franck Thollard, Pierre Dupont, and Colin de la Higuera. Probabilistic
            DFA inference using Kullback-Leibler divergence and minimality. In *Proc.
            17th International Conf. on Machine Learning*, pages 975–982. Morgan
            Kaufmann, 2000.

Fragmentation: Enhancing Identifiability

Henning Fernau

[1] University of Newcastle
School of Electrical Engineering and Computer Science
University Drive, NSW 2308 Callaghan, Australia
fernau@cs.newcastle.edu.au
[2] Wilhelm-Schickard-Institut für Informatik
Universität Tübingen
D-72076 Tübingen, Germany
fernau@informatik.uni-tuebingen.de

Abstract. We introduce the concept of fragmentation in order to adapt the learnability of regular languages towards other regular and non-regular language families. More precisely, rational transducers can be used to implement explicit fragmentation to define new identifiable regular language classes. Context conditions can be used to construe identifiable and characterizable language classes which may contain non-regular languages by means of implicit fragmentation.

1 Introduction

In certain applications, the expected input of a learning algorithm can be analyzed according to existing background knowledge of the subject area. Therefore, we consider the scenario where each input word can be split into two (or several) *fragments*, each of which is given to a known learning algorithm. In this way, new learnable language classes can be constructed, even in the case of the possible simplest learning model of learning in the limit from positive data. For technical reasons, the most interesting fragmentations can be implemented by rational transducers, as we will see.

Let us mention that the idea of fragmentation did appear elsewhere in the huge literature on formal languages, namely in the context of Lindenmayer systems [21], where it was motivated by proliferation processes in "linear" living species which are based on fragmentation.

Besides this method of explicit fragmentation, we will show how the idea of conditional grammars can be used to define characterizable language classes which are learnable from text and which contain non-regular languages. To find such language classes is one of the most challenging problems of current grammatical inference research according to a recent survey of de la Higuera [14]. Conceptually, we may refer to this as a method of implicit fragmentation. Actually, conditional grammars are one of the classical topics in regulated rewriting, rooting in a paper of Navrátil [18]. Further results have been obtained in [4, 5, 9, 17, 19, 20]. Many results are contained in the monograph [6], as well

P. Adriaans, H. Fernau, and M. van Zaanen (Eds.): ICGI 2002, LNAI 2484, pp. 92–105, 2002.
© Springer-Verlag Berlin Heidelberg 2002

as in the third chapter of the second volume of the Handbook of Formal Languages [22].

So again, it proves that many techniques known from formal language theory are useful for constructing learnable language classes. This venue has been taken before, e.g., by using control languages, in [7, 23]. In fact, the paper can also be seen as a supplement to [17], where we discussed learnability issues for certain contextual grammars (which are important for linguistic applications) as well as complexity issues both for contextual and for conditional grammars, but left open the learnability questions concerning conditional grammars.

2   Learning in the Limit

The learning model we adhere to in this paper is usually called *learning from text* or *identification in the limit (from positive data)*. It was introduced by Gold [13] in his seminal paper.

Definition 1. *A language class $\mathcal{L}$ (defined via a class of language describing devices $\mathcal{D}$ as, e.g., grammars or automata) is said to be* identifiable *if there is a so-called* inference machine I *to which as input an arbitrary language $L \in \mathcal{L}$ may be enumerated (possibly with repetitions) in an arbitrary order, i.e., I receives an infinite input stream of words $E(1)$, $E(2)$, ... , where E is an enumeration of L, i.e., a surjection mapping the natural numbers onto L, and I reacts with an output device stream $D_i \in \mathcal{D}$ such that there is an $N(E)$ so that, for all $n \geq N(E)$, we have $D_n = D_{N(E)}$ and, moreover, the language defined by $D_{N(E)}$ equals L.*

An inference machine I obeying the rules of this learning model is also called text learner.

A text learner is termed efficient *if the time needed to compute the nth hypothesis is polynomial in the overall length of the n input samples seen up to this point.*[1]

According to Angluin [2], basically a language family $\mathcal{L}$ (described by the device family $\mathcal{D}$) is identifiable if and only if every language $L \in \mathcal{L}$ contains a *telltale set*, i.e., a finite subset $\chi \subseteq L$ upon seeing which the learner may safely make a hypothesis $D \in \mathcal{D}$ describing L. More precisely, χ has the property that each set $L' \in \mathcal{L}$ with $\chi \subseteq L' \subseteq L$ equals L.

In order to ensure convergence of the learning process in the hypothesis space, it is useful that the device family $\mathcal{D}$ contains one unique *canonical description* for each language $L \in \mathcal{L}$, since the learner will then only utter canonical objects as hypotheses.

---

[1] Sometimes, also the size of the hypotheses is taken into account; since most "natural" text learners produce only hypotheses which are of size polynomial in the overall input length, this seems to be no real restriction. Moreover, our definition avoids several pathological cases which occur with text learners producing exponentially large hypotheses.

This learning model is very simple and natural, but has the drawback that not all regular languages are identifiable. Even more, up to Angluin's papers [1, 3], no *characterizable* non-trivial identifiable class of languages was known.

Here, we will provide a methodology for creating characterizable identifiable language classes based on the concept of fragmentation. The corresponding learning algorithms are—like the learner presented by Angluin [3]—very efficient.

Throughout this paper, we will assume certain background knowledge on formal languages and grammatical inference. We will employ standard notions like ε for the empty word and $\times$ for the product automaton construction. Unexplained algorithmic details on 0-reversible and on function-distinguishable languages are contained in [3, 8, 10].

3   Function Distinguishability and Reversibility

We will show how explicit fragmentation can be used to get new learnable language classes based on the known identifiability of the (0-)reversible languages. Recall that, according to Angluin [3], a regular language is *0-reversible* iff its minimal deterministic automaton is backward deterministic. Let 0-Rev denote the class of 0-reversible languages.

This characterization also defines the corresponding canonical learning objects, i.e., the hypothesis space. We will denote the minimal deterministic automaton of a regular language L by $A(L)$. The same fragmentation methodology can be used to any of the more general classes of function-distinguishable languages [8], where basically any automaton structure of some deterministic automaton A accepting all words over Σ can be used to resolve possible backward nondeterminisms of $A(L) \times A$, where $L \subseteq \Sigma^*$.

Since we need the notion of function distinguishability in what follows, we will provide the corresponding definition.

Definition 2. *Let F be some finite set. A mapping $f : \Sigma^* \to F$ is called a distinguishing function if $f(w) = f(z)$ implies $f(wu) = f(zu)$ for all $u, w, z \in \Sigma^*$.*

To every distinguishing function f, a finite automaton $A_f = (F, \Sigma, \delta_f, f(\lambda), F)$ can be associated by setting $\delta_f(q, a) = f(wa)$, where $w \in f^{-1}(q)$ can be chosen arbitrarily, since f is a distinguishing function. Here, we will formally introduce function distinguishable languages and discuss some formal language properties.

Definition 3. *Let $A = (Q, \Sigma, \delta, q_0, Q_F)$ be a finite automaton. Let $f : \Sigma^* \to F$ be a distinguishing function. A is called f-distinguishable if:*

1. *A is deterministic.*
2. *For all states $q \in Q$ and all $x, y \in \Sigma^*$ with $\delta^*(q_0, x) = \delta^*(q_0, y) = q$, we have $f(x) = f(y)$.*
3. *For all $q_1, q_2 \in Q$, $q_1 \neq q_2$, with either (a) $q_1, q_2 \in Q_F$ or (b) there exist $q_3 \in Q$ and $a \in \Sigma$ with $\delta(q_1, a) = \delta(q_2, a) = q_3$, we have $f(q_1) \neq f(q_2)$.*

A language is f-distinguishable iff it can be accepted by an f-distinguishable automaton. The class of f-distinguishable languages is denoted by f-DL.

We need a suitable notion of a canonical automaton in the following.

Definition 4. *Let $f : \Sigma^* \to F$ be a distinguishing function and let $L \subseteq \Sigma^*$ be a regular set. Let $A(L, f)$ be the stripped subautomaton of the product automaton $A(L) \times A_f$. $A(L, f)$ is called f-canonical automaton of L.*

Theorem 1. *Let $f : T^* \to F$ be some distinguishing function. Then, $L \subseteq T^*$ is f-distinguishable iff $A(L, f)$ is f-distinguishable.* □

This characterization was proved in [8] and used in order to establish the inferability of f-DL. $A(L, f)$ was employed to construct a characteristic sample for L (with respect to f), and moreover, the $A(L, f)$ (note that $A(L, f)$ is usually larger than $A(L)$) are the hypothesis space of the learning algorithm.

4 Explicit Fragmentation

Example 1. The language L given by the regular expression

$$(a^+ \cup b^+)(a|b)^* \tag{1}$$

is not 0-reversible: the minimal automaton $A(L)$ is not 0-reversible, because the final state has more than one ingoing transition labelled a. More generally, for all $L' \subseteq \{a, b\}^*$, $L' \neq \emptyset$, $(a^+ \cup b^+)L' \notin$ 0-Rev for similar reasons.

The previous example shows pretty much of the limitations of the 0-reversible languages (in contrast with the whole class of regular languages which is not identifiable in the limit, see [13]). So, the 0-reversible languages seem to be not apted to learn any non-empty sublanguage of L as given by Eq. (1). But if we knew (due to background knowledge) that only sublanguages of L are of interest to us, we could use a learner for 0-reversible languages in the following manner:

Algorithm 1 (A text learner based on fragmentation).

1. Use a deterministic transducer, i.e., a deterministic finite automaton with additional output labels on the arcs of its transition graph, in order to translate any word $w = a^n v$ of L (where n is maximal for any such representation of w) into $\bar{w} = a^n\$v = w^\alpha\$w^\omega$, where $ is the *fragmentation symbol*).
2. In this way, an input sample $I_+ = \{w_1, \ldots, w_n\}$ is transformed into two input samples $I_+^\alpha = \{w_1^\alpha, \ldots, w_n^\alpha\}$ and $I_+^\omega = \{w_1^\omega, \ldots, w_n^\omega\}$.
3. Both I_+^α and I_+^ω is given to (an instantiation of) a learner for 0-reversible languages; this way, the automata A^α and A^ω are derived. By using our background knowledge again, we might interpret this as the hypothesis language

$$L \cap L(A^\alpha)L(A^\omega).$$

This means that, for any $L' \in$ 0-Rev, $(a^+ \cup b^+)L'$ is identifiable.

In more general terms, we propose the following methodology of explicit fragmentation.

Definition 5. *A deterministic general sequential machine (gsm) M (see [15])
is a* fragmentator *if it either does not accept an input word or it transforms the
input w into $w^\alpha\$w^\omega$, where $w = w^\alpha w^\omega$ and \$, called* fragmentation symbol, *is
not contained in the input alphabet of M.*

Accordingly, w^α and w^ω are called the prefix fragment *and the* suffix fragment
*of w. The morphism μ_{def} mapping \$ onto the empty word and keeping all other
letters the same is called* defragmentator.

Since a gsm translates only successfully if it finally enters an accepting state,
a gsm can be seen as language recognizer when ignoring its output. The language
recognized by a gsm M will be denoted by $L(M)$. So, $M(\Sigma^*) = M(L(M))$ is
the set of possible outputs of M if Σ is the input alphabet of M.

Intuitively speaking, the language $L(M)$ accepted by a fragmentator M defines one part of the background knowledge of the "subject." The other part of
information is where to place the fragmentation symbol. Both parts of information are contained in $M(L(M))$.

By easy modifications of the output function of a fragmentator M, determin-
istic gsm's M^α and M^ω can be built such that $M(w) = M^\alpha(w)\$M^\omega(w)$ for each
$w \in L(M) = L(M^\alpha) = L(M^\omega)$. Since rational transducers preserve regularity,
for each regular language R, $M(R)$, $M^\alpha(R)$ and $M^\omega(R)$ are regular.

Using these two machines, a given sample I_+ yields two new samples $I_+^\alpha =
M^\alpha(I_+)$ and $I_+^\omega = M^\omega(I_+)$. A 0-reversible learner will generalize these samples
to yield the 0-reversible automata $A^\alpha(M, I_+)$ and $A^\omega(M, I_+)$, respectively. The
hypothesis language obtained in this way is

$$L_{hyp,M}(I_+) := \mu_{def}(L(A^\alpha(M, I_+))\$L(A^\omega(M, I_+)) \cap M(L(M))).$$

In a sense, we can interpret the pair $(A^\alpha(M, I_+), A^\omega(M, I_+))$ as the hypothesis of our new learning algorithm 1 (based on the fragmentator M), derived
from the learning algorithms yielding $A^\alpha(M, I_+)$ and $A^\omega(M, I_+)$. Formally, this
means that we can consider the set product of the two hypothesis spaces for the
prefix and suffix fragment languages as our new hypothesis space. In this way,
we would be able to describe languages from the family

$$\mathcal{L}(M) = \{ L_{hyp,M}(I) \mid I \subseteq \Sigma^+ \wedge |I| < \infty \},$$

where Σ is the input alphabet of M. By the identifiability of the 0-reversible
languages, we can immediately deduce:

Lemma 1.

$$\mathcal{L}(M) = \{ \mu_{def}(L^\alpha\$L^\omega \cap M(\Sigma^*)) \mid L^\alpha, L^\omega \in \textit{0-Rev}; L^\alpha, L^\omega \subseteq \Sigma^* \}.$$

Observe that the learning algorithms yielding $A^\alpha(M, I_+)$ and $A^\omega(M, I_+)$
needn't be learning algorithms for 0-Rev. More general, any text learner for
function-distinguishable languages will do. Especially, as we will see through the
proof of Theorem 2, the fragmentation construction suggested in this section can
be recursively applied.

It is quite clear that this new learning algorithm converges iff both original learning algorithms converge. In the following, we will show that $\mathcal{L}(M)$ is identifiable, indeed.

Theorem 2. *For each fragmentator M, $\mathcal{L}(M)$ is an identifiable class of regular languages.*

Proof. We show that, for each M, there is an associated class of function-distinguishable languages $\mathcal{L}$ whose proven identifiability can be used to deduce identifiability of $\mathcal{L}(M)$.

Consider a sample $I_+ \subseteq L \in \mathcal{L}(M)$. To the f-distinguishable learner,

$$I'_+ = M^\alpha(I_+)\{\$\}(\{\varepsilon\} \cup M^\omega(I_+))$$

will be forwarded. So, this learner can cope with languages over $\Sigma \cup \{\$\}$. As distinguishing function f, we use the transition function of $A(M(\Sigma^*))$.

Consider the case when L^α and L^ω are 0-reversible. Let A be the automaton obtained by "concatenating" the automata $A(L^\alpha)$ and $A(L^\omega)$ by an arc labelled $\$$. By considering the product automaton $A \times A(M(\Sigma^*))$, one sees that $L^\alpha\{\$\}L^\omega \cap M(\Sigma^*)$ is f-distinguishable.

This means that any enumeration of $L \in \mathcal{L}(M)$ (transformed to an enumeration of $L' = M^\alpha(L)\{\$\}(\{\varepsilon\} \cup M^\omega(L))$ to the f-distinguishable learner) will converge to a representation $A(L', f)$ of $L^\alpha\{\$\}L^\omega \cap M(\Sigma^*)$, if we consider only states corresponding to final states of $A(M(\Sigma^*))$ as final states of $A(L', f)$. Interpreting $\$$ as ε-inputs, this modified automaton actually accepts L. In other words, a simple re-interpretation of the hypothesis stream of the f-distinguishable learner yields a suitable hypothesis stream for a learner for $\mathcal{L}(M)$, since a valid stream of hypotheses for $\mathcal{L}(M)$ is easily producible.

The proof of the preceding theorem also yields an inference procedure for these languages, but this is not very efficient, since it contains the intermediate construction of function distinguishable automata which might be unnecessarily big. As detailed in [10], the running time of this algorithm may depend exponentially on the size of range of the distinguishing function which, in our case, directly depends on the size of the background knowledge language $L = L(M)$, measured in terms of the number of states of $A(L)$ and $A(M^\alpha(L(M)))$. By way of contrast, the learning algorithm 1 is of the same efficiency as the one for 0-reversible languages and is independent of the state complexity of L.

Let us illustrate this behaviour by continuing with our example:

Example 2. Consider the sample $I_+ = \{ab, aabb, b\}$ as input of the learning algorithm 1 based on fragmentation. We obtain the samples $I^\alpha_+ = \{a, aa, b\}$ and $I^\omega_+ = \{b, bb, \varepsilon\}$ as inputs for a 0-reversible learner. This learner will generalize towards $L^\alpha = \{a, b\}^*$ and $L^\omega = \{b\}^*$. Hence, we get $L_{hyp,M} = (a^+ \cup b^+)b^*$.

The algorithm suggested in the proof of Theorem 2 will produce the sample $I'_+ = \{a\$, aa\$, b\$, a\$b, aa\$bb\}$ as input for an f-distinguishable learning algorithm, with $f(\varepsilon) = 0$, $f(w) = 1$ if $w \in a^+$, $f(w) = 2$ if $w \in b^+$ and $f(w) = 3$

if $w \in M(\Sigma^*) = (a^+ \cup b^+)\$\{a,b\}^*$. This input will be generalized towards an automaton accepting $b\$ \cup a^+\$b^*$, which can be interpreted as the hypothesis $b \cup a^+ b^*$. This it not the same generalization as obtained by the proposed learner, but giving bb (in the form of $bb\$$) as additional bit of information will force the f-distinguishable learner to generalize towards $b^+\$ \cup a^+\$b^*$, so that, according to our interpretation, $L_{hyp,M}$ is correctly learned.

As a general concept, (explicit) fragmentation could be understood more general as defined above. For example, in principle one need not confine one-self to finite automata for implementing the fragmentation. We did this here mainly for technical reasons, since otherwise the sliced off fragments might yield non-regular languages, with which grammatical inference algorithms can hardly cope with, see [14], in particular, when restricting the discussion to 0-reversible languages [16].

5   Conditional Grammars

We now turn to the issue of implicit fragmentation. To get to this point, we need some further notions.

Definition 6. *A grammar with context conditions or conditional grammar is a construct $G = (N, T, P, S)$, where N is a set of nonterminals, T is a set of terminals, $S \in N$ is the start symbol and P is a finite set of rules of the form*

$$(\alpha \to \beta, L).$$

Such a rule is applicable to $x \in (N \cup T)^+$ if

- *α is contained in x, i.e., $\exists x_1, x_2 \in (N \cup T)^* : x = x_1 \alpha x_2$, and*
- *$x \in L$.*

The result of such an application would be $y = x_1 \beta x_2$. This derivation relation is written $x \Rightarrow y$ for short. As usual, we put $L(G) = \{w \in T^* \mid S \overset{*}{\Rightarrow} w\}$.

Usually, one restricts oneself to rules whose *cores* $\alpha \to \beta$ are context-free and whose *context conditions* L are all regular. Every recursively enumerable language can be generated by a grammar with context-free cores and regular context conditions. As exemplified by context-free grammars with permitting and forbidding context symbols (see [6] and [5] for details), several subclasses of regular context conditions have been considered which also possess universal computability. Hence, this mechanism is far too powerful to be used in full generality for learning purposes. Therefore, we will consider a rather restricted form of context condition grammars, mostly confining ourselves to linear core rules and linear context conditions. As shown in [17, Theorem 4], already in this way (surprisingly) non-regular unary languages can be generated. Further language properties of these restricted classes of conditional grammars can be found in [9].

To define identifiable classes, we introduce the following auxiliary notion.

Definition 7. *A context-free grammar* $G = (N, T, P, S)$ *is called a* base gram- mar *provided that* $L(G) = T^*$ *and that* G *is unambiguous.*

Taking, e.g., Earley's algorithm, it is clear that, given some word $w \in T^*$, the unique parse tree of w (for a fixed base grammar) can be obtained in polynomial time. In fact, in what follows, it is the unambiguity which is really needed. If we took some unambiguous grammar G with $L(G) \subsetneq T^*$ as base, then we would automatically restrict the languages obtainable in this way to sublanguages of $L(G)$, which would lead to reasonings similar to those in the preceding section.

Definition 8. *For a fixed base grammar* $G = (N, T, P, S)$ *with* $P = \{A_i \to w_i \mid 1 \le i \le |P|\}$ *and a class of languages* $\mathcal{C}$ *over* $(N \cup T)$, *we can associate the class* $Cond(G, \mathcal{C}) = \{L \subseteq T^* \mid L = L(G')$ *for some grammar* G' *with rules* $(A_i \to w_i, C_i)$, *where each context condition* $C_i \in \mathcal{C}\}$.
   Moreover, if $\bar{C} = (C_1, \ldots, C_{|P|})$ *is a tuple of context conditions from* $\mathcal{C}$, *let* $L(G, \bar{C})$ *denote the conditional language obtained from* G *by using* $C_1, \ldots, C_{|P|}$ *as context conditions.*

In the following argument, we will make use of the following fact:

Fact 1. Let $G = (N, T, P, S)$ be a base grammar. If $\bar{C}$ and $\bar{C}'$ are two tuples of context conditions with $\bar{C} \subseteq \bar{C}'$ (where the inclusion is understood component- wise), then $L(G, \bar{C}) \subseteq L(G, \bar{C}')$. □

Example 3. The rules $S \to 0S0$, $S \to 0S1$, $S \to 1S0$, $S \to 1S1$, $S \to 0$, $S \to 1$, and $S \to \varepsilon$ present a base grammar G. In general, a grammar with context conditions having this base grammar shows the form

$$S \to 0S0, L_0$$
$$S \to 0S1, L_1$$
$$S \to 1S0, L_2$$
$$S \to 1S1, L_3$$
$$S \to 0, T_0$$
$$S \to 1, T_1$$
$$S \to \varepsilon, T_\varepsilon$$

Whenever L_1 as well as T_ε embrace $\{0^n S 1^n \mid n \ge 0\}$ and all other context conditions are are not containing any occurrence of S, then such a grammar will generate $\{0^n 1^n \mid n \ge 0\}$. In particular, this is the case for the regular context conditions $L_1 = T_\varepsilon = 0^* S 1^*$. On the other hand, if

$$L_0 = L_2 = T_0 = T_1 = T_\varepsilon = \{0, 1\}^* S \{0, 1\}^*$$

and if all other context conditions are not containing any occurrence of S, then such a grammar generates all the palindromes over the alphabet $\{0, 1\}$.

Since in the Gold-style learning, convergence is required in the hypothesis space, a normal form representation of $\mathrm{Cond}(G,\mathcal{C})$ is sought for. Taking into account that the sequence of hypotheses given by the inference machine will approach the intended language from below when considering typical text learners for 0-reversible languages and keeping in mind that we would like to use known learning algorithms for $\mathcal{C}$ as sort of sub-programs for learning $\mathrm{Cond}(G,\mathcal{C})$, the natural choice would be to take "the smallest" languages $C_i \in \mathcal{C}$ which are able to define a certain language $L \in \mathrm{Cond}(G,\mathcal{C})$ as context conditions.

As can be easily checked by considering $\mathcal{C}$ as the regular languages and observing the language sequence

$$C_j := \{a,b\}^* \setminus \{a^n b^n \mid 1 \le n \le j\}$$

as a hypothetical way of defining a certain conditional language, there need not be "the smallest" language within $\mathcal{C}$, since obviously the intersection $\bigcap_{j \ge 1} C_j$ is just the complement of $\{a^n b^n \mid 1 \le n\}$ and hence, it is not regular.

Again, we need some more notations: Consider some $L \in \mathrm{Cond}(G,\mathcal{C})$ with $G = (N,T,P,S)$. Since every word $w \in L$ has a unique parse in G, it will give raise to (a possibly empty but finite set of) *condition words* $c_i(w)$ which will belong to the context condition C_i of any tuple of context conditions $\bar{C} = (C_1, \ldots, C_{|P|})$ with $L = L(G, \bar{C})$. Especially, letting

$$c_i(L) := \bigcup_{w \in L} c_i(w)$$

gives a tuple $c(L) := (c_1(L), \ldots, c_{|P|}(L))$ with $L = L(G, c(L))$.

Our discussion suggests the following general way to build text learners for conditional languages:

Algorithm 2 (A sketch of a text learner for conditional languages).

- Choose some base grammar $G = (N,T,P,S)$.
- Choose some identifiable language family $\mathcal{C}$ with languages over $N \cup T$.
- Choose an efficient text learner I for $\mathcal{C}$.

Then, we hope to get an efficient text learner I_G for $\mathrm{Cond}(G,\mathcal{C})$ by the following procedure. Assume $L \in \mathrm{Cond}(G,\mathcal{C})$ is enumerated to I_G. Let $\bar{C} = (C_1, \ldots, C_{|P|})$ be a "minimal tuple of context condition languages" in $\mathcal{C}$ describing L.

Consider one such enumerated word $w \in L$. Upon reading w, I_G computes $c_i(w)$ for $i = 1, \ldots, |P|$. The set $c_i(w)$ is enumerated to the instantiation I_i of I which is aiming at learning C_i. I_G's hypothesis can be taken as the tuple of current hypotheses of I_1 through $I_{|P|}$. If we can assume that I responds with (a sequence of) canonical objects, we can expect that I_G will also react with a (tuple of) canonical objects.

Can we expect that this learning scenario will always converge? If so, we can claim that we indeed constructed a text learner for $\mathrm{Cond}(G,\mathcal{C})$. Unfortunately, this issue is rather subtle, as the following example shows.

Example 4. We continue with the example started in Example 3.

Let us first start with the so-called 2-testable languages (in the strict sense) for which García and Vidal [12] gave an efficient text learner. A *2-testable language* is basically specified as a finite, disjoint union of ε-free languages each given by

- the set of required infixes of length two (and possibly some words of length of at most one) and
- the requirement that all words having as set of infixes of length two the required infixes are contained in that language.

For example, the language 0^*S1^* can be described as the set of words $\{S\} \cup 0^+S \cup S1^+ \cup 0^+S1^+$. The set 0^+S is specified by the infix sets $\{00, 0S\}$ and $\{0S\}$; in particular, since there is no allowed infix starting with S, S must be the last letter of each word in the language. Similarly, $S1^+$ can be described by $\{S1, 11\}$ and $\{S1\}$. Finally, 0^+S1^+ is described by the infix sets $\{00, 0S, S1, 11\}$, $\{0S, S1, 11\}$, $\{00, 0S, S1\}$ and $\{0S, S1\}$. More precisely, $\{00, 0S, S1, 11\}$ describes 00^+S11^+, and the other sets cover other situations. Since the 2-testable languages are a finite language class, the language learning process will converge trivially, irrespectively of the enumerated input language.

This means that, if $\mathcal{C}$ is the class of 2-testable languages, then $\text{Cond}(G, \mathcal{C})$ is a language class which can be inferred efficiently by the learning process described above, making use of (several instantiations of) the text learner of García and Vidal. In particular, $\{0^n1^n \mid n \geq 0\}$ and the palindrome language $\{w \in \{0, 1\}^* \mid w = w^R\}$ (where w^R denotes the *reversal* or *mirror image* of w) can be identified in this way:

If $\{0^n1^n \mid n \geq 0\}$ is enumerated say in increasing order, i.e., $w_n = 0^n1^n$, to this learner, then it would generate no input stream to a learner instantiation for L_0, L_2, L_3, T_0 or T_1 (here and in the following discussion, we carry over the names of the context conditions given in Example 3). So, the empty language is learned in each of these cases. To the contrary, 0^nS1^n is generated as input stream to a learner instantiation for L_1. Hence, we can observe the infix sets $\{S\}$, $\{0S, S1\}$ (each in one case), and $\{00, 0S, S1, S2\}$, which, as explained above, yields

$$L_1 = \{0^nS1^m \mid n, m > 1\} \cup \{0S1, S\}.$$

Similarly, $T_\varepsilon = L_1$ is inferred. As explained in Example 3, we have

$$L(G, (L_0, L_1, L_2, L_3, T_0, T_1, T_\varepsilon)) = \{0^n1^n \mid n \geq 0\}.$$

In the case of the palindrome language, similar observations can be made. For example, when observing the learning of any L_i in this case, we see that the following possible infix sets are found:

- $\{S\}$
- $\{0S, S0\}$, $\{1S, S1\}$,
- $\{00, 0S, S0\}$, $\{11, 1S, S1\}$,
- $\{10, 0S, S0, 01\}$, $\{01, 1S, S1, 10\}$,

- $\{10, 0S, S0, 01, 00\}$, $\{01, 1S, S1, 10, 11\}$,
- $\{10, 0S, S0, 01, 11\}$, $\{01, 1S, S1, 10, 00\}$,
- $\{10, 0S, S0, 01, 00, 11\}$, $\{01, 1S, S1, 10, 11, 00\}$.

As the reader may verify, this way a tuple of context conditions is inferred which correctly describes the palindromes (when taking as base the grammar exhibited in Example 3).

Another popular identifiable class of regular languages are the reversible languages as defined by Angluin [3].

As the reader may verify, $0^*S1^* \in 0\text{-Rev}$. Hence, the reasoning from Example 3 shows that $L = \{0^n1^n \mid n \geq 0\} \in \text{Cond}(G, 0 - \text{Rev})$, where G is the base grammar given in Example 3. Assume now that the words of L are enumerated according to increasing length to a learner for $\text{Cond}(G, 0 - \text{Rev})$ constructed as indicated above. Then, the learner instantiations for L_1 as well as for T_ε will be given $C = \{0^nS1^n \mid n \geq 0\}$ in increasing order, as well. Since each finite language $\{0^nS1^n \mid m \geq n \geq 0\}$ is 0-reversible, as can be easily verified by induction on m, the learning process will not converge.

Observe that the "limit set" $\{0^nS1^n \mid n \geq 0\}$ approximated from below in this way is a context-free, non-regular, proper subset of 0^*S1^*.

Summarizing what we learned from the example, we observe that the sketched venue of building a text learner based on condition languages works as long as the learner which is going to be used as sub-process has only a finite space of (potential) hypotheses.

Fortunately, this does not lead into problems if we use the following fragmentation idea: each context condition contains some nonterminals (if the rule should be applicable at all); if the base grammar is *simple* in the sense that each word w of a context condition contains only the nonterminals A_1 through A_m (in that order, each of them occurring only once), then each such w is naturally fragmented in parts $w = w_0 A_1 w_1 \ldots A_m w_m$. Giving each w_i to some "individual learner" yields a natural learning algorithm for some class of conditional languages which we like to characterize in the following. The exposition will concentrate on 0-reversible languages, again, but is easily extensible to function-distinguishable languages. Hence,

$$C = \{L_0\{A_1\}L_1 \ldots \{A_m\}L_m \mid m \geq 1, L_i \in 0\text{-Rev}, A_i \in N\}.$$

Note that this restriction of C automatically confines the language class to conditional languages of finite index, see [9]. In particular, this means that not all recursively enumerable languages are describable in this way.

To define the last condition of the next lemma, we need a few more technical things:

In each component i, there are only m_i occurrences of nonterminals in each word of $c_i(L)$. By fragmentation, this gives raise to $m_i + 1$ languages $c_i^j(L)$, $1 \leq j \leq m_i + 1$, such that

$$c_i^j(L) = \{v \in T^* \mid \exists u, x \in (N \cup T)^* : uA_jvA_{j+1}x \in c_i(L)\},$$

deliberately neglecting some boundary cases.

We call the pair $(G, \mathcal{C})$ *completely regular* iff, for each $1 \leq i \leq |P|$ and each $0 \leq j \leq m_i$, for all $L \in \mathrm{Cond}(G, \mathcal{C})$, $c_i^j(L)$ is regular.

Lemma 2. *If $G = (N, T, P, S)$ is some simple base grammar and if $(G, \mathcal{C})$ is completely regular, then we can associate to every language $L \in \mathrm{Cond}(G, \mathcal{C})$ a tuple of context conditions $\bar{C} = (C_1, \dots, C_{|P|})$, where each C_i is from $\mathcal{C}$, such that $L = L(G, \bar{C})$ and any tuple of context conditions $\bar{C}' = (C_1', \dots, C_{|P|}') \in \mathcal{C}^{|P|}$ with $L = L(G, \bar{C}')$ obeys $C_i \subseteq C_i'$ for all $1 \leq i \leq |P|$.*

Proof. By assumption, each $c_i^j(L)$ is regular. Due to the approximation properties of 0-reversible languages as exhibited in [16], the enumeration of $c_i^j(L)$ will converge to a minimal 0-reversible language containing $c_i^j(L)$. Setting now

$$C_i(L) := c_i^0(L)\{A_1\}c_i^1(L) \dots \{A_{m_i}\}c_i^{m_i}(L)$$

yields the required normal form.

Based on the preceding lemma and on Fact 1, and taking a slightly modified learning algorithm when compared to Algorithm 2—taking now into account the described implicit form of fragmentation—, we can deduce:

Corollary 1. *If $G = (N, T, P, S)$ is some simple base grammar and $(G, \mathcal{C})$ is completely regular, then then $\mathrm{Cond}(G, \mathcal{C})$ is identifiable.*

Remark 1. The condition of complete regularity is met by a number of base grammars, yielding a bunch of new identifiable language families, even when restricting oneself to $\mathcal{C}$ as being obtained through the class of 0-reversible languages. For instance, the simple base grammar G defined in Example 3 gives a completely regular pair. This base grammar can also be read as a *grammar form*, see [22, Chapter 12 of Volume I] for more details. In this way, by suitable interpretations many completely regular pairs can be defined. More generally, grammars (or grammar forms) whose rules are of the form

$$(S_1 \to xS_1y, C) \text{ or } (S_i \to S_iy, C) \text{ or } (S_j \to x, C)$$

for $i > 1$, $j \geq 1$, $x, y \in T^*$ will yield completely regular pairs. Note that these derivation processes resemble those of linear matrix languages, see [7].

Let us exemplify this venue by continuing with our example:

Example 5. What happens if $L = \{0^n1^n \mid n \geq 0\}$ is enumerated to this learner? Consider the sample

$$I_+ = \{01, 0011, 000111\}.$$

000111 will be parsed as

$$S \Rightarrow 0S1 \Rightarrow 00S11 \Rightarrow 000S111 \Rightarrow 000111.$$

Hence, for language L_1, the samples $S, 0S1, 00S11$ are generated. The corresponding two instances of learners for 0-reversible languages will get

$$I_0 = \{\, \varepsilon, 0, 00 \,\} \quad \text{and} \quad I_1 = \{\, \varepsilon, 1, 11 \,\}$$

as inputs. These inputs are generalized, yielding for L_1 the proposed context condition language 0^*S1^*. After having parsed the other input words, the same context condition will be proposed for T_ε. As we saw in Examples 3 and 4, we have indeed inferred L correctly in this way.

Note that although a certain form of over-generalization can be observed in the learning process of the context conditions, this does not mean that the overall learner over-generalizes, since the overall behaviour of this grammatical mechanism heavily depends on the base grammar.

Similarly, the language of palindromes can be learned.

6   Discussion and Prospect

In this paper, we discussed the concept of fragmentation for grammatical inference purposes. In an explicit fashion, the concept can be used to find new classes of efficiently identifiable regular language classes. In an implicit manner, as exemplified in conditional grammars, the concept is also a useful tool to get identifiable language classes which contain non-regular languages.

In both cases, a certain background knowledge about the envisaged application is assumed on side of the user. Interestingly, this knowledge is sort of contents-dependent: both the selection of "good" fragmentators and of "good" base grammars needs this sort of knowledge. By way of contrast, the concepts of control languages and families of permutations as discussed in [11] are more dedicated to a static knowledge on the domain: the permutations, for instance, are applied to any input word of a certain length, irrespectively of its "contents."

It would be interesting to see applications combining these approaches. We hope that, at the time being, a potential user of grammatical inference techniques has a certain wealth of methodologies to cope with non-regular languages, as well. Now, practical applications and comparisons would be sought for.

References

[1] D. Angluin. Finding patterns common to a set of strings. *Journal of Computer and System Sciences*, 21:46–62, 1980.

[2] D. Angluin. Inductive inference of formal languages from positive data. *Information and Control (now Information and Computation)*, 45:117–135, 1980.

[3] D. Angluin. Inference of reversible languages. *Journal of the ACM*, 29(3):741–765, 1982.

[4] E. Csuhaj-Varjú and A. Meduna. Grammars with context conditions (some results and open problems). *EATCS Bulletin*, 53:199–212, 1994.

[5] J. Dassow and H. Hornig. Conditional grammars with subregular conditions. In *2nd International Colloquium on Words, Languages, and Combinatorics*, pages 71–86. Kyoto Sangyo Unversity (Japan), World Scientific, August 1994.

[6] J. Dassow and Gh. Păun. *Regulated Rewriting in Formal Language Theory*, volume 18 of *EATCS Monographs in Theoretical Computer Science*. Springer, 1989.

[7] H. Fernau. Efficient learning of some linear matrix languages. In T. Asano et al., editors, *COCOON'99*, volume 1627 of *LNCS*, pages 221–230. Springer, 1999.

[8] H. Fernau. Identification of function distinguishable languages. In H. Arimura, S. Jain, and A. Sharma, editors, *Proceedings of the 11th International Conference Algorithmic Learning Theory ALT 2000*, volume 1968 of *LNCS/LNAI*, pages 116–130. Springer, 2000.

[9] H. Fernau and M. Holzer. Conditional context-free languages of finite index. In Gh. Păun and A. Salomaa, editors, *New Trends in Formal Languages*, volume 1218 of *LNCS*, pages 10–26. Springer, 1997.

[10] H. Fernau and A. Radl. Algorithms for learning function distinguishable regular languages. In *Statistical and Syntactical Methods of Pattern Recognition SPR+SSPR*, LNCS. Springer, 2002.

[11] H. Fernau and J. M. Sempere. Permutations and control sets for learning non-regular language families. In A. L. Oliveira, editor, *Grammatical Inference: Algorithms and Applications, 5th International Colloquium (ICGI 2000)*, volume 1891 of *LNCS/LNAI*, pages 75–88. Springer, 2000.

[12] P. García and E. Vidal. Inference of k-testable languages in the strict sense and applications to syntactic pattern recognition. *IEEE Transactions on Pattern Analysis and Machine Intelligence*, 12:920–925, 1990.

[13] E. M. Gold. Language identification in the limit. *Information and Control (now Information and Computation)*, 10:447–474, 1967.

[14] C. de la Higuera. Current trends in grammatical inference. In F. J. Ferri et al., editors, *Advances in Pattern Recognition, Joint IAPR International Workshops SSPR+SPR'2000*, volume 1876 of *LNCS*, pages 28–31. Springer, 2000.

[15] J. E. Hopcroft and J. D. Ullman. *Introduction to Automata Theory, Languages, and Computation*. Reading (MA): Addison-Wesley, 1979.

[16] S. Kobayashi and T. Yokomori. Learning approximately regular languages with reversible languages. *Theoretical Computer Science*, 174(1–2):251–257, 1997.

[17] C. Martin-Vide and Gh. Păun, editors. *Recent topics in mathematical and computational linguistics*, chapter H. Fernau and M. Holzer: External contextual and conditional languages, pages 104–120. Bucharest: The Publishing House of the Romanian Academy, 2000. ISBN 973-27-0770-4.

[18] E. Navrátil. Context-free grammars with regular conditions. *Kybernetika*, 6:118–126, 1970.

[19] Gh. Păun. On the generative capacity of conditional grammars. *Information and Control (now Information and Computation)*, 43:178–186, 1979.

[20] Gh. Păun. A variant of random context grammars: semi-conditional grammars. *Theoretical Computer Science*, 41:1–17, 1985.

[21] G. Rozenberg, K. Ruohonen, and A. K. Salomaa. Developmental systems with fragmentation. *International Journal of Computer Mathematics*, 5:177–191, 1976.

[22] G. Rozenberg and A. Salomaa, editors. *Handbook of Formal Languages (3 volumes)*. Springer, 1997.

[23] Y. Takada. Learning formal languages based on control sets. In K. P. Jantke and S. Lange, editors, *Algorithmic Learning for Knowledge-Based Systems*, volume 961 of *LNCS/LNAI*, pages 317–339. Springer, 1995.

On Limit Points for Some Variants of Rigid Lambek Grammars

Annie Foret and Yannick Le Nir

IRISA, Campus de Beaulieu 35042 Rennes, FRANCE
{foret,ylenir}@irisa.fr
http://www.irisa.fr/prive/foret
http://www.irisa.fr/prive/ylenir

Abstract. In this paper we give some learnability results in the field of categorial grammars. We show that in contrast to k-valued classical categorial grammars, different classes of Lambek grammars are not learnable from strings following Gold's model. The results are obtained by the construction of limit points in each considered class: non associative Lambek grammars with empty sequences and Lambek grammars without empty sequences and without product. Such results express the difficulty of learning categorial grammars from unstructured strings and the need for structured examples.

Keywords: grammatical inference, categorial grammars, Lambek calculus, learning from positive examples, computational linguistic

1 Introduction

Categorial grammars, introduced in [BH53] and extended to Lambek grammars in [Lam58], have been studied in the field of natural language processing. Since they are completely lexicalized, they are well adapted to learning perspectives and an actual way of research is to determine the sub-classes of such grammars that remain learnable in the sense of Gold ([Gol67]). We recall that learning here consist to define an algorithm on a finite set of sentences that converge to obtain a grammar in the class that generates the examples. Let $\mathcal{G}$ be a class of grammars, that we wish to learn from positive examples. Formally, let $\mathcal{L}(G)$ denote the language associated with grammar G, and let V be a given alphabet, a learning algorithm is a function ϕ from finite sets of words in V^* to $\mathcal{G}$, such that for $G \in \mathcal{G}$ with $\mathcal{L}(G) = <e_i>_{i \in N}$ there exists a grammar $G' \in \mathcal{G}$ and there exists $n_0 \in N$ such that : $\forall n > n_0 \; \phi(\{e_1, \ldots, e_n\}) = G' \in \mathcal{G}$ with $\mathcal{L}(G') = \mathcal{L}(G)$. After the initial pessimism following the unlearnability results in [Gol67], there has been a renewed interest due to learnability of non trivial classes from [Ang80] and [Shi90]. Recent works from [Kan98] and [Nic99] have answered the problem for different sub-classes of classical categorial grammars (we recall that the whole class of classical categorial grammars is equivalent to context free grammars; the same holds for the class of Lambek grammars [Pen93] that is thus not learnable

P. Adriaans, H. Fernau, and M. van Zaanen (Eds.): ICGI 2002, LNAI 2484, pp. 106–119, 2002.
© Springer-Verlag Berlin Heidelberg 2002

in Gold's model). The extension of such results for Lambek grammars is an interesting challenge that is adressed by works on logic types from [DSTT01] (these grammars enjoy a direct link with Montague semantics), learning from structures in [BR01], unlearnability results from [FL02] or complexity results from [CF01]. In this paper, we continue in this way and consider the following question : are specific variants of Lambek grammars learnable from strings. The paper is organized as follows. We present two main results on variants of Lambek calculus. The first one, in section 3 gives a construction and a proof of the existence of a limit point for a non associative Lambek grammar allowing empty sequences. Section 4 adresses the construction for Lambek grammars without product and without empty sequences and section 5 concludes.

2   Background

2.1   Categorial Grammars

In this section, we introduce basic definitions concerning categorial grammars. The interested reader may also consult [Cas88, Bus97, Moo97] for an introduction or for further details.

Types. *Types* are constructed from Pr (set of *primitive types*) and three binary connectives $/$, $\backslash$ and $\bullet$ for products. Tp denotes the set of types. Pr contains a *distinguished type*, written S, also called the *principal type*.

Categorial Grammar. Let Σ be a fixed alphabet. A *categorial grammar* over Σ is a finite relation G between Σ and Tp. If $< c, A > \in G$, we say that G *assigns* A to c, and we write $G \ : c \mapsto A$.

Lambek Derivation $\vdash_L$. The relation $\vdash_L$ is the smallest relation $\vdash$ between Tp^+ and Tp, such that for all $\Gamma, \Gamma' \in Tp^+, \Delta, \Delta' \in Tp^*$ and for all $A, B \in Tp$:

$$A \vdash A \qquad \frac{\Gamma, A, \Gamma' \vdash C \quad \Delta \vdash A}{\Gamma, \Delta, \Gamma' \vdash C} \; cut$$

$$\frac{A, \Gamma \vdash B}{\Gamma \vdash A \backslash B} \backslash r \qquad \frac{\Gamma, A \vdash B}{\Gamma \vdash B / A} /r \qquad \frac{\Gamma \vdash A \quad \Gamma' \vdash B}{\Gamma, \Gamma' \vdash A \bullet B} \bullet r$$

$$\frac{\Gamma \vdash A \quad \Delta, B, \Delta' \vdash C}{\Delta, \Gamma, A \backslash B, \Delta' \vdash C} \backslash l \quad \frac{\Gamma \vdash A \quad \Delta, B, \Delta' \vdash C}{\Delta, B / A, \Gamma, \Delta' \vdash C} /l \quad \frac{\Delta, A, B, \Delta' \vdash C}{\Delta, A \bullet B, \Delta' \vdash C} \bullet l$$

Non Associative Lambek Derivation $\vdash_{NL}$**.** In the Gentzen presentation, the derivability relation of NL holds between a term in $\mathcal{S}$ and a formula in Tp, where the term language is $\mathcal{S} ::= Tp|(\mathcal{S}, \mathcal{S})$. Terms in $\mathcal{S}$ are also called *G-terms*. A sequent is a pair $(\Gamma, A) \in \mathcal{S} \times Tp$. The notation $\Gamma[\Delta]$ represents a G-term with a distinguished occurrence of Δ (with the same position in premise and conclusion of a rule). The relation $\vdash_{NL}$ is the smallest relation $\vdash$ between $\mathcal{S}$ and Tp, such that for all $\Gamma, \Delta \in \mathcal{S}$ and for all $A, B, C \in Tp$:

$$ A \vdash A \qquad \frac{\Gamma[A] \vdash C \quad \Delta \vdash A}{\Gamma[\Delta] \vdash C} \; cut $$

$$ \frac{(A, \Gamma) \vdash B}{\Gamma \vdash A \backslash B} \backslash r \qquad \frac{(\Gamma, A) \vdash B}{\Gamma \vdash B / A} /r \qquad \frac{\Gamma \vdash A \quad \Delta \vdash B}{(\Gamma, \Delta) \vdash (A \bullet B)} \bullet r $$

$$ \frac{\Gamma \vdash A \quad \Delta[B] \vdash C}{\Delta[(\Gamma, A \backslash B)] \vdash C} \backslash l \quad \frac{\Gamma \vdash A \quad \Delta[B] \vdash C}{\Delta[(B / A, \Gamma)] \vdash C} /l \quad \frac{\Delta[(A, B)] \vdash C}{\Delta[A \bullet B] \vdash C} \bullet l $$

We write $NL_\emptyset$ for the Non associative Lambek calculus with empty antecedents (left part of the sequent). We also refer to [Bus97, Moo97] for more details on NL.

Note [Cut Elimination]. We recall that the cut rule is admissible in $\vdash_L$ and $\vdash_{NL}$: every derivable sequent has a cut-free derivation.

Language. Let G be a   categorial grammar over Σ. G *generates* a string $c_1 \ldots c_n \in \Sigma^+$ iff there are types $A_1, \ldots, A_n \in Tp$ such that : $G \; : c_i \mapsto A_i$ ($1 \leq i \leq n$) and $A_1, \ldots, A_n \vdash_L S$. The *language of* G, written $\mathcal{L}_L(G)$ is the set of strings generated by G. We define similarly $\mathcal{L}_{NL}(G)$ and $\mathcal{L}_{NL_\emptyset}(G)$ replacing $\vdash_L$ by $\vdash_{NL}$ and by $\vdash_{NL_\emptyset}$ in the sequent where the types are parenthesized in some way.

Notation. In some sections, we may write simply $\vdash$ instead of $\vdash_L$ or $\vdash_{NL}$ or $\vdash_{NL_\emptyset}$. We may simply write $\mathcal{L}(\mathcal{G})$ accordingly.

Rigid and k-valued Grammars. Categorial grammars that assign at most k types to each symbol in the alphabet are called *k-valued grammars*; 1-valued grammars are also called *rigid* grammars.

Example 1. Let $\Sigma_1 = \{John, Mary, likes\}$ and let $Pr = \{S, N\}$ for sentences and nouns respectively. Let $G_1 = \{John \mapsto N, Mary \mapsto N, likes \mapsto N \backslash (S / N)\}$. We get $(John \; likes \; Mary) \in \mathcal{L}_{NL}(G_1)$ since $((N, N \backslash (S / N)), N) \vdash_{NL} S$. G_1 is a rigid (or 1-valued) grammar.

2.2 Some Useful Models

For ease of proof, in next section we use two kinds of models that we now recall
: free groups and powerset residuated groupoids (or semi-groups), a special case
of residuated groupoids (see [Bus97] for details).

Free Group Interpretation. Let FG denote the free group with generators Pr, operation . and with neutral element I. We associate with each formula C an element in FG written $[C]$ as follows : $[p] = p$ for p atomic,
$[C_1 \setminus C_2] = [C_1]^{-1}.[C_2]$, $[C_1 / C_2] = [C_1].[C_2]^{-1}$, $[C_1 \bullet C_2] = [C_1].[C_2]$. We extend the notation to sequents by : $[C_1, C_2, \ldots, C_n] = [C_1].[C_2]. \ldots .[C_n]$. The
following property states that FG are models for L : if $\Gamma \vdash_L C$ then $[\Gamma] =_{FG} [C]$

Powerset Residuated Groupoids and Semi-groups. Let $(M, .)$ be a
groupoid. Let $\mathcal{P}(M)$ denote the powerset of M. A *powerset residuated groupoid*
over $(M, .)$ is the structure $(\mathcal{P}(M), \circ, \Rightarrow, \Leftarrow, \subseteq)$ such that for $X, Y \subseteq M$:
$$X \circ Y = \{x.y : x \in X, y \in Y\}$$
$$X \Rightarrow Y = \{y \in M : (\forall x \in X)x.y \in Y\}$$
$$Y \Leftarrow X = \{y \in M : (\forall x \in X)y.x \in Y\}$$
If $(M, .)$ is a semi-group (. is associative), then the above structure is a *powerset
residuated semi-group*. If $(M, .)$ has a unit I (that is : $\forall x \in M : I.x = x.I = x$),
then the above structure is a *powerset residuated groupoid with unit* (it has $\{I\}$
as unit).

Interpretation. Given a powerset residuated groupoid $(\mathcal{P}(M), \circ, \Rightarrow, \Leftarrow, \subseteq)$, an
interpretation is a map from primitive types p to elements $[[p]]$ in $\mathcal{P}(M)$ that is
extended to types and sequences in the natural way :
$$[[C_1 \setminus C_2]] = [[C_1]] \Rightarrow [[C_2]]$$
$$[[C_1 / C_2]] = [[C_1]] \Leftarrow [[C_2]]$$
$$[[C_1 \bullet C_2]] = [[C_1]] \circ [[C_2]]$$
$$[[C_1, C_2, \ldots, C_n]] = [[C_1]] \circ [[C_2]]. \ldots \circ [[C_n]]$$
If $(M, .)$ is a groupoid with an identity I, we add $[[\Lambda]] = \{I\}$ for the empty
sequence Λ and get a model property for $NL_\emptyset$: if $\Gamma \vdash_{NL_\emptyset} C$ then $[[\Gamma]] \subseteq [[C]]$.
If $(M, .)$ is a semi-group, we have a similar model property for L : if $\Gamma \vdash_L C$
then $[[\Gamma]] \subseteq [[C]]$.

2.3 Learning and Limit Points

We now recall some useful definitions and known properties on learning.

Limit Points. A class $\mathcal{CL}$ of languages has *a limit point* iff there exists an
infinite sequence $< L_n >_{n \in N}$ of languages in $\mathcal{CL}$ and a language $L \in \mathcal{CL}$ such
that : $L_0 \subsetneq L_1 \ldots \subsetneq \ldots \subsetneq L_n \subsetneq \ldots$ and $L = \bigcup_{n \in N} L_n$ (L is *a limit point* of $\mathcal{CL}$).

Limit Points Imply Unlearnability . The following property is important for our purpose. If the languages of the grammars in a class $\mathcal{G}$ have a limit point then the class $\mathcal{G}$ is *unlearnable*. [1]

3   Rigid Limit Points for $NL_\emptyset$

3.1   Construction Overview

Definition. We define the following grammars where p and S are primitive types :
$G_{\langle 1,n \rangle} = \{a \rightarrow p \,/\, p \;;\; c \rightarrow D_{\langle 1,n \rangle}\}$
where $D_{\langle 1,0 \rangle} = S$ and $D_{\langle 1,n \rangle} = D_{\langle 1,n-1 \rangle} \,/\, (p \,/\, p)$
$G_{\langle 1,* \rangle} = \{a \rightarrow p \,/\, p \;;\; c \rightarrow S \,/\, (p \,/\, p)\}$

Language. We get (see proof) $\mathcal{L}(G_{\langle 1,n \rangle}) = \{ca^k / 0 \leq k \leq n\}$
and $\mathcal{L}(G_{\langle 1,* \rangle}) = ca^*$.

Notation. Let $\tau_{\langle 1,n \rangle}$ (and $\tau_{\langle 1,* \rangle}$) denote the type assignment by $G_{\langle 1,n \rangle}$ (by $G_{\langle 1,* \rangle}$ respectively) on $\{a, c\}$ extended to $\{a, c\}^*$ in the natural way; we write $\tau = \tau_{\langle 1,n \rangle}$ on $\{a\}^*$ (independant of $n \geq 0$).

Key Points. We use tautologies of the Lambek calculus allowing empty sequences that ensure one way of type-derivability ($D_{\langle 1,n \rangle} \vdash D_{\langle 1,n-1 \rangle}$). Note that in contrast to [FL02] treatment for the associative calculus L, we do not need here an alternation effect, since non-associativity is enough to block some derivations such as ($D_{\langle 1,n-1 \rangle} \nvdash D_{\langle 1,n \rangle}$). We thus provide a strictly infinite chain of types for $NL_\emptyset$ with respect to $\vdash$.

3.2   Corollaries.

For the Class of Rigid $NL_\emptyset$-grammars . This yields a strictly increasing chain of language of rigid grammars. This shows that the class of rigid grammars has **infinite elasticity** (cf [Kan98] for details). This class also **has a limit point** as follows $c\{a\}^*$ which entails that this class is **not learnable from strings.**

Other Restricted Classes. The same results hold if we restrict to a bounded order, where the order $o(A)$ is :
  $o(p) = 0$ when p is a primitive type
  $o(C_1 \setminus C_2) = max(o(C_1) + 1, o(C_2))$
  $o(C_2 \,/\, C_1) = o(C_1 \setminus C_2)$
In fact the order $o(G_{\langle 1,n \rangle})$ in this construction are not greater than 2. This result also holds for the subclass of unidirectional grammars (we do not use $\setminus$).

---

[1] This implies that the class has infinite elasticity. A class $\mathcal{CL}$ of languages has *infinite elasticity* iff $\exists < e_i >_{i \in N}$ sentences $\exists < L_i >_{i \in N}$ languages in $\mathcal{CL}$ $\forall i \in N$: $e_i \notin L_i$ and $\{e_1, \ldots, e_n\} \subseteq L_{n+1}$ (see [Kan98] for this notion and a use of it).

3.3 Details of Proofs

Our proof is based both on a syntactic reasoning on derivations, and on models.

Proposition 1 (Language description) $\mathcal{L}(G_{\langle 1,n \rangle}) = \{ca^k/0 \le k \le n\}$ and $\mathcal{L}(G_{\langle 1,* \rangle}) = ca^*$.

Notation. For ease of proof, we introduce the following operations : for a word $w = c_1 c_2 c_3 \ldots c_{k-1} c_k$, where c_i denote letters, $l(w)$ is the left bracketed version of w, that is $l(w) = ((\ldots ((c_1 c_2) c_3) \ldots c_{k-1}) c_k)$; similarly for sequences of types $\Gamma = (A_1, A_2, A_3 \ldots A_{k-1}, A_k) : l(\Gamma) = ((\ldots ((A_1, A_2), A_3) \ldots A_{k-1}), A_k)$ that is the left bracketed version of the sequence. We define similarly r on words $r(w)$ and type sequences $r(\Gamma)$, for the right bracketed versions. We also extend the notation l and r to sets (of words or types) in the natural way.

proof of $\{ca^k/0 \le k \le n\} \subseteq \mathcal{L}(G_{\langle 1,n \rangle})$
we show the following left bracketed version of this property, by induction on n :
$$(\forall k : 0 \le k \le n) : l(\tau_{\langle 1,n \rangle}(ca^k)) \vdash S$$
. For $n = 0$ this is an axiom $\tau_{\langle 1,0 \rangle}(c) = S \vdash S$.
. Suppose $n > 0$ and $w' = c.w$ with $w \in \{a^*\}$ and $l(\tau_{\langle 1,n-1 \rangle}(cw)) \vdash S$
- we first show that $l(\tau_{\langle 1,n \rangle}(c.a.w)) \vdash S$:

$$
\vdots
$$

$$
\underbrace{\dfrac{l(D_{\langle 1,n-1 \rangle}, \tau(w)) \vdash S \quad p/p \vdash p/p}{l((D_{\langle 1,n-1 \rangle}/(p/p)), (p/p), \tau(w)) \vdash S}}_{=l(\tau_{\langle 1,n \rangle}(c.a.w))}
$$

- we easily get $l(\tau_{\langle 1,n \rangle}(c.w)) \vdash S$ as follows, we first have $D_{\langle 1,n \rangle} \vdash D_{\langle 1,n-1 \rangle}$ in $NL_\emptyset$ for $n > 0$:

$$
\dfrac{p \vdash p}{\dfrac{\emptyset \vdash p/p \quad D_{\langle 1,n-1 \rangle} \vdash D_{\langle 1,n-1 \rangle}}{D_{\langle 1,n-1 \rangle}/(p/p) \vdash D_{\langle 1,n-1 \rangle}}}
$$

we then infer using the Cut rule on $D_{\langle 1,n-1 \rangle}$:
$\underbrace{l(\tau_{\langle 1,n \rangle}(c.w))}_{=l(D_{\langle 1,n \rangle}, \tau(w))} \vdash S$ from $\underbrace{l(\tau_{\langle 1,n-1 \rangle}(c.w))}_{=l(D_{\langle 1,n-1 \rangle}, \tau(w))} \vdash S$

proof of $\mathcal{L}(G_{\langle 1,n \rangle}) \subseteq \{ca^k/0 \le k \le n\}$ **(main part)**
We consider a powerset residuated groupoid $(\mathcal{P}(M), \circ, \Rightarrow, \Leftarrow, \subseteq)$ over the groupoid $(M, .)$ where . is the concatenation operation and M is the set of bracketed strings over the alphabet $V = \{a, c\}$ with unit ε (empty word). Let us fix n (arbitrary), we define an interpretation as follows : $[[S]] = \{l(ca^k)/k \le n\}$, $[[p]] = \{r(a^k)/0 \le k\}$.

We first remark that $[[p/p]] = \{\varepsilon, a\}$ (since $[[p/p]] = \{z \in M : \forall x \in [[p]], (z.x) \in [[p]]\} = \{z \in M : \forall j, (z.r(a^j)) \in \{r(a^k)/0 \le k\}\}$).

We now show by induction on i that :

$\forall i (0 \leq i \leq n) \quad : \quad [[D_{\langle 1,i \rangle}]] = \{l(c.a^k)/k \leq (n-i)\}$

- case $i = 0 \leq n$ holds since $[[D_{\langle 1,0 \rangle}]] = [[S]] = \{l(c.a^k)/0 \leq k \leq n\}$

- case $(0 < i \leq n)$:

$[[D_{\langle 1,i-1 \rangle} \, / \, (p \, / \, p)]] = \{z \in M : \forall x \in [[p \, / \, p]], (z.x) \in [[D_{\langle 1,i-1 \rangle}]]\}$

$=_{ind.} \{z \in M : \forall x \in \{\varepsilon, a\}, (z.x) \in \{l(c.a^k)/0 \leq k \leq (n-(i-1))\}\}$

$= \{z \in M : z \in \{l(c.a^k)/k \leq (n-i+1)\} \text{ and } (z.a) \in \{l(c.a^k)/k \leq (n-i+1)\}\}$

$= \{l(c.a^k)/k \leq (n-i)\}$ (as desired)

We have thus shown that $[[D_{\langle 1,n \rangle}]] = \{c\}$.

Remark. Note that for each $w \in \{a, c\} : l(w) \in [[l(\tau_{\langle 1,n \rangle}(w))]]$; this holds for atomic words since $l(a) = a \in [[l(\tau_{\langle 1,n \rangle}(w))]] = [[l(p \, / \, p)]] = [[p \, / \, p]] = \{\varepsilon, a\}$ and $l(c) = c \in [[l(\tau_{\langle 1,n \rangle}(c))]] = [[D_{\langle 1,n \rangle}]] = \{c\}$; and for compound types we have : $[[l(\tau_{\langle 1,n \rangle}(c_1 \ldots c_n))]] = [[l(\tau_{\langle 1,n \rangle}(c_1)) \ldots \tau_{\langle 1,n \rangle}(c_k))]]$ includes $l(c_1, c_2 \ldots c_k) = ((c_1.c_2) \ldots c_k)$ (where c_i are atomic).

Let us suppose $\Gamma \vdash S$, where Γ is a bracketed version of $\tau_{\langle 1,n \rangle}(w)$. By models, we have $[[\Gamma]] \subseteq [[S]]$, since $[[S]] = \{l(c.a^k)/k \leq n\}$ has only left bracketed words, Γ must be the left bracketed version of $\tau_{\langle 1,n \rangle}(w)$. Therefore $[[l(\tau_{\langle 1,n \rangle}(w))]] \subseteq [[S]]$, hence $l(w) \in [[S]]$ from a former remark. This corresponds to $w \in \{c.a^k/k \leq n\}$ as desired.

proof of $c\{a\}^* \subseteq \mathcal{L}(G_{\langle 1,* \rangle})$

- We have $c \in \mathcal{L}(G_{\langle 1,* \rangle})$ since in $NL_\emptyset$:

$$\cfrac{\cfrac{p \vdash p}{\vdash p \, / \, p} \quad S \vdash S}{S \, / \, (p \, / \, p) \vdash S}$$

- Let $\Gamma_0 = (p \, / \, p)$ $\Gamma_k = ((p \, / \, p) \, / \, (p \, / \, p), \Gamma_{k-1})$ by induction on k we get $\Gamma_k \vdash (p \, / \, p)$ in $NL_\emptyset$:

$$\cfrac{\cfrac{\vdots}{\Gamma_{k-1} \vdash (p \, / \, p)} \quad (p \, / \, p) \vdash (p \, / \, p)}{\underbrace{((p \, / \, p) \, / \, (p \, / \, p), \Gamma_{k-1})}_{=\Gamma_k} \vdash (p \, / \, p)} \qquad \text{therefore} \qquad \cfrac{\cfrac{\vdots}{\Gamma_k \vdash (p \, / \, p)} \quad S \vdash S}{(S \, / \, (p \, / \, p), \Gamma_k) \vdash S}$$

that shows $c.a^k$ is in the language of $G_{\langle 1,* \rangle}$.

proof of $\mathcal{L}(G_{\langle 1,* \rangle}) \subseteq c\{a\}^*$

We consider the powerset residuated groupoid $(\mathcal{P}(M), \circ, \Rightarrow, \Leftarrow, \subseteq)$ as above but with the following (similar) interpretation : $[[S]] = \{l(c.a^k)/0 \leq k\}$, $[[p]] = \{r(a^k)/0 \leq k\}$ (unchanged)

Let us suppose $\Gamma \vdash_{NL_\emptyset} S$ where Γ is a bracketed version of $\tau_{\langle 1,* \rangle}(w)$.

By models, we have $[[\Gamma]] \subseteq [[S]]$.

We have as before : $[[p \, / \, p]] = \{\varepsilon, a\}$

We here get : $[[S \, / \, (p \, / \, p)]] = \{l(c.a^k)/0 \leq k\} = [[S]]$

$(= \{z \in M : \forall x \in [[p \, / \, p]], z.x \in [[S]]\} = \{z \in M : z \in \{l(c.a^k)/0 \leq k\}$ and $(z.a) \in \{l(c.a^k)/0 \leq k\}\})$

Therefore if $[[l(\tau_{\langle 1,* \rangle}(w))]] \subseteq [[S]] = \{l(c.a^k)/0 \leq k\}$, this also means that $w = cw'$ with $w' \in \{a\}^*$ as desired ∎

4   Rigid Limit Points for L

4.1   Construction Overview

Definition. We define the following types and assignments $\tau_{\langle 2,n\rangle}$, where $A = p \setminus p$, $B = q \setminus q$ and p, q are primitive types :

$$a \to A \ ; \qquad b \to B \ ; \qquad c \to D_{\langle 2,n\rangle}$$

where $D_{\langle 2,0\rangle} = S$

and $D_{\langle 2,n\rangle} = (S\,/\,p) \bullet ((p\,/\,q) \bullet (q\,/\,p))^{n-1} \bullet (p\,/\,q) \bullet q$ if $n > 0$

we write $D'_{\langle 2,n\rangle} = S\,/\,p \bullet (p\,/\,q \bullet q\,/\,p)^n \bullet p$

let $G_{\langle 2,n\rangle}$ denote the grammar defined by $\tau_{\langle 2,n\rangle}$ with alphabet $\{a, b, c\}$

Language. We get (see proof) $\mathcal{L}(G_{\langle 2,n\rangle}) = c(b^*a^*)^n$.

4.2   Details of Proofs

Our proof is based on syntax and models

Lemma 1.
(i) if $\tau_{\langle 2,n\rangle}(w) \vdash S$ is derivable in L then w has exactly one occurrence of c
(ii) if $p, \tau_{\langle 2,n\rangle}(w) \vdash p$ in L then $: w \in a^*$
(iibis) if $q, \tau_{\langle 2,n\rangle}(w) \vdash q$ in L then $: w \in b^*$
(iii) $\tau_{\langle 2,n\rangle}(w_1), S, \tau_{\langle 2,n\rangle}(w_2) \not\vdash S$ (where $w_1.w_2 \in \{a, b\}^+$)

proof of (i) direct by interpretation in free group ($[\tau_{\langle 2,n\rangle}(c)] = S$ and $[\tau_{\langle 2,n\rangle}(a)] = [\tau_{\langle 2,n\rangle}(b)] = I$)

proof of (ii)(iibis)(iii) we consider the powerset residuated semi-group over $M = \{p, q, t, I\}$ equipped with $\circ$ associative:

$\circ \ p \ q \ t \ I$
$p \ p \ t \ t \ p$
$q \ t \ q \ t \ q$
$t \ t \ t \ t \ t$
$I \ p \ q \ t \ I$

we now define $[[p]] = \{p\}, [[q]] = \{q\}$, $[[S]] = I$ and get $[[A]] = \{p, I\}$ and $[[B]] = \{q, I\}$

Suppose $\tau_{\langle 2,n\rangle}(w) \vdash A$, then by models $[[\tau_{\langle 2,n\rangle}(w)]] \subseteq [[A]]$; if w has an occurrence of b, this is impossible since we would have $[[\tau_{\langle 2,n\rangle}(w)]] \ni q$ or $[[\tau_{\langle 2,n\rangle}(w)]] \ni t$ whereas $[[A]] = \{I, p\}$.
Lemma (iibis) is similar.
To show (iii), we just have to consider $w_1.w_2 \in \{a, b\}^+$
to obtain $[[\tau_{\langle 2,n\rangle}(w_1), S, \tau_{\langle 2,n\rangle}(w_2)]] \subseteq \{p, q, t\}$ whereas $[[S]] = \{I\}$ ∎

Lemma 2.
(i)- if $(p\,/\,q, q\,/\,p)^m, p, \tau(w) \vdash p$ in L then $: w \in a^*(b^*a^*)^m$.
(ii)- if $(q\,/\,p, p\,/\,q)^m, q, \tau(w) \vdash q$ in L then $: w \in b^*(a^*b^*)^m$.
(iii)- if $q\,/\,p, (p\,/\,q, q\,/\,p)^m, p, \tau(w) \vdash q$ in L then $: w \in (a^*b^*)^{m+1}$.
(iv)- if $p\,/\,q, (q\,/\,p, p\,/\,q)^m, q, \tau(w) \vdash p$ in L then $: w \in (b^*a^*)^{m+1}$.

proof We show this lemma by reasoning on the possible derivations in L, using a lexicographical induction on m and $s = |w|$ (length of w), with the help of free group interpretation of the sequents in the derivations. See Appendix A for details.

Remark: if $n > 0$ then $\tau(w_1), D_{\langle 2,n \rangle}, \tau(w_2) \vdash S \Leftrightarrow \tau(w_1), S/p, (p/q, q/p)^{n-1}, p/q, q, \tau(w_2) \vdash S$
since $C_1, \cdots, C_n \vdash C_{n+1} \Leftrightarrow C_1 \bullet \cdots \bullet C_n \vdash C_{n+1}$

Proposition 2 (Language description) $\mathcal{L}(G_{\langle 2,n \rangle}) = c(b^*a^*)^n$.

proof of $c(b^*a^*)^n \subseteq \mathcal{L}(G_{\langle 2,n \rangle})$
For n=0, this is an axiom $\tau_{\langle 2,0 \rangle}(c) = S \vdash S$.
For n=1, we have the following deduction :

$$\frac{\qquad \dfrac{p, A \vdash p \quad q, B \vdash q}{S \vdash S \quad p/q, q, B, A \vdash p}}{S/p, p/q, q, B, A \vdash S}$$

Suppose $n > 1$ and $w' = cw = c(b^*a^*)^{n-1} \in \mathcal{L}(G_{\langle 2,n-1 \rangle})$
- we first show that $c.b.a.w \in \mathcal{L}(G_{\langle 2,n \rangle})$

$$\vdots$$

$$\frac{\overbrace{\dfrac{(S/p), ((p/q), (q/p))^{n-2}, (p/q), q, \tau(w) \vdash S \quad p, A \vdash p}{\underbrace{(S/p), ((p/q), (q/p))^{n-1}, p, A, \tau(w) \vdash S}} }^{\Leftrightarrow D_{\langle 2,n-1 \rangle}} /l \quad q, B \vdash q}{\underbrace{(S/p), ((p/q), (q/p))^{n-1}, (p/q), q, \underbrace{B, A, \tau(w)}_{=\tau(b.a.w)} \vdash S}_{=D_{\langle 2,n \rangle}}} /l$$

- we then easily get $c.w \in \mathcal{L}(G_{\langle 2,n \rangle})$ since $D_{\langle 2,n \rangle} \vdash D_{\langle 2,n-1 \rangle}$ in L for $n > 0$.
- we also get $c.a.w \in \mathcal{L}(G_{\langle 2,n \rangle})$ from $D_{\langle 2,n \rangle}, A \vdash D_{\langle 2,n-1 \rangle}$
- we get $c.b.w \in \mathcal{L}(G_{\langle 2,n \rangle})$ from $D_{\langle 2,n \rangle}, B \vdash D_{\langle 2,n-1 \rangle}$
- finally, this is extended to repetitions of each letter a or b separately since $\tau(a), \tau(a) \vdash \tau(a)$ and $\tau(b), \tau(b) \vdash \tau(b)$

proof of $\mathcal{L}(G_{\langle 2,n \rangle}) \subseteq c(b^*a^*)^n$
We have to show : if $\tau(w_1), D_{\langle 2,n \rangle}, \tau(w_2) \vdash S$ in L then   : w_1 is empty and $w_2 \in (b^*a^*)^n$
We show by joined lexicographical induction on n and $s = |w_2|$ that
- (i) if $\tau(w_1), D_{\langle 2,n \rangle}, \tau(w_2) \vdash S$ in L then   : w_1 is empty and $w_2 \in (b^*a^*)^n$
- (ii) if $\tau(w_1), D'_{\langle 2,n \rangle}, \tau(w_2) \vdash S$ in L then   : w_1 is empty and $w_2 \in a^*(b^*a^*)^n$
See Appendix B for details.

4.3   New Types Without Product

Key Points. We now transform our types assignments to obtain product free types by curryfication. We use type raising properties to use the previous result on $\tau_{\langle 2,n \rangle}$.

Notation. We write $A^{l,X}$ the type raising of A: $X / (A \setminus X)$

Definition. We define the following types assignments where $A = p \backslash p$, $B = q \backslash q$ and p, q are primitive types :

$\tau_{\langle 3,n \rangle}$: $a \to A$; $b \to B$; $c \to D_{\langle 3,n \rangle}$ where $D_{\langle 3,n \rangle} = D_{\langle 2,n \rangle}{}^{l,S}$
let $G_{\langle 3,n \rangle}$ denote the grammar defined by $\tau_{\langle 3,n \rangle}$ with alphabet $\{a, b, c\}$ and principal type S.
Let $G_{\langle 3,* \rangle}$ denote the grammar, with type assignment $\tau_{\langle 3,* \rangle}$ defined by :
$G_{\langle 3,* \rangle} = \{a \to A; b \to A; c \to S / A\}$

Proposition 3 (Language description)
$\mathcal{L}(G_{\langle 3,n \rangle}) = c(b^*a^*)^n - \{c\}$ in L for $n \geq 0$ and $\mathcal{L}(G_{\langle 3,* \rangle}) = c\{a, b\}^+$ in L

proof of $c(b^*a^*)^n - \{c\} \subseteq \mathcal{L}(G_{\langle 3,n \rangle})$
We know from proposition 2 that for $n \geq 0$, $D_{\langle 2,n \rangle}, \tau(w) \vdash S$ where $w \in (b^*a^*)^n$
Moreover,

$$\cfrac{S \vdash S \quad \cfrac{D_{\langle 2,n \rangle}, \tau(w) \vdash S}{\tau(w) \vdash D_{\langle 2,n \rangle} \setminus S} \backslash r(\text{ if } \tau(w) \neq \varepsilon)}{S / (D_{\langle 2,n \rangle} \setminus S), \tau(w) \vdash S} /l \qquad \text{thus } c(b^*a^*)^n - \{c\} \subseteq \mathcal{L}(G_{\langle 3,n \rangle})$$

proof of $\mathcal{L}(G_{\langle 3,n \rangle}) \subseteq c(b^*a^*)^n - \{c\}$ in L
Using free group interpretation, we show there is exactly one c in every word of $\mathcal{L}(G_{\langle 3,n \rangle})$.
$\tau_{\langle 3,n \rangle}(w) \vdash S$ is then equivalent to $\tau_{\langle 3,n \rangle}(w_1), D_{\langle 3,n \rangle}, \tau_{\langle 3,n \rangle}(w_2) \vdash S$ where $w = w_1.c.w_2$
By definition, we obtain $\tau_{\langle 3,n \rangle}(w_1), D_{\langle 2,n \rangle}{}^{l,S}, \tau_{\langle 3,n \rangle}(w_2) \vdash S$
thus $\tau_{\langle 3,n \rangle}(w_1), D_{\langle 2,n \rangle}, \tau_{\langle 3,n \rangle}(w_2) \vdash S$ and $\tau_{\langle 2,n \rangle}(w_1), D_{\langle 2,n \rangle}, \tau_{\langle 2,n \rangle}(w_2) \vdash S$
By proposition 2, w_1 is empty and $w_2 \in (b^*a^*)^n$.
Moreover, for $n \geq 0$, $\tau_{\langle 3,n \rangle}(c) \nvdash S$ in L since $C^{l,S} \nvdash S$ in L for any formula C
We have $\mathcal{L}(G_{\langle 3,n \rangle}) \subseteq c(b^*a^*)^n - \{c\}$ as desired.
By curryfication $D_{\langle 3,n \rangle}$ is equivalent to a type without product :

$$\overbrace{\qquad\qquad\qquad}^{n-1 \ times}$$
$$D_{\langle 3,n \rangle} \equiv S / (q \setminus ((p / q) \setminus ((q / p) \setminus \cdots \setminus ((p / q) \setminus ((S / p) \setminus S)) \cdots))).$$

The previous property is then true for L without product.
We now have to prove that $\mathcal{L}(G_{\langle 3,* \rangle}) = c\{a, b\}^+$ to obtain a limit point.

proof of $c\{a, b\}^+ \subseteq \mathcal{L}(G_{\langle 3,* \rangle})$
- We have $ca, cb \in \mathcal{L}(G_{\langle 3,* \rangle})$ since $S / A, A \vdash S$
- We then get $c\{a, b\}^+ \in \mathcal{L}(G_{\langle 3,* \rangle})$ since $A, A \vdash A$

proof of $\mathcal{L}(G_{\langle 3,* \rangle}) \subseteq c\{a, b\}^+$
We consider the powerset residuated semi-group $(\mathcal{P}(V^+), \circ, \Rightarrow, \Leftarrow, \subseteq)$ with the following interpretation : $[[S]] = c\{a, b\}^*$ and $[[p]] = a^*$ thus $[[A]] = a^*$ and $[[S / A]] = c\{a, b\}^*$, therefore if $[[\tau_{\langle 3,* \rangle}(w)]] \subseteq [[S]] = c\{a, b\}^*$, this also means that $w = cw'$ with $w' \in \{a, b\}^*$.
Moreover $S / A \nvdash S$ in L thus $w' \in \{a, b\}^+$ as desired ∎

4.4   Non-learnability for Subclasses.

From the constructions in previous sections we get the following propositions as corollaries :

Proposition 4 (non-learnability) *The class of languages of rigid (or k-valued for an arbitrary k) Non associative Lambek grammars with empty sequence admits a limit point ; the class of rigid (or k-valued for an arbitrary k) Non associative Lambek grammars with empty sequence is not learnable from strings.*

Proposition 5 (non-learnability) *The class of languages of rigid (or k-valued for an arbitrary k) Lambek grammars without product and without empty sequence admits a limit point ; the class of rigid (or k-valued for an arbitrary k) Lambek grammars without product and without empty sequence is not learnable from strings.*

4.5   Future Work

Our results indicate the necessity of using structures as input of learning algorithms. We have shown that with empty sequence, non associative Lambek grammars are not learnable from strings. It would now be very interesting to extend this result to the case without empty sequence before searching structures that are sufficient to obtain learning algorithms. The second result gives a lower bound to the complexity of structures we need to learn Lambek grammars in Gold's model. An upper bound, that is the full proof tree structures of examples is obtained by the algorithm from [BR01], on the same class of grammars. An intermediate structure should then be a good alternative between insufficient structures (strings) and linguistic unrealistic structures (full proof tree structures).

References

[Ang80]   Dana Angluin. Inductive inference of formal languages from positive data. *Information and Control*, 45:117–135, 1980.

[BH53]   Y. Bar-Hillel. A quasi arithmetical notation for syntactic description. *Language*, 29:47–58, 1953.

[BR01]   Roberto Bonato and Christian Retoré. Learning rigid lambek grammars and minimalist grammars from structured sentences. *Third workshop on Learning Language in Logic, Strasbourg*, 2001.

[Bus97]   W. Buszkowski. Mathematical linguistics and proof theory. In van Benthem and ter Meulen [vBtM97], chapter 12, pages 683–736.

[Cas88]   Claudia Casadio. Semantic categories and the development of categorial grammars. In R. Oehrle, E. Bach, and D. Wheeler, editors, *Categorial Grammars and Natural Language Structures*, pages 95–124. Reidel, Dordrecht, 1988.

[CF01]   C. Costa Florêncio. Consistent Identification in the Limit of the Class k-valued is NP-hard. In *LACL*, 2001.

[DSTT01] Dudau-Sofronie, Tellier, and Tommasi. Learning categorial grammars from semantic types. In *13th Amsterdam Colloquium*, 2001.

[FL02]   Annie Foret and Yannick Le Nir. Rigid lambek grammars are not learnable from strings. Coling 2002. http://www.irisa.fr/prive/foret/learn.ps.

[Gol67]   E.M. Gold. Language identification in the limit. *Information and control*, 10:447–474, 1967.

[Kan98]   Makoto Kanazawa. *Learnable classes of categorial grammars*. Studies in Logic, Language and Information. FoLLI & CSLI, 1998. distributed by Cambridge University Press.

[Lam58]   Joachim Lambek. The mathematics of sentence structure. *American mathematical monthly*, 65:154–169, 1958.

[Moo97]   Michael Moortgat. Categorial type logic. In van Benthem and ter Meulen [vBtM97], chapter 2, pages 93–177.

[Nic99]   Jacques Nicolas. Grammatical inference as unification. Rapport de Recherche RR-3632, INRIA, 1999. http://www.inria.fr/RRRT/publications-eng.html.

[Pen93]   Mati Pentus. Lambek grammars are context-free. In *Logic in Computer Science*. IEEE Computer Society Press, 1993.

[Shi90]   T. Shinohara. Inductive inference from positive data is powerful. In *The 1990 Workshop on Computational Learning Theory*, pages 97–110, San Mateo, California, 1990. Morgan Kaufmann.

[vBtM97] J. van Benthem and A. ter Meulen, editors. *Handbook of Logic and Language*. North-Holland Elsevier, Amsterdam, 1997.

Appendix

A   Proof of Lemma 2

By symmetry, we do not treat part (ii) and (iv).

- if $m = 0$, then (i) is $p, \tau(w) \vdash p$ and $w \in a^*$; (iii) is $q \, / \, p, p, \tau(w) \vdash q$ with antecedents $p, \tau(w_1) \vdash p$ and $q, \tau(w_2) \vdash q$ where $w = w_1.w_2$; from lemma 1

- if $m > 0$, part (i) :

    - if the last introduction is on $p \, / \, q$ then the only correct antecedents (this can be seen by free group interpretation) are $(p \, / \, q, q \, / \, p)^i, p, \tau(w_2) \vdash p$ and $q \, / \, p, (p \, / \, q, q \, / \, p)^{m-i-1}, p, \tau(w_1) \vdash q$ where $0 \le i < m$ and $w = w_1.w_2$

    - if the last introduction is on $q \, / \, p$ then the only correct antecedents are $(p \, / \, q, q \, / \, p)^i, p \, / \, q, q, \tau(w_2) \vdash p$ and $(p \, / \, q, q \, / \, p)^{m-i-1}, p, \tau(w_1) \vdash p$ where $0 \le i < m$ and $w = w_1.w_2$

    - if the last introduction is on $p \backslash p$ ($s \ge 1$) then the only correct antecedents are $(p \, / \, q, q \, / \, p)^i, p, \tau(w_1) \vdash p$ and $(p \, / \, q, q \, / \, p)^{m-i}, p, \tau(w_2) \vdash p$ where $0 \le i \le m$ and $w = w_1.a.w_2$ (If $i = m$ then $|w_1| < |w|$)

    - if the last introduction is on $q \backslash q$ ($s \ge 1$) then the only correct antecedents are $q \, / \, p, (p \, / \, q, q \, / \, p)^i, p, \tau(w_1) \vdash q$ and $(p \, / \, q, q \, / \, p)^{m-i-1}, p \, / \, q, q, \tau(w_2) \vdash p$ where $0 \le i < m$ and $w = w_1.b.w_2$

In all these cases, by induction we have $w \in a^*(b^*a^*)^m$.

- if $m > 0$, part (iii) :

- if the last introduction is on p / q then the only correct antecedents are $q / p, (p / q, q / p)^i, p, \tau(w_2) \vdash q$ and $q / p, (p / q, q / p)^{m-i-1}, p, \tau(w_1) \vdash q$ where $0 \le i < m$ and $w = w_1.w_2$

- if the last introduction is on q / p then the only correct antecedents are $(q / p, p / q)^i, q, \tau(w_2) \vdash q$ and $(p / q, q / p)^{m-i}, p, \tau(w_1) \vdash p$ where $0 \le i \le m$ and $w = w_1.w_2$. We apply part (i) and (ii) up to m as shown above.

- if the last introduction is on $p \backslash p$ ($s \ge 1$) then the only correct antecedents are $q / p, (p / q, q / p)^i, p, \tau(w_2) \vdash q$ and $(p / q, q / p)^{m-i}, p, \tau(w_1) \vdash p$ where $0 \le i \le m$ and $w = w_1.a.w_2$ (If $i = m$ then $|w_2| < |w|$)

- if the last introduction is on $q \backslash q$ ($s \ge 1$) then the only correct antecedents are $(q / p, p / q)^i, q, \tau(w_2) \vdash q$ and $q / p, (p / q, q / p)^{m-i}, p, \tau(w_1) \vdash p$ where $0 \le i \le m$ and $w = w_1.b.w_2$ (If $i = 0$ then $|w_1| < |w|$)
In all these cases, by induction we have $w \in (a^*b^*)^{m+1}$

B   Proof of $\mathcal{L}(G_{\langle 2,n \rangle}) \subseteq c(b^*a^*)^n$

For ease of proof we consider sequence version of $D_{\langle 2,n \rangle}$ and $D'_{\langle 2,n \rangle}$ with commas instead of products.
case $n = 0$, (i) is $\tau(w_1), S, \tau(w_2) \vdash S$ and has already be proved in lemma 1 and (ii) is $\tau(w_1), S / p, p, \tau(w_2) \vdash S$ and is obtained from (i) and lemma 1 (see after). We know that the last rule is an introduction on the left and that, from free group interpretation, introduction in such deduction is impossible on $\tau(w_1)$. We deduce the following forms for deductions, where $w_2 = w_{21}.w_{22}$, from free group interpretation.
case $n > 0$ (i) :
- if the last introduction is on S / p we obtain the following deduction

$$\frac{\tau(w_1), S, \tau(w_{22}) \vdash S \quad p / q, (q / p, p / q)^{n-1}, q, \tau(w_{21}) \vdash p}{\tau(w_1), \underbrace{S / p, p / q, (q / p, p / q)^{n-1}, q, \tau(w_2)}_{\Leftrightarrow D_{\langle 2,n \rangle}} \vdash S}$$

w_1, w_{22} are empty from lemma 1(iii) and $w_{21} \in (b^*a^*)^n$ from lemma 2.
- if the last introduction is on q / p, $0 \le i < n - 1$, we obtain the following deduction

$$\frac{\tau(w_1), \overbrace{S / p, p / q, (q / p, p / q)^i, q, \tau(w_{22})}^{\Leftrightarrow D_{\langle 2,i+1 \rangle}} \vdash S \quad p / q, (q / p, p / q)^{n-i-2}, q, \tau(w_{21}) \vdash p}{\tau(w_1), S / p, p / q, (q / p, p / q)^{n-1}, q, \tau(w_2) \vdash S}$$

w_1 is empty, $w_{22} \in (b^*a^*)^{i+1}$ (induction) and $w_{21} \in (b^*a^*)^{n-i-1}$ (lemma 2).
- if the last introduction is on p / q, $0 \le i < n$, we obtain the following deduction

$$\frac{\tau(w_1), \overbrace{S / p, (p / q, q / p)^i, p, \tau(w_{22})}^{\Leftrightarrow D'_{\langle 2,i \rangle}} \vdash S \quad (q / p, p / q)^{n-i-1}, q, \tau(w_{21}) \vdash q}{\tau(w_1), S / p, p / q, (q / p, p / q)^{n-1}, q, \tau(w_2) \vdash S}$$

w_1 is empty, $w_{22} \in a^*(b^*a^*)^i$ (induction) and $w_{21} \in b^*(a^*b^*)^{n-i-1}$ (lemma 2).

- if the last introduction is on $p \backslash p$, $0 \le i < n$, we obtain the following deduction

$$\frac{\tau(w_1), S\,/\,p, (p\,/\,q, q\,/\,p)^i, p, \tau(w_{22}) \vdash S \quad (p\,/\,q, q\,/\,p)^{n-i-1}, p\,/\,q, q, \tau(w_{21}) \vdash p}{\tau(w_1), S\,/\,p, p\,/\,q, (q\,/\,p, p\,/\,q)^{n-1}, q, \tau(w_{21}), p \backslash p, \tau(w_{22}) \vdash S}$$

w_1 is empty, $w_{22} \in a^*(b^*a^*)^i$ (induction) and $w_{21} \in (b^*a^*)^{n-i}$ (lemma 2).

- if the last introduction is on $q \backslash q$, $0 \le i < n$, we obtain the following deduction

$$\frac{\tau(w_1), S\,/\,p, (p\,/\,q, q\,/\,p)^i, p\,/\,q, q, \tau(w_{22}) \vdash S \quad (q\,/\,p, p\,/\,q)^{n-i-1}, q, \tau(w_{21}) \vdash q}{\tau(w_1), S\,/\,p, (p\,/\,q, q\,/\,p)^{n-1}, p\,/\,q, q, \tau(w_{21}), q \backslash q, \tau(w_{22}) \vdash S}$$

w_1 is empty, $w_{22} \in (b^*a^*)^{i+1}$ (induction) and $w_{21} \in b^*(a^*b^*)^{n-i-1}$ (lemma 2).

case $n \ge 0$ (ii) :

- if the last introduction is on $S\,/\,p$ we obtain the following deduction

$$\frac{\tau(w_1), S, \tau(w_{22}) \vdash S \quad (p\,/\,q, q\,/\,p)^n, p, \tau(w_{21}) \vdash p}{\tau(w_1), \underbrace{S\,/\,p, (p\,/\,q, q\,/\,p)^n, p, \tau(w_2)}_{\Leftrightarrow D'_{\langle 2,n \rangle}} \vdash S}$$

w_1, w_{22} are empty from lemma 1(iii) and $w_{21} \in a^*(b^*a^*)^n$ from lemma 2.

- if the last introduction is on $q\,/\,p$, $0 \le i < n$, we obtain the following deduction

$$\frac{\overbrace{\tau(w_1), S\,/\,p, (p\,/\,q, q\,/\,p)^i, p\,/\,q, q, \tau(w_{22})}^{\Leftrightarrow D_{\langle 2,i+1 \rangle}} \vdash S \quad (p\,/\,q, q\,/\,p)^{n-i-1}, p, \tau(w_{21}) \vdash p}{\tau(w_1), S\,/\,p, (p\,/\,q, q\,/\,p)^n, p, \tau(w_2) \vdash S}$$

w_1 is empty, $w_{22} \in (b^*a^*)^{i+1}$ (induction), $w_{21} \in a^*(b^*a^*)^{n-i-1}$ (lemma 2).

- if the last introduction is on $p\,/\,q$, $0 \le i < n$, we obtain the following deduction

$$\frac{\overbrace{\tau(w_1), S\,/\,p, (p\,/\,q, q\,/\,p)^i, p, \tau(w_{22})}^{\Leftrightarrow D'_{\langle 2,i \rangle}} \vdash S \quad q\,/\,p, (p\,/\,q, q\,/\,p)^{n-i-1}, p, \tau(w_{21}) \vdash q}{\tau(w_1), S\,/\,p, (p\,/\,q, q\,/\,p)^n, p, \tau(w_2) \vdash S}$$

w_1 is empty, $w_{22} \in a^*(b^*a^*)^i$ (induction) and $w_{21} \in (a^*b^*)^{n-i}$ (lemma 2).

- if the last introduction is on $p \backslash p$, $0 \le i \le n$, we obtain the following deduction

$$\frac{\tau(w_1), S\,/\,p, (p\,/\,q, q\,/\,p)^i, p, \tau(w_{22}) \vdash S \quad (p\,/\,q, q\,/\,p)^{n-i}, p, \tau(w_{21}) \vdash p}{\tau(w_1), S\,/\,p, (p\,/\,q, q\,/\,p)^n, p, \tau(w_{21}), p \backslash p, \tau(w_{22}) \vdash S}$$

either $n \ne i$ or $|w_{22}| < |w_2|$ thus w_1 is empty and $w_{22} \in a^*(b^*a^*)^i$ by induction and $w_{21} \in a^*(b^*a^*)^{n-i}$ from lemma 2.

- if the last introduction is on $q \backslash q$, $0 \le i < n$, we obtain the following deduction

$$\frac{\tau(w_1), S\,/\,p, (p\,/\,q, q\,/\,p)^i, p\,/\,q, q, \tau(w_{22}) \vdash S \quad q\,/\,p, (p\,/\,q, q\,/\,p)^{n-i-1}, p, \tau(w_{21}) \vdash q}{\tau(w_1), S\,/\,p, (p\,/\,q, q\,/\,p)^n, p, \tau(w_{21}), q \backslash q, \tau(w_{22}) \vdash S}$$

w_1 is empty, $w_{22} \in (b^*a^*)^{i+1}$ (induction) and $w_{21} \in (a^*b^*)^{n-i}$ (lemma 2).

Generalized Stochastic Tree Automata for Multi-relational Data Mining

Amaury Habrard, Marc Bernard, and François Jacquenet

EURISE – Université de Saint-Etienne – 23, rue du Dr Paul Michelon
42023 Saint-Etienne cedex 2 – France
{Amaury.Habrard,Marc.Bernard,Francois.Jacquenet}@univ-st-etienne.fr

Abstract. This paper addresses the problem of learning a statistical distribution of data in a relational database. Data we want to focus on are represented with trees which are a quite natural way to represent structured information. These trees are used afterwards to infer a stochastic tree automaton, using a well-known grammatical inference algorithm. We propose two extensions of this algorithm: use of sorts and generalization of the infered automaton according to a local criterion. We show on some experiments that our approach scales with large databases and both improves the predictive power of the learned model and the convergence of the learning algorithm.

Keywords. Stochastic tree automata, multi-relational data mining, generalization, sorts.

1   Introduction

For many years, the use of relational databases is continually increasing in all domains of activities. Companies want to store more and more information in their databases and their activities now really depend on them. It is now well known that a large amount of knowledge may be hidden inside these large databases. That is the reason why machine learning and knowledge discovery in databases have known a fast expansion during the last decade.

Most of existing techniques work on a flat representation of the database, that is on one table built from a join on multiple tables [9, 2, 20]. Unfortunately, flattening data leads to lose some information since each example must have the same representation. A few attempts have been made to learn from databases without flattening data [12, 10, 16]. That leads to the emergence of an active field of research, called multi-relational learning [11]. For example the ILP framework [21] allows learning from a representation of the database as a subset of first order logic, keeping the structuring of data. [13] proposed the concept of probabilistic relational models that extends the standard attribute-based Bayesian network representation to take into account the relational structure on different entities.

Our approach can be placed in the same context. We try to collect in a tree all the information relative to each example. This is done using relations between

P. Adriaans, H. Fernau, and M. van Zaanen (Eds.): ICGI 2002, LNAI 2484, pp. 120–133, 2002.
© Springer-Verlag Berlin Heidelberg 2002

tables. This kind of representation is quite natural and allows to have trees of variable size for various examples, depending on the information we have about them. In this paper we present a method for learning a distribution of data stored in a particular table of a relational database, taking into account the related information stored in other tables. Our method follows several steps. We first generate a learning sample containing one tree per record of the table we want to focus on. Then we infer a stochastic tree automata following the distribution of the learning sample. We improve the inference algorithm proposing the use of sorts during the inference, and introducing a local generalization technique. We illustrate the relevance of these two contributions on some experiments.

The paper focuses on grammatical inference aspects of this approach. We first present the generation of trees from a relational database. Then we define the inference of stochastic many-sorted tree automata and we introduce generalized tree automata. Finally we evaluate our approach on a relational database of the PKDD'01 discovery challenge [4].

2 Capturing the Information in a Tree

A relational database stores information about multiple entities. In order to learn some knowledge from one entity of the database, we focus on a particular table that we call the root table. We use a tree structure to capture in a tree all the information related to one row of the root table. The basic idea to build such a tree is to generate a root node labelled with the name of the root table. Then for each attribute value of the row we construct a subtree. The process computes recursively the subtrees corresponding to foreign keys. For example we may want to discover some knowledge about products stored in the database relying on the schema of figure 1.

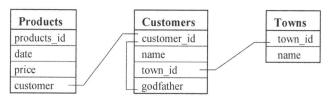

Fig. 1. Example database

If the database contains data of figure 2, the information related to the product 1 is represented by the tree of figure 3.

Products			
product_id	date	price	customer
1	11/11/2001	120	2
...	...	...	...

Customers			
customer_id	name	town_id	godfather
1	Jones	2	
2	Smith	1	1
...	...	...	...

Towns	
town_id	name
1	hills
2	city
...	...

Fig. 2. Data example

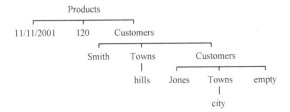

Fig. 3. Generated tree

To present the algorithm which computes the generation of trees we introduce some notations. We consider a database $\mathcal{T}$ with n tables $T_1, \ldots, T_n$. Each table is made up of a set of attributes $A(T_i) = \{a_{i_1}, \ldots, a_{i_{n(i)}}\}$ where $n(i)$ is the number of attributes of the table T_i. We denote $T_i.a_{i_k}$ the attribute a_{i_k} of the table T_i. We define the set of foreign keys $F(T_i) = \{a_{i_1}, \ldots, a_{i_m}\}$ such that $F(T_i) \subseteq A(T_i)$ and each $a_{i_k} \in F(T_i)$ is a reference to an attribute $T_j.a_{j_l}$ (what we denote $T_i.a_{i_k} : T_j.a_{j_l}$).

Algorithm 1 describes the construction of a tree associated with one row of the root table. For example the tree of figure 3 is obtained calling Generate_tree($Products, product\_id, 1$).

Generate_tree($T_i, target\_attribute, value$)

Result: Node
begin

     $p_1, \ldots, p_{n(i)} \leftarrow$ SELECT $a_{i_1}, \ldots, a_{i_{n(i)}}$ FROM T_i
                 WHERE $T_i.target\_attribute = value$
     $N \leftarrow T_i(p_1, \ldots, p_{n(i)})$
     foreach $a_{i_k} \in F(T_i)$ such that $T_i.a_{i_k} : T_j.a_{j_l}$ **do**
         $p_k \leftarrow$ Generate_tree(T_j, a_{j_l}, p_k)
     end
     Return N

end

Algorithm 1: Tree generation

A bias language, that we do not detail here, allows us to control the generation of trees. A SQL query can be specified to select only a part of rows of the root table. We may ignore a subset of attributes of each table. We can also bound the depth of trees to avoid infinite trees.

Generating trees from the database produces a training set of trees representing a concept stored in the database. Based on this set we now aim at learning a probabilistic tree grammar represented by a stochastic tree automaton.

3   Inference of Stochastic Tree Automata

Tree automata [15, 8] define a regular language on trees as finite automata define a regular language on strings. Note that we consider ordered trees, that is trees where left to right order between siblings is significant. Stochastic tree automata are an extension of tree automata which define a statistical distribution on the tree language recognized by the automata. Learning tree automata has received many attention for some years. For example [14] and [19] proposed some algorithms for learning tree automata. In the probabilistic framework, [23] proposed a framework for inducing probabilistic grammars. In the context of tree automata, [6] proposed an efficient algorithm to learn stochastic tree automata. [1] dealt with learning stochastic tree grammars to predict protein secondary structure. [22] presented a generalization of k-gram models for stochastic tree languages.

   Our inference procedure is an extension of [6], that takes sorts into account, defining stochastic many-sorted tree automata (SMTA). We briefly present SMTA before their inference procedure.

Definition 1 *A signature Σ is a 4-tuple (S, X, α, σ). S is a finite set whose elements are called sorts. X is a finite set whose elements are called function symbols. α is a mapping from X into $\mathbb{N}$. $\alpha(f)$ will be called the arity of f. σ is a mapping from X into S. $\sigma(s)$ will be called the sort of s.*

Note that in our approach the signature is learned from the learning sample using a basic procedure [3]. A symbol a appears at position (f, n) if it is the nth argument of a tree constructed on the symbol f. We define equivalence classes in the following way: two symbols are equivalent if they appear at least one time at the same position. A sort is then associated with each equivalence class.

   A set of sorted trees can be recognized by a stochastic many-sorted tree automaton.

Definition 2 *A stochastic many-sorted tree automaton is a 5-tuple $(\Sigma, Q, r, \delta, p)$. Σ is a signature (S, X, α, σ). $Q = \cup_{s \in S} Q^s$ is a finite set of states, each state having a sort in S. $r : Q \longrightarrow [0, 1]$ is the probability for the state to be an accepting state. $\delta : X \times Q^* \longrightarrow Q$ is the transition function. $p : X \times Q^* \longrightarrow [0, 1]$ is the probability of a transition.*

   A SMTA parses a tree using a bottom-up strategy. A state and a probability are associated with each node of the tree. The labelling of each node is defined by the transition function. The tree is accepted if the probability of its root node is strictly positive. Given a SMTA A, the probability of a tree t is computed as follows:

$$p(t \mid A) = r(\delta(t)) \times \pi(t)$$

where $\pi(f(t_1, \ldots, t_n))$ is recursively computed by:

$$\pi(t) = p(f, \delta(t_1), \ldots, \delta(t_n)) \times \pi(t_1) \times \cdots \times \pi(t_n)$$

```
1.0 :  a ⟶ q1
1.0 :  b ⟶ q2
0.5 :  f(q1,q2) ⟶ q3
0.5 :  f(q1,q1) ⟶ q3
1.0 :  g(q3) ⟶ q4
Final state : r(q4) = 1.0
```

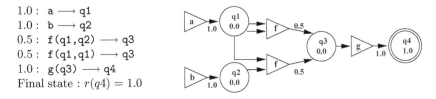

Fig. 4. An example of stochastic tree automaton

Example The automaton defined on figure 4 recognizes the tree $t = g(f(a,b))$ with the following probability:

$$
\begin{aligned}
p(t|A) &= r(\delta(g(f(a,b)))) \times \pi(g(f(a,b))) \\
&= r(q4) \times p(g, \delta(f(a,b))) \times \pi(f(a,b)) \\
&= r(q4) \times p(g,q3) \times p(f, \delta(a), \delta(b)) \times \pi(a) \times \pi(b) \\
&= r(q4) \times p(g,q3) \times p(f, q1, q2) \times p(a) \times p(b) \\
&= 1.0 \times 1.0 \times 0.5 \times 1.0 \times 1.0 \\
&= 0.5
\end{aligned}
$$

We are interested in producing consistent SMTA. Such automata define a statistical distribution over all trees built on a given alphabet. Therefore we have to ensure the sum of the probabilities of all these trees equals to one.

Algorithm 2 gives an idea of the main steps of inference. We do not detail the procedure here, the interested reader may refer to [6]. The input of the algorithm is a training set S of trees and the output is a SMTA which respects the distribution over S. The algorithm computes the transition function considering all the subtrees of the training set. A total order is defined on subtrees comparing their depth. Each subtree is mapped to a state, taking into account the fact that if two subtrees are similar in the training set, then they have the same state. We denote $[t]$ the state mapped to the subtree t. To compute the similarity of two subtrees (*comp* function), the algorithm uses a statistical test [18] depending on a parameter $0 \le \alpha \le 1$. Intuitively α represents a tolerance parameter for the merging of two trees on a same state. The probabilities are then computed counting the subtree occurrences on the training set. The algorithm has the following properties: it is polynomial in the number of different subtrees of the training set, it infers a consistent automaton [7], and it converges to the limit under the Gold paradigm [17].

As we consider many-sorted trees, the algorithm only computes the similarity of subtrees built from symbols of same sort. Thus using sorts speeds up the convergence of the algorithm and improves its predictive power as experimentally shown in section 6.

Data: S: a training set,
   $\Sigma = (X, S, \sigma, \alpha)$: a signature
Result: $A = (\Sigma, Q, \delta, p, r)$: a SMTA
begin
   $W \leftarrow$ Subtrees of S
   $States \leftarrow \emptyset$
   while $W \neq \emptyset$ **do**
      $x \leftarrow g(t_1, \ldots, t_n) = min\ W$
      $W \leftarrow W \backslash \{x\}$
      if $\exists y \in States \mid \sigma(x) = \sigma(y)\ and\ comp(x, y, \alpha)$ **then**
         $\delta(g, [t_1], \ldots, [t_n]) = y$
      else
         $States \leftarrow States \cup \{x\}$
         $\delta(g, [t_1], \ldots, [t_n]) = x$
      end
   end
   $compute\_probabilities(S, \delta, p, r)$
end

Algorithm 2: Inference of a SMTA

4   Generalization of SMTA

A SMTA generalizes examples of the learning sample. Nevertheless, it is possible to generalize even more. Actually, looking at the transition rules of a learned SMTA, we may observe local regularities. For example if we consider $R_{f,q}$, the set of all rules of the form $f(q_1, \ldots, q_n) \rightarrow q$:

$$R_{f,q} = \{f(q1, q2, q3) \rightarrow q,\ f(q1, q4, q3) \rightarrow q,\ f(q1, q5, q3) \rightarrow q\}$$

Here we can see that whatever the state at position $(f, 2)$ is, we reach the state q given that $q1$ is in position $(f, 1)$ and $q3$ is in position $(f, 3)$. Therefore we would like to generalize these three rules in the rule $f(q1, X, q3) \rightarrow q$. This leads us to introduce generalized stochastic many-sorted tree automata which locally generalize SMTA. Note the α parameter of the inference algorithm is set globally and thus cannot have the local effect we described above.

4.1   Generalized SMTA

Definition 3 *A generalized SMTA is 6-tuple $(\Sigma, Q, \delta, p, r, V)$. $\Sigma = (S, X, \sigma, \alpha)$ is a signature. Q is a finite set of states, each state having a sort in S. $r : Q \rightarrow [0, 1]$ is the probability for a state to be an accepting state. $\delta : X \times \{Q \cup V\}^* \rightarrow Q$ is the transition function. $p : X \times \{Q \cup V\}^* \rightarrow [0, 1]$ is the probability of a transition. V is a set of variables such that $V \cap X = \emptyset$.*

The parsing of a tree with a generalized SMTA is similar to the one performed by a SMTA. It processes a tree using a bottom-up strategy, trying to label each node with a state. A variable stands for any state or any unrecognized state. In our framework, the parsing is deterministic. If two rules or more can be used, we choose the one of highest probability.

Given a generalized tree automaton A, the probability associated with a tree $t = f(t_1, \ldots, t_n)$ is defined by:

$$p(t \mid A) = r(\delta(t)) \times \pi'(t_1) \times \ldots \times \pi'(t_n)$$

where π' is recursively computed by:

$$\pi'(t) = p(f, \delta(t_1), \ldots, \delta(t_n)) \times \nu_1(\pi'(\delta(t_1))) \times \ldots \times \nu_n(\pi'(\delta(t_n)))$$

where

$$\nu_i(b) = \begin{cases} 1 \text{ if } \delta(t_i) \text{ instantiates a variable} \\ b \text{ otherwise} \end{cases}$$

Example Let A be the generalized automaton defined by:

$$
\begin{array}{lll}
f(q1, X, q2) \to q3 : 0.4 & a \to q1 & : 0.2 \\
b \to q2 \qquad\qquad\quad : 0.1 & r(q3) = 1.0 &
\end{array}
$$

The probability associated with the tree $f(a, f(a, b, c), b)$ is:

$$p(f(a, f(a, b, c), b) \mid A) = 1.0 \times 0.4 \times 0.2 \times 1.0 \times 0.1 = 0.008$$

4.2   Generalization Algorithm

We propose a method to generalize a stochastic tree automata A according to a parameter γ ($0 \leq \gamma \leq 1$). The idea consists in locally generalizing the tree automaton by replacing a set of rules $R_{f,q}$ with more general rules.

Definition 4 *Let r_1 and r_2 be two rules: $r_1 = f(x_1, \ldots, x_n) \to q$ and $r_2 = f(x'_1, \ldots, x'_n) \to q'$ such that $x_i \in Q \cup V$ and $x'_i \in Q \cup V$. r_1 is more general than r_2 (we note $r_1 > r_2$) if and only if there exists a substitution θ such that $f(x_1, \ldots, x_n) \theta = f(x'_1, \ldots, x'_n)$. We say that r_1 subsumes r_2.*

Definition 5 *A rule r is called a generalized rule if there exists a rule r' in $R_{f,q}$ such that $r > r'$.*

This generalization relation defines an upper semi-lattice for each set $R_{f,q}$. The upper bound is the rule containing only variables and the lower bounds are the rules of $R_{f,q}$.

The lattice is traversed searching for the maximally specific general rules having a score greater than γ. The score of a generalized rule is equal to the sum of the probabilities of all less general rules.

Example Consider the set of rules $R_{f,q}$ of a stochastic tree automaton:

$$f(q1, q2, q3) \rightarrow q : 0.3 \qquad f(q1, q4, q3) \rightarrow q : 0.3$$
$$f(q1, q2, q4) \rightarrow q : 0.2 \qquad f(q5, q2, q3) \rightarrow q : 0.2$$

The generalized rules having a score greater than 0.6 are:

$$f(\_,\_,\_) : 1.0 \qquad f(q1,\_,\_) : 0.8 \qquad f(q1,\_, q3) : 0.6$$
$$f(\_,\_, q3) : 0.8 \qquad f(\_, q2,\_) : 0.7$$

As we only keep the maximally specific generalized rules, we only keep the rules $f(q1,\_, q3)$ and $f(\_, q2,\_)$ for state q and symbol f. Note that we use the symbol '$\_$' to denote any anonymous variable. The lattice associated with $R_{f,q}$ is represented on figure 5.

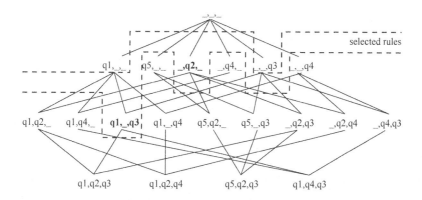

Fig. 5. Lattice of generalization

Algorithm 3 generalizes a SMTA. It first constructs a set of generalized rules. In this set, some rules may subsume some others. In this case the more general rule is deleted. When two generalized rules, reaching a different state, subsume the same non generalized rule, one of the two general rules is deleted. Finally all the rules of the SMTA that are not subsumed by generalized rules are added to the set of transitions of the generalized SMTA.

Then the probabilities of generalized rules are computed from their scores using the function *update_probabilities*. If a rule r of the initial automaton is subsumed by n generalized rules $r_1, \ldots, r_n$, its probability is shared among the generalized rules. Therefore the score $p(r_i)$, $1 \leq i \leq n$, must be updated adding $\frac{p(r)}{n} - p(r)$.

Data: $A = (\Sigma, Q, \delta, p, r_s)$: a SMTA
     γ: a generalization parameter
Result: $A_g = (\Sigma, Q, \delta_g, p_g, r_s, V)$: a generalized SMTA
begin
    $F \leftarrow \emptyset$
    foreach $R_{f,q}$ *such that* $q \in Q, f \in X, \alpha(f) > 1$ **do**
        $E \leftarrow \{\, f(q_1, \ldots, q_n) \mid f(q_1, \ldots, q_n) \rightarrow q \,\}$
        $F_{f,q} \leftarrow find\_rules(E, \gamma)$
        $F \leftarrow F \cup F_{f,q}$
    end
    $F \leftarrow F \backslash \{r \mid r \in F_{f,i}, \exists r' \in F_{f,j}, i \neq j, r' > r\}$
    $F \leftarrow F \backslash \{r \mid r \in F_{f,i}, \exists r' \in F_{f,j}, i \neq j, \exists d \in \delta \text{ such that } r > d, r' > d\}$
    $F \leftarrow F \cup \{d \in \delta \mid \nexists r \in F, r > d\}$
    $p_g \leftarrow update\_probabilities(F)$
    $\delta_g \leftarrow F$
    Return A_g
end

Algorithm 3: SMTA generalization

The function $find\_rules$ searches for all most specific rules of $R_{f,q}$ with a score greater than γ.

5   Experimental Evaluation

We have evaluated our approach using a relational database in the medical domain. The database was collected at Chiba University Hospital and stores data about collagen diseases and thrombosis. The original version is available on the UCI repository [4]. In this paper we use a more recent version of this database proposed for the PKDD'01 discovery challenge[1].

5.1   Perplexity

The evaluation of non-probabilistic models is often based on the classification rate. Probabilistic models are rather assessed on their ability to correctly predict the probability of a test sample. In this paper we evaluate the learned automata by measuring the perplexity criterion.

In the case of tree automata, the quality of a model A can be evaluated by the average likelihood on a set of trees S relatively to the distribution defined by A:

---

[1] http://lisp.vse.cz/challenge/pkdd2001/

$$LL = \left(\frac{1}{\|S\|} \sum_{j=1}^{|S|} \log P(t_j)\right)$$

This is linked to the Kullback-Leibler divergence which compares the distribution of an unknown target to a distribution evaluated on a training set [5]. A perfect model can predict each element of the sample with a probability equal to one, and so $LL = 0$. In a general way we consider the perplexity of the test set which is defined by $PP = 2^{LL}$. A minimal perplexity $(PP = 1)$ is reached when the model can predict each element of the test sample. Therefore we consider that a model is more predictive than another if its perplexity is lower.

A problem occurs when a tree of the test sample cannot be recognized by the automaton. Actually the probability of this example is 0 and the perplexity cannot be computed. To avoid this problem we smooth the distribution of the learned model. We define a universal (generalized) SMTA A_0 with only one state s. The probabilities of the rules are computed from the training set. If a transition involves an unknown symbol, its probability is fixed to a small ratio of the size of the training set. In the smoothed model, a tree t has the probability:

$$\hat{P}(t) = \beta . p(t|A) + (1 - \beta) . p(t|A_0)$$

where $0 \le \beta \le 1$. The results presented below are computed with $\beta = 0.9$.

5.2 Experimental Results

The database is made up of seven relations. The table *patient_info* stores information about patients. The three tables *antibody_exam*, *ana_pattern* and *lab_exam* report laboratory examinations. The table *thrombosis* stores data about all thrombosis attacks. The table *diagnosis* lists all diseases a patient is suffering from. Finally, the table *disease* includes all the diseases diagnosed at the hospital.

The idea is to learn a distribution on the patient examinations, taking into account information stored in other tables. Thus we focus our experiments on the *lab_exam* table. The table has 57542 records that we split into a set of 30000 trees and a test set of 17542 trees. 30000 trees are used during the training phases and the remaining ones form the test set. For each perplexity measure we consider five random learning samples of size 1000 to 30000. For each learned model we assess the perplexity according to the size of the learning sample.

In a first series of experiments, we aim at measuring the benefit of sorts in tree automata. For each training sample we represent examples either with trees or many-sorted trees. This leads to learn either stochastic tree automata or stochastic many-sorted tree automata. Figure 6 shows that perplexity is significantly reduced when we used many-sorted trees.

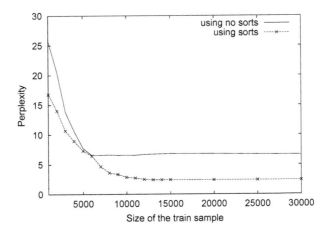

Fig. 6. Contribution of sorts

In a second series of experiments, we measure the predictive ability of the generalized SMTA comparing the one of SMTA. Let us recall the generalization depends on a parameter γ. Figure 7 and 8 show the evolution of the perplexity with various values of γ. In order to improve the readability we present these results on four charts. We may observe that for some values of γ, the generalized model performs better than ungeneralized one. First it improves the predictive power of the automaton and secondly it requires less examples to converge. These two points seem to show the interest of local generalization.

6   Conclusion

In this paper we have presented a grammatical inference approach to learn probabilistic models on relational databases. This approach is based on the inference of stochastic many-sorted tree automata. Experiments have shown our approach is able to address large amount of data (up to 30000 trees which corresponds to 230000 records of the database). We have shown that incorporating sorts really improves the efficiency of the learned automaton and speeds up the convergence of the inference algorithm. Moreover we have proposed generalized stochastic many-sorted tree automata which locally generalize stochastic many-sorted tree automata. The experiments have shown that this concept improves both the predictive power of the learned model and the convergence of the learning algorithm. We now aim at refining the local generalization studying various strategies to select generalized rules and to compute their probabilities.

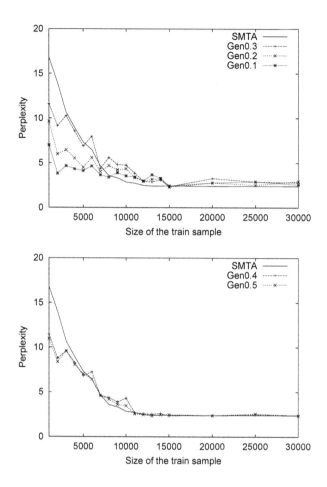

Fig. 7. Evaluation of the generalized SMTA

References

[1] N. Abe and H. Mamitsuka. Predicting protein secondary structure using stochastic tree grammars. *Machine Learning*, 29:275–301, 1997.
[2] R. Agrawal and R. Srikant. Fast algorithms for mining association rules. In J. B. Bocca, M.s Jarke, and C. Zaniolo, editors, *Proc. 20th Int. Conf. Very Large Data Bases, VLDB*, pages 487–499. Morgan Kaufmann, 12–15 1994.
[3] M. Bernard and C. de la Higuera. Apprentissage de programmes logiques par Inférence Grammaticale. *Revue d'Intelligence Artificielle*, 14(3–4):375–396, 2000. Hermes Sciences.
[4] C.L. Blake and C.J. Merz. University of California Irvine repository of machine learning databases. http://www.ics.uci.edu/~mlearn/, 1998.
[5] J. Calera-Rubio and R. C. Carrasco. Computing the relative entropy between regular tree languages. *Information Processing Letters*, 68(6):283–289, 1998.

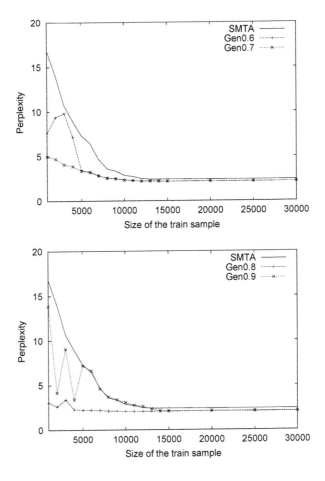

Fig. 8. Evaluation of the generalized SMTA

[6] R. C. Carrasco, J. Oncina, and J. Calera. Stochastic Inference of Regular Tree Languages. *Machine Learning*, 44(1/2):185–197, 2001.

[7] R. Chaudhuri and A. N. V. Rao. Approximating grammar probabilities: Solution of a conjecture. *Journal of the Association for Computing Machinery*, 33(4):702–705, 1986.

[8] H. Comon, M. Dauchet, R. Gilleron, F. Jacquemard, D. Lugiez, S. Tison, and M. Tommasi. Tree Automata Techniques and Applications . Available on: `http://www.grappa.univ-lille3.fr/tata`, 1997.

[9] G. F. Cooper and E. Herskovits. A bayesian method for the induction of probabilistic networks from data. *Machine Learning*, 9:309–347, 1992.

[10] V. Crestana-Jensen and N. Soparkar. Frequent itemset counting across multiple tables. In *4th Pacific-Asian conference on Knowledge Discovery and Data Mining (PAKDD 2000)*, pages 49–61, April 2000.

[11] L. De Raedt. Data mining in multi-relational databases. In *4th European Conference on Principles and Practice of Knowledge*, 2000. Invited talk.

[12] L. Dehaspe and H. Toivonen. Discovery of frequent DATALOG patterns. *Data Mining and Knowledge Discovery*, 3(1):7–36, 1999.

[13] N. Friedman, L. Getoor, D. Koller, and A. Pfeffer. Learning probabilistic relational models. In *16th International Joint Conference on Artificial Intelligence (IJCAI)*, pages 1300–1307. Morgan Kaufmann, 1999.

[14] P. Garcia and J. Oncina. Inference of recognizable tree sets. Research Report DSIC - II/47/93, Departamento de Sistemas Informáticos y Computación, Universidad Politécnica de Valencia, 1993.

[15] F. Gécseg and M. Steinby. *Tree Automata*. Akadémiai Kiadó, Budapest, 1984.

[16] L. Getoor, N. Friedman, D. Koller, and B. Taskar. Learning probabilistic models of relational structure. In *18th International Conference on Machine Learning*, pages 170 – 177, Williamston, MA, June 2001. Morgan Kaufmann.

[17] E. M. Gold. Language identification in the limit. *Information and Control*, 10(n5):447–474, 1967.

[18] W. Hoeffding. Probabilities inequalities for sums or bounded random variables. *Journal of the American Association*, 58(301):13–30, 1963.

[19] T. Knuutila and M. Steinby. Inference of tree languages from a finite sample: an algebraic approach. *Theoretical Computer Science*, 129:337–367, 1994.

[20] H. Mannila, H. Toivonen, and A. I. Verkamo. Efficient algorithms for discovering association rules. In U. M. Fayyad and R. Uthurusamy, editors, *AAAI Workshop on Knowledge Discovery in Databases (KDD-94)*, pages 181–192, Seattle, Washington, 1994. AAAI Press.

[21] S. Muggleton and L. De Raedt. Inductive Logic Programming: Theory and Methods. *Journal of Logic Programming*, 19–20:629–679, 1994.

[22] J. R. Rico-Juan, J. Calera, and R. C. Carrasco. Probabilistic k-Testable Tree-Languages. In A. L. Oliveira, editor, *5th International Colloquium on Grammatical Inference (ICGI 2000), Lisbon (Portugal)*, volume 1891 of *Lecture Notes in Computer Science*, pages 221–228, Berlin, September 2000. Springer.

[23] A. Stolcke and S. Omohundro. Inducing probabilistic grammars by bayesian model merging. In *2nd International Colloquium on Grammatical Inference (ICGI'94)*, volume 862 of *Lecture Notes in Artificial Intelligence*, pages 106–118, Alicante, Spain, 1994. Springer Verlag.

On Sufficient Conditions to Identify in the Limit Classes of Grammars from Polynomial Time and Data

Colin de la Higuera[1] and Jose Oncina[2]

[1] EURISE, Université de Saint-Etienne, 23 rue du Docteur Paul Michelon,
42023 Saint-Etienne, France
cdlh@univ-st-etienne.fr,
http://eurise.univ-st-etienne.fr/~cdlh
[2] Departamento de Lenguajes y Sistemas Informáticos,
Universidad de Alicante, Ap.99. E-03080 Alicante, Spain
oncina@dlsi.ua.es,
http://www.dlsi.ua.es/~oncina

Abstract. Linearity and determinism seem to be two essential conditions for polynomial learning of grammars to be possible. We propose a general condition valid for certain subclasses of the linear grammars given which these classes can be polynomially identified in the limit from given data. This enables us to give new proofs of the identification of well known classes of grammars, and to propose a new (and larger) class of linear grammars for which polynomial identification is thus possible.

Keywords: Polynomial identification in the limit, linear grammars.

1 Introduction

The main focus of research in the field of grammatical inference has been set on learning regular grammars or deterministic finite automata (*dfa*). Algorithms have been provided dealing with learning such grammars in a variety of settings: when both examples and counter-examples are provided [OG92, dlH97, LPP98], or when the learning algorithm is allowed to question some teacher [Ang87]. Reasons justifying that most attention has been spent on this class of grammars are that this problem may seem simple enough but theoretical results make it already too hard for usual *Machine Learning* settings [KV89, PW93]; on the other hand the class of *dfa* seems to be in some way maximal for certain forms of polynomial learning. In the framework of *active learning* it is known that *dfa* can be inferred through a polynomial use of a *Minimal Adequate Teacher* [Ang87]. It is conjectured [Ang01] not to be the case for richer classes. In the setting of learning from a bunch of examples, this is even clearer as *dfa* can be polynomially identified from time and data, but not context-free grammars or non-deterministic finite automata.

P. Adriaans, H. Fernau, and M. van Zaanen (Eds.): ICGI 2002, LNAI 2484, pp. 134–148, 2002.
© Springer-Verlag Berlin Heidelberg 2002

Yet, even if all this seems to induce that the harder question of learning context-free grammars may only yield negative answers, there are many practical issues that induce us to continue research in this direction. Context-free grammars are much more general than regular grammars and can model many situations that are not within reach of the regular patterns: stacks, palindromes, parenthesis... Grammatical inference will only be able to tackle a certain number of applications if it can cope with some form of context-free grammars. This is probably even more the case with recent applications such as:

- XML grammars [Fer01]. XML documents can be described by special sorts of context-free grammars. Learning such grammars would enable to find specific documents type definitions for certain XML documents.
- In computational linguistics it is generally argued that the structure of natural language cannot be represented by automata, and that at least context-free grammars are needed [Sto95].
- There is a variety of problems linking grammatical inference with bio-informatics [BJVU98]. Problems related with secondary structure require a tree-like representation [Sak90], involving context-free grammars.

A survey on grammatical inference (with special interest on context-free grammar learning) can be found in [Sak97] and a specific survey covering a wide range of context-free grammar learning results can be found in [Lee96]. In order to extend positive results in grammatical inference to sub-classes of context-free grammars, one should analyze the reasons the main algorithms work:

- Determinism of the grammar is a necessary condition: in terms of grammars, this will be called *strong unambiguity*: at any one point of a parse, at most one rule should be applicable. This condition ensures that merging non-terminals wrongfully can be refuted.
- Linearity of the grammars is also an essential feature: it is easy [dlH97] to construct very simple non linear grammars that only generate exponentially (in the size of the grammar) long strings. Learning such grammars requires teaching sets too large to be considered.

Combining these two conditions with a third condition corresponding roughly to the existence of some constructive filter on the shape of the production rules, we obtain a sufficient condition for subclasses of linear grammars to be learned. We use here as learning paradigm that of *identification in the limit from polynomial time and data*: the learning algorithm must run in time polynomial in the learning data and there must always exist a data set of polynomial size from which identification is achieved. Moreover this is monotonic, in the sense that the inclusion of this *characteristic set* in the learning sample is sufficient.

The existence of sufficient conditions for polynomial learning to be possible has been shown in other settings: for active learning [HPRW96] conditions are given for a polynomial number of membership and equivalence queries to be sufficient for identification; in the context of learning from text (only positive examples are available) [Fer00] proposes the existence of distinguishing functions to define sub-classes of regular languages that could be identifiable.

2   Definitions

2.1   Languages and Grammars

An alphabet Σ is a finite nonempty set of symbols. Σ^* denotes the set of all finite strings over Σ, $\Sigma^+ = \Sigma^* \setminus \{\lambda\}$. A language L over Σ is a subset of Σ^*. In the following, unless stated otherwise, symbols are indicated by $a, b, c \ldots$, strings by $u, v, \ldots, z$, and the empty string by λ. $\mathbb{N}$ is the set of non negative integers.

The length of a string u will be denoted $|u|$, so $|\lambda| = 0$. Let S be a finite set of strings, $|S|$ denotes the number of strings in the set and $\|S\|$ denotes the total sum of the lengths of all strings in S.

Let $u, v \in \Sigma^*, u^{-1}v = w$ such that $v = uw$ (undefined if u is not a prefix of v) and $uv^{-1} = w$ such that $u = wv$ (undefined if v is not a suffix of u). Let L be a language and $u \in \Sigma^*$, $u^{-1}L = \{v : uv \in L\}$ and $Lu^{-1} = \{v : vu \in L\}$; $u^{-1}Lv^{-1} = \{w : uwv \in L\}$. The symmetric difference between two languages L_1 and L_2 will be denoted $L_1 \ominus L_2$.

A *context-free grammar* G is a quadruple $\langle \Sigma, V, P, S \rangle$ where Σ is an alphabet, V is a finite alphabet (of variables or non-terminals), $P \subset V \times (\Sigma \cup V)^*$ is a finite set of production rules, and $S(\in V)$ is the axiom. Unless stated otherwise, strings in $(\Sigma \cup V)^*$ are denoted by $\alpha, \beta, \ldots$.

We will denote $uTv \rightarrow uwv$ when $(T \rightarrow w) \in P$. $\xrightarrow{*}$ is the reflexive and transitive closure of $\rightarrow$. We denote by $L_G(T)$ the language $\{w \in \Sigma^* : T \xrightarrow{*} w\}$. When T is the axiom, we will also denote the language $L(G)$. Two grammars are equivalent if they generate the same language. A context-free grammar $G = \langle \Sigma, V, P, S \rangle$ is *linear* if $P \subset V \times (\Sigma^* V \Sigma^* \cup \Sigma^*)$.

We will be needing to speak of the *size* of a grammar. Without entering into a lengthy discussion, the size has to be a quantity polynomially linked with the number of bits needed to encode a grammar [Pit89]. We will consider here the size of G denoted $\|G\| = \sum_{(T,\alpha) \in P(G)} (|\alpha| + 1)$.

Example 1. We will consider as a running example the class of even linear grammars, *i.e.* those grammars[1] for which $P \subset V \times \Sigma^* \cup \Sigma V \Sigma$. The fact that this class could be identified from polynomial time and data has been proved by [Tak88, SG94]. We will use the following normal form for the grammars: $P \subset V \times \Sigma \cup \{\lambda\} \cup \Sigma V \Sigma$ and $(T \rightarrow aT'b) \in P \wedge (T \rightarrow aT''b) \in P \implies T' = T''$.

The learning model we will be working in (and which will be properly defined in the next sub-section) considers both examples of the language to be learned and counter-examples.

A *sample* X is a pair of sets (X_+, X_-) where $X_+ \cap X_- = \emptyset$. $\mathbb{S}$ is the set of all finite samples over Σ. If $X, X' \in \mathbb{S}$, we will write $X \subseteq X'$ if $X_+ \subseteq X'_+$ and $X_- \subseteq X'_-$

$X \in \mathbb{S}$ is a sample of a language L if $X \subseteq (L, \Sigma^* \setminus L)$. The set of all samples of L is denoted $\mathbb{S}_L$ or $\mathbb{S}_G$ when G is a grammar generating language L. Let $\mathcal{G}$ a

---

[1]   Other characterisations are possible, but lead to the same class.

class of grammars, $\mathbb{S}_{\mathcal{G}}$ is the set of all samples of languages that can be generated by grammars in $\mathcal{G}$.

Different learning paradigms have been examined and used in the literature of machine learning [Val84, Gol78]. We will use identification in the limit from polynomial time and data [dlH97] as our learning model.

Definition 1. *A class $\mathcal{G}$ of grammars is identifiable in the limit from polynomial time and data if there exist two polynomials $p()$ and $q()$ and an algorithm $\mathcal{A}$ such that:*

1. *for each grammar G in $\mathcal{G}$, there exists a characteristic sample $(X_{c,+}, X_{c,-})$ of size less than $q(\|G\|)$ for which, if $X_{c,+} \subseteq X_+$, $X_{c,-} \subseteq X_-$, $\mathcal{A}$ returns a grammar G' equivalent with G;*
2. *given any sample (X_+, X_-) of some language $L(G)$ with G in $\mathcal{G}$, $\mathcal{A}$ returns a grammar G in $\mathcal{G}$ compatible with (X_+, X_-) in $O(p(\|X_+\| + \|X_-\|))$ time.*

With this definition it is known that deterministic finite automata [OG92] are identifiable in the limit from polynomial time and data whereas non-deterministic finite automata and linear (and hence context-free) grammars are not [dlH97].

3   Results

3.1   About Compatibility and Consistency

In a state-merging algorithm the basic operation consists in knowing if 2 states (or non-terminals) can be merged or not. A merge may be refused for different reasons: because there is no way, once the merge is done, to reach any grammar in the class (compatibility), or to reach some grammar consistent with the learning sample.

Definition 2 (Strongly unambiguous grammar). *Let $p \in P, Z_p = \{w\}$ if $p = (A \rightarrow w)$, $Z_p = u\Sigma^*v$ if $p = (A \rightarrow uBv)$. A linear grammar G is strongly unambiguous if $\forall (A \rightarrow \alpha), (A \rightarrow \beta) \in P$ $Z_{(A \rightarrow \alpha)} \cap Z_{(A \rightarrow \beta)} = \emptyset \iff \alpha \neq \beta$.*

That is, during the parse of any string, at any point there is at most one rule that can apply.

Example 2. Consider $G = \langle \{a, b\}, \{S\}, \{S \rightarrow aSa, S \rightarrow bSb, S \rightarrow \lambda\}, S \rangle$ (a grammar for even palindromes). G is strongly unambiguous: a string is either λ, and will be parsed if possible by the appropriate rule, or of non null length where again there is at most one rule that applies. This is true in general for any grammar in the normal form (example 1).

Lemma 1. *Let G be a strongly unambiguous grammar, let $A, B \in V : L(A) \neq L(B)$ then $\exists x \in L(A) \ominus L(B) : |x|$ is linear with $\|G\|$.*

Proof. Let us construct the grammar G_d in the following way:

$\forall A \to a_1 \ldots a_n B b_1 \ldots b_k \in P_G$ add the rules $A_{a_1 \ldots a_{i-1}} \to a_i A_{a_1 \ldots a_i}$ $1 \leq i \leq n$, and $A_{a_1 \ldots a_n b'_1 \ldots b'_{i-1}} \to b'_i A_{a_1 \ldots a_n b'_1 \ldots b'_i}$ $1 \leq i \leq k$ to G_d, and $\forall A \to a_1 \ldots a_n \in P_G$ add the rules $A_{a_1 \ldots a_{i-1}} \to a_i A_{a_1 \ldots a_i}$ $1 \leq i \leq n$ $A_{a_1 \ldots a_n} \to \lambda$, where the symbols b' are new symbols, each one corresponding to each symbol $b \in \Sigma$ and $A_\lambda = A$ and $A_{a_1 \ldots a_n b'_1 \ldots b'_k} = B$.

As the grammar G is strongly unambiguous, the associated grammar G_d is a deterministic regular grammar (the grammar representation of a *dfa*, see section 4.1 for details). Moreover, for each $x \in L(G)$ we can associate a single string $x' \in L(G_d)$ obtained by using the rules corresponding to those used during the parse of x. The converse also holds, so $x \in L(G) \iff x' \in L(G_d)$.

Let $A, B \in V_G : L(A) \neq L(B)$, as G_d is regular and deterministic we know that $\exists w' \in L_{G_d}(A) \ominus L_{G_d}(B)$ such that $|w'|$ is linear with $\|G\|$, then the corresponding string $w \in L_G(A) \ominus L_G(B)$, and $|w| = |w'|$.

Grammars may only partially parse strings: what is left will be called unparsed and can be linearly computed:

Definition 3 (Unparsed strings). *Let* $Y \subseteq \Sigma^*$, *let* G *be a strongly unambiguous linear grammar and let* $A \in V_G$, *then* $\mathbf{unparsed}(Y, G, A) = \{uxv : u'uxvv' \in Y \wedge S \xrightarrow{*} u'Av' \wedge \nexists A \to uBv \in P_G\}$.

Definition 4 (Related states). *Let* G, G' *be two strongly unambiguous linear grammars, non-terminal* A *of* G' *is related with the non-terminal* B *of* G *($B = r(A)$) if* $\forall \{u_i\}, \{v_i\} : S_{G'} \to_{G'} u_1 A_1 v_1 \to_{G'} \cdots \to_{G'} u_n A v_n$ *then* $S_G \to_G u_1 B_1 v_1 \to_G \cdots \to_G u_n B v_n$.

For a given grammar it is possibly to consider the grammars that may lead, through merges to this grammar. Such grammars are composed of 2 types of non-terminals: *kernel* ones (in $\bar{K}$) that constitute the core of the grammar, and *frontier* ones (in $\bar{F}$) that are only used in the right-hand of one rule:

Definition 5. $\bar{G} = \langle \Sigma, \bar{K}, \bar{F}, \bar{P}, \bar{S} \rangle$ *is a* half-way *grammar of the strongly unambiguous linear grammar* $G = \langle \Sigma, N, P, S \rangle$ *($\bar{G} \in \mathrm{hw}(G)$) if:*

1. $\forall A \in \bar{K}, \exists u, v : \bar{S} \xrightarrow{*} uAv$
2. $\forall A \in \bar{K}, A \to uBv \in \bar{P} \iff r(A) \to u \, r(B) v \in P$
3. $\forall B \in \bar{F} \; \exists! A \in \bar{K} : A \to uBv \in \bar{P}$
4. $\forall B \in \bar{F} \; \nexists B \to uCv \in \bar{P}$

We shall denote $\bar{V} = \bar{K} \cup \bar{F}$, *and use* $\bar{G}$ *as a linear grammar when convenient.*

Definition 6. *By extension, let* $\mathcal{G}$ *be a class of strongly unambiguous linear grammars,* $\bar{G} \in \mathrm{hw}(\mathcal{G})$ *if* $\exists G \in \mathcal{G} : \bar{G} \in G$.

Example 3. $\bar{G} = \langle \{a, b\}, \{\bar{S}\}, \{\bar{T}\}, \{\bar{S} \to a\bar{T}a, \bar{S} \to b\bar{S}b\}, \bar{S} \rangle$ is a half-way grammar of G (from example 2), with $\bar{S}$ in the kernel and $\bar{T}$ as a frontier non-terminal. Let $X_+ = \{abba, baab, bb\}$ and $X_- = \{aba, baaa, bbab\}$. $\mathbf{unparsed}(X_+, \bar{G}, \bar{T}) = \{bb, \lambda\}$

Definition 7 (merge function). *Let G an strongly unambiguous linear grammar, Let $\bar{G} \in \mathrm{hw}(G)$, let $A \in \bar{F}, B \in \bar{K}$ then, $\bar{G}' = merge(\bar{G}, B, A)$ if*

1. $\bar{\Sigma}' = \bar{\Sigma}$
2. $\bar{K}' = \bar{K}$
3. $\bar{F}' = \bar{F} \setminus \{A\}$
4. $\bar{S}' = \bar{S}$
5. $\bar{P}' = \bar{P} \setminus \{C \to uAv\} \cup \{C \to uBv\}$

Note that as $\bar{G} \in \mathrm{hw}(G)$, if $A \in \bar{F}$, non-terminal C of point 5 is unique.

Lemma 2. *Let $\bar{G} \in \mathrm{hw}(G)$, $A \in \bar{F}, B \in \bar{K} : \mathrm{r}(A) = \mathrm{r}(B)$ then $merge(\bar{G}, B, A) \in \mathrm{hw}(G)$.*

Proof. Let $\bar{G}' = merge(\bar{G}, B, A)$. As $A \in \bar{F}$ we know, by definition of half-way (def. 5.3) that $\exists! C \in \bar{K} : C \to uAv \in \bar{P}$. Then, by 5.2 we know that $\mathrm{r}(C) \to u\,\mathrm{r}(A)v \in P$, and as $\mathrm{r}(B) = \mathrm{r}(A)$, $\mathrm{r}(C) \to u\,\mathrm{r}(B)v \in P$. Then substituting the rule $C \to uAv \in \bar{P}$ by $C \to uBv$ implies that 5.2 is met.

Definition 8 (Consistent with a sample). *Let $\bar{G} \in \mathrm{hw}(\mathcal{G})$, let $X \in \mathbb{S}_G$, $\bar{G}$ is consistent with the sample X (consistent$(X, \bar{G})$) if $\forall A \in \bar{V}$, unparsed$(X_+, \bar{G}, A) \cap$ unparsed$(X_-, \bar{G}, A) = \emptyset$.*

Lemma 3. *Let $\bar{G} \in \mathrm{hw}(G)$ and $X \subseteq \mathbb{S}_G$ then consistent$(X, \bar{G})$.*

Proof. By contradiction.

Example 4. $\bar{G} = \langle \{a, b\}, \{\bar{S}\}, \{\bar{T}\}, \{\bar{S} \to a\bar{T}a, \bar{S} \to b\bar{S}b\}, \bar{S} \rangle$ is consistent with sample $X_+ = \{abba, baab, bb\}$ and $X_- = \{aba, baaa, bbab\}$.

Definition 9 (Compatible non-terminals). *Let $\bar{G} \in \mathrm{hw}(\mathcal{G})$, let $A \in \bar{F}, B \in \bar{K}$, we say that the non-terminals A and B are compatible (and write compatible$(\bar{G}, B, A)$) if $merge(\bar{G}, B, A) \in \mathrm{hw}(\mathcal{G})$.*

By extension: Let $G \in \mathcal{G}$, non-terminals $A, B \in V$ are compatible in G if $\forall \bar{G} \in \mathrm{hw}(G) \exists A' \in \bar{F}, \mathrm{r}(A') = A, \exists B' \in \bar{K}, \mathrm{r}(B') = B \Rightarrow$ compatible$(\bar{G}, B', A')$.

Example 5. For the class of even linear grammars compatible is a trivial function that always returns true.

Definition 10 (Non-redundant grammar in a class). *A grammar G is non-redundant in the class $\mathcal{G}$ if $\forall A, B \in V$, $A \neq B$, compatible$(G, A, B) \Rightarrow L(A) \neq L(B)$.*

Lemma 4. *Let G be a non-redundant strongly unambiguous linear grammar in the class $\mathcal{G}$, with $\bar{G} \in \mathrm{hw}(G)$ and $A \in \bar{F}, B \in \bar{K}$ then $\exists X_{\bar{G},B,A} \in \mathbb{S}_G : \forall X \in \mathbb{S}_G, X_{\bar{G},B,A} \subseteq X$:*

$$r(A) = r(B) \iff \texttt{compatible}(\bar{G}, B, A) \wedge \texttt{consistent}(X, \bar{G}).$$

Moreover, $\|X_{\bar{G},B,A}\|$ is linear in $\|G\|$.

Proof. There are 2 cases:

$r(A) = r(B) \Rightarrow \texttt{compatible}(\bar{G}, B, A) \wedge \texttt{consistent}(X, \texttt{merge}(\bar{G}, B, A))$. By lemma 2 we have that $\texttt{merge}(\bar{G}, B, A) \in \mathrm{hw}(G)$, so $\texttt{compatible}(\bar{G}, B, A)$ and by lemma 3 $\forall X \in \mathbb{S}_G, \texttt{consistent}(X, \texttt{merge}(\bar{G}, B, A))$.

$r(A) \neq r(B) \Rightarrow \neg \texttt{compatible}(\bar{G}, B, A) \vee \neg \texttt{consistent}(L, \texttt{merge}(\bar{G}, B, A))$. We are going to show that $\exists X_{\bar{G},B,A} \in \mathbb{S}_G : \forall X \in \mathbb{S}_G, X_{\bar{G},B,A} \subseteq X$
$r(A) \neq r(B) \wedge \texttt{compatible}(\bar{G}, B, A) \Rightarrow \neg \texttt{consistent}(L, \texttt{merge}(\bar{G}, B, A))$.
Let $\bar{G}' = \texttt{merge}(\bar{G}, B, A)$. As G is non-redundant in the class, by definition of non-redundancy (def. 10), we know that $L(r(A)) \neq L(r(B))$. Then $\exists x \in L(r(A)) \ominus L(r(B))$, suppose $x \in L(r(B))$ but $x \notin L(r(A))$ (without loss of generality; the other case is similar). Let $\bar{S} \overset{*}{\to} u_A A v_A$ and $\bar{S} \overset{*}{\to} u_B B v_B$, then let $X_{\bar{G},B,A}$ such that $u_B x v_B \in X_{\bar{G},B,A,+}$ and $u_A x v_A \in X_{\bar{G},B,A,-}$.
Let $C : \texttt{unparsed}(\{u_B x v_B\}, \bar{G}', C) \neq \emptyset$, but in the grammar $\bar{G}', S \overset{*}{\to} u_A B u_A$. Then $\texttt{unparsed}(\{u_A x v_A\}, \bar{G}', C) = \texttt{unparsed}(\{u_B x v_B\}, \bar{G}', C) \neq \emptyset$ holds and $\texttt{unparsed}(X_+, \bar{G}', C) \cap \texttt{unparsed}(X_-, \bar{G}', C) \neq \emptyset \ \forall X \supseteq X_{\bar{G},B,A}$ follows. Moreover, as in the derivation of the non-terminal symbols A and B we can avoid repetitions of the intermediate non-terminals, the lengths of the strings u_A, v_A, u_B, u_B are linear in $\|G\|$. And by lemma 1 the length of x is also linear in $\|G\|$.

3.2 Guessing the Next Rules

If we are capable of refuting a given rule, all we need to do is choose the new possible rules in an economical manner. Suppose we have a function (called $\texttt{next}$) which takes a finite sample as input, and returns a set of pairs (u_i, v_i) with intended meaning that $\forall i : T \to u_i T' v_i$ is a possible rule, what properties does this function have to respect in order to make identification possible?

Definition 11 (next function). *Let $\texttt{next}$ be a function taking as arguments a finite set of strings, a half-way grammar and a frontier non-terminal, and returning a finite set of pairs of strings. We say that the $\texttt{next}$ function is good for a class of grammars $\mathcal{G}$ if $\forall \bar{G} \in \mathrm{hw}(\mathcal{G}), \forall A \in \bar{F}$:*

1. *$\forall X_+ \subseteq \Sigma^* \forall \{(u_i, v_i), (u_j, v_j)\} \subseteq \texttt{next}(X_+, \bar{G}, A) u_i \Sigma^* v_i \cap u_j \Sigma^* v_j = \emptyset \forall i \neq j$*
2. *$\forall X_+ \subseteq \Sigma^*, \forall (u, v) \in \texttt{next}(X_+, \bar{G}, A), \exists u x v \in \texttt{unparsed}(X_+, \bar{G}, A)$*
3. *$\texttt{next}(X_+, \bar{G}, A)$ works in time polynomial in $\|X_+\|$ and $\|\bar{G}\|$.*
4. *$\exists X_{\bar{G},A} \subseteq \Sigma^* : \forall X_+ \in \Sigma^*, X_{\bar{G},A} \subseteq X_+ \subseteq L(G)$*
   $(u, v) \in \texttt{next}(X_+, \bar{G}, A) \iff \exists B : r(A) \to uBv \in P$
5. *$\|X_{\bar{G},A}\|$ is polynomial in $\|G\|$.*

By condition 1 function `next` can only create rules that lead to strong unambiguity. Notice that if $\mathcal{G}$ contains linear grammars that are not strongly unambiguous, no good `next` function can exist. No rules can be invented out of thin air because of condition 2. A characteristic set from which all rules can be guessed must exist (condition 4): in practice this condition with the condition 2 are easy to meet; it is sufficient to have strings that use the rules of the intended grammar. The computation of the candidate rules must obviously take place in polynomial time (condition 3), and the characteristic sets must also have polynomial time (condition 5).

Example 6. `next` can be computed for even linear grammars as $\mathtt{next}(X_+, \bar{G}, A) = \{(a, b) : uawbv \in X_+ \wedge \bar{S} \xrightarrow{*} uAv\}$.

Definition 12 (good **class of grammars**). *Let $\mathcal{G}$ be a strongly unambiguous class of linear grammars, $\mathcal{G}$ is a* good *class of grammars if:*

1. *there is a* good `next` *function for the class;*
2. *there is a polynomial* `compatible` *function;*
3. *$\forall G \in \mathcal{G}$ there is a non-redundant grammar $G' \in \mathcal{G}$ such that $L(G) = L(G')$.*
4. *there is a polynomial algorithm $\mathcal{A}_{trivial}$ such that: $\forall X \in \mathbb{S}_{\mathcal{G}} \mathcal{A}_{trivial}(X) = G \in \mathcal{G} : X \subseteq (L(G), \Sigma^* \setminus L(G))$*

Example 7 (Proving that all the conditions are met for even linear grammars).

1. `next` only introduces strongly unambiguous rules (11.1);
2. pairs (a, b) introduced by `next` correspond to strings in X (definition 11.2);
3. `next` given by algorithm 6 is polynomial (11.3);
4. `next` has a polynomial characteristic set: it is sufficient to introduce one string per rule (11.3 and 11.5);
5. function `compatible` is the trivial (and thus polynomial) function that always returns `true`; (12.2)
6. there is always a non-redundant normal form which is not too large (12.3). It also can be argued that when choosing to represent these languages by more general even linear grammars, this remains true, enabling the class of grammars that is identifiable to be larger;
7. any finite set of strings is a regular language, hence also an even linear language of which a polynomial grammar can be directly constructed.

Lemma 5. *Let $\mathcal{G}$ be a good class of grammars, let $G \in \mathcal{G}$ and let $X \in \mathbb{S}_G$, then algorithm 1 halts and gives a strongly unambiguous linear grammar G' such that $X \in \mathbb{S}_{G'}$.*

Proof. Suppose that in an iteration, in the **while** line, we have a half-way grammar $\bar{G}$ of a strongly unambiguous linear grammar G such that `consistent`$(X, \bar{G})$.
    Let us call
$$1_{\#}(\bar{G}) = \sum_{\forall A \in \bar{V}} \| \mathtt{unparsed}(X_+, \bar{G}, A) \|.$$
Take now a non-terminal A from F (`extract` line).

Algorithm 1 Infer

Require: $X \in \mathbb{S}_G$
Ensure: $\bar{G} = \langle \Sigma, \bar{K}, \bar{F}, \bar{S}, \bar{P} \rangle$
   $A = \text{newNT}$
   $\bar{S} = A$
   $\bar{K} = \emptyset$
   $\bar{P} = \emptyset$
   $\bar{F} = A$
   while $\bar{F} \neq \emptyset$ **do**
     $A = \text{extract}(\bar{F})$
     if $\exists B \in \bar{K} : \text{compatible}(\bar{G}, B, A) \wedge \text{consistent}(X, \text{merge}(\bar{G}, B, A))$ **then**
       $\bar{G} = \text{merge}(\bar{G}, B, A)$
     else
       $\bar{K} = \bar{K} \cup \{A\}$
       for all $(u, v) \in \text{next}(X_+, \bar{G}, A)$ **do**
         $B = \text{newNT}$
         $\bar{P} = \bar{P} \cup \{A \to uBv\}$
         $\bar{F} = \bar{F} \cup B$
       end for
     end if
   end while
   for all $A \in \bar{K}$ **do**
     for all $w \in \text{unparsed}(X_+, \bar{G}, A)$ **do**
       $\bar{P} = \bar{P} \cup \{A \to w\}$
     end for
   end for

There are two cases:

1. If $\exists B \in \bar{K} : \text{compatible}(\bar{G}, B, A) \wedge \text{consistent}(X, \text{merge}(\bar{G}, B, A))$
   Let us call $\bar{G}' = \text{merge}(\bar{G}, B, A)$. It is obvious that $\bar{G}'$ is a strongly unambiguous linear grammar and is consistent with the sample. Observe that once A and B are merged $|\bar{F}'| = |\bar{F}'| - 1$ and $l_\#(\bar{G}') \leq l_\#(\bar{G})$.
2. If $\nexists B \in \bar{K} : \text{compatible}(\bar{G}, B, A) \wedge \text{consistent}(X, \text{merge}(\bar{G}, B, A))$
   Then a new non-terminal is added to $\bar{K}$ and the grammar is expanded in such a way that it is compatible with the sample. By definition of next (def. 11.1) it is a half-way grammar of a strongly unambiguous linear grammar. Let us call $\bar{G}'$ such grammar. Observe that for each rule added there are some strings in $\text{unparsed}(X_+, \bar{G}, A)$ and $\text{unparsed}(X_-, \bar{G}, A)$ (def. 11.2) that are going to use it, then $l_\#(\bar{G}') < l_\#(\bar{G})$ but $|\bar{F}'| \geq |\bar{F}| - 1$.

In one case $|\bar{F}|$ diminishes but $l_\#(\bar{G})$ can be stable, in the other case $|\bar{F}|$ can increase but then $l_\#(\bar{G})$ has to decrease. As $l_\#(\bar{G})$ can not be lower than zero, there must exist an iteration when $|\bar{F}| = 0$ and the loop will stop.

At the end of the **while** loop we have a half-way grammar such that $\bar{F} = \emptyset$.

In the last **for** loop all the rules of the form $A \to w$ will be added in such a way that the entire positive sample will be accepted.

Lemma 6. *Let $\mathcal{G}$ be a* good *class of linear grammars, let $G \in \mathcal{G}$, then $\exists X_c : \forall X \in \mathbb{S}_G, X_c \subseteq X$, let G_X be the grammar obtained by algorithm 1 using X, then $L(G_X) = L(G)$. Moreover, $\|X_c\|$ is polynomial in $\|G\|$.*

Proof. We are going to show that for any grammar G from some good class $\mathcal{G}$, there exists a sample $X_c \in \mathbb{S}_G$ of size polynomial in $\|G\|$, such that from any $X \in \mathbb{S}_G : X_c \subseteq X$, algorithm 1 returns a grammar G_X such that $L(G_X) = L(G)$.

Suppose that G is non-redundant in the class. If it is not, we know that there is a non-redundant grammar in the class that accepts the same language. Suppose that in an iteration, in the **while** line, we have a half-way grammar $\bar{G} \in \mathrm{hw}(G)$.

Take now a non-terminal A from $\bar{F}$ (line 7).

If we suppose that all the $X_{\bar{G},B,A} \subseteq X_c \forall B \in \bar{K}$, by lemma 4 we know that $\mathtt{compatible}(\bar{G}, B, A) \wedge \mathtt{consistent}(X, \mathtt{merge}(\bar{G}, B, A)) \iff \mathrm{r}(A) = \mathrm{r}(B)$.

There are now two cases:

1. $\exists B \in \bar{K} : \mathtt{compatible}(\bar{G}, B, A) \wedge \mathtt{consistent}(X, \mathtt{merge}(\bar{G}, B, A))$.
   Then we know that $\mathrm{r}(A) = \mathrm{r}(B)$ and the algorithm merges both non-terminals obtaining a new half-way grammar of G (lemma 2) (observe that if such a non-terminal B exists, it is unique).
2. $\nexists B \in \bar{K} : \mathtt{compatible}(\bar{G}, B, A) \wedge \mathtt{consistent}(X, \mathtt{merge}(\bar{G}, B, A))$.
   Then $\forall B \in \bar{K} : \mathrm{r}(A) \neq \mathrm{r}(B)$, that is, A is an unseen non-terminal and it is added to the $\bar{K}$ set.
   Then condition 2 of def. 5 possibly does not hold anymore.
   If **next** is good, and $X_{c,+} \subseteq X_{\bar{G},A}$, as **next** is good (def. 11) all the rules needed to meet point 2 of the half-way definition (def. 5) are added and the new non-terminals added to $\bar{F}$ are added in a way that points 3 and 4 of half-way hold.
   Then we have a new half-way grammar of G.

At the end of the **while** loop we have a half-way grammar such that $F = \emptyset$, moreover **next** function has added all the rules of the form $A \rightarrow uBv$ and then all the non-terminals of G are in $\bar{G}$.

If $\forall A \rightarrow w \in P$ we have a string $uwv \in X_{c,+}$ such that $\bar{S} \xrightarrow{*} uAv$ then, in the last **for** loop all the rules of the form $A \rightarrow w$ will be added (note that $|u|$ and $|v|$ can be linear in $\|G\|$).

In the process we have called at most $|V| \cdot |P|$ times the $\mathtt{compatible}$ function, and $|V|$ times the **next** function. As we have seen, in order to identify the grammar a number of at most $|V| \cdot |P|$ sets $X_{\bar{G},A,B}$ is needed for $\mathtt{compatible}$ to work properly, a number of $|V|$ sets $X_{\bar{G},A}$ is needed so that function **next** works properly and $|V|$ strings are also needed in order to include all the $A \rightarrow w$ rules. As all those sets have a polynomial size, there exists a characteristic sample of polynomial size.

Theorem 1. *Any* good *class of grammars is identifiable in the limit from polynomial time and data.*

Proof. Condition 1 of definition 1 is that there must be a characteristic set. Here it is a consequence of lemma 6. Now in the general case (corresponding to condition 2 of definition 1, algorithm 1 is polynomial and returns a strongly unambiguous grammar. But this grammar may be incorrect (not in $\mathcal{G}$). In this case by condition 4 of definition 12 we can run the alternative algorithm $\mathcal{A}_{trivial}$ in order to return simply a consistent solution.

4   Examples

We have provided in the previous section the elements to prove that the class of (deterministic) even linear grammars are good. We will in this section give the main lines of the proof that (deterministic) regular grammars, deterministic linear grammars and alternated linear grammars are identifiable from polynomial time and data. In the first case the result is well known [OG92], the second is a recent result [dlHO02], and the last corresponds to a class of grammars for which no result was up to now known.

4.1   Regular Grammars

Regular deterministic grammars correspond exactly to deterministic finite automata. They are regular grammars for which $P \subset \Sigma V \cup \{\lambda\}$ and $(T \to aT') \in P \wedge (T \to aT'') \in P \implies T' = T''$. Checking conditions from definitions 11 and 12 is straightforward: $\mathtt{next}(X_+, \bar{G}, A) = \{(a, \lambda) : uaw \in X_+ \wedge \bar{S} \xrightarrow{*}_{\bar{G}} uA\}$.

1. $\mathtt{next}$ clearly introduces strongly unambiguous rules only (definition 11.1);
2. $\mathtt{next}$ only introduces sustained rules (definition 11.2);
3. $\mathtt{next}$ can be computed in polynomial time (definition 11.3);
4. in all contexts, a set of strings exists (one string for each a) from which $\mathtt{next}$ finds all new rules (definition 11.4 and 11.5);
5. $\mathtt{next}$ has a polynomial characteristic set (definition 11.5);
6. the class admits a $\mathtt{compatible}$ function which is polynomial: in this case it is the function that always returns true (definition 12.2);
7. there is always a non-redundant normal form which is not too large (definition 12.3);
8. any finite set of strings is a regular language (definition 12.4).

4.2   Deterministic Linear Languages

There is a variety of classes linked with deterministic one-turn pushdown automata. In [dlHO02] we study the identification of the following class:

Definition 13 (Deterministic linear grammars). *A deterministic linear (DL) grammar* $G = \langle \Sigma, V, P, S \rangle$ *is a linear grammar where all rules are of the form* $(T \to aT'u)$ *or* $(T \to \lambda)$ *and* $\forall (T \to a\alpha), (T \to a\beta) \in P \implies \alpha = \beta$ *with* $\alpha, \beta \in V\Sigma^*$.

A canonical form for these grammars is obtained by choosing systematically the longest possible suffix:

The *longest common suffix* (lcs(L)) of L is the longest string u such that $(Lu^{-1})u = L$.

For the class of deterministic linear languages $\mathtt{next}(X_+, \bar{G}, A) = \{(a, w) : a^{-1}\mathtt{unparsed}(X_+, \bar{G}, A) \neq \emptyset \text{ with } w = \mathrm{lcs}(a^{-1}(\mathtt{unparsed}(X_+, \bar{G}, A) \cap a\Sigma^*))\}$.

And again all conditions from definitions 11 and 12 hold.

4.3   Alternated Linear Languages

The class of grammars proposed in the previous sub-section can generate all regular languages and certain non regular ones (for instance palindromes, $a^n b^n$) but suffer from an asymmetrical definition. To generalize the previous class we propose:

Definition 14 (Alternated linear grammars). *An* alternated linear grammar $G = \langle \Sigma, V_E \cup V_O, P, S \rangle$ *is a linear grammar where* $V_E \cap V_O = \emptyset$, $S \in V_E$ *and*

if $T \in V_E$:
1. $T \to \alpha \in P \implies \alpha \in \Sigma V_O \Sigma^* \cup \{\lambda\}$
2. *if* $T \to a\alpha \in P$ *and* $T \to a\beta \in P$ *then* $\alpha = \beta$
3. *either* $T \to \lambda \in P$ *or* $|\{a : T \to aT'w \in P\}| > 1$

if $T \in V_O$:
1. $T \to \alpha \in P \implies \alpha \in \Sigma^* V_E \Sigma \cup \{\lambda\}$
2. *if* $T \to \alpha a \in P$ *and* $T \to \beta a \in P$ *then* $\alpha = \beta$
3. *either* $T \to \lambda \in P$ *or* $|\{a : T \to wT'a \in P\}| > 1$

A canonical form for these grammars is obtained by choosing systematically the longest possible prefix or suffix depending on the parity of the non-terminal.

The *longest common prefix* (lcp(L)) of L is the longest string u such that $u(u^{-1}L) = L$. Compatibility is not a trivial function this time, as we have to avoid merging an *even* (V_E) non-terminal with an *odd* (V_O) one. In a half-way grammar $\bar{G}$ computing the parity of the non-terminals is straight-forward: axiom is even, and parity changes with each application of a rule.

$$\mathtt{next}(X_+, \bar{G}, A) =$$
$$\begin{cases} \{(a, w) : U = a^{-1}\mathtt{unparsed}(X_+, \bar{G}, A), U \neq \emptyset, w = \mathrm{lcs}(U)\} \text{ if } A \in V_E, \\ \{(a, w) : U = \mathtt{unparsed}(X_+, \bar{G}, A)a^{-1}, U \neq \emptyset, w = \mathrm{lcp}(U)\} \text{ if } A \in V_O \end{cases}$$

Example 8. $\{(aa+bb)^n(c+d)^n : n \in \mathbb{N}\}$ is a language that cannot be generated by any regular, even or deterministic linear grammar. Yet the following alternated linear grammar generates it:
$\langle \{a, b, c, d\}, \{S, T\}, \{S \to aT + bT + \lambda, T \to aSc + aSd\}, S \rangle$ with $V_E = \{S\}$ and $V_O = \{T\}$.

To prove that the class is identifiable in the limit from polynomial time and data it is sufficient to notice that:

1. `next` only introduces strongly unambiguous rules (11.1): in both cases the function acts as in the linear deterministic one;
2. `next` only introduces pairs corresponding to strings in X_+ (definition 11.2);
3. `next` given by algorithm 6 is polynomial (11.3);
4. `next` has a polynomial characteristic set (definition 11.5): for each even accessible non-terminal A of some half-way grammar $\bar{G}$ of G, it is sufficient to introduce two strings $uavwz$ and $uav'wz$ such that $S_{\bar{G}} \xrightarrow{*}_{\bar{G}} uAz$, $\mathrm{lcs}\{v,v'\} = \lambda$ and $r(A) \to_G ar(B)w \in P$. The case where A is odd is symmetrical;
5. the class admits a `compatible` function which is polynomial (12.2);
6. there is always a non-redundant normal form which is not too large (12.3);
7. it is easy to build an alternated linear grammar that only accepts the positive sample.

5 Conclusion

We provide in this paper a reasonable way to check if some linear language class can be identified from polynomial time and data. On the other hand necessary conditions are given in [dlH97]. Between the possible follow-ups of this work we can propose:

- Adaptation of these results to classes of tree grammars is certainly feasible, but, as often is the case, technical.
- Our generic algorithm, because of its genericity, may be slow for particular classes. Speeding-up can take place by avoiding to repeatedly call functions `unparsed` and `compatible`.
- Tightening the complexity bounds would be of certain use. This may apply in a more general way to many other grammatical inference algorithms.
- The reasons for only considering linear grammars are that through them we have a direct relationship between the size of the grammar and the length of the characteristic examples. Nevertheless, even if general context-free grammars are still out of reach for our techniques, certain subclasses (such as that of multi-linear grammars) may not be. Practically the difficulty is to be able to parse in an unambiguous way (and without lookahead) strings through the rules given by the `next` function.

References

[Ang87]   D. Angluin. Learning regular sets from queries and counterexamples. *Information and Control*, 39:337–350, 1987.

[Ang01]   D. Angluin. Queries revisited. In *Proceedings of ALT 2001*, pages 12–31. Springer-Verlag, 2001.

[BJVU98] A. Brazma, I. Jonassen, J. Vilo, and E. Ukkonen. Pattern discovery in
          biosequences. In V. Honavar and G. Slutski, editors, *Grammatical Infer-
          ence, ICGI '98*, number 1433 in LNCS, pages 257–270, Berlin, Heidelberg,
          1998. Springer-Verlag.
[dlH97]   C. de la Higuera. Characteristic sets for polynomial grammatical inference.
          Machine Learning, 27:125–138, 1997.
[dlHO02] C. de la Higuera and J. Oncina. Learning deterministic linear languages.
          In R. H. Sloan J. Kivinen, editor, *Proceedings of COLT 2002*, volume 2375
          of *LNCS*, pages 185–200. Springer-Verlag, 2002.
[Fer00]   H. Fernau. Identification of function distinguishable languages. In S. Jain
          H. Arimura and A. Sharma, editors, *Proceedings of the 11th International
          Conference on Algorithmic Learning Theory (ALT 2000)*, volume 1968,
          pages 116–130, Berlin, Heidelberg, 2000. Springer-Verlag.
[Fer01]   H. Fernau. Learning XML grammars. In P. Perner, editor, *Machine Learn-
          ing and Data Mining in Pattern Recognition MLDM'01*, number 2123,
          pages 73–87. Springer-Verlag, 2001.
[Gol78]   E. M. Gold. Complexity of automaton identification from given data.
          Information and Control, 37:302–320, 1978.
[HPRW96] Lisa Hellerstein, Krishnan Pillaipakkamnatt, Vijay Raghavan, and Dawn
          Wilkins. How many queries are needed to learn? *Journal of the ACM*,
          43(5):840–862, 1996.
[KV89]   M. Kearns and L. Valiant. Cryptographic limitations on learning boolean
          formulae and finite automata. In *21st ACM Symposium on Theory of
          Computing*, pages 433–444, 1989.
[Lee96]   S. Lee. Learning of context-free languages: A survey of the literature.
          Technical Report TR-12-96, Center for Research in Computing Technol-
          ogy, Harvard University, Cambridge, Massachusetts, 1996.
[LPP98]   K. J. Lang, B. A. Pearlmutter, and R. A. Price. Results of the Abbadingo
          one DFA learning competition and a new evidence-driven state merging
          algorithm. In *Grammatical Inference*, number 1433 in LNCS, pages 1–12.
          Springer-Verlag, 1998.
[OG92]   J. Oncina and P. García. Identifying regular languages in polynomial
          time. In H. Bunke, editor, *Advances in Structural and Syntactic Pattern
          Recognition*, volume 5 of *Series in Machine Perception and Artificial In-
          telligence*, pages 99–108. World Scientific, 1992.
[Pit89]   L. Pitt. Inductive inference, DFA's, and computational complexity. In
          Analogical and Inductive Inference, number 397 in LNCS, pages 18–44.
          Springer-Verlag, Berlin, 1989.
[PW93]   L. Pitt and M. Warmuth. The minimum consistent DFA problem cannot
          be approximated within any polynomial. *Journal of the Association for
          Computing Machinery*, 40(1):95–142, 1993.
[Sak90]   Y. Sakakibara. Learning context-free grammars from structural data in
          polynomial time. *Theoretical Computer Science*, 76:223–242, 1990.
[Sak97]   Y. Sakakibara. Recent advances of grammatical inference. *Theoretical
          Computer Science*, 185:15–45, 1997.
[SG94]   J. M. Sempere and P. García. A characterisation of even linear lan-
          guages and its application to the learning problem. In R. C. Carrasco
          and J. Oncina, editors, *Grammatical Inference and Applications, ICGI-94*,
          number 862 in LNCS, pages 38–44, Berlin, Heidelberg, 1994. Springer-
          Verlag.

[Sto95]   A. Stolcke. An efficient probablistic context-free parsing algorithm that computes prefix probabilities. *Comp. Linguistics*, 21(2):165–201, 1995.

[Tak88]   Y. Takada. Grammatical inference for even linear languages based on control sets. *Information Processing Letters*, 28(4):193–199, 1988.

[Val84]   L. G. Valiant. A theory of the learnable. *Communications of the Association for Computing Machinery*, 27(11):1134–1142, 1984.

Stochastic Grammatical Inference with Multinomial Tests

Christopher Kermorvant[1] and Pierre Dupont[2]

[1] EURISE, Université Jean Monnet, Saint-Etienne, France
kermorva@univ-st-etienne.fr
[2] INGI, University of Louvain, Louvain-la-Neuve, Belgium
pdupont@ingi.ucl.ac.be

Abstract. We present a new statistical framework for stochastic grammatical inference algorithms based on a state merging strategy. We propose to use multinomial statistical tests to decide which states should be merged. This approach has three main advantages. First, since it is not based on asymptotic results, small sample case can be specifically dealt with. Second, all the probabilities associated to a state are included in a single test so that statistical evidence is cumulated. Third, a statistical score is associated to each possible merging operation and can be used for best-first strategy. Improvement over classical stochastic grammatical inference algorithm is shown on artificial data.

1 Introduction

The aim of stochastic regular grammatical inference is to learn a stochastic regular language from examples, mainly through learning the structure of a stochastic finite state automaton and estimating its transition probabilities. Several learning algorithms have been proposed to infer the structure of a stochastic automaton from a sample of words belonging to the target language [2, 13, 3, 14]. These algorithms are based on the same scheme: they start by building a tree which stores exactly the sample set and test possible state merging according to a fixed order. The two key points of these algorithms are the order in which the possible merging operations are evaluated and the compatibility function which evaluates whether or not two states can be merged.

The order chosen to evaluate candidate merging operations is usually hierarchical: states are ordered according to their depth in the tree and for a given depth according to the symbol labeling their incoming edge, the symbols of the alphabet being ordered according to an arbitrary order. Alternative strategies, named data-driven [5] or evidence-driven [7] have been proposed to explore the tree. However these strategies have been applied in a non probabilistic framework and are not directly dependent on the statistical significance of a merging operation.

Merging compatibility function which have been proposed are based either on local statistical tests [2, 13, 3] or on a global test [14]. This global test is derived from the Kullback-Leibler divergence and the merged states are chosen

P. Adriaans, H. Fernau, and M. van Zaanen (Eds.): ICGI 2002, LNAI 2484, pp. 149–160, 2002.

in order to balance the divergence from the sample distribution and the size of the inferred automaton. The global test has been shown to yield better results on a language modeling task, but its complexity is significantly higher than local tests. In the present work, we will restrict our attention to local tests.

Local compatibility tests evaluate a candidate pair of states to be merged according to two criteria:

- the compatibility of probabilities associated with outgoing transitions labeled by the same symbol
- the compatibility of states final probabilities

For a given transition, Carrasco and Oncina [2] proposed to use Hoeffding bounds to evaluate an upper bound of the difference between the transition probability estimated on the sample set and the theoretical probability. From this bound, they derive a compatibility criterion for two estimated transition probabilities. However, the proposed tests suffer from the following limitations:

- the transition compatibility test is derived from an asymptotic bound and is therefore designed for large sample sets. The case of small sample sets is not addressed whereas it is particularly important for real life applications.
- the state compatibility test is based on several independent transition compatibility tests, and no cumulated evidence is used.
- the compatibility test does not interact with the evaluation order, even if data or evidence based order is used.

Solutions were proposed only for the first limitation. In [13], states with too low frequencies are not considered during the inference and afterward are merged into special *low frequency* states. In [16], a statistical test is used to separate low frequency states, which are merged at the end of the inference according to heuristics.

We propose a new compatibility test based on a classical multinomial goodness of fit test. For each state, the set of outgoing transitions probabilities may be modeled by a multinomial probability distribution on the alphabet. In this framework, for each state, the set of observed frequencies for these transitions is the realization of a multinomial random variable. The compatibility test between two states is then a classical statistical test : given the observed transition frequencies, test the hypothesis that the two states share the same underlying multinomial probability distribution. The advantages of this approach are:

- small value frequencies can be specifically dealt with, using exact tests.
- all outgoing transitions probabilities are considered in a single test, such that evidence is cumulated.
- by normalizing the test score, several merging operations can be compared and the evaluation order can be modified accordingly.

The structure of this paper is as follows : first we recall the definition of probabilistic finite state automata and present the Alergia inference algorithm. Then we present a new multinomial framework for the inference algorithm and propose solutions for small sample case and evidence driven search strategy. Finally, the proposed tests and strategies are compared on artificial data.

2   Probabilistic Finite State Automaton

We consider probabilistic finite state automata (PFSA), which are a probabilistic extension of finite state automata. A PFSA $\mathcal{A}$ is defined by $< Q, \Sigma, \delta, \tau, q_0, F >$ where

- Q is a finite set of states
- Σ is the alphabet
- $\delta : Q \times \Sigma \to Q$ is a transition function
- $\tau : Q \times \Sigma \to]0, 1]$ is a function which returns the probability associated with a transition
- q_0 is the initial state,
- $F : Q \to [0..1]$ is a function which returns the probability for a state to be final

Furthermore, we only consider PFSA which are structurally deterministic. This constraint comes from the learning algorithm. This means that given a state q and a symbol s, the state reached from the state q by the symbol s is unique if it exits.

In order to define a probability distribution on Σ^* (the set of all words built on Σ), τ and F must satisfy the following consistency constraint :

$$\forall q \in Q , \left[\sum_{a \in \Sigma} \tau(q, a) \right] + F(q) = 1$$

A string $a_0 \cdots a_{l-1}$ is generated by an automaton $\mathcal{A}$ iff there exists a sequence of states $e_0 \cdots e_l$ such that

- $e_0 = q_0$
- $\forall i \in [0, l-1]$, $\delta(e_i, a_i) = e_{i+1}$
- $F(e_l) \neq 0$.

The automaton assigns to the string the probability

$$P_{PFSA}(a_0 \cdots a_{l-1}) = \left[\prod_{i=0}^{l-1} \tau(e_i, a_i) \right] * F(e_l)$$

Note that PFSA are a particular case of Markov models with discrete emission probabilities on transitions and with final probabilities.

2.1   Learning Algorithm

Several algorithms have been proposed to infer PFSA from examples [2, 13, 14]. All these algorithms are based on the same scheme, which is presented as algorithm 1.

Given a set of positive examples I_+, the algorithm first builds the probabilistic prefix tree acceptor (PPTA). The PPTA is an automaton accepting all

---

Algorithm 1 Generic PFSA induction algorithm

Input:
  I_+, training set (sequences)
  α, a precision parameter
Output: a Probabilistic Finite State Automata
  A $\leftarrow$ *build_PPTA(I_+)*
  while $(q_i, q_j) \leftarrow$ *choose_states*(A) **do**
    if *is_compatible(q_i, q_j, α)* **then**
      merge(A,q_i, q_j)
    end if
  end while
  return A

---

examples of I_+, in which the states corresponding to common prefixes are merged and such that each state and each transition is associated with the number of times it is used while parsing the sample set. This count is then used to define the function τ: if $C(q)$ is the number of times the state q is used while parsing I_+, and $C(q, a)$ is the number of times the transition (q, a) is used while parsing I_+, then $\tau(q, a) = \frac{C(q,a)}{C(q)}$. Similarly, if $C_f(q)$ is the number of times q is used as final state in I_+ for each state q, we have $F(q) = \frac{C_f(q)}{C(q)}$. The second step of the algorithm consists in running through the PPTA (function *choose_states(A)*), and testing whether the states are compatible as a function of the precision parameter α (*is_compatible(q_i, q_j, α)*). If the states are compatible, they are merged (function *merge(A,q_i, q_j)*). Usually, several consecutive merging operations are done in order to keep the automaton structurally deterministic. The algorithm stops when no more merging is possible. In the case of the Alergia algorithm [2], the compatibility of two states is based on three different tests : the compatibility of their outgoing probabilities on the same letter, the compatibility of their probability to be final and the recursive compatibility of their successors.

More formally, the compatible test is derived from Hoeffding bounds [6]. Two states q_1 and q_2 are compatible iff:

$$\forall a \in \Sigma \quad \left| \frac{C(q_1, a)}{C(q_1)} - \frac{C(q_2, a)}{C(q_2)} \right| < \sqrt{\frac{1}{2} \ln \frac{2}{\alpha}} \left(\frac{1}{\sqrt{C(q_1)}} + \frac{1}{\sqrt{C(q_2)}} \right) \quad (1)$$

$$\left| \frac{C_f(q_1)}{C(q_1)} - \frac{C_f(q_2)}{C(q_2)} \right| < \sqrt{\frac{1}{2} \ln \frac{2}{\alpha}} \left(\frac{1}{\sqrt{C(q_1)}} + \frac{1}{\sqrt{C(q_2)}} \right) \quad (2)$$

$$\forall a \in \Sigma, \delta_Q(q_1, a) \text{ and } \delta_Q(q_2, a) \quad \text{are compatible} \quad (3)$$

However, these compatibility tests suffer from several limitations. First the tests 1 and 2 are done independently and no cumulated evidence is used. Second, theses tests derived from Hoeffding bounds which are asymptotic results. Their behavior on finite and limited data is not considered. They are used to prove the identification in the limit of the structure of the target automaton by the algorithm , but might not be adapted for small sample cases.

	letter a	letter b	total
state q_1	$C(q_1, a)$ $H_{1a} = C(q_1)\hat{\tau}_a^q$	$C(q_1, b)$ $H_{1b} = C(q_1)\hat{\tau}_b^q$	$C(q_1)$
state q_2	$C(q_2, a)$ $H_{2a} = C(q_2)\hat{\tau}_a^q$	$C(q_2, b)$ $H_{2b} = C(q_2)\hat{\tau}_b^q$	$C(q_2)$
total	$C(a) = C(q_1, a) + C(q_2, a)$	$C(b) = C(q_1, b) + C(q_2, b)$	$N = C(q_1) + C(q_2)$

Fig. 1. Observed and expected transition frequencies on a two letters alphabet for two states under H_0 hypothesis

The search order followed by the Alergia algorithm can also be improved. This algorithm searches for possible merging between states of the PPTA using a hierarchical order. States are ordered according to their depth in the tree and for a given depth according to the symbol labeling their incoming edge, the symbols of the alphabet being ordered according to an arbitrary order. When sufficient data is available, the order in which merging operations are done at a given depth is not critical, since only relevant state pairs are compatible. However, in the case of limited data, it is important to perform first the merging operations supported by the most evidence.

In section 3, we propose a framework for compatibility tests dealing with these limitations.

3   Multinomial State Model

Each state of the automaton is associated with a multinomial distribution modeling the outgoing transition probabilities and the final probability. In other words, each state is associated with a multinomial random variable with parameter $\tau = \{\tau_1, \tau_2, \cdots, \tau_K\}$, each τ_i corresponding to the transition probability on the ith letter of the alphabet including a special final state symbol. If a transition on a given letter does not exist from a given state, its probability is set to zero. In the PPTA, each state q is seen as a realization of the multinomial random variable $\tau^q = \{\tau_1^q, \tau_2^q, \cdots, \tau_K^q\}$ of the state in the target automaton it corresponds to. The problem of identifying the target automaton is the same as finding the states in the PPTA which correspond to the same states in the target automaton and thus must be merged. In our framework, states of the PPTA which are assumed to be the realization of the same random variable can be checked for compatibility according to a statistical test.

3.1   Multinomial Compatibility Test

We consider the H_0 hypothesis that two states q_1 and q_2 of the PPTA must be merged. In this case, they are both a realization of the same multinomial random variable associated with the state of the target automaton they correspond to, $\tau^q = \{\tau_1^q, \tau_2^q, \cdots, \tau_K^q\}$. Using notations of section 2.1, for each state the expected frequency for each transition i is respectively $C(q_1)\tau_i^q$ and $C(q_2)\tau_i^q$. The unknown parameters of the random variables τ^q can be estimated by maximum likelihood:

$$\hat{\tau}_i^q = \frac{C(q_1, i) + C(q_2, i)}{C(q_1) + C(q_2)}$$

The expected frequencies H_{qi} are then

$$C(q_1)\hat{\tau}_i^q = C(q_1)\frac{C(q_1, i) + C(q_2, i)}{C(q_1) + C(q_2)} \quad \text{and} \quad C(q_2)\hat{\tau}_i^q = C(q_1)\frac{C(q_1, i) + C(q_2, i)}{C(q_1) + C(q_2)}$$

Figure 1 summarizes these results for a two letters alphabet in a contingency table.

The Pearson statistic [11] is one of the most classical statistics to test the H_0 hypothesis:

$$X^2 = \sum_k \left(\frac{C(q_1, k) - H_{1k}}{H_{1k}} + \frac{C(q_2, k) - H_{2k}}{H_{2k}} \right)$$

Several other statistics have been proposed like the log-likelihood ratio statistics [15] or the power-divergence statistics family [4]. All these statistics follow asymptotically a χ^2 distribution with $K - 1$ degrees of freedom. The H_0 hypothesis will be rejected with confidence α if the test statistic X^2 is larger than $\chi^2(K - 1, \alpha)$. This statistic can be used in the following conditions:

- the sample set must be large enough to allow a multinormal approximation of the multinomial distribution. Typically, $C(q)$ must be larger than 20 and $C(q, i)$ must be larger than 5 for all letters.
- the dimension of the multinomial random variables must be constant with respect to the sample size.

In particular, the first condition implies that this statistic can not be used to compare two states as soon as a transition is observed in one of them and not observed in the other. Section 3.2 proposes a solution to this problem, common in real data.

3.2   Small Sample Case

In the case where χ^2 statistics can not be applied due to too small observed frequencies, the Fisher exact test can be used. Given two states and their transition frequencies summarized in a contingency table, as show on Figure 1, this test consists in computing the probability of all the contingency tables with the same marginal counts as the tested table (same values for $C(q_i), C(q_j), C(a), C(b)$) and at least as unfavorable to H_0. For fixed marginal counts, the probability of a contingency table is given by an hypergeometric distribution. To compute the Fisher exact test, we enumerate all the contingency tables with the same marginal counts as the tested table and at least as unfavorable to H_0, we add their probability computed by the hypergeometric distribution and directly compare this sum to the confidence threshold α to accept or reject H_0.

Algorithm 2 Recursive contingency table enumeration algorithm

---

Input:
   a $2 \times c$ contingency table: $x[2][c]$
   current position in table : j
   line and column table sums : $n_0, n_1, C_0, \cdots, C_r$
   partial column sum for current position sc
   partial cell sum for cells already set sx
   total table sum N
Output: enumerate all tables with same marginal counts
   $lj \leftarrow max(sc + n_0 + C_j - sx - N, 0)$ {set minimal value}
   $uj \leftarrow min(n_0 - sx, c_j)$ {set maximal value}
   for $x(1, j) = lj$ to uj **do**
      $x(2, j) \leftarrow C_j - x(1, j)$ {set line 2 value}
      $sc \leftarrow sc + C_j$ {update sc}
      $sx \leftarrow sx + x(1, j)$ {update sx}
      if $j \neq c - 1$ **then**
         Enumerate_table($x[2][c], j + 1, n_0, n_1, C_0, \cdots, C_r, sc, sx, N$) {recursive call}
      else
         $x(1, j) \leftarrow n_0 - sx$ {set line 1 value}
         $x(2, j) \leftarrow C_j - x(1, j)$ {set line 2 value}
         output table
      end if
      $sc \leftarrow sc - C_j$ {update sc}
      $sx \leftarrow sx - x(1, j)$ {update sx}
   end for

March [8] proposed an iterative algorithm to enumerate all the contingency tables at least as unfavorable to H_0. We propose a recursive version of this algorithm in case of $2 \times k$ tables (see algorithm 2). This algorithm only enumerates the tables with correct marginal counts. It consists in a loop on all cells of the table, in which all possible values are enumerated. Given a cell and a possible value for this cell, the possible values for all other cells are computed with a recursive call to the enumeration function.

3.3   Algorithmic Complexity of the Test

Using the multinomial compatibility test does not increase the initial complexity of the inference algorithm since χ^2 values can be tabulated. When using the Fisher exact test, the number of contingency tables we need to evaluate in order to compute is exponential in the number of degree of freedom in the table, which is the size of the alphabet. However, several solutions have been proposed to evaluate the Fisher exact test without a complete enumeration of the possible tables using properties of the multinomial distributions [10] or with dynamic programming methods [9]. An hybrid algorithm, using both exact tests and normal approximations has also been proposed [1].

Algorithm 3 Evidence driven state merging

Input: a Probabilistic Prefix Tree Acceptor
Output: a Probabilistic Finite State Automata
  set the initial state to red
  set the direct successors of the initial state to blue
  while there is a blue node **do**
    evaluate all red/blue merging
    if there exists a blue node incompatible with all red node **then**
      promote the shallowest such blue node to red
    else
      perform the highest score red/blue merging
    end if
  end while

3.4 Evidence Driven Search Strategies

Alternative search strategies have been proposed in the framework of deterministic finite automaton induction from positive and negative examples [5, 7]. Data-dependent strategy [5] is based on the idea that merging operations that are supported by the most evidence must be done first. A variant of this strategy, successfully implemented with an additional merging order constraint by Lang [7], is known as the Blue-Fringe algorithm (see Algorithm 3). This algorithm consists in maintaining a set of states already checked (red states) and a set of states candidate for a possible merging operation (blue states). Blue states are states directly accessible from a red state. All red/blue states pairs are considered. If at least one blue state is incompatible with all the red states, the such blue node with lowest depth is promoted to red. Otherwise, the red/blue merging operation with the highest score is done. Red and blue sets are updated and all red/blue states pairs are considered again. The algorithm stops when there is no more blue state.

We propose here an extension of the Blue-Fringe algorithm to infer probabilistic automata. In the case of a multinomial compatibility test, we need to compare the χ^2 values of all possible merging operations between a red and a blue state. It is not possible to directly compare χ^2 values since they depend both on the number of observations and the size of the contingency table.

To compare the possible merging operations, we propose to use the p-value, the significance level of the test. The p-value is the smallest value of α for which H_0 is rejected. A possible merging operation with a high p-value denotes a strong association between the two states whereas a small p-value denotes a weak association. Other χ^2 results comparison coefficients, like Cramer's V coefficient, could be used, but they should be adapted to take into account the case when the Fisher test is used. With a multinomial compatibility test in algorithm 3, the merging operation with the highest score is the one with the highest p-value.

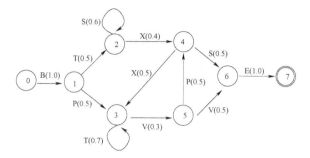

Fig. 2. The SDFA corresponding to the Reber grammar

4   Experiments

In order to compare our approach with previously published results [2, 3], we have tested the multinomial based inference on artificial data. We used the Reber grammar [12], presented on Figure 2, as the target automaton. We have inferred automata on randomly generated learning sample sets of size varying from 5 to 100 strings (about 100 to 2000 symbols). All results presented in this section are averaged over 50 different runs of the experiments. The inference algorithms tested were Alergia [2], the proposed inference algorithm based on the multinomial compatibility function, denoted as Malergia, and the evidence-driven variation, denoted as Blue-Malergia.

Since our goal is to improve inference when available data is limited, we do not present inference results in the limit (when the learning set size grows to infinity) but rather on small size learning sets.

All presented inference algorithms depend on a learning parameter (α in algorithm 1). For each algorithm, this parameter has been tuned to the value leading to the fastest convergence to an automaton with the same number of states as the target automaton ($\alpha = 0.1$ for Alergia and $\alpha = 0.005$ for Malergia and $\alpha = 0.001$ for Blue-Malergia). Note that , if we use standard thresholds on frequencies to decide when to apply exact tests, the number of parameters needed when using multinomial tests is the same as Alergia.

Figure 3 shows the number of states of the inferred automaton as a function of the size of the training set for the three algorithms. The two versions of Malergia show a faster convergence to the correct number of states.

We have evaluated the statistical distance between the target language and the inferred language. On a large sample S of the target language (10 000 words, 96232 symbols), we have computed the average difference between the probability P_t assigned by the target automaton and the probability P_i assigned by the inferred automaton:

$$\bar{L}1 = \frac{1}{|S|} \sum_{w \in S} |P_t(w) - P_i(w)|$$

Figure 4 shows the value of $\bar{L}1$ when the size of the learning sample is increasing. The use of multinomial tests significantly reduce the average error made when

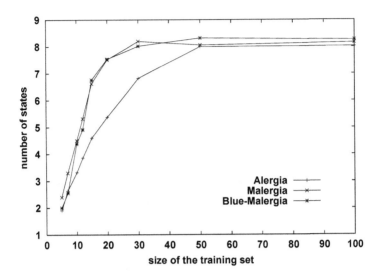

Fig. 3. Number of states of the inferred automaton for increasing learning set size for Alergia, Malergia and Blue-Malergia.

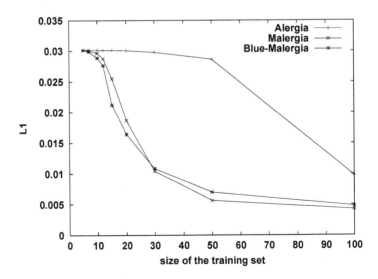

Fig. 4. Value of $\bar{L}1$ for increasing learning set size for automata inferred with Alergia, Malergia and Blue-Malergia

assigning a probability to a word in the target language with the inferred automaton. However , on this task, the advantage of using evidence driven strategy is not shown. This point should be further explored.

5   Conclusion

We have proposed a new statistical framework for grammatical inference algorithms based on a state merging strategy. Each state is considered as a realization of a multinomial distribution and a merging operation of two states is evaluated with a χ^2 test. In this framework, small sample case can be particularly dealt with, all frequencies concerning two states to be merged are used in a single test so that statistical evidence is cumulated and possible merging operations can be compared. Further evaluations of this framework should be conducted, in particular on real data.

References

[1] J. Baglivo, D. Olivier, and M. Pagano. Methods for analysis of contingency tables with large an small cell counts. *Journal of the American Statistical Association*, 83(404):1006–1013, 1988.

[2] R. C. Carrasco and J. Oncina. Learning stochastic regular grammars by means of a state merging method. In *Proc. Int. Coll. on Grammatical Inference*, volume 862 of *Lecture Notes in Artificial Intelligence*, pages 139–152. Springer Verlag, 1994.

[3] R. C. Carrasco and J. Oncina. Learning deterministic regular grammars from stochastic samples in polynomial time. *RAIRO (Theoretical Informatics and Applications)*, 33(1):1–20, 1999.

[4] N. Cressie and T.R.C. Read. Multinomial goodness-of-fit tests. *Journal of the Royal Statistical Society Series B*, 46:440–464, 1984.

[5] C. de la Higuera, J. Oncina, and E. Vidal. Identification of DFA: data-dependent vs data-independent algorithms. In Laurent Miclet and Colin de la Higuera, editors, *Proceedings of the Third International Colloquium on Grammatical Inference (ICGI-96): Learning Syntax from Sentences*, volume 1147 of *LNAI*, pages 313–325, Berlin, September 25–27 1996. Springer.

[6] W. Hoeffding. Probability inequalities for sums of bounded random variables. *Journal of the American Statistical Association*, 58(301):13–30, March 1963.

[7] Kevin J. Lang, Barak A. Pearlmutter, and Rodney A. Price. Results of the Abbadingo One DFA learning competition and a new evidence-driven state merging algorithm. In Springer-Verlag, editor, *Proc. Int. Coll. on Grammatical Inference*, volume 1433 of *LNAI*, pages 1–12, 1998.

[8] D.L. March. Exact probability for $r \times c$ contingency tables. *Communications of the ACM*, 15(11):991–992, November 1972.

[9] C. Mehta and N.R. Patel. A network algorithm for performing fisher's exact test in $r \times c$ contingency tables. *Journal of the American Statistical Association*, 78(382):427–434, 1983.

[10] M. Pagano and K. Taylor Halvorsen. An algorithm for finding the exact significance levels of $r \times c$ contingency tables. *Journal of the American Statistical Association*, 76(376):931–934, 1981.

[11] K. Pearson. On the criterion that a given system of deviations from the probable in the case of a correlated system of variables is such that it can be reasonably supposed to have arisen from random sampling. *Philosophy Magazine*, 50:157–172, 1900.

[12] A.S. Reber. Implicit learning of artificial grammars. *Journal of verbal learning and verbal behaviour*, 6:855–863, 1967.

[13] D. Ron, Y. Singer, and N. Tishby. On the learnability and usage of acyclic probabilistic automata. In *Proceedings of the Eighth Annual Conference on Computational Learning Theory*, pages 31–40, Santa Cruz, CA, 1995. ACM Press.

[14] F. Thollard and P. Dupont. Probabilistic DFA inference using Kullback-Leibler divergence and minimality. In *Proc. Int. Conf. on Machine Learning*, pages 975–982. Morgan Kaufmann, San Francisco, CA, 2000.

[15] S.S. Wilks. The large-sample distribution of the likelihood ratio for testing composite hypotheses. *Annals of Mathematical Statistics*, 9:60–62, 1938.

[16] M. Young-Lai and F. WM. Tompa. Stochastic grammatical inference of text database structure. *Machine Learning*, 40:111–137, 2000.

Learning Languages with Help

Christopher Kermorvant and Colin de la Higuera*

EURISE, Université Jean Monnet, Saint Etienne, France
kermorva,cdlh@univ-st-etienne.fr

Abstract. Grammatical inference consists in learning formal grammars for unknown languages when given learning data. Classically this data is raw: strings that belong to the language and eventually strings that do not. We present in this paper the possibility of learning when presented with additional information such as the knowledge that the hidden language belongs to some known language, or that the strings are typed, or that specific patterns have to/can appear in the strings. We propose a general setting to deal with these cases and provide algorithms that can learn deterministic finite automata in these conditions. Furthermore the number of examples needed to correctly identify can diminish drastically with the quality of the added information. We show that this general setting can cope with several well known learning tasks.

1 Introduction

Grammatical inference consists in learning formal grammars for unknown languages when given learning data. In a classification type of approach one wants to learn a language from a presentation of this language. The presentation may include only instances of the language (we will be learning from *text*) or both examples and counter-examples with their respective labels (learning from a *complete presentation*). In this setting it is unusual to have any more information than these strings and the added bias of the class of grammars from which one should select the candidate from. If no extra hypothesis is taken a succesful algorithm for the case of *deterministic finite automata* (dfa) learning has been RPNI[1][17]. Heuristics in which the order in which hypothesis are made depends on the quantity of data that sustains it have been proposed under the names of *data driven* or *evidence driven* algorithms [7, 15]. If one is allowed to ask questions about the unknown language the setting is that of *active learning* for which the L^* algorithm [1] has been proposed. In the absence of a source of reliable counter-examples the possibilities of learning become smaller [13]. Additional information that may help in that case is the actual structure of the strings [19]; this is equivalent to been given the skeleton of the parse tree for each example. Partial structure may also help, as shown in [20]. An interesting alternative is

---

* This work was done when the second author visited the Departamento de Lenguajes y Sistemas Informáticos of the University of Alicante, Spain. The visit was sponsored by the Spanish Ministry of Education.

[1] Regular Positive and Negative Inference

P. Adriaans, H. Fernau, and M. van Zaanen (Eds.): ICGI 2002, LNAI 2484, pp. 161–173, 2002.
© Springer-Verlag Berlin Heidelberg 2002

to consider the hypothesis that not only is the language regular, but that the distribution also is. In such a case one needs to learn a *Stochastic Finite Automaton*. A better known algorithm for this task is ALERGIA [4]. Data-driven versions have been provided in [12, 22].

In other areas of machine mearning, on the other hand, succesfull techniques have been invented to be able to learn with much more additional information: a typical example is that of *inductive logic programming* (ILP) [16]. ILP is concerned with learning logic programs from data that is also presented as facts. Furthermore some *background knowledge* can be presented to the system using the same representation language (first order logics) as the data or the program to be learned. The field has used this possibility with great success. The generalization methods may then include different techniques, between which one may even encounter grammatical inference [3, 6]. The possibility of being able to use such background knowledge in a systematic way in grammatical inference would lead to the following advantages, that we give for the special case of dfa learning.

First, the search space of the dfa identification task is well defined [8]. The space depends on the learning data one is presented, and can be extremely large. Typing, or excluding specific automata as solutions allows for the reduction of the search space. Second, convergence of dfa learning algorithms depends on the presence of characteristic elements in the learning sets. Some of these elements can be substituted by specific knowledge. Third and more importantly, in practical cases, the alphabet does not consist of 0s and 1s: one has an alphabet where certain symbols appear in certain positions only, independently of the particular language one is faced with. For instance, in a task involving well formed boolean expressions the sequence "¬)" should not appear. But it will neither appear in the correctly labelled examples (those that will evaluate to true), nor in those that will evaluate to false. If - as would be the case with a typical state merging algorithm - one depends on the presence of a counter-example containing "¬)" in the characteristic set for identification to be possible (for some specific merge not to take place), then we would really have no hope to identify. If on the other hand we have background knowledge that no string can contain "¬)" as a substring, then this merge would not take place and identification could take place even when some counter example cannot *par nature* be given.

The idea of using this sort of extra information is not new in grammatical inference. [18] propose an algorithm to learn stochastic finite automata. For theoretical reasons they restrict themselves to the class of acyclic automata. They prove that these admit a normalized level form: each state is assigned a unique integer, which corresponds to the shortest length of the strings that reach that state. The restriction can be translated as a specific automaton which has to be used as the backbone of the dfa to be inferred. [12] use algorithm ALERGIA [4] to learn automata for web-oriented tasks. The authors note that a data driven heuristics [7] and a typed approach give better results. The typed approach consists in noting that locally certain symbols may not follow each other and thus forcing the automaton to respect such rules. This is tested on several benchmarks with clear success. [9] uses *distinguishing functions* to define specific classes of dfa that can be identified in the limit from text. The distinguishing function is another dfa that is used in a manner similar to the one presented in this paper, to reduce the search space. [6] propose an ILP system called GIFT[2] that learns a tree automaton from a set of terms. This automaton is later translated into a logic program. The system is applied to real world data, and a typing of the data is also infered (for instance rules that state that a person has two parents one of which is male and the other female). This type is used to avoid testing for impossible merges (a *man* with a *woman*). A stochastic version (learning stochastic logic programs by means of stochastic tree automata) is proposed in [2]. [10] suggests the task of learning XML grammars from positive data. A very general XML grammar is known, and the idea is to find a better fitting grammar (but that takes into account the general one).

In the next section, definitions will be given for the paper to be self-contained. The inference of typed automata will be proved feasible in section 4. The new information is used to infer a solution, but incorrectly typed data whether positive or negative is unavailable. Applications of these methods are presented in section 5.

2   Introductory Example: Natural Language Modeling

In tasks involving the learning of a natural language model, typing may be used to introduce extra-information, such as grammatical knowledge. For example, typing may be used to make a difference between syntactically correct sentences and semantically correct ones. An approximative hypothesis would be to consider that every semantically correct sentence is syntactically correct. Typing can thus reduce the search space by allowing us to consider only sentences that can be parsed through a very general grammar that could be used as a first filter. Typically, this very general grammar can be built from the information provided by a part-of-speech tagger. Let us consider for example the alphabet $\{John, Mary, loves, the, woman\}$ and the set of sorts $S = \{Start, D, N, V, PN\}$ that can be interpreted as determinant, noun, verb and proper noun. In this example *symbols* of the alphabets are english words and *words* are english sentences. A possible type automaton is

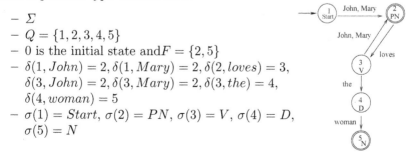

- Σ
- $Q = \{1, 2, 3, 4, 5\}$
- 0 is the initial state and $F = \{2, 5\}$
- $\delta(1, John) = 2, \delta(1, Mary) = 2, \delta(2, loves) = 3,$
  $\delta(3, John) = 2, \delta(3, Mary) = 2, \delta(3, the) = 4,$
  $\delta(4, woman) = 5$
- $\sigma(1) = Start, \sigma(2) = PN, \sigma(3) = V, \sigma(4) = D,$
  $\sigma(5) = N$

---

[2] Grammatical Inference For Terms

For examples, sentences *"John loves Mary"*, *"John loves the woman"* and *"John loves Mary loves Mary"* are correctly typed. The sentences *"the woman loves John"* and *"loves the Mary"* are not correctly typed since they can not be parsed by the type automaton. The grammatical extra-information, introduced into the automaton by typing, may be used during the inference of the language model to prevent from learning sentences which are known to be grammatically incorrect. In this example, negative examples (grammatically incorrect sentences) are remplaced by a priori knowledge (grammatical rules for correct sentences), so that incorrect sentences are not learned and we do not expect the learning algorithm to discover what we already know about grammatically correct sentences.

3   Basic Definitions

3.1   Languages and Automata

An alphabet Σ is a finite nonempty set of symbols. Σ^* denotes the set of all finite strings over Σ, $\Sigma^+ = \Sigma^* \backslash \{\lambda\}$. A language L over Σ is a subset of Σ^*. In the following, unless stated otherwise, symbols are indicated by $a, b, c \ldots$, strings by $u, v, \ldots$, and the empty string by λ. $\mathbb{N}$ is the set of non negative integers.

The length of a string u will be denoted $|u|$, so $|\lambda| = 0$. Let X be a finite set of strings, $|X|$ denotes the number of strings in the set and $\|X\|$ denotes the total sum of the lengths of all strings in X. Let L be a language, the *prefix set* is $\mathrm{Pref}(L) = \{x : xy \in L\}$. Let $u \in \Sigma^*$ and $L \subseteq \Sigma^*$, $u^{-1}L = \{v : uv \in L\}$. By extension $L_1^{-1}L_2 = \{v : \exists u \in L_1 \land uv \in L_2\}$.

Definition 1 (Deterministic finite automata). *A deterministic finite automaton(dfa) $\mathcal{A} = < \Sigma, Q, F, \delta, q_0 >$ is a quintuple where Σ is a finite alphabet, Q is a finite set of states, $F \subset Q$ is the set of final states, $q_0 \in Q$ is the initial state, $\delta : Q \times \Sigma \to Q$ is the transition function*

The above definition allows dfa to have inaccessible states or states that do not lead to any acceptable string. We will not consider such automata in this paper. In the sequel, we will admit that $\forall q \in Q, \exists w \in \Sigma^* : \delta(q_0, w) = q$ and $\forall q \in Q, \exists w \in \Sigma^* : \delta(q, w) \in F$. This constraint is not restrictive, as any dfa can be simply transformed into a dfa with no useless states [3]. We extend δ to a function $Q \times \Sigma^* \to Q$ by $\forall q \in Q : \delta(q, \lambda) = q$ and $\forall q \in Q, \forall a \in \Sigma, \forall u \in \Sigma^* : \delta(q, au) = \delta(\delta(q, a), u)$. Let $\mathcal{A} = < \Sigma, Q, F, \delta, q_0 >$ be a dfa. The language recognized by $\mathcal{A}$, $L(\mathcal{A})$ is $\{w \in \Sigma^* : \delta(q_0, w) \in F\}$. The language $L_{\mathcal{A}}(q_i) = \{w \in \Sigma^* : \delta(q_0, w) = q_i\}$. The *size* of $\mathcal{A}$ denoted $\|\mathcal{A}\|$ is $|Q|\|\Sigma|$. q is a *predececessor* of q' iff $\exists a \in \Sigma : \delta(q, a) = q'$.

---

[3] The dfa for the empty language will nevertheless, for technical reasons, have one single (initial) state

3.2 Polynomial Identification in the Limit from Given Data

The question of learning grammars or automata with help can be tackled in a variety of learning models. Due to the difficulty of the PAC-learning[4] model [21] in the case of languages, and the fact that the active learning setting [1] already makes use of external help through the use of queries, we will turn to the polynomial variant of identification in the limit [14, 5].

In this setting the learner is asked to learn from a learning *sample* $I = (I_+, I_-)$, composed of two finite sets of strings, I_+ being the sub-sample of positive instances and I_- the sub-sample of negative ones.

Definition 2 (Polynomial identification in the limit from given data).
A class $\mathbb{A}$ of automata is polynomially identifiable in the limit from given data iff there exist two polynomials $p()$ and $q()$ and a learning algorithm $\mathcal{L}$ such that:

1. *Given any sample (I_+, I_-), $\mathcal{L}$ returns an automaton $\mathcal{A}$ in $\mathbb{A}$ compatible with (I_+, I_-) in $\mathcal{O}(p(\|I_+\| + \|I_-\|))$ time;*
2. *for each automaton $\mathcal{A}$ in $\mathbb{A}$ of size n, there exists a characteristic sample (CI_+, CI_-) of size less than $q(n)$ for which, from $I_+ \supseteq CI_+$, $I_- \supseteq CI_-$, $\mathcal{L}$ returns a grammar $\mathcal{A}'$ equivalent to $\mathcal{A}$.*

In this setting it is known that deterministic finite automata are polynomially identifiable in the limit from given data, whereas context-free grammars and non deterministic finite automata are not [5].

3.3 Learning Regular Languages: A Generic Algorithm

A variety of algorithms identifying dfa can be considered. We give (figure 1 and 2) a generic algorithm, dependent of a function Choose, which we will suppose deterministic. The proof that this algorithm complies with the conditions of definition 2 can be found in [7]. Algorithm 1 depends on the choice of function Choose. Provided it is a deterministic function (such as one that chooses the minimal $\langle i, a \rangle$ in lexicographic order), convergence is insured.

4 Inferring Typed Automata

Between the additional information one may have about the language to be inferred, we consider here that information is not only about inclusion (all strings should belong to such language), but also structural. In many cases information is about how strings are meant to belong. Typically this can be dealt with by typing.

---

[4] Probably Approximatively Correct

Algorithm 1 Infer $\mathcal{A}$

Require: $I = (I_+, I_-)$, functions Compatible, Choose
Ensure: $L(\mathcal{A}) = L$ if I is characteristic, some compatible language if not where
$\quad \mathcal{A} = <\Sigma, Q, F, \delta, q_0>$
$\quad Q = \{q_0\}$
$\quad i = 1$
$\quad$ Candidates $= \{\langle 0, a \rangle : a\Sigma^* \cap I_+ \neq \emptyset\}$
$\quad$ **while** Candidates $\neq \emptyset$ **do**
$\quad\quad \langle k, a \rangle = $ Choose(Candidates)
$\quad\quad$ Candidates $= $ Candidates $- \{\langle k, a \rangle\}$
$\quad\quad$ **if** $\exists q_j \in Q :$ Compatible$(k, a, j, \mathcal{A}, I)$ **then**
$\quad\quad\quad \delta(q_k, a) = q_j$
$\quad\quad$ **else**
$\quad\quad\quad Q = Q \cup \{q_i\}$
$\quad\quad\quad \delta(q_k, a) = q_i$
$\quad\quad\quad$ Candidates $= $ Candidates $\cup \{\langle i, a \rangle : a\Sigma^* \cap L_A(q_i)^{-1}I_+ \neq \emptyset\}$
$\quad\quad\quad i{+}{+}$
$\quad$ **for all** $q_i \in Q$ **do**
$\quad\quad$ **if** $\lambda \in (L_A(q_i))^{-1}I_+$ **then** $F = F \cup \{q_i\}$

Algorithm 2 Compatible$(i, a, j, \mathcal{A}, I)$

Require: $I = (I_+, I_-)$
$\quad \delta(q_i, a) = q_j$
$\quad$ **for all** $q_k \in Q$ **do**
$\quad\quad$ **if** $(L(q_k))^{-1})I_+ \not\subseteq \{\lambda\} \vee (L(q_k))^{-1})I_+ \cap (L(q_k))^{-1})I_- \neq \emptyset$ **return false**
$\quad$ **return true**

4.1   Type Automaton

Definition 3. *A type automaton $\mathcal{T}$ is defined by $<\Sigma, Q, q_0, F, \delta, S, \sigma>$ where Σ is an alphabet, Q is a finite set of states, q_0 is the initial state, $\delta : Q \times \Sigma \to Q$ is the transition function, S is a set of elements called sorts, $\sigma : Q \to S$ is the typing (total) function, $F \subset Q$ is the set of final states such that $\forall q_1, q_2 \in Q$, $\sigma(q_1) = \sigma(q_2) \implies (q_1 \in F \iff q_2 \in F)$.*

It should be noticed that a type automaton is a dfa with types. The intended meaning of the type automaton is to describe how strings are constructed. Final states are used to indicate which are the sorts of the objects in the language. Classically, $L(\mathcal{T})$, the language defined by a type automaton $\mathcal{T}$, is the set of all words w in Σ^* such that $\delta(q_0, w) = q$ with $q \in F$. We define the extension of σ to words such that for all $w \in \text{Pref}(L(\mathcal{T}))$, $\sigma(w) = \sigma(\delta(q_0, w))$.

Definition 4. *A type automaton $L(\mathcal{T}) = <\Sigma, Q, q_0, F, \delta, S, \sigma>$ is minimal if $\forall q, q' \in Q$ such that $q \neq q'$, $\exists w \in \Sigma^* : \sigma(\delta(q, w)) \neq \sigma(\delta(q', w))$*

In the sequel, we will only consider type automaton that are minimal.

Definition 5. *A dfa $\mathcal{A} = <\Sigma, Q, q_0, F, \delta>$ is compatible with a type automaton $\mathcal{T} = <\Sigma, Q_\mathcal{T}, q_{0\mathcal{T}}, F_\mathcal{T}, \delta_\mathcal{T}, S_\mathcal{T}, \sigma_\mathcal{T}>$, noted $\mathcal{A}$ is $\mathcal{T}$-compatible, if*

1. $\forall u, v \in \mathrm{Pref}(L(\mathcal{A})), \ \delta(q_0, u) = \delta(q_0, v) \implies \sigma_T(u) = \sigma_T(v)$
2. $\forall u \in L(\mathcal{A}), \ u \in L(T)$

The type automaton T might be too general relatively to a given dfa $\mathcal{A}$ so that only a part of this automaton is used to type $\mathcal{A}$. Therefore we can define the pruning of the type automaton T relatively to $\mathcal{A}$:

Definition 6. *Let* $T = < \Sigma, Q_T, q_{0T}, F_T, \delta_T, S_T, \sigma_T >$ *be a type automaton and* $\mathcal{A} = < \Sigma, Q, q_0, F, \delta >$ *be a dfa.* $T_\mathcal{A} = < \Sigma, Q_{T\mathcal{A}}, q_{0T\mathcal{A}}, F_{T\mathcal{A}}, \delta_{T\mathcal{A}}, S_{T\mathcal{A}}, \sigma_{T\mathcal{A}} >$, *the automaton obtained by pruning* T *relatively to* $\mathcal{A}$ *is defined by :*

- $Q_{T\mathcal{A}} = \{ q \in Q_T : \exists u, v \in \Sigma^*, \ \delta_T(q_{0T}, u) = q \wedge uv \in L(\mathcal{A}) \}$
- $F_{T\mathcal{A}} = \{ q \in F_T : \exists u \in L(\mathcal{A}), \ \delta_T(q_{0T}, u) = q \}$
- $\delta_{T\mathcal{A}}$ *is such that* $\forall q \in Q_{T\mathcal{A}}, \forall a \in \Sigma, \ \delta_{T\mathcal{A}}(q, a) = q'$ *if* $\exists u, v \in \Sigma^*$: $\delta_T(q_{0T}, u) = q \wedge uav \in L(\mathcal{A})$
- $S_{T\mathcal{A}} = \{ s \in S_T : \exists q \in Q_{T\mathcal{A}}, \ \sigma_T(q) = s \}$
- $\sigma_{T\mathcal{A}}$ *is the restriction of* σ_T *to* $Q_{T\mathcal{A}}$

$T_\mathcal{A}$ is also a type automaton.

Proposition 1. $\mathcal{A} = < \Sigma, Q, q_0, F, \delta >$ *is compatible with a minimal type automaton* $T = < \Sigma, Q_T, q_{0T}, F_T, \delta_T, S, \sigma >$ *if and only if*

- $\forall u, v \in \mathrm{Pref}(L(\mathcal{A})), \ \delta(q_0, u) = \delta(q_0, v) \Rightarrow \delta_T(q_0, u) = \delta_T(q_0, v)$
- $\forall u \in L(\mathcal{A}), \ u \in L(T)$

Proof. A state in T has unique type, thus the condition is sufficient. Conversily suppose we have $u, v \in \mathrm{Pref}(L(\mathcal{A}))$ such that $\delta(q_0, u) = \delta(q_0, v) \wedge \sigma_T(u) = \sigma_T(v) \wedge \delta_T(q_{0T}, u) \neq \delta_T(q_{0T}, v)$ Then as T is minimal $\exists w \in \Sigma^*$ such that $\sigma_T(\delta_T(q_{0T}, uw)) \neq \sigma_T(\delta_T(q_{0T}, vw)$. But as $\delta(q_0, u) = \delta(q_0, v)$, $\delta(q_0, uw) = \delta(q_0, vw)$. So in that case by compatibility $\sigma_T(uw)) \neq \sigma_T(vw)$, which is a contradiction.

The definition of a T-compatible automaton induces the definition of a T-compatible language :

Definition 7. *A language* L *is* T-*compatible if there exists a* T-*compatible dfa* $\mathcal{A}$ *such that* $L(\mathcal{A}) = L$.

It is possible to know if a dfa is compatible with a given type automaton as stated in the following proposition:

Proposition 2. *Let* $T = < \Sigma, Q_T, q_{0T}, F_T, \delta_T, S_T, \sigma_T >$ *be a type automaton and* $\mathcal{A} = < \Sigma, Q, q_0, F, \delta >$ *be an dfa. It can be decided in* $O(\|\mathcal{A}\|)$ *time if* $\mathcal{A}$ *is* T-*compatible.*

The proof of this proposition is given by algorithm 3. This algorithm performs a breadth-first search through the automaton $\mathcal{A}$ and runs in parallel through the automaton T. It associates to each state of $\mathcal{A}$ the sort of the corresponding state in T, through the typing function ϕ. Each state of $\mathcal{A}$ must be associated with a unique sort. Should a state be associated with two different sorts, the algorithm returns false. At the end of the procedure, if all the states are associated with a sort, then the automaton is fully typed and the algorithm return true. Otherwise the algorithm returns false.

Algorithm 3 The automata typing algorithm

Require: $\mathcal{A} =< \Sigma, Q, q_0, F, \delta >$, an automaton and
  $\mathcal{T} =< \Sigma, Q_T, q_{0T}, F_T, \delta_T, S_T, \sigma_T >$, a type automaton
Ensure: return true if $\mathcal{A}$ is $\mathcal{T}$ compatible, false if not.
  let $\phi : Q \to S_T$ be a typing function
  $T \leftarrow \{q_0\}$
  $\phi(q_0) = \sigma(q_{0T})$
  $Enqueue((q_0, q_{0T}))$
  while $(q_i, q_{iT}) \leftarrow Dequeue$ **do**
    for all $a \in \Sigma$ such that $\delta(q_i, a) = q_j$ **do**
      if $q_j \notin T$ **then**
        let $q_{jT} = \delta_T(q_{iT}, a)$
        $\phi(q_j) = \sigma(q_{jT})$
        $T = T \cup \{q_j\}$
        $Enqueue((q_j, q_{jT}))$
      else
        if $\phi(q_j) \neq \sigma(\delta_T(q_{iT}, a))$ **then return false**
  if $T = Q$ **then return** true **else return** false

4.2   The Search Space for Typed Languages

The problem of regular inference may be viewed as a search in the regular automata space. The search space has been characterized by Dupont *et al.* [8] as a partition lattice. In this section, we propose an extension of this framework to typed languages inference.

Let $\mathcal{A} =< Q, \Sigma, \delta, q_0, F >$ be a dfa and π a partition of Q the set of states. This partition induces an equivalence relation on the states. The quotient automaton $\mathcal{A}/\pi =< Q_\pi, \Sigma, \delta_\pi, q_{\pi 0}, F_\pi >$ is defined as :

- $Q_\pi = Q/\pi$ is the set of equivalence classes defined by the partition π
- δ_π is a function $Q_\pi \times \Sigma \to 2^{Q_\pi}$ such that $\forall q_\pi, q'_\pi \in Q_\pi \; \forall a \in \Sigma$,
  $\delta_\pi(q_\pi, a) = q'_\pi \iff \exists q \in q_\pi \; \exists q' \in q'_\pi, \; \delta(q, a) = q'$
- $q_{\pi 0}$ is the equivalence class to which belongs q_0.
- F_π is the set of equivalence classes to which belong at least one state q such that $q \in F$.

We define the following relation on the set of all possible quotient automata of a deterministic automaton :

Definition 8. *Let $\mathcal{A} =< Q, \Sigma, \delta, q_0, F >$ be a deterministic automaton and π_1 and π_2 be two partitions on Q. We say that $\mathcal{A}/\pi_2$ derives from $\mathcal{A}/\pi_1$, noted $\mathcal{A}/\pi_2 \preceq \mathcal{A}/\pi_1$, if π_1 is finer than π_2.*

This relation is a partial order on the set of all possible deterministic quotient automata of a deterministic automaton and we have the following proposition [11]:

Proposition 3. *If an automaton $\mathcal{A}/\pi_j$ derives from an automaton $\mathcal{A}/\pi_i$ then $L(\mathcal{A}/\pi_i) \subseteq L(\mathcal{A}/\pi_j)$.*

Definition 9 (Positive and negative $\mathcal{T}$-compatible sample set). *Let $\mathcal{T}$ be a type automaton. A positive $\mathcal{T}$-compatible sample set I_+ of a $\mathcal{T}$-compatible language L is a finite subset of L. A negative $\mathcal{T}$-compatible sample set I_- is a finite subset of $L(\mathcal{T})\backslash L$.*

It should be noted that the counter-examples may not be taken from $\Sigma^* \setminus L$ but from $L(\mathcal{T})\backslash L$: unstructured objects, or badly typed sentences make no sense. This will be explicit in the next section.

Definition 10 (Structural completeness). *A sample set I_+ is structurally complete relatively to a dfa $\mathcal{A} =< Q, \Sigma, \delta, q_0, F >$ if and only if*

1. $\forall q \in Q \ \forall a \in \Sigma, \ \delta(q, a) = q' \implies \exists u, v \in \Sigma^* : \delta(q_0, u) = q \wedge uav \in I_+$
2. $\forall q \in F \ \exists u \in I_+ : \delta(q_0, u) = q$

Definition 11 ($\mathcal{T}$-compatible Prefix Tree Acceptor). *Let I_+ be a $\mathcal{T}$-compatible sample set and $\mathcal{T}$ a type automaton. The $\mathcal{T}$-compatible prefix tree acceptor of I_+ according to $\mathcal{T}$ is the smallest $\mathcal{T}$-compatible dfa accepting exactly I_+ in which each state has at most one predecessor.*

Proposition 4. *Let L be a $\mathcal{T}$-compatible language for some type automaton $\mathcal{T}$. Then $\mathrm{PTA}(I_+)$ is $\mathcal{T}$-compatible.*

Proof. Suppose this is not the case. Then, by proposition 1 $\exists u, v \in \mathrm{Pref}(I_+)$ such that $\delta(q_0, u) = \delta(q_0, v) \wedge \delta_{\mathcal{T}}(q_{0\mathcal{T}}, u) = \delta_{\mathcal{T}}(q_{0\mathcal{T}}, v)$. But as $PTA(I_+)$ is a tree, necessarily $u = v$. Thus a contradiction.

We extend the definition of a partition to $\mathcal{T}$-compatible dfa.

Definition 12 ($\mathcal{T}$-compatible partition). *Let $\mathcal{T}$ be a type automaton and let $\mathcal{A}$ be a $\mathcal{T}$-compatible dfa. A partition π of Q is $\mathcal{T}$-compatible if $\mathcal{A}/\pi$ is $\mathcal{T}$-compatible.*

For a partition to be $\mathcal{T}$-compatible it is sufficient for determinism to be preserved and that each class of states is uniquely typed:

Proposition 5. *Let $\mathcal{A} =< Q, \Sigma, \delta, q_0, F >$ be a $\mathcal{T}$-compatible dfa and π be a partition of Q. π is $\mathcal{T}$-compatible iff*

1. $\mathcal{A}/\pi$ *is deterministic*
2. $\forall q, q' \in Q$ *with* $w, w' \in \Sigma^*$ *such that* $\delta(q_0, w) = q$ *and* $\delta(q_0, w') = q'$, $q \in q_\pi$ *and* $q' \in q_\pi \implies \sigma_{\mathcal{T}}(\delta_{\mathcal{T}}(q_{0\mathcal{T}}, w)) = \sigma_{\mathcal{T}}(\delta_{\mathcal{T}}(q_{0\mathcal{T}}, w'))$.

Proof. Straightforward

The relation $\preceq$ is a partial order on the set of $\mathcal{T}$-compatible deterministic automata derived from a $\mathcal{T}$-compatible dfa $\mathcal{A}$. We consider the restriction of $\preceq$ to the set of $\mathcal{T}$-compatible deterministic quotient automata, denoted $\preceq_{\mathcal{T}}$. Then we have the following proposition :

Proposition 6. *Let $\mathcal{A}_{\mathcal{T}}$ be a $\mathcal{T}$-compatible dfa. The set of all $\mathcal{T}$-compatible quotient automata of $\mathcal{A}_{\mathcal{T}}$ together with the partial order $\preceq_{\mathcal{T}}$ is a finite lattice denoted $Lat_{\mathcal{T}}(\mathcal{A}_{\mathcal{T}})$ for which $\mathcal{A}_{\mathcal{T}}$ is the lowest upper bound and the type automaton $\mathcal{T}_{\mathcal{A}}$ is the greatest lower bound.*

Proof. The set of all deterministic automata is a sub-lattice of $Lat(PTA(I_+))$[8]. In turn $Lat_{\mathcal{T}}(PTA(I_+))$ is a sub-lattice of $Lat(PTA(I_+))$, and so a lattice. $\mathcal{T}_{\mathcal{A}}$ is the greatest lower bound since it derives from $\mathcal{A}_{\mathcal{T}}$ with the largest type compatible partition, defined by $\forall q, q' \in Q_{\mathcal{A}_{\mathcal{T}}}, q \equiv q' \Leftrightarrow \sigma_{\mathcal{A}_{\mathcal{T}}}(q) = \sigma_{\mathcal{A}_{\mathcal{T}}}(q')$.

We can now define the problem of the inference of a $\mathcal{T}$-compatible regular language in the framework of $\mathcal{T}$-compatible deterministic automata lattice :

Corollary 1. *Let $\mathcal{T}$ a type automaton and I_+ be a sample set structurally complete relatively to some $\mathcal{T}$-compatible dfa $\mathcal{A}$; then $\mathcal{A}$ belongs to $Lat_{\mathcal{T}}(PTA(I_+))$.*

Proof. Clearly, as I_+ is structurally complete $\mathcal{T}_{\mathcal{A}} = \mathcal{T}_{PTA(I_+)}$. By [8] $\mathcal{A}$ is in $Lat(PTA(I_+))$; as furthermore it is $\mathcal{T}$-compatible, it is in $Lat_{\mathcal{T}}(PTA(I_+))$.

4.3   Inference of Typed Languages

It is now necessary to provide an algorithm that will visit $Lat_{\mathcal{T}}(PTA(I_+))$, without considering badly types automata, for which no negative data is available. Algorithm 1 will be used, but function compatible (algorithm 2) will be slightly modified in order to test $\mathcal{T}$-compatibility. For this it will call algorithm 3. As the different algorithms are all polynomial it is clear that the entire algorithm runs in time polynomial in $\|I_+ \cup I_-\|$. The characteristic set is included in the characteristic set necessary in the case where the automata are untyped, and so its size is bounded by this one.

In the worse case (where the type automaton just contains one state, thus one type) the complexity of our algorithm and the size of the characteristic set are the same as those for the untyped case, so typing does not gain anything. But in a case (which should correspond to most applications) where typing leads to the definition of some non trivial type automaton, the gain will be that of all those pairs of states of different types that do not require specific strings to be separated. A more precise analysis seems difficult, as even in this case it is possible to come up with a complex type automaton, but for which on some specific target, only one state is really used, thus presenting us with a complexity similar to that of the untyped case.

5   Applications

We visit or revisit a number of applications where typing is possible, with diverse formalisms, and propose the type automaton for each case.

DNA family representation: when one is trying to detect genes or promoters in DNA sequences, the information that the coding unit (codons) is a triplet of nucleotides can be introduced by the type automaton $< \Sigma, Q, q_0, F, \delta, S, \sigma >$ defined as :

- $\Sigma = \{A, G, C, U\}$
- $Q = \{0, 1, 2\}$
- 0 is the initial state and $F = Q$
- $\forall x \in \Sigma \delta(0, x) = 1, \delta(1, x) = 2, \delta(2, x) = 0$
- $S = \{0, 1, 2\}$
- $\forall q \in Q : \sigma(q) = q$

Many-Sorted Terms: In [6], system GIFT was implemented in order to learn recursive PROLOG programs, and discover new predicates. To do so tree automata were inferred from terms representing the examples. In turn the tree automaton would be translated into a readable logic program. When defining correct terms, typing was used. The same typing was also used during inference to avoid merging 2 uncomparable states. As a simple example, and without giving the formal definitions, suppose we intend to model stacks of objects. Each object has a shape (cube or ball) and a colour (red or blue). A stack is represented by a term such as $ontop(object(blue, ball), ontop(object(red, cube), nothing))$ which would describe a blue ball on top of a red cube. The following type automaton defines correct stacks:

- $\Sigma = \{ontop, nothing, red, blue, ball, cube, object\}$
- $Q = \{0, 1, 2, 3, 4\}$
- 0 is the initial state and $F = \{4\}$
- $\delta(\lambda, red) = \delta(\lambda, blue) = 1,$
  $\delta(\lambda, cube) = \delta(\lambda, ball) = 2,$
  $\delta(12, object) = 3,$
  $\delta(\lambda, nothing) = \delta(34, ontop) = 4$
- $S = \{\bar{0}, \bar{1}, \bar{2}, \bar{3}, \bar{4}\}$
- $\forall q \in Q : \sigma(q) = \bar{q}$

Loop-free automata: in [18], it is proved that any loop-free dfa is equivalent to another automaton which has the following property : $\delta(q_0, u) = \delta(q_0, v) \implies |u| = |v|$. As the result does not depend on the probabilities, it can be applied both to the dfa case and the PFA case. To obtain loop-free automata it is thus sufficient to restrict ourselves to the following typed automata :

where Q = any initial segment of $\mathbb{N}$, 0 is the initial state and $F = Q$, $\forall x \in \Sigma, \delta(i, x) = i + 1$ and $\forall q \in Q : \sigma(q) = q$.

Conclusion

The typing formalism presented in this paper is just a first step in a direction we not only find promising but also necessary: that of using extra information in the task of learning languages. The formalism we propose needs to be better compared with the one of distinguishing functions [9]. The ideas for an extension to tree automata precede this paper and can be found in [6]. A more general question than the one we answer in this paper is that of learning languages when we know of some inclusion. Namely: we know that $L_1 \subset L_2$, we have examples from L_1 and eventually counter-examples from $L_2 \setminus L_1$; how do we find L_1?

Acknowledgements

The authors wish to thank Jean-Christophe Janodet for many discussions over the ideas in this paper. Amaury Habrard and Marc Bernard also contributed with motivating examples, whereas Jose Oncina did the same with just as motivating counter-examples.

References

[1] D. Angluin. Learning regular sets from queries and counterexamples. *Information and Control*, 39:337–350, 1987.

[2] M. Bernard and A. Habrard. Learning stochastic logic programs. Int. Conf. on Inductive Logic Programming, Work in progress session, 2001.

[3] H. Boström. Theory–Guided Induction of Logic Programs by Inference of Regular Languages. In *Int. Conf. on Machine Learning*, 1996.

[4] R. Carrasco and J. Oncina. Learning stochastic regular grammars by means of a state merging method. In *ICGI'94*, number 862 in LNAI, pages 139—150, 1994.

[5] C. de la Higuera. Characteristic sets for polynomial grammatical inference. *Machine Learning*, 27:125–138, 1997.

[6] C. de la Higuera and M. Bernard. Apprentissage de programmes logiques par inférence grammaticale. *Revue d'Intelligence Artificielle*, 14(3):375–396, 2001.

[7] C. de la Higuera, J. Oncina, and E. Vidal. Identification of DFA: data dependent versus data independent algorithm. In *ICGI'96*, number 1147 in LNAI, pages 313–325, 1996.

[8] P. Dupont, L. Miclet, and E. Vidal. What is the search space of the regular inference? In *ICGI '94*, number 862 in LNAI, pages 25–37, 1994.

[9] H. Fernau. Identification of function distinguishable languages. In *Int. Conf. on Algorithmic Learning Theory*, volume 1968 of *LNCS*, pages 116–130, 2000.

[10] H. Fernau. Learning xml grammars. In *Machine Learning and Data Mining in Pattern Recognition MLDM'01*, number 2123 in LNCS, pages 73–87, 2001.

[11] K. S. Fu and T. L. Booth. Grammatical inference: Introduction and survey. part i and ii. *IEEE Transactions on Syst. Man. and Cybern.*, 5:59–72 and 409–423, 1975.

[12] T. Goan, N. Benson, and O. Etzioni. A grammar inference algorithm for the world wide web. In *Proc. of AAAI Spring Symp. on Machine Learning in Information Access.*, 1996.

[13] E. M. Gold. Language identification in the limit. *Information and Control*, 10(5):447–474, 1967.

[14] E. M. Gold. Complexity of automaton identification from given data. *Information and Control*, 37:302–320, 1978.

[15] K. J. Lang, B. A. Pearlmutter, and R. A. Price. Results of the Abbadingo one DFA learning competition and a new evidence driven state merging algorithm. In *ICGI'98*, number 1433 in LNAI, pages 1–12, 1998.

[16] S. Muggleton. Inductive Logic Programming. In *The MIT Encyclopedia of the Cognitive Sciences (MITECS)*. MIT Press, 1999.

[17] J. Oncina and P. García. Identifying regular languages in polynomial time. In *Advances in Structural and Syntactic Pattern Recognition*, pages 99–108. 1992.

[18] D. Ron, Y. Singer, and N. Tishby. On the learnability and usage of acyclic prob abilistic finite automata. In *Proc. of COLT 1995*, pages 31–40, 1995.

[19] Y. Sakakibara. Recent advances of grammatical inference. *Theoretical Computer Science*, 185:15–45, 1997.

[20] Y. Sakakibara and H. Muramatsu. Learning context free grammars from partially structured examples. In *ICGI'00*, number 1891 in LNAI, pages 229–240, 2000.

[21] L. G. Valiant. A theory of the learnable. *Com. of the ACM*, 27(11):1134–1142, 1984.

[22] M. Young Lai and F. W. Tompa. Stochastic grammatical inference of text database structure. *Machine Learning*, 40(2):111–137, 2000.

Incremental Learning of Context Free Grammars

Katsuhiko Nakamura and Masashi Matsumoto

School of Science and Engineering,
Tokyo Denki University, Hatoyama-machi, Saitama-ken,
350-0394 Japan.
nakamura@k.dendai.ac.jp

Abstract. This paper describes inductive inference for synthesizing context free grammars from positive and negative sample strings, implemented in *Synapse* system. For effective inference of grammars, Synapse employs the following mechanisms.

1. A rule generating method called "inductive CYK algorithm," which generates minimum production rules required for parsing positive samples.
2. Incremental learning for adding newly generated rules to previously obtained rules.

Synapse can synthesize both ambiguous grammars and unambiguous grammars. Experimental results show recent improvement of Synapse system to synthesize context free grammars.

Keywords: incremental learning, inductive CYK algorithm, context free language, unambiguous grammar, iterative deepening

1 Introduction

Inductive inference, or automatic synthesis, of context free grammars is generally considered as a fundamental and important subject in machine learning, and yet as a difficult problem requiring a high degree of computational complexity. There have been few works on this subject compared with those for regular grammars and other more restricted grammars.

In this paper, we investigate inductive inference for synthesizing context free grammars from positive and negative sample strings. This grammatical inference is implemented in *Synapse* (Synthesis by Analyzing Positive String Examples) system. For solving the computational complexity problem, we employ the following approaches.

– **Inductive CYK algorithm** Synapse generates production rules for each positive sample string by a rule generation method called inductive CYK algorithm. When the sample string is derived from the set of rules, the process of the algorithm succeeds as the usual CYK algorithm (Hopcroft & Ullman, 1979). Otherwise, the process generates minimum production rules and adds them to the set of rules, from which the sample string is derived. An important feature of this method is that the system only generates the rules that are applied in the bottom-up parsing by CYK algorithm.

P. Adriaans, H. Fernau, and M. van Zaanen (Eds.): ICGI 2002, LNAI 2484, pp. 174–184, 2002.

- **Incremental learning** Production rules generated by inductive CYK algorithm for a positive sample are added to a set of previously obtained rules.
  This feature is used not only for learning a grammar from its samples, but
  also for learning a grammar based on the other grammars of similar or related
  languages.
- **Iterative deepening** Synapse searches for the set of rules, from which
  all the positive samples, but no negative samples, are derived by iterative
  deepening: The sets of rules are searched within a limited number of rules.
  When the search fails, the system iterates the search with larger limits. The
  iterative deepening is widely used for finding the optimum solution by the
  search as inductive logic programming.

The incremental learning in Synapse is used in two ways. First, for learning
a grammar from its sample strings, the positive samples are given to the rule
generation by inductive CYK algorithm in order, until all the positive samples
are derived from the set of rules. Strictly speaking, this approach might not
be called incremental learning, since it is different from the usual incremental
learning as in [4] in that the system checks all the negative samples each time it
finds a set of rules for a positive sample. This process continues until the system
finds a set of rules from which all the positive samples, but none of the negative
samples are derived. We employ this approach because checking negative samples
requires less time than generating rules for positive samples.

The second use of incremental learning is to synthesize a grammar by adding
rules to the rules of previously learned similar languages. We show some examples
for this type of grammatical inference in Section 5.2.

The first version of Synapse system is described in [3]. In the latest version, the inductive CYK algorithm has been improved, and some heuristics were
implemented as described in Sections 3 and 4.

Only a few research papers on practical algorithms for synthesizing context
free grammars have published so far. GRIDS system by Langley and Stromsten
[2] uses two operators to create new nonterminal symbols and to merge rules for
inducing grammars. This system is different from Synapse in that natural languages are assumed the object language and that it is not intended to synthesize
simple grammars for general context free languages. Sakakibara et. al. [5,6] presented methods based on both genetic algorithm and the CYK algorithm. Their
use of CYK algorithm is different from our approach in that possible tables of
symbol sets are generated and tested in every generation of the GA process.

2   Context Free Grammars and Languages

A *context free grammar* (CFG) is a system $G = (N, T, P, S)$, where N and T
are finite sets of nonterminal symbols and terminal symbols, respectively; P
is a finite set of production rules (or simply rules) of the form $A \rightarrow \beta$ with
$A \in N, \beta \in (N \cup T)^*$; and $S \in N$ is a starting symbol.

For any $B \in N$ and $w \in (N \cup T)^*$, we write $B \overset{*}{\Rightarrow}_G w$, if w can be derived from B by the rules in G, and equivalently there is the syntax tree with the root with label B and the result w. The *language* of G is the set

$$L(G) = \{w \in T^* | \ S \overset{*}{\Rightarrow}_G w\}.$$

A CFG is *ambiguous*, if there is a string w such that there are two or more different syntax trees with the result w and the root labeled by S.

For any set P of rules is a *variant* of a set Q of rules, if there is a one-to-one correspondence between the set of nonterminal symbols of P and that of Q and P is converted to Q by replacing all the nonterminal symbols in P with the corresponding symbols.

Any CFG $G = (N, T, P, S)$ can be transformed to Chomsky normal form such that all the productions have the forms $A \to BC$ and $A \to a$, where A, B and C are nonterminal and a is a terminal symbol. To simplify the inductive inference, we use the *revised Chomsky normal form*

$$A \to \beta\gamma \ (\beta, \gamma \in N \cup T).$$

We can restrict the CFG to have this revised normal form without loss of generality, since the class of languages defined by this grammar includes all the context free languages of strings with the lengths two or more. We can simplify not only the sets of rules but also grammatical inference by omitting the rules of the form $A \to a$, in the case where the number of terminal symbols is not large. A "coding" technique is used in Section 5.1 to make up for the problem that this form of grammars does not have the rules of the form $A \to a$.

3   Inductive CYK Algorithm

We assume that all the production rules are of the revised Chomsky normal form and that S is the starting symbol in every grammar. Inductive CYK algorithm works similarly as usual CYK algorithm when a given string is derived from the set of rules. This algorithm represents the process for generating necessary rules for deriving a given string and adding them to the set of rules, when the string is not derived from the set of rules.

Figure 1 shows a nondeterministic procedure for the inductive CYK algorithm. For inputs of a string w and a set P of rules, the procedure outputs a set of rules P_V and a set N_V of nonterminal symbols in P_V such that w is derived from P_V. The procedure is nondeterministic: It has choice points, or nondeterministic branches, to which the control backtracks. By nondeterministic selection, we mean that the elements are selected from the set in a predefined order, and the next elements are selected by the backtracking.

This procedure includes a sub-procedure for CYK algorithm. In the sub-procedure, the variable TS is used to keep the *test set* of symbol pairs (β, γ), which are tested whether any rule $A \to \beta\gamma$ can be applied in the execution of the CYK algorithm. Each of the pairs is a candidate of a right part of a newly generated rule. Note that the symbol S is assumed to be the starting symbol in this program.

The algorithm can be used to synthesize rules for unambiguous grammars as well as for ambiguous grammars. For generating unambiguous grammars, when ambiguity is detected, the process fails and causes backtracking as shown in Step 1, 1 (b) of the algorithm in Figure 1.

Inductive CYK Algorithm

Input w: a string, P_0: a set of rules; N: a set of nonterminal symbols in P_0; and K: an integer (the limit of the number of rules).

Output A set of rules from which w is derived and a set of nonterminal symbols in the rules.

Procedure Initialize the variables $P \leftarrow P_0$ (the set of rules), $M \leftarrow |P_0|$ (the limit of the number of rules), and $TS \leftarrow \emptyset$ (the test set).

Repeat Steps 1 and 2 until w is derived from the set of rules. If no set of rules is obtained within the limit M and $M < K$ then $M \leftarrow M + 1$ and restart the process, otherwise the process fails.

Step 1 (Parsing by CYK algorithm: Test whether w is derived from P, and at the same time generate a test set TS, which is used in Step2.)

1. Consider w as the string $a_1 a_2 \cdots a_n$. Find each element $T[i,j]$ of a 2-dimensional array T such that $A \Rightarrow^* a_i \cdots a_{i+j-1}$ for all $A \in T[i,j]$ by iterating the following processes for $2 \le j \le n$ and for $1 \le i \le n - j + 1$.
   (a) $T[i,j] \leftarrow \emptyset$;
   (b) For all k $(1 \le k \le j - 1)$, $B \in T[i,k]$, and $C \in T[i+k, j-k]$, if $(A \to BC) \in P$ then
      - For generating unambiguous grammars, if $A \in T[i,j]$ then backtrack to the previous choice point.
      - $T[i,j] \leftarrow T[i,j] \cup \{A\}$;
      - $TS \leftarrow TS \cup \{(B,C)\}$
2. If $S \in T[1,n]$ (w is derived from P) then output the values P and N.
3. If $|P| = M$ then backtrack to previous choice point.

Step 2 (Generation of rules: Generate a rule $A \to BC$ and add it to P, where (B,C) is a pair contained in the test set TS.)

1. † Nondeterministically select a pair $(B,C) \in TS$.
2. † Nondeterministically select a nonterminal symbol $A \in N$ such that $(A \to BC) \notin P$, or generate a new nonterminal symbol A and add it to N by $N \leftarrow N \cup \{A\}$.
3. $P \leftarrow P \cup \{(A \to BC)\}$.

† Choice points for backtracking.

Fig. 1. Nondeterministic Procedure for Inductive CYK Algorithm

---

The algorithm contains the control for iterative deepening on the number of rules to be generated for each positive sample as follows. In the process of inductive CYK algorithm, the limit (M) on the number of rules is restricted to that of the input set of rules at first. When the system fails to derive the input string from the set of rules within the limit, the system increases the limit by one until the limit K given by the top-level procedure, which is described later.

Inductive CYK algorithm has the following "completeness" property for finding sets of rules.

Theorem 1. *Let w be a string in TT^+, and $G = (N_0, T, P_0, S)$ be any revised Chomsky normal form CFG. Suppose that w is not derived from G, but there is a set P_1 of rules with $P_0 \cap P_1 = \emptyset$ such that w is derived from the CFG $(N_1, T, P_0 \cup P_1, S)$ and all the rules in P_1 are used in the derivation of w. Then, a variant of $P_0 \cup P_1$ in the variable P and a variant of N_1 in N is a result of executing the algorithm with the initial values w, P_0 and N_0.*

If the inputs are $P_0 = \emptyset$ and $N_0 = \{S\}$, a variant of P_1 is a possible result. Note that if P_1 is the minimum set of rules such that w is derived from $P_0 \cap P_1$, then all the rules in P_1 are used in the derivation.

Proof. We prove this theorem by the induction on the number of rules in P_1. For the case that the set P_1 contains exactly one rule $A \rightarrow \beta\gamma$, the algorithm can generate a variant of this rule, since the test set contains the pair (β, γ) at the point after the CYK algorithm fails to obtain S in $T[1, n]$ in the execution with the input values P_0 and N_0. Suppose that the proposition holds for the case $|P_1| = I$ for any $I \geq 1$ and consider the case $|P_1| = I + 1$. Since the test set contains at least a pair (β, γ) for a rule $A \rightarrow \beta\gamma$ in P_1 at the point after the CYK algorithm fails to obtain S in the execution, the algorithm can generate a variant of this rule. By the inductive hypothesis, the algorithm can generate the other rules of P_1. □

In the execution of the inductive CYK algorithm, when the test by CYK algorithm fails, every rule $A \rightarrow \beta\gamma$ is generated for each (β, γ) in the test set TS and for each $A \in N_k$, where N_k is the value of the variable N. The number of possibly generated rules equals to $|TS| \cdot |N_k|$. Hence, the number of all rules which can be generated in the execution is bounded by $(v|N|)^r = O(|N|^{3r})$, where $v \leq (|N| + |T|)^2$ is the maximum number of pairs in the test set, r is the number $|P_1|$ of result rules, and T is the set of terminal symbols. The computation time and the number r are further discussed in Section 5.1.

4   The Search for Sets of Rules and Synapse System

Figure 2 shows the top-level procedure of Synapse. It has inputs of sequences S_P and S_N of positive and negative sample strings, respectively, and an initial set of rules for incremental learning of the grammars.

For learning a grammar only from its positive and negative samples, the empty set is assigned to the initial set of rules. For learning a grammar not only from its samples but also based on the rules of other languages, the rules are given to the top-level procedure as an initial set of rules.

Top-Level Search Algorithm

Input S_P: an ordered set of positive sample strings; S_N: an ordered set of negative
   sample strings; P_0: an initial set of rules; and K_{max}: the limit of the number of
   rules.

Output A set P of rules such that all the strings in S_P are derive from P but
   no string in S_N is derived from P.

Procedure

   Step 1: Initialize variables $P \leftarrow P_0$ (the set of rules), $N \leftarrow \{S\}$ (the set of
   nonterminal symbols), and $K \leftarrow |P_0|$ (the limit of the number of rules).

   Step 2: For each $w \in S_P$, iterate the following steps.

   1. Find a set of rules by calling inductive CYK algorithm with the inputs w,
      P, N and K. Assign the results to P and N.
   2. For each $v \in S_N$, test whether v is derived from P by CYK algorithm. If
      there is a string v derived from P, then backtrack to the previous choice
      point.

   If no set of rules is obtained, then

   1. If $K \geq K_{max}$ terminate (no set of rules is obtained within the limit K_{max}).
   2. Otherwise, add 1 to K and restart Step 2.

   Step 3: Output the result P.

   For finding all the solutions, backtrack to the previous choice point. For finding
   a solution, terminate.

Fig. 2. Nondeterministic Procedure for the Search

For inputs of any sets S_P and S_N of positive and negative sample strings,
respectively, with $S_P, S_N \subseteq TT^*, S_P \cap S_N = \emptyset$, and an initial set of rules P_0,
the top-level procedure searches for the set P of rules and set N of nonterminal
symbols such that $S_P \subseteq L(G)$ and $S_N \cap L(G) = \emptyset$ for a CFG $G = (N, T, P \cup
P_0, S)$. If the procedure of inductive CYK algorithm includes the ambiguity check
then the CFG G is weakly ambiguous for the strings in S_P.

The procedure contains a control for iterative deepening on the number of
rules to be generated. First, the number of the rules in the initial set of rules
is assigned to the limit (K) of the number of rules. When the system fails to
satisfy the samples within this limit, it increases the limit by one and iterates
the search. By this control, it is assured that the procedure finds a grammar
with the minimum number of rules at the expense that the system repeats the
same search each time the limit is increased.

Synapse system is an implementation of the procedures in the previous section. In addition to heuristics described so far, the system employs the following
heuristics to improve the search efficiency.

1. **Intelligent backtracking** This is a well-known technique in logic programming for efficient computation using backtracking. Consider the case that by
   adding two or more newly generated rules, a positive sample is derived from
   the set of rules but some negative sample is also derived from this set of
   rules. In this case, instead of a rule R of the generated rules, another rule

may be generated in redoing process, but the rule R is not be used in the derivation of the negative sample. To avoid this ineffectiveness, the system tests each of the rules in backtracking whether the negative sample is not derived from the set of rules without this rule, and regenerates a rule, only if the test succeeds. By adding this heuristics, the synthesis speed increased by several times as fast as before.

2. **Limitation on the form of generated rules** In inductive CYK algorithm, when the system generates a rule with a new symbol in the left hand side, this rule is not effective until a rule containing A in the right hand side is also generated. Therefore, after generating a rule of the form $A \to \beta\gamma$ with a new symbol A, we can restrict the rule generation not to terminate until a rule of the form either $B \to A\eta$ or $B \to \eta A$ is generated. This implies that when the system generates a rule containing a new nonterminal symbol, it needs to generate at least two rules. By adding this heuristics, the synthesis speed increased by a factor of two to twenty in most cases.

5 Performance Results

In all the experiments, we used Synapse system written in C++ and compiled by Windows version Borland C++ Compiler running on AMD Athron processor with 1 GHz clock. We checked the correctness of all the synthesized grammars.

5.1 Learning Grammars Only from Their Sample Strings

Table 1 shows ambiguous and unambiguous grammars synthesized by Synapse and the computation time in seconds. In the experiments, the positive and negative samples are sequences of all strings within a certain length, typically from five to seven. The sequences are sorted by their length. For example, the positive and negative samples for the language (a), $a^m b^n (1 \le m \le n)$, are as follows.

$$\text{Positive}: ab, abb, aabb, abbb, aabbb, abbbb, aaabbb, \cdots,$$
$$\text{Negative}: aa, ba, bb, aaa, aab, aba, baa, bab, bba, bbb, \cdots,$$

The grammars for the languages (b), (c), (d) and (e) are solutions to exercise problem in the textbook by Hopcroft & Ullman (1979), where the language (e) is the set of strings over $\{a, b\}^+$ containing the same number of a's and b's, and (f) is the set of strings containing twice as many b's as a's. In the grammar for the language (c) of the set of regular expression, symbols a and b are denoted by aa and bb, respectively, to reduce the number of the rules in revised Chomsky normal form.

Synapse found only ambiguous grammars for the languages (e) and (f) and it could not find any unambiguous grammars for these languages. We have a conjecture that the languages (e) and (f) are strictly ambiguous. Although Synapse found an unambiguous grammar of the regular expressions (c), we would need some additional information other than the sample strings for synthesizing a proper unambiguous grammar for this language.

Table 1. Grammars synthesized by Synapse (Computation time in second).

Language		Set of rules	R	Time	GR	r
(a) $a^m b^n$ $(1 \leq m \leq n)$	A	$S \rightarrow ab \mid Sb \mid aC,\ C \rightarrow Sb$	4	< 1	73	2
	U	$S \rightarrow ab \mid aD \mid cB,$ $C \rightarrow ab \mid Cb,\ D \rightarrow Sb$	6	< 1	1498	3
(b) balanced parentheses	A	$S \rightarrow (\ ) \mid C\ ) \mid SS,\ C \rightarrow (\ S$	4	< 1	245	2
	U	$S \rightarrow (\ ) \mid C\ ),$ $C \rightarrow S(\ \mid (\ S \mid DS,\ D \rightarrow S($	6	4	18023	2
(c) regular expressions	A	$S \rightarrow aa \mid bb \mid S* \mid SS \mid G\ ) \mid HS,$ $G \rightarrow (\ S,\ H \rightarrow S+$	8	2	56672	2
(d) $w = w^R$ $w \in \{a,b\}\{a,b\}^+$	A	$S \rightarrow aa \mid bb \mid bD \mid Ca,$ $C \rightarrow aa \mid ab \mid aS,$	10	13	9.4×10^4	2
	(U)	$D \rightarrow ab \mid bb \mid Sb$	(7)	(7)	(5.9×10^4)	(2)
(e) $\#_a(w) = \#_b(w)$	A	$S \rightarrow ab \mid ba \mid bC \mid Cb \mid SS,$ $C \rightarrow aS \mid Sa$	7	2	6534	2
(f) $2\#_a(w) = \#_b(w)$	A	$S \rightarrow bC \mid Cb \mid SS,$ $C \rightarrow ab \mid ba \mid bD \mid Db,$ $D \rightarrow aS \mid Sa$	9	75	1.4×10^6	2

A: ambiguous grammar.   U: unambiguous grammar.
w^R: the reversal of w. $\#_a(w)$: the number of a's in the string w.
R: the number of rules in the grammar.   GR: the number of all generated rules.
r: the maximum number of rules generated for one positive sample.

The results of the experiments can be summarized as follows.

1. **Computation time** The computation time varies considerably depending on the samples, especially the number and the selection of the negative sample strings. By selecting proper samples, we can reduce the computation time shown in Table 1.
2. **Parameters determining the computation time** The computation time is closely related to two parameters. One is the number of generated rules, GR, which represents the size of nodes in the search tree. This value is not so dependent on the number of samples as the computation time, unless the samples are insufficient to synthesize the grammars. The other is the maximum number r of rules which are generated for satisfying one positive sample. To keep this parameter small, shorter positive samples are placed before the longer strings. If longer positive samples are given first, the parameter r has larger values and the computation time increases in general.
3. **Ambiguous and unambiguous grammars** In general, unambiguous grammars require more rules than ambiguous grammars, and synthesis of unambiguous grammars requires longer time. The language (d) of balanced parentheses is an exception: The result of synthesizing an ambiguous grammar is the same as that of unambiguous grammar and the computation time for the ambiguous grammar is longer. We consider that this is because the

condition for the ambiguity in the CYK algorithm is effective in restricting the search.

5.2   Learning Grammars Based on Grammars of Similar Languages

Example 1: Languages composed of two subset languages This is also a language of the problems in Hopcroft & Ullman. Synapse could not directly synthesize the language

$$\{a^i b^j c^k \mid i = j \text{ or } j = k, \ i, j, k \geq 1\}$$

in a reasonable amount of time. On the other hand, by giving the grammars of its subsets,

$$L_1 = \{a^i b^i c^k \mid \ i, k \geq 1\},$$
$$L_2 = \{a^i b^j c^j \mid \ i, j \geq 1\}$$

as the initial set of rules, the system generates the grammar of $L_1 \cup L_2$. Each of the following grammars of L_1 and L_2 are obtained in less than one second (GR = 691).

$$L_1 : S_1 \rightarrow aF \mid aS_1, \ F \rightarrow bc \mid Gc, \ G \rightarrow bF.$$
$$L_2 : S_2 \rightarrow Dc \mid S_2c, \ D \rightarrow ab \mid Eb, \ E \rightarrow aD.$$

Given these grammars and the sample strings, Synapse found the remaining rules

$$S \rightarrow aF \mid aS_1 \mid Dc \mid S_2c$$

of the grammar of $L_1 \cup L_2$ in approximately 10 seconds (GR = 3.8×10^5).

Example 2: The set of strings containing more b's than a's For the language

$$\{w \in \{a, b\}^+ \mid \#_a(w) < \#_b(w), \ |w| \geq 2\},$$

Synapse generates the following set of rules in approximately 35 seconds (GR = 4.3×10^5).

$$S \rightarrow SC \mid Sb \mid bb \mid bC \mid Cb, \ C \rightarrow Sa \mid aS \mid ab \mid ba$$

By giving the grammar for the similar language (e), the set of strings containing the same number of a's and b's, as the initial set of rules, Synapse generated the following additional rules in less than one second (GR = 2524).

$$S \rightarrow Sb \mid SS_1 \mid bb \mid bS_1 \mid S_1b,$$

where S_1 is the starting symbol of the grammar for language (e). Note that the number of the total rules $7 + 5 = 9$ is larger, but the total computation time is much less, than those of the directly obtained grammar.

6   Conclusion

We described methods of synthesizing context free grammars, which is a revised and improved version of that presented in our previous paper [3]. Our grammatical inference is based on inductive CYK algorithm, incremental learning and search with iterative deepening to generate sets of effective production rules for deriving positive sample strings.

The most important feature of our approach would be incremental learning to synthesize new grammars by adding production rules to any existing grammars. Synapse not only synthesizes a grammar from its sample strings, but also synthesizes a grammar from grammars of similar or related languages in addition to the samples as shown in the previous section. This can be considered as a method for dividing problems into sub-problems, or the learning based on background knowledge.

Synapse system can synthesize several ambiguous and unambiguous context free grammars in a rather short time. Synthesized grammars include those of five languages among six exercise problems in the text book by Hopcroft and Ullman[1] [1]. In one of the problems, the grammar of the language $\{a^i b^j c^k \mid i = j \text{ or } j = k, \ i, j, k \geq 1\}$ was synthesized by the incremental learning from its subsets as shown in the previous section.

As far as the authors know, no other practical system can synthesize the example CFGs in the previous section. By improving the inductive CYK algorithm and introducing the heuristics described in Sections 3 and 4, the computation speed in the latest version of Synapse is more than 100 times faster than the first version reported in [3], and hence it can synthesize a broader class of CFGs. A current restriction of Synapse is that it has not synthesized grammars with more than about 12 rules only from their samples. An approach to solve this problem is the incremental learning based on the similar grammars.

We are working on improving Synapse system written in C++ and developing another version of Synapse system written in Prolog. The other future problems and/or open problems are as follows.

- Improving the efficiency of the system and theoretical analysis of the synthesis methods.
- Extending the induction methods in order to synthesize other classes of grammars including regular grammars and CFGs with standard Chomsky normal form.
- Developing methods for representing semantics in sample strings. This is necessary, for example, to synthesize an unambiguous CFG of arithmetic expressions as well as the regular expressions as mentioned in Section 5.1.
- Applying our approaches to other machine learning such as inductive logic programming.

---

[1] The remaining language in the exercise problems is the complement of the double word language $\{ww \mid w \in \{a, b\}^+\}$.

Acknowledgements

The author thanks Professor Yasubumi Sakakibara for his encouragement and valuable discussions, and Takashi Ishiwata and Satoru Yoshioka for their help in writing and testing Synapse system.

References

1. J. E. Hopcroft, and J. E. Ullman, *Introduction to Automata Theory, Languages, and Computation*, Addison-Wesley (1979).
2. P. Langley and S. Stromsten, Learning Context-Free Grammars with a Simplicity Bias, *Machine Learning: ECML 2000*, LNAI 1810, Springer-Verlag, 220 – 228 (2000).
3. K. Nakamura, and Y. Ishiwata, Synthesizing context free grammars from sample strings based on inductive CYK algorithm, *Fifth International Colloquium on Grammatical Inference (ICGI 2000)*, LNAI 1891, Springer-Verlag, 186 – 195 (2000).
4. R. Parekh, and V. Honavor, An incremental interactive algorithm for regular grammar inference, *Third International Colloquium on Grammatical Inference (ICGI-96)*, 222–237 (1996).
5. Y. Sakakibara, Recent advances of grammatical inference, *Theoretical Computer Science, 185*, 15–45 (1997).
6. Y. Sakakibara, and M. Kondo, GA-based learning of context-free grammars using tabular representations, *Proc. 16th International Conference of Machine Learning*, 354–360 (1999).
7. Y. Sakakibara, and H. Muramatsu, Learning of context-free grammars partially structured examples, *Fifth International Colloquium on Grammatical Inference (ICGI 2000)*, LNAI 1891, Springer-Verlag, 229 – 240 (2000).

Estimating Grammar Parameters
Using Bounded Memory

Tim Oates[1] and Brent Heeringa[2]

[1] Department of Computer Science and Electrical Engineering. University of Maryland
Baltimore County. 1000 Hilltop Circle. Baltimore, MD 21250
oates@eecs.umbc.edu
[2] Department of Computer Science. University of Massachusetts, Amherst.
Amherst, MA 01003
heeringa@cs.umass.edu

Abstract. Estimating the parameters of stochastic context-free grammars
(SCFGs) from data is an important, well-studied problem. Almost without exception, existing approaches make repeated passes over the training data. The
memory requirements of such algorithms are ill-suited for embedded agents exposed to large amounts of training data over long periods of time. We present a
novel algorithm, called HOLA, for estimating the parameters of SCFGs that computes summary statistics for each string as it is observed and then discards the
string. The memory used by HOLA is bounded by the size of the grammar, not
by the amount of training data. Empirical results show that HOLA performs as
well as the Inside-Outside algorithm on a variety of standard problems, despite
the fact that it has access to much less information.

1   Introduction

Stochastic context-free grammars (SCFGs) are perhaps best known as a tool for ex-
pressing the syntactic structure of natural languages. However, their utility extends well
beyond this one domain. In recent years SCFGs have been widely applied to problems
in computational biology, such as modeling the secondary structure of RNA families
[1]. Other applications include visual recognition of activities and language modeling
for speech recognition [2].

A problem of central importance in each of these applications is inducing SCFGs
from data. Solutions to this problem almost always have the following two properties:
(1) they make multiple passes through the data, often expending significant computation during each pass and (2) they require large amounts of data to accurately estimate
production probabilities. One experiment reported in the literature used the 30 million
word Wall Street Journal corpus to estimate the parameters of an English grammar [3].
The memory requirements of such algorithms are ill-suited for embedded agents exposed to large amounts of training data over long periods of time. If children induced
syntax in this manner they would have to memorize a large number of the utterances to
which they are exposed, decide at some point to run an algorithm for inducing a grammar from these utterances, and then suddenly have knowledge of the syntax of their
native language.

P. Adriaans, H. Fernau, and M. van Zaanen (Eds.): ICGI 2002, LNAI 2484, pp. 185–198, 2002.

The goal of our work is to develop algorithms for inducing SCFGs from data that have bounded memory requirements and that learn via incremental computation. The former requirement implies that the amount of memory consumed by the algorithm must remain fixed, regardless of the number of strings supplied as input. The latter requirement implies that improvement in the grammar can occur with small amounts of computation and that the quality of the grammar improves monotonically as more computation is allocated to learning. This paper introduces an algorithm called HOLA that satisfies both of these requirements. The novel approach taken by HOLA is justified theoretically, and empirical results show that HOLA performs just as well as the Inside-Outside algorithm in estimating the parameters of SCFGs from data despite the fact that it has access to a bounded amount of information.

2 Background

Following Hopcroft and Ullman [4], a *context-free grammar* (CFG) is a four-tuple $G = (N, \Sigma, P, S)$ where N is a finite set of non-terminals, Σ is a finite set of terminals, P is a finite set of productions or rules, and $S \in N$ is the start symbol. N and Σ are disjoint. Elements of P are of the form $X \to \alpha$ where $X \in N$ and $\alpha \in (N \cup \Sigma)^*$. The language accepted by G, denoted $L(G)$, is a subset of Σ^*. A grammar is said to be *ambiguous* if for some string $w \in L(G)$ there is more than one way to derive w from S.

A stochastic context-free grammar is a CFG where each production is augmented with a probability. The probability associated with production $X \to \alpha$ is denoted $p(X \to \alpha)$. The probabilities of all the productions that expand any given non-terminal must sum to one. The CFG underlying a SCFG is called the SCFG's *structure*, and the probabilities are called its *parameters*. The parameters of a SCFG are denoted Θ. SCFGs define a probability distribution over strings. The probability of a string given a SCFG is the sum over each derivation of the string of the product of the probabilities of the productions used in the derivation.

Given the structure of an unambiguous SCFG it is easy to determine the maximum likelihood parameters for a given training set, i.e. those parameters that maximize the probability of the data given the grammar. Let D be a derivation of some string in the training data and let $c(X \to \alpha | D)$ be the number of times that production $X \to \alpha$ occurs in D. The maximum likelihood estimate of a production's probability is as follows:

$$\hat{p}(X \to \alpha) = \frac{\sum_D c(X \to \alpha | D)}{\sum_D \sum_{X \to \beta} c(X \to \beta | D)}$$

When a grammar is ambiguous there may be many derivations for a given string in the training data and there is no way to know which one was actually used to generate the string. Strings are observable but the actual derivation used to generate a string is hidden. The Inside-Outside algorithm [5, 6] uses Expectation Maximization [7] to solve this hidden data problem. In the expectation step, a weighted sum is computed for each production of the number of times it occurs in the derivations of strings in the training data, with derivation probabilities serving as the weights:

$$\hat{c}(X \to \alpha) = \frac{\sum_D p(D|G) c(X \to \alpha | D)}{\sum_D p(D|G)}$$

In the maximization step, these expected counts are used to compute new parameter estimates:

$$\hat{p}(X \rightarrow \alpha) = \frac{\hat{c}(X \rightarrow \alpha)}{\sum_{X \rightarrow \beta} \hat{c}(X \rightarrow \beta)}$$

The Inside-Outside algorithm is the gold standard for accuracy of parameter estimates. Other algorithms have been devised for estimating the parameters of SCFGs, such as HOLA, that address limitations of Inside-Outside. But no algorithm has been shown to do consistently better with respect to parameter estimation.

Two approaches that are especially relevant to the research described herein are Neal and Hinton's incremental EM [8] and Boyen and Koller's online EM [9]. The idea behind incremental EM is to speed the convergence of standard EM by running a complete M step after the expected value of each hidden variable is computed, corresponding to a single data item, rather than waiting until the expected values of all hidden variables are computed. Doing so makes information available to the M step more quickly and is shown empirically to speed convergence. That is, incremental EM requires fewer passes through the data than standard EM. The algorithm can be used in an online setting by repeatedly obtaining a new data item, running a partial E step, and discarding the item. However, this greatly increases the total number of data items that must be observed and may not be practical when large amounts of data are required for batch parameter estimation. As previously noted, accurately estimating the parameters of SCFGs often requires large amounts of training data, thereby making incremental EM less attractive.

Boyen and Koller's online EM is based on Neal and Hinton's incremental EM and therefore shares its shortcomings with respect to SCFG parameter estimation. In addition, online EM was applied to parameter learning in dynamic Bayesian networks, a representation that admitted effective belief state approximations, and it is unclear whether the approach is feasible for SCFGs as well.

3 Motivation

The number of times a grammar's productions occur in derivations of strings in the training data plays an important role in parameter estimation. For unambiguous grammars these counts are sufficient for recovering the maximum likelihood parameter estimates. For ambiguous grammars the Inside-Outside algorithm weights the counts by derivation probabilities, a computation that requires storage linear in the size of the training data.

The idea behind HOLA is to use unweighted counts to drive the search for parameters, regardless of whether the grammar is ambiguous or unambiguous. The counts are a function of two things – the structure of the grammar and the training data. The parameters of the learned grammar do not enter into their computation. However, because the training data are sampled according to the distribution over strings defined by the target grammar, the parameters of that grammar do affect the counts. HOLA attempts to find a set of parameters that, given a fixed structure, will generate strings that yield the same (or similar) counts as the training data. Because HOLA keeps a counter for each production in the grammar rather than a set of derivations for the strings in the training data, its memory requirements are linear in the size of the grammar regardless of the size of the training corpus.

The natural way to formulate the search for a set of parameters is in terms of gradient descent. Doing so requires a function that maps from grammars (both structure and parameters) and counts to an error term that indicates how similar the counts are to those that would result from sampling from the grammar. Taking the partial derivative of this function with respect to the parameters of the grammar would make it possible to perform gradient descent in parameter space. The main result of this section is a proof that such a function is not computable and must therefore be approximated.

Given a set of counts, C_1, and a grammar, G, we want to compute the counts, C_2, that would result from sampling from G so that C_1 and C_2 may be compared.

Definition 1. *Let $\phi(X \rightarrow \alpha, G)$ be a function that computes the expected number of times production $X \rightarrow \alpha$ will occur in the derivation(s) of a string in $L(G)$ sampled according to the distribution over strings defined by stochastic context-free grammar G:*

$$\phi(X \rightarrow \alpha, G) = \sum_{s \in L(G)} p(s|G) \left(\sum_{D \text{ of } s} c(X \rightarrow \alpha|D) \right)$$

The following lemma will be useful in proving the main theoretical result of this section. It says that for any stochastic context-free grammar G it is possible to create a new grammar G' that has certain desirable properties.

Lemma 1. *Let $G = (N, \Sigma, P, S)$ be a SCFG. Create grammar $G' = (N', \Sigma', P', S')$ from G as follows. Let $N' = N \cup S'$ where $S' \notin N$ and S' is the start symbol of G'. Let $\Sigma' = \Sigma$ and let $P' = P \cup S' \rightarrow S$ where $p(S' \rightarrow S) = 1$. The following are true:*

(1) $L(G') = L(G)$
(2) $p(w|G') = p(w|G)$ for all $w \in L(G)$
(3) $c(S' \rightarrow S|D) = 1$ for any valid derivation D

Proof: By construction, every derivation of a string in $L(G')$ starts by expanding S' to S, where S is the start symbol of G. Therefore, any string that can be derived from S can be derived from S'. Because the productions of G' are identical to those of G except for the one involving S', the derivation(s) of w from S and S' will be identical except for the initial application of $S' \rightarrow S$ in the latter case. Because the derivation(s) are the same (after generating S in G') for the two grammars and because $p(S' \rightarrow S) = 1$ the probabilities of the strings will be the same. □

Now we are in a position to prove the following theorem.

Theorem 1. *The function ϕ is not computable for an arbitrary production in an arbitrary stochastic context-free grammar.*

Proof: Suppose that ϕ is computable. Let G' be the grammar constructed as described in Lemma 1 for some stochastic context-free grammar G. The construction of G' ensures that $c(S' \rightarrow S) = 1$ for every derivation. Consider $\phi(S' \rightarrow S, G')$, if G is unambiguous

Θ	observed	norm	sample	norm
$S \rightarrow A$ [0.5]	4	0.57	3	0.60
$S \rightarrow B$ [0.5]	3	0.43	2	0.40
$A \rightarrow y$ [0.5]	1	0.25	1	0.33
$A \rightarrow z$ [0.5]	3	0.75	2	0.67
$B \rightarrow z$ [1.0]	3	1.00	2	1.00

Fig. 1. A grammar that generates the language $\{y\,z\}$. Both observed and normalized counts are provided for a bag of strings containing one y and three z's.

then so is G', in which case the inner sum in Definition 1 is one for all strings in $L(G')$ and we have the following:

$$\phi(S' \rightarrow S, G') = \sum_{s \in L(G')} p(s|G')$$
$$= 1$$

If G is ambiguous then there is more than one derivation for some string in $L(G)$ and thus more than one derivation for some string in $L(G')$, in which case the inner sum in Definition 1 is greater than one for that string and $\phi(S' \rightarrow S, G') > 1$. That is, we can use the value of $\phi(S' \rightarrow S, G')$ to decide whether or not G is ambiguous. However, it is undecidable whether an arbitrary CFG is ambiguous [4]. This is a contradiction, so ϕ is not computable. □

The import of Theorem 1 is that we cannot hope to perform gradient descent in parameter space analytically. As described in the next section, HOLA uses sampling to overcome this hurdle.

4   Algorithm Description

This section outlines the HOLA algorithm, gives examples of its execution, and discusses enhancements and improvements. In contrast to other learning algorithms, HOLA does not use the observation (i.e., training) data directly to estimate grammar parameters. Rather, learning is done indirectly by finding parameters that generate strings similar to the those observed. To this end, HOLA exploits the generative nature of grammars as a means for learning.

The HOLA algorithm is given in Figure 2. HOLA attempts to recover the parameters of the grammar generating the observation data. We call this the *target* grammar. The structure of the target grammar is given to the algorithm, but the initial parameters are set by random assignment or pre-training. We call the structure and current parameter estimates the *learning* grammar. Given a learning grammar G and a set of strings S generated from the target grammar, HOLA learns a set of parameters that generate strings statistically equivalent to the observed data.

First, HOLA finds the derivation of each string in S with respect to the grammar. This process is called parsing and occurs in the HOLACOUNT subroutine of the algorithm.

HOLA(*scfg,strings*)
1. HOLACOUNT(*scfg,strings*)
2. UNLESS STOPPINGCRITERION(*scfg*)
3.   HOLAITERATION(*grammar*)

HOLACOUNT(*scfg,strings*)
1. *derivations* ← PARSE(*scfg,S*)
2. FOREACH *d* in *derivations*
3.   FOREACH *r* in *scfg.rules*
4.   *r.observed* ← *r.observed* + COUNT(*r, d*)
5. NORMALIZEOBSERVEDCOUNTS(*scfg*)

HOLAITERATION(*scfg*)
1. *sampleStrings* ← SAMPLE(*scfg*)
1. *derivations* ← PARSE(*scfg,sampleStrings*)
2. FOREACH *d* in *derivations*
3.   FOREACH *r* in *scfg.rules*
4.   *r.sample* ← *r.sample* + COUNT(*r, d*)
5. NORMALIZESAMPLECOUNTS(*scfg*)
6. UPDATEPARAMETERS(*scfg*)

Fig. 2. The HOLA algorithm.

Parsing is a function of the grammar structure, not the parameters. When the grammar is ambiguous, multiple derivations may exist for a single string. For example, consider the grammar in Figure 1 and the set of strings $\{y\,z\,z\,z\}$. The string y has a single derivation, $S \to A \to y$, but z has two derivations, $S \to A \to z$ and $S \to B \to z$. Each possible derivation indicates what rules were used in generating the string. HOLA finds the total occurrences of each rule in all the derivations, records them, and then disposes of them. We call these *observed* counts since they come from the observed data. Because HOLA searches for parameter estimates that produce strings with counts similar to those observed, we need a general way to compare counts. For comparison, HOLA normalizes the counts with respect to rules with the same left-hand-side. Only the normalized count for each rule is stored. The observed counts are not updated, but stay fixed throughout the rest of HOLA's execution. Both the observed and normalized counts for the data discussed above are given in Figure 1.

Next, HOLA iterates through a generate and update cycle until a stopping criterion is met. This corresponds to the HOLAITERATION subroutine in the algorithm. This procedure is nearly identical to HOLACOUNT except for two differences. First, the observed data is replaced with a small sample of strings generated from the grammar. This sample reflects the current parameter estimates. For example, generating a sample of size three from the grammar in Figure 1 will probably result in two z's and one y. Second, counts taken from the sample are stored separately from the observed counts. At the end of the generation phase, each rule r has two counts $r.observed$ and $r.sample$. The pairwise similarity of these counts indicates the similarity in the current parameter estimates and the target parameters. HOLA updates each rule according to these differences:

$$p(r) = p(r) * (1 + \alpha * (r.observed - r.sample))$$

Note that when the sample counts are smaller than the observed counts, the rule probability increases. When the sample counts are larger, the rule probability decreases. The change in parameter estimates potentially changes the strings we would expect to see when generating a sample from the grammar during the next iteration. These changes in turn move the parameters toward more likely estimates. The step-size parameter α helps learning narrow in on the correct parameter estimates. However, since each iteration generates a set of strings, convergence to maximum likelihood estimates probably does not happen because of sample variance.

5   Experiments

This section shows empirically that HOLA learns good parameter estimates using bounded memory. We performed three experiments: two on unambiguous grammars generating English phrases and palindromes and one on a small ambiguous grammar. In each experiment we fixed the structure of the target grammar and conducted 50 independent trials, randomly generating the target parameters in each case. A trial consists of generating 1000 strings of observation data from the target grammar. Next a learning grammar is created by taking the structure of the target grammar and reinitializing it with new random parameters. Finally, copies of the learning grammar are handed along with the observation data to both HOLA and the Inside-Outside algorithm.

The Inside-Outside algorithm is known to converge to a set of parameters that locally maximize the likelihood of the data. We show HOLA performs comparably to the Inside-Outside algorithm even though it uses less information and requires only bounded memory. This evaluation of the learned parameter estimates is accomplished by finding the log-likelihood of the data given the grammar and the learned parameters.

5.1   English Phrases

We used the English phrase grammar taken from Cook, Rosenfeld and Aronson [10] in Figure 3 in our first experiment. This grammar is unambiguous and does not contain any recursive rules, however, it is comparable in size to other grammars used in the literature for grammatical inference (e.g., [11]). We ran HOLA for 100 iterations using a sample size of 100 and decreasing the step-size parameter by 10% every 10 iterations. We allowed the Inside-Outside algorithm to run until convergence. HOLA performed well in comparison to the Inside-Outside algorithm in all trials. Figure 4 gives the percentage difference between HOLA and the Inside-Outside algorithm with respect to the log-likelihood of the data given the learned parameters. In all trials the difference in performance was less than one percent; in over half the trials, the difference was less than two-tenths of one percent. The mean difference was 0.166 percent, the variance only 0.017 percent. In most cases the total difference in true log-likelihood was fractional. We expect the differences will converge to zero once a suitable method for reducing sample variance is incorporated into HOLA. Empirically, though, HOLA tends to find parameter estimates strikingly similar to those found by the Inside-Outside algorithm.

$$
\begin{array}{rcl}
S & \rightarrow & I \quad am \; A \\
S & \rightarrow & he \quad T \\
S & \rightarrow & she \quad T \\
S & \rightarrow & it \quad T \\
S & \rightarrow & they \quad V \\
S & \rightarrow & you \quad V \\
S & \rightarrow & we \quad V \\
S & \rightarrow & this \quad C \\
S & \rightarrow & that \quad C \\
T & \rightarrow & is \quad A \\
V & \rightarrow & are \quad A \\
Z & \rightarrow & man \\
Z & \rightarrow & woman \\
A & \rightarrow & there \\
A & \rightarrow & here \\
C & \rightarrow & is \quad a \; Z \\
C & \rightarrow & Z \quad T
\end{array}
$$

Fig. 3. A grammar generating English strings from Book, Rosenfeld and Aronson

HOLA is also robust to differences in initial parameter settings. Applying linear regression to the trials plotted as a function of performance difference and sorted initial loglikelihood results in a near horizontal line (see Figure 5 with $r^2 = 0.03$. This means little correlation exists between HOLA's performance and the initial log-likelihood.

Figure 6 shows the learning curve over 100 iterations for trial 1. Note that by iteration 40, HOLA has settled in on good parameter estimates. Each subsequent iteration walks locally around the maximum likelihood probably due to sample variance.

5.2 Palindromes

The second experiment involved the palindrome-generating grammar in Figure 7. This grammar is unambiguous and contains two self-referential rules. HOLA ran for 300 iterations while decreasing the step-size by 5% every 10 trials. The results in Figure 8 show that in all trials, HOLA's performance differs from the Inside-Outside algorithm by less than one-half of one percent. In three quarters of the trials, the performance difference was less than one-tenth of one percent. The mean percentage difference is 0.07, the variance 0.009. Like the first experiment, HOLA learns parameter estimates only fractions away from those learned by Inside-Outside algorithm.

5.3 Ambiguous Grammars

Our final experiment used the simple ambiguous grammar discussed previously in Figure 1. We ran HOLA for 100 iterations with the step-size parameter decreasing every 10 iterations by 5%. Like in the other experiments, HOLA performs almost identically to the Inside-Outside algorithm. In all the trials, save three, the percentage difference in log-likelihood was less than half a percent. In an overwhelming majority of cases, the

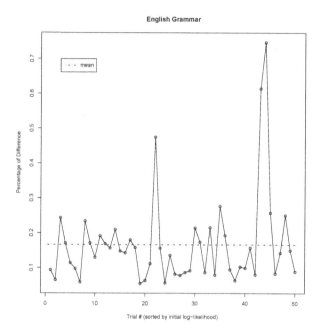

Fig. 4. The percentage difference in log-likelihood between HOLA and the Inside-Outside algorithm for 50 trials using the English phrase grammar.

difference was less than one-tenth of one percent. The mean difference in percentage was 0.17, however, if we remove the three outliers the mean falls to 0.03. The variance was 0.34, however, removing the outliers significantly reduces it to 0.002.

The higher difference in the three outliers occurs because learning isn't finished. For example, consider the farthest outlier, trial 2. Here, the negative log-likelihood after 100 iterations is around 192. The local maximum likelihood is 186.56. If we allow learning to continue for 200 more iterations, HOLA finds better parameter estimates resulting in a negative log-likelihood of 186.82 – only fractionally different from those found by the Inside-Outside algorithm.

6   Discussion

Consider again the example grammar given in Figure 10. We know every SCFG defines a probability distribution over the language of the grammar. In this case the distribution is $p(y) = .3$ and $p(z) = .7$. Said differently, if we generate 10 sentences from our grammar, we expect to see three y's and seven z's. In fact, the bag of strings containing three y's and seven z's is the smallest corpus completely representative of the probability distribution provided by Θ. That said, note that the observed counts of each rule, when suitably normalized, are poor estimators of the original parameters. This is because the grammar is ambiguous. Furthermore, setting Θ to the normalized counts yields a com-

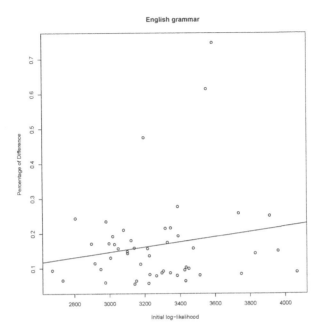

Fig. 5. Percentage of difference in performance versus sorted initial log-likelihood on the English phrase grammar. The line is a linear fit of the data.

pletely different probability distribution over the language; $p(y) \approx .18$ and $p(z) \approx .82$. But, recall that HOLA does not use the counts directly, but rather attempts to find parameter estimates where the sample normalized counts are equivalent to the observed normalized counts—parameters that result in the *observed* probability distribution over the language.

If we let $p_1 = p(S \rightarrow A)$ and $p_2 = p(A \rightarrow y)$ then $1 - p_1 = p(S \rightarrow B)$ and $1 - p_2 = p(A \rightarrow z)$. Any parameterization $p_1, p_2 \in [0, 1]$ satisfying $p_1 p_2 = 0.30$ results in a probability distribution over the language where y's occur 30% of the time and z's 70%. Clearly these parameters may vary significantly from those in Θ. However, from a generative view, they are good estimators since the expected output is equivalent to the generating grammar.

One natural question is: *Does a parameterization Θ' exist for a grammar such that the normalized counts are the same but the probability distribution over the language is different?* For the grammar at hand the answer is 'no.' The only way y can be generated is through an application of $A \rightarrow y$, so we know the normalized count for $A \rightarrow y$ is $p(y)$. This means the normalized count for $A \rightarrow z$ is $p(z) = 1 - p(y)$. Since $S \rightarrow B$ is counted with the same frequency as $A \rightarrow z$, its normalized count is $p(z)/(1.0 + p(z))$; the 1.0 in the denominator is added because $S \rightarrow A$ can derive the entire language. This means $S \rightarrow A$ has a normalized count of $1/(2 - p(y))$. It's clear for this grammar that the probability distribution over the language corresponds linearly with the nor-

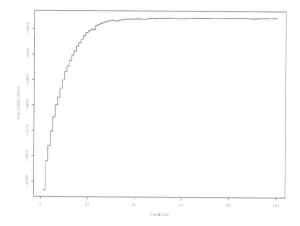

Fig. 6. HOLA's learning curve in trial 1 of the English phrase grammar.

$$
\begin{array}{ccl}
S & \to & A\ S\ A \\
S & \to & B\ S\ B \\
S & \to & A\ A \\
S & \to & B\ B \\
S & \to & A \\
S & \to & B \\
A & \to & y \\
B & \to & z \\
\end{array}
$$

Fig. 7. A grammar generating palindromes over the alphabet $\{y\ z\}$

malized counts. This means fixing the counts results in only one possible probability distribution over the language. To the best of our knowledge, whether this is true for all stochastic context-free grammars is still an open question. We suspect that grammars exist where multiple parameter estimates lead to different probability distributions over the language while still resulting in identical rule counts, but these estimates locally maximize the likelihood of the data.

7 Conclusion

The HOLA algorithm raises and addresses some interesting theoretical and empirical questions. First, it incrementally learns likely parameter estimates of stochastic context-free grammars using bounded space. Such algorithms are developmentally more plausible and applicable in domains where large amounts of data are encountered and processed over long periods of time. Second HOLA shows that using the generative nature of grammars helps capriole the hurdle of analytically determing rule counts. At the same time, sample variance hinders convergence but we're confident that future work will address and solve this problem. Still, empricial evidence shows that the Inside-Outside algorithm, known to converge to parameters that are locally maximum, performs only fractionally better than HOLA. Finally, we discussed the quality of the learned estimates,

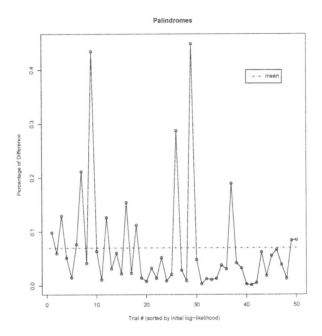

Fig. 8. The percentage difference in log-likelihood between HOLA and the Inside-Outside algorithm for 50 trials with the palindrome grammar.

specifically asking where in parameter space estimates that produce counts similar to the data lie. While emprically the estimates move toward local maximum likelihood locations, in the future we hope to show theoretical proof of such convergence.

8   Acknowledgements

Mark Johnson supplied a nice implementation of the inside-outside algorithm.

This research is supported by DARPA/USASMDC under contract number DASG60-99-C-0074. The U.S. Government is authorized to reproduce and distribute reprints for governmental purposes notwithstanding any copyright notation hereon. The views and conclusions contained herein are those of the authors and should not be interpreted as necessarily representing the official policies or endorsements either expressed or implied, of DARPA/USASMDC or the U.S. Government.

References

[1] Sakakibara, Y., Brown, M., Highey, R., Mian, I.S., Sjolander, K., Haussler, D.: Stochastic context-free grammars for tRNA modeling. Nucleic Acids Research **22** (1994) 5112–5120
[2] Jurafsky, D., Wooters, C., Segal, J., Stolcke, A., Fosler, E., Tajchman, G., Morgan, N.: Using a stochastic context-free grammar as a language model for speech recognition. In: Proceedings of ICASSP. (1995) 189–192

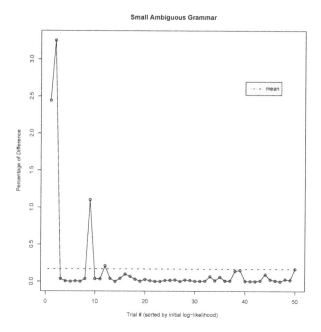

Fig. 9. The percentage difference in log-likelihood between HOLA and the Inside-Outside algorithm for 50 trials with an ambiguous grammar.

[3] Schabes, Y., Roth, M., Osborne, R.: Parsing the Wall Street Journal with the inside-outside algorithm. In: Proceedings of the 6th Conference of the European Chapter of the Association for Computational Linguistics. (1993) 341–346

[4] Hopcroft, J.E., Ullman, J.D.: Introductin to Automata Theory, Languages, and Computation. Addison Wesley (1979)

[5] Lari, K., Young, S.J.: The estimation of stochastic context-free grammars using the inside-outiside algorithm. Computer Speech and Language **4** (1990) 35–56

[6] Lari, K., Young, S.J.: Applications of stochastic context-free grammars using the inside-outside algorithm. Computer Speech and Language **5** (1991) 237–257

[7] Dempster, N.M., Laird, A.P., Rubin, D.B.: Maximum likelihood from incomplete data via the EM algorithm. Journal of the Royal Statistical Society B **39** (1977) 185–197

	Θ	*observed*	*normalized*
$S \rightarrow A$	[0.6]	10/17	0.59
$S \rightarrow B$	[0.4]	7/17	0.41
$A \rightarrow y$	[0.5]	3/10	0.30
$A \rightarrow z$	[0.5]	7/10	0.70
$B \rightarrow z$	[1.0]	7/7	1.0

Fig. 10. A grammar that generates the language $\{y\,z\}$

[8] Neal, R.M., Hinton, G.E.: A view of the EM algorithm that justifies incremental, sparse, and other variants. In Jordan, M.I., ed.: Learning in Graphical Models, Kluwer Academic (1998)

[9] Boyen, X., Koller, D.: Approximate learning of dynamic models. In: Neural Information Processing Systems. (1998)

[10] Cook, C.M., Rosenfeld, A., Aronson, A.: Grammatical inference by hill climbing. Informational Sciences **10** (1976) 59–80

[11] Stolcke, A., Omohundro, S.: Inducing probabilistic grammars by bayesian model merging. In Carrasco, R.C., Oncina, J., eds.: Grammatical Inference and Applications, Berlin, Heidelberg, Springer (1994) 106–118

Stochastic k-testable Tree Languages and Applications

Juan Ramón Rico-Juan, Jorge Calera-Rubio, and Rafael C. Carrasco⋆

Departament de Llenguatges i Sistemes Informàtics, Universitat d'Alacant,
E-03071 Alacant, Spain
{juanra, calera, carrasco}@dlsi.ua.es

Abstract. In this paper, we describe a generalization for tree stochastic languages of the k-gram models. These models are based on the k-testable class, a subclass of the languages recognizable by ascending tree automata. One of the advantages of this approach is that the probabilistic model can be updated in an incremental fashion. Another feature is that backing-off schemes can be defined. As an illustration of their applicability, they have been used to compress tree data files at a better rate than string-based methods.

Keywords: tree grammars, stochastic models, backing-off, data compression

1   Introduction

Stochastic models based on k-grams have been widely used in natural language modeling [1, 14], speech recognition [10] and data compression [18]. Indeed, stochastic models can be used to predict the next symbol in a sequence and, therefore, they are a key component of arithmetic data compression algorithms [23, 7]. In classification tasks, the need of stochastic models often arises when the Bayes' decision rule for minimum error rate is applied: given a sequence $S = s_1 s_2 \ldots$ of observations, the stochastic model M that maximizes the conditional probability $P(M|S)$ also maximizes $P(S|M)P(M)$ and, therefore, a model $P(S|M)$ for the generation of sequences is needed. If the stochastic model is of the form $P(S = s_1 s_2 \ldots s_t | M) = p_M(s_1)p_M(s_2|s_1) \cdots p_M(s_t|s_1 s_2 \ldots s_{t-1})$ and the conditional probabilities are assumed to depend only on the last $k-1$ words, $p_M(s_t|s_1 \ldots s_{t-1}) = p_M(s_t|s_{t-k+1} \ldots s_{t-1})$, the resulting Markov chain model [5] is known as k-gram model.

¿From a theoretical point of view, k-gram models can be regarded as a probabilistic extension of locally testable languages [9, 24]. Informally, a string language L is locally testable if every string w can be recognized as a string in L just by looking at all the substrings in w of length at most k.

⋆ Work supported by the Spanish Comisión Interministerial de Ciencia y Tecnología through grant TIC2000-1599-C02.

On the other hand, previous work [12, 11, 8] has proposed identification algorithms for locally testable tree languages. Trees are a more natural representation of the input when hierarchical relations are established among the pattern components. In particular, stochastic tree grammars have been widely used to tackle ambiguity in natural language parsing [3, 21]. In this paper, we explore the applicability of stochastic locally testable models to describe tree data. Some notation is introduced in the following section and a description of the model can be found in section 3. We have checked (section 4) that using these models for adaptive compression of tree data results in an improved performance compared to the traditional string-based arithmetic compression. How a backing-off scheme can be defined for classification tasks is described in section 5.

2   Trees and Tree Automata

Given an *alphabet*, that is, a finite set of symbols $\Sigma = \{\sigma_1, \ldots, \sigma_{|\Sigma|}\}$, the set Σ^T of Σ-trees is defined as the language generated by the context-free grammar $G = (\Sigma', \{T, F\}, T, R)$, where the alphabet Σ' contains Σ plus the left and right parenthesis and whose set of productions R contains the rules:

- $T \longrightarrow \sigma(F)$ for all $\sigma \in \Sigma$
- $F \longrightarrow \lambda \mid TF$

In this definition, λ represents the empty string. For brevity, we will write σ whenever $\sigma(\lambda)$ is generated by G. The *depth* of a tree t is

$$\text{depth}(t) = \begin{cases} 0 & \text{if } t = \sigma \in \Sigma \\ 1 + \max_{j=1}^{m}\{\text{depth}(t_j)\} & \text{if } t = \sigma(t_1 \ldots t_m) \text{ with } m > 0 \end{cases} \quad (1)$$

For instance, the Σ-tree $a(a(a(ab))b)$ belongs to $\{a, b\}^T$ and its depth is 3. Its graphical representation is depicted in Fig.1.

A *deterministic finite-state tree automaton* (DTA) is defined as a four-tuple $A = (Q, \Sigma, \Delta, F)$, where $Q = \{q_1, \ldots, q_{|Q|}\}$ is a finite set of states, $\Sigma = \{\sigma_1, \ldots, \sigma_{|\Sigma|}\}$ is the alphabet, $F \subseteq Q$ is the subset of accepting states and $\Delta = \{\delta_0, \delta_1, \ldots, \delta_M\}$ is a collection of transition functions of the form $\delta_m : \Sigma \times Q^m \to Q$. For all trees $t \in \Sigma^T$, the result $\delta(t) \in Q$ of the operation of A on t is

$$\delta(t) = \begin{cases} \delta_0(\sigma) & \text{if } t = \sigma \in \Sigma \\ \delta_m(\sigma, \delta(t_1), \ldots, \delta(t_m)) & \text{if } t = \sigma(t_1 \ldots t_m) \text{ with } m > 0 \end{cases} \quad (2)$$

The tree language $L(A)$ recognized by the automaton A is the subset of Σ^T

$$L(A) = \{t \in \Sigma^T : \delta(t) \in F\}. \quad (3)$$

Every language that can be recognized by a DTA is called a *rational tree language* [17] and generalize the *ascending tree automata* described by Nivat and Podelsky [15].

For instance, if $\Sigma = \{a, b\}$ and Δ contains the transitions $\delta_0(a) = q_1$, $\delta_0(b) = q_2$, $\delta_2(a, q_1, q_2) = q_2$ and $\delta_1(a, q_2) = q_1$, the result of the operation of A on tree $t = a(a(a(ab))b)$, plotted in Fig.1, is $\delta(t) = \delta_2(a, \delta(a(a(ab))), \delta(b))$. Recursively, one gets $\delta(b) = q_2$ and $\delta(a(a(ab))) = q_1$. Then, $\delta(t) = \delta(a, q_1, q_2) = q_2$. By convention, undefined transitions lead to absorption states, that is, to unaccepted trees. Stochastic tree automata generate a probability distribution over

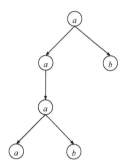

Fig. 1. A graphical representation of the tree $t = a(a(a(ab))b)$.

the trees in Σ^T. A stochastic DTA incorporates a probability for every transition in the automaton, with the normalization that the probabilities of the transitions leading to the same state $q \in Q$ must add up to one. In other words, there is a collection of functions $P = \{p_0, p_1, p_2, \dots, p_M\}$ of the type $p_m : \Sigma \times Q^m \rightarrow [0, 1]$ such that they satisfy, for all $q \in Q$,

$$\sum_{\sigma \in \Sigma} \sum_{m=0}^{M} \sum_{\substack{q_1, \dots, q_m \in Q: \\ \delta_m(\sigma, q_1, \dots, q_m) = q}} p_m(\sigma, q_1, \dots, q_k) = 1 \tag{4}$$

In addition to these probabilities, every *stochastic deterministic tree automaton* $A = (Q, V, \delta, P, \rho)$ provides a function $\rho : Q \rightarrow [0, 1]$ which, for every $q \in Q$, gives the probability that a tree satisfies $\delta(t) = q$ and extends, in the definition of the DTA, the subset of accepting states[1]. Then, the probability of a tree t in the language generated by the stochastic DTA A is given by the product of the probabilities of all the transitions used when A operates on t, times $\rho(\delta(t))$:

$$p(t|A) = \rho(\delta(t))\, \pi(t) \tag{5}$$

with $\pi(t)$ recursively given by

$$\pi(t) = \begin{cases} p_0(\sigma) & \text{if } t = \sigma \in \Sigma \\ p_m(\sigma, \delta(t_1), \dots, \delta(t_m))\, \pi(t_1) \cdots \pi(t_m) & \text{if } t = \sigma(t_1 \dots t_m) \text{ with } m > 0 \end{cases} \tag{6}$$

---

[1] We may define accepting states as those $q \in Q$ such that $\rho(q) > 0$

The equations (5) and (6) define a probability distribution $p(t|A)$ which is consistent if

$$\sum_{t \in \Sigma^T} p(t|A) = 1. \tag{7}$$

As shown by Chaudhuri et al. [4] and Sánchez and Benedí [20], context-free grammars whose probabilities are estimated from random samples are always consistent. It is easy to show [19] that identifying a DTA is equivalent to identifying a context-free grammar from structural descriptions. In the following, the probabilities of the DTA will be extracted from random samples and, therefore, consistency is always preserved.

3 Stochastic Extension of Locally Testable Tree Languages

Locally testable languages, in the case of strings, are characterized by defining the set of substrings of length k together with prefixes and suffixes of length strictly smaller than k to check near the string boundaries [9, 24]. In the case of trees, the k-fork plays the role of the substrings and the k-root and k-subtrees are used to check near the tree boundaries. These concepts are formally defined below.

For all $k > 0$ and for all trees $t = \sigma(t_1 \ldots t_m) \in \Sigma^T$, the k-root of t is the tree in Σ^T defined as

$$r_k(\sigma(t_1 \ldots t_m)) = \begin{cases} \sigma & \text{if } k = 1 \\ \sigma(r_{k-1}(t_1) \ldots r_{k-1}(t_m)) & \text{otherwise} \end{cases} \tag{8}$$

Note that in case $m = 0$, that is $t = \sigma \in \Sigma$, then $r_k(\sigma) = \sigma$.

On the other hand, the set $f_k(t)$ of k-forks and the set $s_k(t)$ of k-subtrees are defined for all $k > 0$ as follows:

$$f_k(\sigma(t_1 \ldots t_m)) = \cup_{j=1}^m f_k(t_j) \cup \begin{cases} \emptyset & \text{if } 1 + \text{depth}(\sigma(t_1 \ldots t_m)) < k \\ r_k(\sigma(t_1 \ldots t_m)) & \text{otherwise} \end{cases} \tag{9}$$

$$s_k(\sigma(t_1 \ldots t_m)) = \cup_{j=1}^m s_k(t_j) \cup \begin{cases} \sigma(t_1 \ldots t_m) & \text{if } \text{depth}(\sigma(t_1 \ldots t_m)) < k \\ \emptyset & \text{otherwise} \end{cases} \tag{10}$$

In the particular case $t = \sigma \in \Sigma$, then $s_k(t) = f_1(t) = \sigma$ and $f_k(t) = \emptyset$ for all $k > 1$.

For instance, if $t = a(a(a(ab))b)$ then one gets $r_2(t) = \{a(ab)\}$, $f_3(t) = \{a(a(a)b), a(a(a(b)))\}$ and $s_2(t) = \{a(ab), a, b\}$.

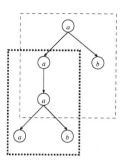

Fig. 2. Set of 3-forks generated in $a(a(a(ab))b)$.

The above definitions allow one to define formally the class of k-testable tree languages. A tree language T is a *strictly k-testable* language (with $k \geq 2$) if there exist three finite subsets $\mathcal{R}, \mathcal{F}, \mathcal{S} \subseteq \Sigma^T$ such that

$$t \in T \Leftrightarrow r_{k-1}(t) \subseteq \mathcal{R} \wedge f_k(t) \subseteq \mathcal{F} \wedge s_{k-1}(t) \subseteq \mathcal{S}. \tag{11}$$

It is straightforward [12, 11, 8] to build a DTA $A = (Q, \Sigma, \Delta, F)$ that recognizes a strictly k-testable tree language T. For this purpose, it suffices to choose:

- $Q = \mathcal{R} \cup r_{k-1}(\mathcal{F}) \cup \mathcal{S}$;
- $F = \mathcal{R}$;
- $\delta_m(\sigma, t_1, \dots, t_m) = \sigma(t_1 \dots t_m)$ for all $\sigma(t_1 \dots t_m) \in \mathcal{S}$
- $\delta_m(\sigma, t_1, \dots, t_m) = r_{k-1}(\sigma(t_1 \dots t_m))$ for all $\sigma(t_1 \dots t_m) \in \mathcal{F}$

Furthermore, under the assumption that the tree language L is k-testable, the DTA recognizing L can be identified from positive samples [12, 11, 8], that is, from sets made of examples of trees in the language. Given a positive sample S, the procedure to obtain the DTA essentially builds the automaton A using $r_{k-1}(S)$, $f_k(S)$ and $s_{k-1}(S)$ instead of $\mathcal{R}, \mathcal{F}$ and $\mathcal{S}$ respectively in the above definitions for Q, F and Δ.

For instance, for the single example sample $S = \{a(a(a(ab))b)\}$ and $k = 3$ one gets the set of sates $Q = r_2(S) \cup r_2(f_3(S)) \cup s_2(S) = \{a(ab), a(a), a, b\}$ with final subset $F = \{a(ab)\}$ and transitions $\delta_0(a) = a$, $\delta_0(b) = b$ and $\delta_2(a, a, b) = a(ab)$ on the one hand and $\delta_2(a, a(a), b) = a(ab)$ and $\delta_1(a, a(ab)) = a(a)$ on the other hand.

Now we can extend this learning procedure to the case where the sample is stochastically generated. A stochastic sample $S = \{\tau_1, \tau_2, \dots \tau_{|S|}\}$ consists of a sequence of trees generated according to a given probability distribution. If our model is a stochastic DTA, the distribution $p(t|A)$ is given by equations (5–6). The assumption that the underlying transition scheme (that is, the states Q and the collection of transition functions Δ) correspond to a k-testable DTA allows one to infer a stochastic DTA from a sample in a simple way. For this purpose, one should note that the likelihood of the stochastic sample S is maximized [14] if the stochastic model assigns to every tree τ in the sample a probability equal to the relative frequency of τ in S. In other words, every transition in Δ will be assigned a probability which coincides with the relative number of times the rule is used when the trees in the sample are parsed. Therefore, the procedure to infer a stochastic DTA from a stochastic sample $S = \{\tau_1, \tau_2, \ldots, \tau_{|S|}\}$ works as follows. The set of states is built as:

$$Q = r_{k-1}(S) \cup r_{k-1}(f_k(S)) \cup s_{k-1}(S); \tag{12}$$

for every $t = \sigma(t_1, \ldots, t_m) \in s_{k-1}(S)$, Δ contains a transition

$$\delta(\sigma, t_1, ..., t_m) = \sigma(t_1, ..., t_m); \tag{13}$$

for every $t = \sigma(t_1, \ldots, t_m) \in f_k(S)$, Δ contains a transition

$$\delta(\sigma, t_1, ..., t_m) = r_{k-1}(\sigma(t_1, ..., t_m)); \tag{14}$$

for all $t = \sigma(t_1, \ldots, t_m) \in s_{k-1}(S) \cup f_k(S)$ the transition probabilities in P are estimated as

$$p_m(\sigma, t_1, \ldots, t_m) = \frac{C^{[k]}(\sigma(t_1, \ldots, t_m), S)}{C^{[k-1]}(r_{k-1}(\sigma(t_1, \ldots, t_m)), S)} \tag{15}$$

where $C(t, S) = \sum_{i=1}^{|S|} C(t, \tau_i)$ and $C(t, \tau_i)$ counts the number of k-forks and $(k-1)$-subtrees[2] isomorphic to t found in τ_i; finally, the subset of accepting states is $F = r_{k-1}(S)$ and the probabilities $\rho(t)$ are estimated for every $t \in F$ as

$$\rho(t) = \frac{1}{|S|} D^{[k]}(t, S) \tag{16}$$

where $D^{[k]}(t, S) = \sum_{i=1}^{|S|} D^{[k]}(t, \tau_i)$ and $D^{[k]}(t, \tau_i) = 1$ if $r_{k-1}(\tau) = t$ and zero otherwise.

It is useful to store the above probabilities as the quotient of two terms, as given by equations (15) and (16). In this way, if a new tree (or subtree) τ is provided, the automaton A can be easily updated to account for the additional information. For this incremental update, it suffices to increment each term in the equations with the partial sums obtained for τ.

4   An Application: Tree Data Compression

In this section, we explore the application of the class of models considered here to the task of tree data compression. Because stochastic modeling becomes a key ingredient in arithmetic compression [23, 22], one expects that probabilistic tree models that provide a better description of the file content will allow for a more effective file compression. Conversely, compression performance can be used as a measure of the quality of the stochastic model.

---

[2] Note that a tree τ may contain, depending on the depth of t, either k-forks or $(k-1)$-subtrees isomorphic to t but not both simultaneously.

Recall that an arithmetic encoder uses at step n the cumulative range of probabilities $[l(e_n), h(e_n)[$ that the model assigns to the event e_n having probability $h(e_n) - l(e_n)$. Starting with $low_0 = 0$ and $high_0 = 1$, a new interval is iteratively computed as follows

$$low_{n+1} = low_n + (high_n - low_n)l(e_n)$$
$$high_{n+1} = low_n + (high_n - low_n)h(e_n) \tag{17}$$

Implementing this computation using integer arithmetics is a subtle task as shown by Witten et al. [23]. An important issue is that the probabilistic model should never assign a null probability to any event that can be observed, that is, $h(e_n) - l(e_n)$ has to be always strictly positive.

The procedure to compress tree data follows the guidelines of prediction by partial matching (PPM, Cleary and Witten [6]). Similarly to the case of strings, a probabilistic model $M^{[k]}$ predicts the next code to be transmitted based on the previous context. In this case, the context is given by the $(k-1)$-fork (or when appropriate by the $(k-1)$-root or $(k-1)$-subtree) in the tree above the node. For instance, if $k = 3$, the possible expansions of the nodes shadowed in Fig. 3 depend on the whole context marked with a square. In that case, the probability $p_2(a, a(a), b)$ of the expansion $t = a(a(a)b)$ given the observed state $q = r_2(t) = a(ab)$ is needed. In the following, we will call a tree t expansion if $t \in f_k(S) \cup s_{k-1}(S)$ and root expansion if $t \in r_{k-1}(S)$.

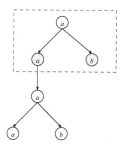

Fig. 3. Trailing context $(k = 3)$ for the expansion of the shadowed node.

In case the k-testable model $M^{[k]}$ contains no information about the expansion $t = \sigma(t_1, ..., t_m)$, the $(k-1)$-order model $M^{[k-1]}$ is used instead to compute the probabilities of the subexpansions $t_1, ..., t_m$. This backing-off procedure is repeated recursively till either a) a suitable model is found for the subexpansion under consideration or b) $k = 1$ and the ground model $M^{[1]}$ is applied. On the return, when each state expansion is known, the models $M^{[1]}$ to $M^{[k]}$ are updated.

Some important features differentiate the procedure form the standard string PPM compression and are worth to comment:

1. In contrast to strings, where left-to-right processing is the natural choice, different orders are possible to perform a walk on the tree. Breadth-first traversal offers the advantage that the model can be updated before the whole tree is expanded. This improves compression of files consisting of a single tree or a small amount of them.

2. Each model $M^{[k]}$ with $k > 1$ consists of a collection of counters $C^{[k]}(t)$ and $D^{[k]}(t)$ needed for the estimates (15) and (16) respectively. There is a counter for every different argument t, where t is a k-fork or $(k-1)$-subtree in the first case and a $(k-1)$-root in the second case. In addition, one needs counters for the escape codes: $D^{[k]}(\epsilon_r)$ for the root escape code ϵ_r and $C^{[k]}(\epsilon_q)$ for the escape code ϵ_q associated to the state q. All these counters are initialized to zero, updated with the processed part of the tree and they will be used to estimate the probabilities as follows. The probability in model $M^{[k]}$ of the expansion t from state $q = \sigma(t_1, ..., t_m)$ is given by

$$\alpha(k, t) = \frac{C^{[k]}(t)}{C^{[k-1]}(q) + C^{[k]}(\epsilon_q)} \qquad (18)$$

The above formula can also be used for the escape probabilities $\alpha(k, \epsilon_q)$. On the other hand, the probability in $M^{[k]}$ of the root expansion t is

$$\beta(k, t) = \frac{D^{[k]}(t)}{|S| + D^{[k]}(\epsilon_r)} \qquad (19)$$

This equation is also holds for the escape code probability $\beta(k, \epsilon_r)$.

3. The ground model $M^{[1]}$ is used when no information is available about a expansion $t = \sigma(a_1, ..., a_m)$ with $a_1, ..., a_m \in \Sigma$ or $t = \sigma$. In such case, $q = r_1(t) = \sigma$ and one needs to code the number m of descendents together with, if $m > 0$, their labels $a_1, ..., a_m$. Therefore, this ground model has two components. On the one hand, a collection of counters $E_\sigma(m)$ stores how many nodes labeled σ expanded m subtrees. As the maximal tree-width M is in advance unknown, we initially use M counters per symbol, $E_\sigma(0), ..., E_\sigma(M-1)$ plus an additional one $E_\sigma(\epsilon_\sigma)$ that stores how often M additional counters are needed. Then, the probability that a node labeled σ has m descendents is computed as follows

$$\gamma(\sigma, m) = \frac{1 + E_\sigma(m)}{1 + ME_\sigma(\epsilon_\sigma) + \Sigma_{i=0}^{ME_\sigma(\epsilon_\sigma)} E_\sigma(i)} \qquad (20)$$

The same equation holds for $\gamma(\sigma, \epsilon_\sigma)$.

On the other hand, $M^{[1]}$ keeps a counter $C^{[1]}(\sigma)$ storing the number of nodes labeled with σ in the sample. They are used to assign a probability to every symbol

$$\alpha(1, \sigma) = \frac{1 + C^{[1]}(\sigma)}{|\Sigma| + \Sigma_{a \in \Sigma} C^{[1]}(a)} \qquad (21)$$

```
algorithm tcompress(k, τ)          [for k > 1]
    r_encode(r_{k-1}(τ))
    do (∀x subtree of τ in breadth-first order)
        t ← r_k(x)
        if (1 + depth(t) ≥ k - 1) then
            f_encode(k, t)
        endif
    enddo
endalgorithm
```

Fig. 4. Main tree compression algorithm.

With all these ingredients, the tree compression algorithm executes repeatedly a function, tcompress schematically represented in Fig. 4, for every tree τ in the input and the maximal order $k_{\max}$ allowed for the models. The tcompress algorithm calls a function f_encode (plotted in Fig. 5) that encodes the k-forks and $(k-1)$-subtrees[3] and a similar function r_encode (plotted in Fig. 7) that encodes the $(k-1)$-root. All these functions use a generic procedure send(φ, η, x) where $\varphi \in \{\alpha, \beta, \gamma\}$, η is a k- or σ- value and x is a tree or m-value. Both φ and η specify the table to be used (that is, the equation (18–21 and first argument) while x is the parameter that selects the table entry (the second argument in these equations). The function send generates the input for the arithmetic encoder, that is, the cumulative range of probabilities assigned to the event by the model.

The corresponding decoding functions are implemented in a similar fashion and can be found in [16]. We checked this model with a 6.129 Mbyte file consisting of parse trees (with structural and part-of-speech tags) contained in the Penn Tree-bank [13]. The compression rate obtained, 13.94, is to be compared with 7.08 obtained using gzip with best compression options, 10.92 obtained with bzip2 with longest block-size or 9.08 using trigram-based arithmetic compression.

5   Multilevel Smoothing of Tree Languages

A standard procedure to avoid null probabilities is the backing-off method that has been extensively studied for string models (see, for instance, Ney et al. [14]). In this section we introduce a backing-off procedure that has been succesfully used in classification tasks. Different schemes are possible but the results are not very sensitive to the detailed structure [14] and our main purpose is to illustrate the difficulties and differences with the string case. Indeed, the most important diference comes from the fact that the number of descendents of a node is not bounded: on the one hand a special ground model is needed and, on the other hand, care has to be taken when calculating the normalization factors

---

[3] this means that the argument t for f_encode satisfies $k - 1 \leq 1 + depth(t) \leq k$.

```
function f_encode(k, t)
    q ← r_{k-1}(t)                      [k > 1 is always true]
    if (C^{[k]}(t) > 0) then            [t found in M^{[k]}]
        send(α, k, t)
        update(k, t)
    else                    [t not found in M^{[k]}]
        send(α, k, ε_q)
        inc(C^{[k]}(ε_q))
        if (k > 2) then                    [use M^{[k-1]} for t = σ(t_1, ..., t_m)]
            do (j = 1, ..., m)
                if (1 + depth(t_j) ≥ k − 2) then
                    f_encode(k − 1, t_j)
                endif
            enddo
        else                [use M^{[1]} for t = σ(a_1, ..., a_m)]
            do (while m ≥ ME_σ(ε_σ))
                send(γ, σ, ε_σ)
                inc(E_σ(ε_σ))
            enddo
            send(γ, σ, m)
            inc(E_σ(m))
            do (j = 1, ..., m)
                send(α, 1, a_j)
                inc(C^{[1]}(a_j))
            enddo
        endif
        inc(C^{[k]}(t))
    endif
endfunction
```

Fig. 5. Encoding function. The command inc increments the counter by one. Function update is expanded in Fig. 6.

as the number of unseen events is not known. Following the standard approach a discounting function λ such that $0 < \lambda < 1$ is used for every case that originates a discount term Λ with a normalizing factor F. In the following we will use counters $C^{[k]}$, $D^{[k]}$ and E_σ with the same meaning as in previous section.

The probability of a tree $\tau = \sigma(\tau_1, ..., \tau_m)$ in model $M^{[k]}$ is computed using the definitions (5) and (6) adapted to a k-testable language, so that $p(\tau|M^{[k]}) = \rho^{[k]}(r_{k-1}(\tau))\pi^{[k]}(\tau)$ and

$$
\pi^{[k]}(\tau) = \begin{cases} p_m^{[k]}(\sigma, r_{k-1}(\tau_1), ..., r_{k-1}(\tau_m)) \ \prod_{i=1}^{m} \pi^{[k]}(\tau_i) \\ \qquad\qquad\qquad\qquad \text{if } \tau = \sigma(\tau_1, ..., \tau_m) \wedge m > 0 \\ p_0^{[k]}(\sigma) \qquad\qquad\qquad \text{if } \tau = \sigma \in \Sigma \end{cases}
$$

$$(22)$$

```
function update(k, t)
    if (k > 2) then                    [t = σ(t₁, ..., tₘ)]
        do (j = 1, ..., m)
            if (1 + depth(tⱼ) ≥ k − 2) then update(k − 1, tⱼ)
        enddo
    else                               [t = σ(a₁, ..., aₘ)]
        inc(Eσ(m))
        do (j = 1, ..., m)
            inc(C[1](aⱼ))
        enddo
    endif
    inc(C[k](t))
endfunction
```

Fig. 6. Function update.

```
function r_encode (k, t)
    if (D[k](t) > 0) then               [use M[k]]
        send(β, k, t)
        do(i = 2, ..., k)
            inc(D[i](rᵢ₋₁(t)))
            update(i − 1, rᵢ₋₁(t))
        enddo
    else                    [use M[k−1]]
        send(β, k, εᵣ)
        inc(D[k](εᵣ))
        if (k > 2) then                  [t = σ(t₁, ..., tₘ)]
            r_encode (k − 1, rₖ₋₁(t))
            if(1 + depth(t) ≥ k − 1) f_encode (k − 1, t)
        else                    [t = σ]
            send(α, 1, σ)
            inc(C[1](σ))
        endif
        inc(D[k](t))
    endif
endfunction
```

Fig. 7. Root encoding function.

Where the probabilities of type $p_m^{[k]}$ with $k > 2$ and $m > 0$, given $t = \sigma(t_1, ..., t_m)$ with $t_i = a_i(s_{i1}, ..., s_{im_i})$, are defined as

$$p_m^{[k]}(\sigma, t_1, ..., t_m) = \begin{cases} \dfrac{C^{[k]}(t)}{C^{[k-1]}(r_{k-1}(t))} \left(1 - \lambda^{[k]}(t)\right) & \text{if } C^{[k]}(t) > 0 \\ \dfrac{\Lambda^{[k]}(r_{k-1}(t))}{F^{[k]}(r_{k-1}(t))} \prod_{i=1}^{m} p_{m_i}^{[k-1]}(a_i, s_{i1}, ..., s_{im_i}) & \text{otherwise} \end{cases}$$

(23)

where

$$\Lambda^{[k]}(q) = \frac{1}{C^{[k-1]}(t)} \sum_{u:C^{[k]}(u)>0 \wedge r_{k-1}(u)=q} C^{[k]}(u)\lambda^{[k]}(u) \tag{24}$$

and the normalization factor is

$$F^{[k]}(\sigma(\tau_1, ..., \tau_m)) = 1 - \sum_{\substack{u_1,...,u_m: \\ C^{[k]}(\sigma(u_1,...,u_m))>0 \wedge r_{k-2}(u_i)=\tau_i}} \prod_{i=1}^{m} p_{m_i}^{[k-1]}(a_i, v_{i1}, ..., v_{im_i}) \tag{25}$$

where $u_i = a_i(v_{i1}, ..., v_{im_i})$.

The root probabilities $\rho^{[k]}$ are also needed and a possible discounting scheme in case $k > 2$ is, for $t = \sigma(t_1, ..., t_m)$,

$$\rho^{[k]}(\sigma(t_1, ..., t_m)) = \begin{cases} \frac{D^{[k]}(t)}{|S|}\left(1 - \theta^{[k]}(t)\right) & \text{if } D^{[k]}(\sigma(t_1, ..., t_m)) > 0 \\ \frac{\Theta^{[k]}}{G^{[k]}}\, \rho^{[k-1]}(r_{k-2}(t))\, p_m^{[k-1]}(\sigma, t_1, ..., t_m) & \text{otherwise} \end{cases} \tag{26}$$

where

$$\Theta^{[k]} = \frac{1}{|S|} \sum_{u:D^{[k]}(u)>0} D^{[k]}(u)\, \theta^{[k]}(u) \tag{27}$$

and the suitable normalizing factor is

$$G^{[k]} = 1 - \sum_a \sum_m \sum_{\substack{u_1,...,u_m: \\ D^{[k]}(a(u_1,...,u_m))>0}} \rho^{[k-1]}(r_{k-2}(a(u_1, ..., u_m)))\, p_m^{[k-1]}(a, u_1, ..., u_m) \tag{28}$$

In case $k = 1$ (the ground model) or $k = 2$ (the model that calls the ground one) different equations are needed[16]. Especial care has to be taken because, in contrast to the case of strings, the number of descendents of a node is *a priori* unbounded. However, all these equations provide an efficient backing-off scheme that guarantees that no event is assigned a null probability.

6   Conclusion

We have described a probabilistic extension of the k-testable tree languages that can be also regarded as a generalization of k-grams for tree languages. The models of this type can be updated incrementally and may work with medium-sized samples, where some state merging methods [2] tend to output too simple models. The higher compression rates achieved when processing tree data files show that this class of models can be suitable for practical purposes. We also showed that a discounting scheme can be easily defined for this class of models.

References

[1] Peter F. Brown, Vincent J. Della Pietra, Peter V. deSouza, Jenifer C. Lai, and Robert L. Mercer. Class-based n-gram models of natural language. *Computational Linguistics*, 18(4):467–479, 1992.

[2] Rafael C. Carrasco, Mikel L. Forcada, M. Ángeles Valdés-Muñoz, and Ramón P. Ñeco. Stable encoding of finite-state machines in discrete-time recurrent neural nets with sigmoid units. *Neural Computation*, 12(9):2129–2174, 2000.

[3] Eugene Charniak. *Statistical Language Learning*. MIT Press, 1993.

[4] R. Chaudhuri, S. Pham, and O.N. Garcia. Solution of an open problem on probabilistic grammars. *IEEE Transactions on Computers*, 32(8):758–750, 1983.

[5] K. L. Chung. *Markov Chains with Stationary Transition Probabilities*. Springer, Berlin, 2 edition, 1967.

[6] John G. Cleary and Ian H. Witten. Data compression using adaptive coding and partial string matching. *IEEE Transactions on Communicaton*, 32(4):396–402, 1984.

[7] Thomas M. Cover and Joy A. Thomas. *Elements of Information Theory*. Wiley Series in Telecommunications. John Wiley & Sons, New York, NY, USA, 1991.

[8] Pedro García. Learning k-testable tree sets from positive data. Technical Report DSIC-ii-1993-46, DSIC, Universidad Politécnica de Valencia, 1993.

[9] Pedro García and Enrique Vidal. Inference of k-testable languages in the strict sense and application to syntactic pattern recognition. *IEEE Transactions on Pattern Analysis and Machine Intelligence*, 12(9):920–925, sep 1990.

[10] Frederick Jelinek. *Statistical Methods for Speech Recognition*. The MIT Press, Cambridge, Massachusetts, 1998.

[11] T. Knuutila and M. Steinby. The inference of tree languages from finite samples: an algebraic approach. *Theoretical Computer Science*, 129:337–367, 1994.

[12] Timo Knuutila. Inference of k-testable tree languages. In H. Bunke, editor, *Advances in Structural and Syntactic Pattern Recognition (Proc. Intl. Workshop on Structural and Syntactic Pattern Recognition, Bern, Switzerland)*. World Scientific, aug 1993.

[13] Mitchell P. Marcus, Beatrice Santorini, and Mary Ann Marcinkiewicz. Building a large annotated corpus of english: the penn treebank. *Computational Linguistics*, 19:313–330, 1993.

[14] H. Ney, U. Essen, and R. Kneser. On the estimation of small probabilities by leaving-one-out. *IEEE Trans. on Pattern Analysis and Machine Intelligence*, 17(12):1202–1212, 1995.

[15] Maurice Nivat and Andreas Podelski. Minimal ascending and descending tree automata. *SIAM Journal on Computing*, 26(1):39–58, 1997.

[16] J.R. Rico-Juan, J. Calera-Rubio, and R.C. Carrasco. Stochastic k-testable tree languages and applications. http://www.dlsi.ua.es/~calera/fulltext02.ps.gz, 2002.

[17] G. Rozenberg and A. Salomaa, editors. *Handbook of Formal Languages*. Springer, 1997.

[18] Frank Rubin. Experiments in text file compression. *Communications of the ACM*, 19(11):617–623, 1976.

[19] Yasubumi Sakakibara. Efficient learning of context-free grammars from positive structural examples. *Information and Computation*, 97(1):23–60, March 1992.

[20] J.A. Sánchez and J.M. Benedí. Consistency of stochastic context-free grammars from probabilistic estimation based on growth transformations. *IEEE Transactions on Pattern Analysis and Machine Intelligence*, 19(9):1052–1055, 1997.

[21] Andreas Stolcke. An efficient context-free parsing algorithm that computes prefix probabilities. *Computational Linguistics*, 21(2):165–201, 1995.

[22] I. H. Witten, A. Moffat, and T. C. Bell. *Managing Gigabytes: Compressing and Indexing Documents and Images*. Morgan Kauffman Publishing, San Francisco, 2nd edition, 1999.

[23] I. H. Witten, R. M. Neal, and J. G. Cleary. Arithmetic coding for data compression. *Communications of the ACM*, 30(6):520–540, 1987.

[24] Takashi Yokomori. On polynomial-time learnability in the limit of strictly deterministic automata. *Machine Learning*, 19(2):153–179, 1995.

Fast Learning from Strings of 2-Letter Rigid Grammars

Yoav Seginer

ILLC, Universiteit van Amsterdam, The Netherlands

Abstract. It is well-known that certain classes of classical categorial grammars are learnable, within Gold's paradigm of identification in the limit, from positive examples. In the search for classes which can be learned efficiently from strings, we study the class of 2-letter rigid grammars, which is the class of classical categorial grammars with an alphabet of two letters, each of which is assigned a single type. The (non-trivial) structure of this class of grammars is studied and it is shown that grammars in this class can be learned very efficiently. The algorithm given for solving this learning problem runs in time linear in the total length of the input strings. After seeing two or more strings in a language, the algorithm can determine precisely the (finite) set of grammars which can generate those strings.

1 Introduction

It is well-known that certain classes of classical categorial grammars are learnable, within Gold's paradigm of identification in the limit, from positive examples. In [3], Kanazawa showed that the class of k-valued categorial grammars, in which every letter in the alphabet (lexicon) is assigned at most k types, is learnable from positive example strings (sequences of letters generated by the grammar). While this general result guarantees that k-valued grammars are learnable, it does not guarantee that this can be done efficiently. In fact, Kanazawa's approach is based on learning from a richer input - structural examples. Structural examples give the learner not only the strings but also the tree structure for each string. For k-valued grammars with $2 \leq k$ it has been shown in [1] that the learning problem from structural examples (under reasonable assumptions) is NP-hard. To extend this method of learning to strings, one needs to try out all possible tree structures for each string. Even for 1-valued grammars (also called *rigid* grammars), where learning from structural examples can be done in polynomial time, the associated method for learning from strings is intractable.

There may be, of course, other methods for learning grammars from strings. These methods may have to be tailored specifically for each class of grammars we wish to learn. To find them, we must both identify grammar classes for which this can be done and find an algorithm that learns the grammars in the class. In this paper we examine what is probably one of the simplest classes of classical categorial grammars - rigid grammars over an alphabet of two letters. We will

P. Adriaans, H. Fernau, and M. van Zaanen (Eds.): ICGI 2002, LNAI 2484, pp. 213–224, 2002.

see that this class of grammars, which produces a non-trivial class of languages, has a combinatorial structure which allows very efficient learning.

Languages generated by 2-letter rigid grammars may have finite or infinite overlaps with each other or even be contained in each other. The language class does not have the property of finite thickness - there are strings which belong to infinitely many different languages (but, as shown by Kanazawa, the class does have finite elasticity). Many of the languages in this class are not regular.

Underneath this complex surface structure, there are properties which allow for very quick learning. All learning algorithms used here run in time linear in the size of the input strings. Moreover, the algorithms learn all that can be learned from any given input. This means that the algorithms can always give exactly the family of grammars whose languages contain the input strings. When these languages are contained in each other, the minimal language is given (which implies conservative learning).

The exact sequence in which strings are presented to the learner may influence how quickly the algorithms converge to a correct grammar. For every language there is a pair of strings which allows the algorithms to converge immediately to a correct grammar.

In what follows, we confine our attention to rigid grammars over two letters. We begin, in Sect. 2, by giving a labeled graph representation of these grammars. We then characterize the structure of the graphs. This will serve as the basis for the rest of the analysis. In Sect. 3 we give the learning algorithm for these grammars, step by step. At each step, an additional parameter in the structure of the associated graph will be inferred. Even when such inference is not complete, it is shown to be sufficient for the next step in the algorithm to be carried out.

2   A Graph Representation for Grammars

In classical categorial grammars, each string is associated with a type. These types determine the way in which strings may be combined together (by concatenation) into longer strings. The set of types consists of *primitive types* (which include the *distinguished type* t) and *functor types*, which are formed by combining types. For any two types t_1 and t_2, the functor types t_1/t_2 and $t_2 \backslash t_1$ are defined. The type t_2 is the *argument type* of the functor types t_1/t_2 and $t_2 \backslash t_1$.

If string s_1 has type t_1/t_2 and string s_2 has type t_2, the concatenation $s_1 s_2$ may be formed. Similarly, if s_1 has type $t_2 \backslash t_1$, the concatenation $s_2 s_1$ is formed. In both cases, the concatenation is assigned the type t_1. We call this operation a *functor application*. The direction of the slash determines the order in which the two strings are concatenated. When we wish to ignore the direction of the slash, we write $t_1 | t_2$ for both functor types t_1/t_2 and $t_2 \backslash t_1$.

A categorial grammar is defined over an alphabet (set of letters). Each letter in the alphabet is assigned one or more types. The language generated by a grammar is the set of strings of type t that can be generated from the alphabet by functor applications. A *rigid* grammar is a grammar in which each letter in the alphabet is assigned exactly one type.

In this paper, we work over the alphabet $\{a, b\}$ and use directed graphs to represent rigid grammars over this alphabet. A graph has a single node for every type which can be generated by the corresponding categorial grammar. The nodes, however, are not labeled by types (there is always some arbitrariness possible in the choice of types and we wish to avoid it).

Two kinds of directed edges are used in constructing the graphs, *argument edges* (dashed arrows in diagrams) and *functor edges* (solid arrows in diagrams). An argument edge connects a node representing a functor type with the node representing the argument type of that functor (e.g. $t_1/t_2 \dashrightarrow t_2$). A functor edge connects a node representing a functor type with the node representing the type which is the result of the application of that functor (e.g. $t_1/t_2 \to t_1$).

The construction of the graph corresponding to a categorial grammar begins with two nodes which are labeled by the letters a and b and by the type assigned to each of these letters by the grammar (the type labeling of nodes is only temporary and is not part of the final graph). We call these two nodes the *start nodes*. At each step in the construction we look for two nodes which are labeled by types t_2 and $t_1|t_2$ but are not yet connected by an argument edge. We first add an argument edge from the node labeled $t_1|t_2$ to the node labeled t_2. If there is no node yet labeled t_1, we create such a node. We then add a functor edge from the node labeled $t_1|t_2$ to the node labeled t_1. We repeat this process until no more edges and nodes can be added (the process must terminate).

Next, we look for a node labeled by the distinguished type t. We select this node to be the *terminal node* (if no such node exists, the categorial grammar generates an empty language and is not interesting). We also assign slashes to nodes which have edges leaving them. Such nodes must be labeled by a functor type and we assign each such node the main slash of its type (i.e. if the type is t_1/t_2, assign / and if the type is $t_2 \backslash t_1$, assign \). Finally, we remove all type labeling. For an example, see Fig. 1. When the slashes are removed from a graph G, we get the *edge structure* of G, which we denote by $E(G)$.

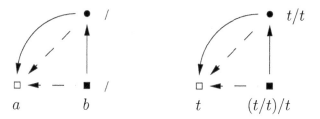

Fig. 1. The graph for the categorial grammar $a \mapsto t, b \mapsto (t/t)/t$. On the left appears the graph as constructed. On the right the nodes of the graph are labeled by the corresponding types (which are not part of the graph). Start nodes are indicated by squares and the terminal node is indicated by a hollow node (in this particular case, the left start node).

Strings can be generated at the graph nodes by a simple rule. Whenever a configuration $\nu_1 \leftarrow\!\!\text{--} \nu_2 \rightarrow \nu_3$ of three nodes has strings s_1 and s_2 already generated at nodes ν_1 and ν_2, the concatenation of s_1 and s_2 is generated at ν_3 (s_1s_2 or s_2s_1 depending on the direction of the slash on ν_2). The process begins with the strings a and b at the start nodes. It is not difficult to see that the strings generated at the terminal node of a graph are exactly the language generated by the grammar that the graph represents. We write $L(G)$ for the language generated at the terminal node of the graph G.

2.1   Characterizing the Graphs of 2-Letter Rigid Grammars

There is a simple characterization of the structure of graphs representing 2-letter rigid grammars. We define a *functor path* to be a directed path (in a graph) consisting of functor edges only. Since the graphs contain no directed loops, it is possible to number the nodes along a functor path. We write $p(i)$ for the i'th node on functor path p. The graphs for 2-letter rigid grammars are then characterized by the next theorem (see Fig. 2 for typical examples). Note that this characterization is given only in terms of the edge structure of the graph. Any slash assignment to the nodes is possible.

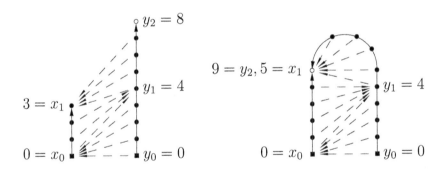

Fig. 2. Typical graphs for 2-letter rigid grammars. A loopless graph (*left*) and a looping graph (*right*). The nodes labeled by x_i and y_j are as in Theorem 1. In diagrams, we always have p_α on the left and p_β on the right.

Theorem 1. *A graph represents a 2-letter rigid categorial grammar iff:*

1. *All graph nodes lie on two functor paths p_α and p_β, which begin at the two start nodes. The two functor paths either do not meet at all or meet only once, at the last node of both paths. The terminal node is the last node on a functor path.*
2. *There are two strictly increasing sequences of natural numbers $\{x_i\}_{0 \le i \le m}$ and $\{y_j\}_{0 \le j \le n}$, with $0 \le n-1 \le m \le n$ such that $x_0 = y_0 = 0$, the last node in path p_α is $p_\alpha(x_m)$ and the last node in path p_β is $p_\beta(y_n)$. All argument edges are given by:*

(a) *If* $i + 1 \leq n$ *then for* $y_i \leq l < y_{i+1}$ *there is an argument edge from* $p_\beta(l)$ *to* $p_\alpha(x_i)$.

(b) *If* $i + 1 \leq m$ *then for* $x_i \leq l < x_{i+1}$ *there is an argument edge from* $p_\alpha(l)$ *to* $p_\beta(y_{i+1})$.

2.2 Looping and Loopless Graphs

From the theorem we see that there are two types of graphs. Graphs in which the two functor paths meet we call *looping graphs*. Graphs in which the two functor paths do not meet we call *loopless graphs*. In the analysis of looping graphs, we look separately at the *base* and the *loop* of the looping graph (see Fig. 3). The base of a looping graph is a loopless graph.

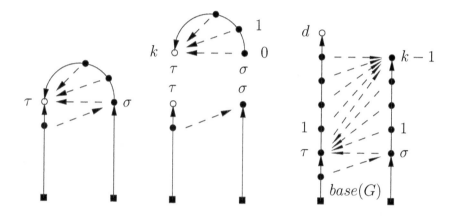

Fig. 3. A looping graph G (*left*), its base (*center bottom*), its loop (*center top*) and the graph $NL(G, d)$ (*right*) which generates a string with the same letter count as strings generated by G. Only the last nodes and argument edge of the base are shown.

In loopless graphs (and therefore also in the base of looping graphs) strings are generated strictly from the bottom up, that is, when a string is generated at a node, it is a concatenation of strings generated at lower nodes. Therefore, only one string is generated at each node of a loopless graph. On the loop, however, the strings generated at the terminal node can be used to generate additional strings on the loop.

In looping graphs, a loop is attached on top of a base. The generation of strings in these graphs therefore begins by generating two strings s_τ and s_σ at the top nodes τ and σ of the base. These two strings then serve as input for the concatenations which take place on the loop. Any string generated on the loop must be a concatenation of copies of the two strings s_τ and s_σ. One can think of s_τ and s_σ as the two words of the language, which the loop then combines into sentences.

A simple consequence of this description of the way strings are generated by a graph is a simple method for distinguishing between languages generated by looping and by loopless graphs. A language generated by a loopless graph consists of only one string, while a language generated by a looping graph is infinite.

3   Learning 2-Letter Rigid Grammars

Since the languages of loopless grammars consist of only one string, they are not interesting in terms of learnability. We therefore concentrate on learning languages generated by looping graphs. However, because the base of a looping graph is a loopless graph, we will return to the analysis of loopless graphs.

To learn the language generated by a looping graph G, a learner must deduce several parameters of the graph G from a sample of strings generated by G. The structure of the class of graphs for 2-letter rigid grammars is such that the learning process has two main stages. First, the learner has to discover the two strings s_τ and s_σ (the words of the language). These two strings are determined by the base of the graph. Having learned s_τ and s_σ, the learner can then learn the way these two strings are put together (on the loop) to construct the final strings (sentences) of the language.

The rest of this paper is concerned with answering these two questions based on a sample of strings from $L(G)$. Answering these questions requires answering a sequence of sub-questions. This can be done efficiently because the questions do not need to be answered simultaneously, but can be answered in sequence. The answer to one question then makes answering the next question in the sequence easy. Very often there remains some uncertainty as to the answer to a certain question. This uncertainty is such, however, that it does not effect the ability to answer the next question in the sequence.

3.1   Letter Assignment to the Start Nodes

The learning procedure is based on the graph representation as given in Theorem 1. The representation given in this theorem is not symmetric, however. There is always an argument edge from the start node of the path p_β (right in the diagrams) to the start node of the path p_α (left in the diagrams) and never the other way around.

There are, therefore, two ways of assigning the letters of the alphabet to the start nodes. The *standard assignment of letters* assigns a to p_α and b to p_β. The inverse assignment creates languages which are "negatives" of the languages with the standard assignment. The learner can distinguish languages with the standard and the inverse assignment of letters by counting the number of a's and b's in the sample strings.

We write $\#_a(s)$ for the number of a's in a string s and $\#_b(s)$ for the number of b's in the string. The pair $[\#_a(s), \#_b(s)]$ which we also denote by $[s]$, we call the *letter count* of the string s. As will be seen in the next section, a great part of the structure of a grammar can be deduced from the letter counts of the strings in its language. At this stage we only observe that strings generated by graphs with the standard assignment of letters [1] have $\#_b(s) < \#_a(s)$, while strings generated by graphs with the inverse letter assignment have $\#_a(s) < \#_b(s)$. The learner can, therefore, easily distinguish the two types of languages. From now on we assume that the grammar has the standard assignment (for the inverse assignment, we simply have to exchange the roles of a and b).

3.2   Inferring the Strings s_{τ_0} and s_{σ_0}

According to our original plan, we now need to find the strings s_τ and s_σ. This, however, cannot always be done. What we can do, is find two strings s_{τ_0} and s_{σ_0}. The strings s_τ and s_σ are either equal to s_{τ_0} and s_{σ_0} or composed of concatenations of s_{τ_0} and s_{σ_0} (in which case s_{τ_0} and s_{σ_0} are the "syllables" within the words s_τ and s_σ). In either case, every string in $L(G)$ is a concatenation of copies of s_{τ_0} and s_{σ_0} and therefore, these string will do just as well as s_τ and s_σ.

The discovery of s_{τ_0} and s_{σ_0} involves two basic steps. First, the letter counts $[s_{\tau_0}]$ and $[s_{\sigma_0}]$ are determined. Next, strings with these letter counts are extracted from the ends of the available sample strings of $L(G)$.

Since the letter counts of strings generated by a graph G are independent of the slashes assigned to the nodes of G, letter counts of strings generated at the nodes of G can be determined from the edge structure $E(G)$. We therefore attempt to discover the edge structure $E(G)$. As a first step in this direction, we show that the edge structure of a loopless graph can be inferred from the letter count of the single string generated by the graph.

Inferring the Edge Structure of Loopless Graphs. The process of generating a string on a loopless graph begins with the two strings a and b which have letter counts $[1, 0]$ and $[0, 1]$. The generation then proceeds by going "up" the graph, each time concatenating two previously generated strings. Concatenation of strings amounts to the vector addition of their letter counts. This process is very similar to what happens in the so-called Stern-Brocot tree. The edge structure of every loopless graph is equivalent to a branch in the Stern-Brocot tree and the letter count of the string generated by a loopless graph is the same as the vector on the corresponding branch in the tree (see [2] for details about the Stern-Brocot tree).

The Stern-Brocot tree has several interesting properties which translate immediately to properties of loopless graphs. In the Stern-Brocot tree every branch produces a different vector and there is an algorithm which, given a vector in the Stern-Brocot tree, calculates the branch of that vector. We give a version of this algorithm which takes as input a string letter count and outputs an edge structure which generates a string with this letter count. The translation from loopless graphs to tree branches matches two loopless graphs with every branch

---

[1] This fails for one (simple) graph and the three strings b,ab,ba, which can be dealt with separately.

in the right half of the Stern-Brocot tree. These two graphs are very similar and we fix a representative graph from each such pair, which we call the *standard loopless graph*. The algorithm returns the standard loopless graph.

Algorithm 1. *The algorithm takes as input a letter count $[x, y]$ of some string generated by a loopless graph with the standard letter assignment (so $x \le y$). Let c_1 and c_2 be variables, which have nodes as their values. We begin with two start nodes and let c_1 be the start node labeled by a and c_2 the start node labeled by b.*

1. *Create a new node, ν. Add an argument edge from c_2 to c_1 and a functor edge from c_2 to ν.*
2. *If $[x, y] = [1, 1]$, stop.*
3. *If $x > 2y$ or $[x, y] = [2, 1]$, set $[x, y] := [x - y, y]$, $c_2 := \nu$ and repeat the algorithm.*
4. *If $x < 2y$, set $[x, y] := [y, x - y]$, $c_2 := c_1$, $c_1 := \nu$ and repeat the algorithm.*

Inferring the Edge Structure of the Base of a Looping Graph. We cannot use Algorithm 1 directly to discover the edge structure of the base of the looping graph G, because the sample strings are generated on the loop of G and not in the base. Fortunately, it turns out that for every string $s \in L(G)$, there is a $0 \le d$ such that the *loopless* graph $NL(G, d)$, given in Fig. 3, generates a string with the same letter count as s (but not necessarily the exact same string).

Since Algorithm 1 only looks at the letter count of the input string and not at the order of the letters within the string, applying the algorithm to a string $s \in L(G)$ results [2] in the edge structure of the graph $NL(G, d)$, for some d. We are looking for the edge structure of the base of G, and, as can be seen in Fig. 3, the base of G is the bottom of the graph $NL(G, d)$. To get the base of G, all we need to do is remove a few nodes off the top of the graph $NL(G, d)$. The question is how many nodes off the top of $NL(G, d)$ should be removed.

We say that several nodes belong to the same *node sequence* if the nodes just below these nodes (along the functor path) are all connected with argument edges to the same node. This property can be read off a graph directly. Looking at the diagram in Fig. 3, we see that to obtain the base of G, all we need to do is remove the last node sequence from each functor path in $NL(G, d)$.

There remain two slight problems. The first is that when $k = 1$, a node sequence has to be removed only from one functor path, while when $1 < k$, node sequences have to be removed from both functor paths. Since we do not know the value of k, we do not know how many nodes to remove. A second problem is that when $k = 1$, the nodes which should be removed and some nodes in the base of G (which should not be removed) belong to the same node sequence (this can be seen in Fig. 3, since, when $k = 1$, the node labeled $k - 1$ and the node labeled σ in the figure are the same node).

---

[2] Because Algorithm 1 returns a standard loopless graph and $NL(G, d)$ is not always standard, the graph returned may be slightly different from $NL(G, d)$, but, using two strings from the sample, this problem can easily be solved.

Despite these problems, our algorithm always removes the last node sequence from each of the functor paths of the graph $NL(G, d)$. Note that this results in the same graph for every value of d and therefore we can denote the resulting (edge structure) graph by $\mathcal{B}(G)$. When $1 < k$, $\mathcal{B}(G)$ is exactly the base of G. When $k = 1$, however, too many nodes are removed by the algorithm and, as a result, $\mathcal{B}(G)$ is only the bottom part of the base of G. The missing part, though, is not too large. It is only the two last nodes sequences of the base of G.

Let τ_0 and σ_0 be the top nodes of $\mathcal{B}(G)$. Since string letter counts do not depend on the slashes assigned to a graph, it is possible to calculate, from the edge structure $\mathcal{B}(G)$, the letter counts $[s_{\tau_0}]$ and $[s_{\sigma_0}]$ of the strings s_{τ_0} and s_{σ_0} which are generated at τ_0 and σ_0 (that is, generated after we assign slashes to the edge structure).

In case $1 < k$, the strings s_{τ_0} and s_{σ_0} are exactly the strings s_τ and s_σ. When $k = 1$, because s_{τ_0} and s_{σ_0} are generated lower down in the base of G than s_τ and s_σ, the strings s_τ and s_σ must be concatenations of copies of s_{τ_0} and s_{σ_0}. In either case, every string in $L(G)$ must be a concatenation of copies of the strings s_{τ_0} and s_{σ_0}.

Finally, we note that when the loop length of G is $1 < k$, the length of the node sequence removed above the node σ is $k - 1$. Therefore, once we deduce that indeed $1 < k$, we can immediately deduce the number k.

Extracting s_{τ_0} and s_{σ_0} from the Prefixes of Sample Strings. Let $s \in L(G)$ be a string in the sample available to the learner. The string s is a concatenation of copies of s_{τ_0} and s_{σ_0}. Therefore, s must have at least one of the strings s_{τ_0} or s_{σ_0} as a prefix. It is not known, however, which of the two strings is such a prefix and at which end (left or right) of the string s. Knowing $[s_{\tau_0}]$ and $[s_{\sigma_0}]$, we know not only the lengths of the prefixes we are looking for, but also their letter counts. However, it may happen that a string s has a prefix with letter count $[s_{\tau_0}]$, but that this prefix is not equal to s_{τ_0}. The same can happen with s_{σ_0}.

By looking at Fig. 3, one sees that s_{τ_0} is a concatenation of several copies of s_{σ_0} with a single copy of some other string s_{π_0} which is generated at some node in the base of G. It turns out that this fact guarantees that *at least* one of the three methods described in the next algorithm must succeed in finding at least one of the strings s_{τ_0} or s_{σ_0}:

Algorithm 2. *Given is a string $s \in L(G)$ and the letter counts $[s_{\tau_0}]$ and $[s_{\sigma_0}]$ deduced for G.*

1. *If the left and right prefixes of s of length $|s_{\tau_0}|$ are identical, then this is the string s_{τ_0}.*
2. *If the left and right prefixes of s of length $|s_{\sigma_0}|$ are identical, then this is the string s_{σ_0}.*
3. *If the letter counts of the left and right prefixes of s of length $|s_{\tau_0}|$ are different, then one of these letter counts must be equal to $[s_{\tau_0}]$. The corresponding prefix is s_{τ_0}. The prefix of length $|s_{\sigma_0}|$ at the other end of s must be the string s_{σ_0}.*

Example 1. Let G be a graph with loop length 2 which has $s_{\sigma_0} = s_\sigma = a$, $s_{\pi_0} = s_\pi = b$ and $s_{\tau_0} = s_\tau = s_\sigma s_\sigma s_\pi = aba$ (it is simple to construct the appropriate base for G). Assume both slashes on the loop of G are forward slashes (/). The language $L(G)$ then contains the two strings $s_\sigma s_\tau s_\tau = aabaaba$ and $s_\sigma(s_\sigma s_\tau s_\tau)s_\tau = aaabaabaaba$. The $|s_{\tau_0}|$-length left and right prefixes of the first string are aab and aba. Both have letter count $[s_{\tau_0}] = [2, 1]$ and therefore the algorithm cannot determine which of them is the string s_{τ_0}. For the second string, the prefixes are aaa and aba. Since aaa does not have letter count $[s_{\tau_0}]$, the algorithm can determine that $s_{\tau_0} = aba$. For both strings the algorithm can determine s_{σ_0} since $|s_{\sigma_0}| = 1$ and all prefixes of that length are the single letter a.

3.3   Inferring the Loop Structure

The loop of the graph G generates strings by concatenating copies of s_τ and s_σ. To infer the structure of the loop, we must first parse strings in the sample as concatenations of s_{τ_0} and s_{σ_0} (which are either equal to s_τ and s_σ or substrings of s_τ and s_σ).

Parsing Strings. In order to parse a sample string s as a concatenation of s_{τ_0} and s_{σ_0}, it is enough to know one of the two strings s_{τ_0} or s_{σ_0}. ¿From now on, we assume the learner found s_{τ_0}. The treatment of the case in which the learner discovers s_{σ_0} is similar, in principle, though some of the technical details differ.

To parse a sample string s, the learner simply tries to match s_{τ_0} with segments of s. This begins at one end (left or right) of s. Each time the compared segment of s is identical to s_{τ_0}, that segment is marked as u_τ. When the match fails, the learner assumes an s_{σ_0} was reached and marks the appropriate segment (of known length $|s_{\sigma_0}|$) as u_σ. The process then continues to the next segment. The segments marked u_τ are clearly identical to s_{τ_0}. It is less obvious, but true, that the segments marked u_σ are always identical to each other and have the same letter count as $[s_{\sigma_0}]$. However, depending on the direction of the parse (from the right or left), different parses may result and the string marked by u_σ may differ, as in the following example, where $s_{\tau_0} = baaba$. The parse from the left is given above the string and the parse from the right is given below the string:

$$
\begin{array}{ccccc}
 & \overbrace{\quad}^{u_\tau} & & \overbrace{\quad}^{u_\tau} & \\
u_\tau & & u_\sigma & & u_\sigma \\
baaba & baa & ba & aba & baa & ba & aba \\
u_\tau & u_\sigma & & u_\sigma & \\
 & \underbrace{\quad}_{u_\tau} & & \underbrace{\quad}_{u_\tau} &
\end{array}
$$

Whether the two parses are identical or different is a property of the strings s_{τ_0} and s_{σ_0}, and therefore is the same for all strings in $L(G)$. The two parses can differ only by a "shift" of one u_τ. When different, the right to left parse can be transformed into the left to right parse by removing one u_τ from the right end and attaching it at the left end (as in the example). Note that at least one parse must be a *correct* parse, which reflects the way the string was generated by the graph.

Completing the Language Inference. Let l and r be the number of backslashes (\\) and forward slashes (/), respectively, assigned to the loop of a graph G (so $l + r = k$). The language $L(G)$ generated by the loop of a graph G is easily seen to consist of the string s_τ and strings of the form $s_1 \ldots s_l s_\sigma s_{l+1} \ldots s_{l+r}$, where $s_1, \ldots, s_{l+r}$ are strings in $L(G)$. We outline the way in which the numbers l and r can be deduced from the parses described in the previous section. Since the parses also give an hypothesis for the string s_{σ_0}, this completes the language inference. The uncertainties involved in the inference procedure may result in a graph being hypothesized which is slightly different from the original graph G that generated the sample. The language hypothesized, however, is always correct.

A language generated by a graph of loop length 1 must have one of the following forms (where k is the number deduced when calculating $\mathcal{B}$ in Sect. 3.2):

1. $L(G) = \{ s_{\tau_0}^i (s_{\sigma_0} s_{\tau_0}^{k-1})^{q+n} s_{\sigma_0} s_{\tau_0}^{k-i} \mid 0 \le n \}$.
2. $L(G) = \{ s_{\tau_0}^i s_{\sigma_0} (s_{\tau_0}^{k-1} s_{\sigma_0})^{q'} s_{\tau_0} (s_{\tau_0}^{k-1} s_{\sigma_0})^{q+n} s_{\tau_0}^{k-1-i} \mid 0 \le n \}$.
3. $L(G) = \{ s_{\tau_0}^i (s_{\sigma_0} s_{\tau_0}^{k-1})^{q+n} s_{\tau_0} (s_{\sigma_0} s_{\tau_0}^{k-1})^{q'} s_{\sigma_0} s_{\tau_0}^{k-1-i} \mid 0 \le n \}$.

When all parses of strings in the sample match one of these forms, the corresponding language is hypothesized. Since no more than one of the above forms can fit the same two strings, any two strings from the sample are sufficient in order to construct such a hypothesis. Any graph of loop length greater than 1, which generates strings with such parses, generates a language which strictly contains this hypothesized language. Therefore, as long as the sample does not contain a string whose parse does not fit the loop length 1 hypothesis, this hypothesis can be safely maintained.

Only one uncertainty remains. The parameter n in the above forms is added to some constant q. For the parses of the sample strings, it is possible to determine $q + n$, but not q and n separately. The solution is to assume that the shortest string in the sample has $n = 0$. This guarantees that the hypothesized language is contained in the language $L(G)$. When new strings are added to the sample, a shorter string may require the hypothesized parameter q to be decreased.

Once the sample contains strings whose parses cannot be interpreted as being generated by a loop length 1 graph, the learner can deduce that the language was generated by a graph of loop length greater than 1. This means that $s_{\tau_0} = s_\tau$ and $s_{\sigma_0} = s_\sigma$. Moreover, from the algorithm in Sect. 3.2, the learner also knows the length k of the loop.

Once k is known, there is a linear time algorithm which can determine those values of l, r which can generate the sample. For some samples there may be more than one such pair (some languages overlap). We do not give here the full algorithm, but only a partial algorithm (based on the same principles). This algorithm only finds upper bounds for the numbers l and r. To calculate an upper bound for l, the algorithm should be applied to a parse from left to right. To calculate an upper bound for r, it should be applied from right to left.

Algorithm 3. *Let k be the loop length of G. Given is a parse P of a string $s \in L(G)$. The algorithm begins at one end of P and advances one by one along the symbols of P. The bound calculated by the algorithm is returned in the variable ρ. The algorithm begins with $\rho := k$ and $\delta := 0$.*

1. *If the current symbol in the parse is u_τ, increase δ by 1 and continue to the next symbol in the parse.*
2. *If the current symbol in the parse is u_σ, set $\rho := min(\rho, \delta)$ and then $\delta := max(0, \delta - (k-1))$.*

We conclude by commenting that in every language there is a string from which even the simple Algorithm 3 can calculate the values of l and r exactly. When the left and right parses are identical, the simple string $s_\tau^l s_\sigma s_\tau^r$ will do. When the left and right parses are different, a more complicated string disambiguates the language. For example, if the correct parse is from left to right and $2 \le l$, then the string $s_\tau^l s_\sigma s_\tau^l s_\sigma s_\tau^{2r+l-2} s_\sigma s_\tau^{2l+r-2} s_\sigma s_\tau^r s_\sigma s_\tau^r$ will always do. Applying Algorithm 3 to the incorrect parse of this string will result in the pair $l-1, r$, which does not sum together to k. This allows the learner to reject the parse.

4   Conclusion

Even the very simple class of 2-letter rigid grammars has a complex structure. While learning a grammar in this class can be done efficiently, it is not a trivial task. The learning algorithm must be carefully devised to make use of the special properties of the class of grammars being learned. Moreover, receiving the "wrong" input may delay (indefinitely) learning the correct grammar. At the same time, receiving the "right" input can lead to very fast convergence to the correct grammar.

The properties of the 2-letter rigid grammars which were used here cannot be easily extended to other classes of grammars (but do apply to any 2-letter sub-language of a rigid grammar). Even the 3-letter rigid grammars are already a more complex class. However, one may try to identify other classes of grammars which can be characterized by parameters which can be solved sequentially. These parameters may be hidden below the surface of the standard representation of categorial grammars through types.

References

1. Costa Florêncio C. *Consistent Identification in the Limit of any of the Classes k-Valued is NP-Hard*, In de Groote P., Morril G., Retoré C., Eds., Logical Aspects of Computational Linguistics, vol. 2099 of Lecture Notes in Artificial Intelligence, p. 125-138, Springer, 2001.
2. Graham R., Knuth D., Potashnik O. *Concrete Mathematics*, 2nd ed. Addison-Wesley, 1994.
3. Kanazawa M. *Learnable Classes of Categorial Grammars*, Studies in Logic Language and Information, CSLI Publications, 1998.

Learning Locally Testable Even Linear Languages from Positive Data*

José M. Sempere and Pedro García

Departamento de Sistemas Informáticos y Computación
Universidad Politécnica de Valencia
Valencia, Spain
{jsempere,pgarcia}@dsic.upv.es

Abstract. Learning from positive data is a center goal in grammatical inference. Some language classes have been characterized in order to allow its learning from *text*. There are two different approaches to this topic: (i) reducing the new classes to well known ones, and (ii) designing new learning algorithms for the new classes. In this work we will use reduction techniques to define new classes of even linear languages which can be inferred from positive data only. We will center our attention to inferable classes based on local testability features. So, the learning processes for such classes of even linear languages can be performed by using algorithms for locally testable regular languages.
Keywords: *Learning from positive data, local testability, even linear languages.*

1 Introduction

Grammatical inference [AS83, Sa97] is the inductive learning approach where target concepts are represented through objects from Formal Language theory (typically finite automata, formal grammars and Turing machines-like acceptors or generators). Learning new language classes from different information protocols is one of the most important goals in grammatical inference. Along the time, there have been characterized many language classes that can be inferred from only positive data. Learning from positive data [An80] is one of the most attractive information protocols for grammatical inference. It excludes negative information and all the problems concerning its characterization in terms of noisy or incomplete data. Nevertheless, the main problem with learning from positive data is the *overgeneralization* effect to formulate hypotheses. Anyway, some subclasses of regular languages have been characterized and proved to be inferred from positive data. First, talking about regular languages, we can mention, among others, reversible languages [An82, Mä00], k-testable languages in the strict sense [GVO90], different subfamilies of testable languages including k-testable languages [Ru97], terminal distinguishable languages [Fe99, RN87a, RN87b] and generalizations of k-testable plus terminal distinguishable languages [Fe00a]. Talking about even linear languages, we can refer

---

* Work supported by the Spanish CICYT under contract TIC2000-1153.

P. Adriaans, H. Fernau, and M. van Zaanen (Eds.): ICGI 2002, LNAI 2484, pp. 225–236, 2002.

to terminal distinguishable even linear languages [RN88, Fe99] and deterministic even linear languages which are an extension of regular reversible ones [KMT97]. A generalization to function distinguishable language learning can be found in [Fe00b]. Finally, for other language classes, there have been different approaches to the same direction [EST96, EST98, EST00].

In this work, we will explore how k-testability can be extended to act over even linear languages and, therefore, can be taken into account to design new learning algorithms based on old ones. Our success criterion will be Gold's *identification in the limit* [Go67] and the information protocol will be only positive strings of the target language. We will propose some front-end transformations in order to carry out the learning methods.

The structure of this work is as follows: First, we will give the definitions and results that we will use in order to define new language classes. We will introduce different classes of even linear languages whose definitions depend on how the reductions to regular languages are performed. For every language class we will propose an integrated protocol to efficiently learn target languages of every class.

2   Basic Concepts and Notation

The basic concepts of formal language theory that we will use can be consulted in [HU79]. First, Σ will denote an alphabet and $card(\Sigma)$ its cardinality. Σ^* will be the set of words over Σ. The empty string will be denoted by λ. The reversal of a string x will be denoted by x^r. The product of the strings x and y will be denoted by xy. The set of strings with length less than or equal to k (resp. less than k, equal to k) will be denoted by $\Sigma^{\leq k}$ (resp. $\Sigma^{<k}$, Σ^k). Given any string $x \in \Sigma^*$, its length will be denoted by $|x|$. A language L defined over Σ is any subset of Σ^*.

A grammar is a construct $G = (N, \Sigma, P, S)$ where, N and Σ are two disjoint alphabets of nonterminal and terminal symbols, P is a finite set of production rules and $S \in N$ is the axiom of the grammar. The relationship between strings of symbols that can eventually appear during a derivation process in the grammar will be denoted by $\overset{*}{\underset{G}{\Rightarrow}}$. So, the language obtained by the grammar G is the set $L(G) = \{x \in \Sigma^* : S \overset{*}{\underset{G}{\Rightarrow}} x\}$. The class of regular languages will be denoted by $\mathcal{REG}$ and the class of context-free languages will be denoted by $\mathcal{CF}$.

Even linear language class ($\mathcal{ELL}$) was first introduced by Amar and Putzolu in [AP64]. An even linear grammar $G = (N, \Sigma, P, S)$ is characterized through the forms in which every production appears in the grammar. There are two possible forms for every production in G:

1. $A \rightarrow xBy$ with $A, B \in N$ and $x, y \in \Sigma^k$ for any $k > 0$
2. $A \rightarrow x$ with $A \in N$ and $x \in \Sigma^*$

The following normal form of the productions can be applied to any even linear grammar to obtain an equivalent one:

1. $A \rightarrow aBb$ with $A, B \in N$ and $a, b \in \Sigma$
2. $A \rightarrow x$ with $A \in N$ and $x \in \Sigma \cup \{\lambda\}$

From now on we will work with grammars in the previously defined normal form. It is well known that $\mathcal{REG} \subset \mathcal{ELL} \subset \mathcal{CF}$. Amar and Putzolu [AP64] proved that any even linear language can be characterized by a finite index *quasi-congruence* over pair of strings (x, y). Later, Takada [Ta88] showed how any even linear language can be obtained from a regular control set together with a predefined universal grammar. He designed an inference protocol for even linear languages based on a reduction of the input sample to a different one which induces a regular language. Sempere and García [SG94] defined a transformation $\sigma : \Sigma^* \rightarrow (\Sigma\Sigma)^* \Sigma \cup \lambda$ in the following way

1. $(\forall a \in \Sigma \cup \{\lambda\})\ \sigma(a) = a$
2. $(\forall a, b \in \Sigma)\ (\forall x \in \Sigma^*)\ \sigma(axb) = [ab]\sigma(x)$

The transformation σ^{-1} was defined in a similar way:

1. $(\forall a \in \Sigma \cup \{\lambda\})\ \sigma^{-1}(a) = a$
2. $(\forall a, b \in \Sigma)\ (\forall x \in \Sigma^*)\ \sigma^{-1}([ab]x) = a\sigma^{-1}(x)b$

Sempere and García [SG94] showed that L is an even linear language iff $\sigma(L)$ is regular. So, in a similar manner as Takada did, they reduced the problem of learning even linear languages to the problem of learning regular ones.

3   Locally Testable Even Linear Languages

Locally testable languages were first introduced by McNaughton and Papert [McP71]. We will give some definitions to establish the characteristics of such languages.

Definition 1. *Let $k > 0$ and for every string $x \in \Sigma^*$ we define the k-testable vector of x as the tuple $v_k(x) = (i_k(x), t_k(x), f_k(x))$ where*

$$i_k(x) = \begin{cases} x & \text{if } |x| < k \\ u : x = uv, |u| = k - 1 & \text{if } |x| \geq k \end{cases}$$

$$f_k(x) = \begin{cases} x & \text{if } |x| < k \\ v : x = uv, |v| = k - 1 & \text{if } |x| \geq k \end{cases}$$

$$t_k(x) = \{v : x = uvw, u \in \Sigma^*, w \in \Sigma^*, |v| = k\}$$

Definition 2. *For every $k > 0$, we define the equivalence relation $\equiv_k \subseteq \Sigma^* \times \Sigma^*$ as follows:*

$$(\forall x, y \in \Sigma^*) \quad x \equiv_k y \Longleftrightarrow v_k(x) = v_k(y)$$

It has been proved that $\equiv_k$ is a finite index relation and $\equiv_{k+1}$ refines $\equiv_k$.

Definition 3. *We will say that $L \subseteq \Sigma^*$ is k-testable iff it is the union of some equivalence classes of $\equiv_k$. L is locally testable if it is k-testable for any $k > 0$.*

We will denote the family of k-testable languages by k-$\mathcal{TL}$ and the class of locally testable languages by $\mathcal{LT}$. It is proved that $\mathcal{LT} \subset \mathcal{REG}$

Another language class which is intimately related to $\mathcal{LT}$ is the class of locally testable languages in the strict sense [Ga88]. We will define it as follows:

Definition 4. *Let Σ be an alphabet and $Z_k = (\Sigma, I_k, F_k, T_k)$ where $I_k, F_k \subseteq \Sigma^{\leq k-1}$ and $T_k \subseteq \Sigma^k$. Then, L is a k-testable language in the strict sense if it is defined by the following expression*

$$L = (I_k \Sigma^*) \cap (\Sigma^* F_k) - (\Sigma^* T_k \Sigma^*)$$

We will say that L is locally testable in the strict sense if it is k-testable in the strict sense for any $k > 0$.

We will denote the family of k-testable languages in the strict sense by k-$\mathcal{LTSS}$ and the class of locally languages in the Strict Sense by $\mathcal{LTSS}$. It is proved that $\mathcal{LTSS} \subset \mathcal{REG}$. Furthermore, k-$\mathcal{LT}$ is the boolean closure of k-$\mathcal{LTSS}$. Observe that both classes, k-$\mathcal{LT}$ and k-$\mathcal{LTSS}$ are closed under reversal.

In order to work with even linear languages we must use σ transformation together with a morphism $g : (\Sigma\Sigma) \cup \Sigma \rightarrow \Delta$, where Δ is an alphabet such that $card(\Delta) \geq card(\Sigma)^2 + 2 \cdot card(\Sigma)$. So, if $\Sigma = \{a_1, a_2, \cdots, a_n\}$ and $\Delta = \{b_1, b_2, \cdots, b_m\}$ then g will be defined as follows

1. $(\forall a_i \in \Sigma) \, g(a_i) = b_i$
2. $(\forall a_i, a_j \in \Sigma) \, g([a_i a_j]) = b_{n+i \cdot n + j}$

Definition 5. *Let $L \in \mathcal{ELL}$. Then, L is a locally testable even linear language iff $g(\sigma(L)) \in \mathcal{LT}$. We will say that L is a locally testable even linear language in the strict sense iff $g(\sigma(L)) \in \mathcal{LTSS}$.*

We will denote the class of locally testable even linear languages as $\mathcal{LT}_{\mathcal{ELL}}$ and the class of locally testable even linear languages in the strict sense as $\mathcal{LTSS}_{\mathcal{ELL}}$. From the last definition, we can design a reduction technique to learn languages from $\mathcal{LT}_{\mathcal{ELL}}$ or $\mathcal{LTSS}_{\mathcal{ELL}}$ by applying learning algorithms for $\mathcal{LT}$ or $\mathcal{LTSS}$. Let us suppose that the learning algorithm for $\mathcal{LT}$ is $A_{\mathcal{LT}}$ as described in [Ru97], then the script for such a reduction is showed in Figure 1.

Input: A finite sample R
Method:
$$S = \emptyset$$
$$\forall x \in R$$
$$S = S \cup g(\sigma(x))$$
$$\mathcal{H} = A_{\mathcal{LT}}(S)$$
Output: $\sigma^{-1}(g^{-1}(\mathcal{H}))$

Figure 1. *A method to infer languages from* $\mathcal{LT_{ELL}}$

The script to learn languages from $\mathcal{LTSS_{ELL}}$ is similar to the previous one. In this case, we should use a method to infer languages from $\mathcal{LTSS}$ as in [GVO90]. Let us suppose that such a method is $A_{\mathcal{LTSS}}$, then the inferring method is showed in Figure 2

Input: A finite sample R
Method:
$$S = \emptyset$$
$$\forall x \in R$$
$$S = S \cup g(\sigma(x))$$
$$\mathcal{H} = A_{\mathcal{LTSS}}(S)$$
Output: $\sigma^{-1}(g^{-1}(\mathcal{H}))$

Figure 2. *A method to infer languages from* $\mathcal{LTSS_{ELL}}$

Example 1. Let us suppose that sample R is defined by the set

$$R = \{10, 10001110, 111000111000, 11100001111000\}$$

then $\sigma(R)$ equals to the set

$$\{[10], [10][01][01][01], [10][10][10][01][01][01], [10][10][10][01][01][01][01]\}$$

If we apply the morphism g such that $g([10]) = a$ and $g([01]) = b$ then $g(\sigma(R)) = \{a, abbb, aaabbb, aaabbbb\}$. Now, by applying $A_{\mathcal{LTSS}}(S)$ to $g(\sigma(R))$, with $k = 2$, we obtain an hypothesis $\mathcal{H}$ such that $\sigma^{-1}(g^{-1}(\mathcal{H}))$ is the following even linear grammar: $S \rightarrow 1A0;\ A \rightarrow 1A0 \mid 0B1 \mid \lambda;\ B \rightarrow 1A0 \mid 0B1 \mid \lambda$.

A Characterization of Locally Testable Even Linear Grammars

Now, once we have efficiently solved the problem of learning locally testable even linear languages, we can take profit of the reductions we have applied in order to describe some features that makes an even linear grammar a locally testable one. Let us formalize such characteristics.

Property 1. Let $k > 0$ and let $G = (N, \Sigma, P, S)$ be an even linear grammar such that the following condition holds: $(\forall A \in N)$ if $S \overset{*}{\underset{G}{\Rightarrow}} x_1 A y_1$ and $S \overset{*}{\underset{G}{\Rightarrow}} x_2 A y_2$ then $\forall w \in \Sigma^*\ g(\sigma(x_1 w y_1)) \equiv_k g(\sigma(x_2 w y_2))$. Then $L(G) \in k - \mathcal{LT_{ELL}}$.

Proof.

Let us suppose that the grammar G holds the condition that the property states. Then, obviously, the strings of the language $L(G)$ can be obtained by $\mathcal{O}(card(N))$ equivalence classes according to $\equiv_k$.

$\square$

A similar result can be obtained in order to characterize those even linear grammars that generate languages from $\mathcal{LTSS}_{ELL}$.

4   More on Locally Testable Even Linear Languages

We have showed some relationships between even linear and regular languages through the transformations σ and g. Now, we will change the front-end string interface in order to characterize new language classes inside $\mathcal{ELL}$ that benefits from local testability in a different manner as described before.

Half-splitting Strings

Take notice that, in every even linear language, all the strings can be separated by right and left sides with equal length and a (possibly λ) centered string. The sides of every string can be mapped to derivations in even linear grammars

So, we will define a new transformation HalfSplit over strings which will separate them in two halves with the same length. For every string $x \in \Sigma^*$, we will define $\text{HalfSplit}(x) = \{x_1, a, x_2^r\}$ with $x = x_1 a x_2$ and $|x_1| = |x_2|$ and $a \in \Sigma \cup \{\lambda\}$.

Now, we will extend the operation over any finite sample S.

$$\text{HalfSplit}(S) = \{L(S), M(S), R(S)\}$$

where
$L(S) = \{x_1 \in \Sigma^* : \exists x \in S, \text{HalfSplit}(x) = \{x_1, a, x_2\}\},$
$R(S) = \{(x_2)^r \in \Sigma^* : \exists x \in S, \text{HalfSplit}(x) = \{x_1, a, x_2\}\}$ and
$M(S) = \{a \in \Sigma \cup \{\lambda\} : \exists x \in S, \text{HalfSplit}(x) = \{x_1, a, x_2\}\}.$

Synchronized Vs. Non Synchronized Half-splitting

With the help of HalfSplit, we can obtain hypotheses called *constructors* which will guide the learning process to obtain the final hypothesis. In Figure 3 we show the scripting method to obtain constructors from HalfSplit operation by using learning algorithms for $\mathcal{LT}$ language class.

Input: A finite sample S
Method:
$$T_L = L(S) \in \texttt{HalfSplit}(S)$$
$$T_R = R(S) \in \texttt{HalfSplit}(S)$$
$$T_M = M(S) \in \texttt{HalfSplit}(S)$$
$$\mathcal{H}_L = A_{\mathcal{LT}}(T_L)$$
$$\mathcal{H}_R = A_{\mathcal{LT}}(T_R)$$
$$\mathcal{H}_M = T_M$$
Output: $\{\mathcal{H}_L, \mathcal{H}_M, \mathcal{H}_R\}$

Figure 3. *A method to infer constructors for synchronized and non synchronized half-splitting*

Example 2. Let $S = \{abbaabab, abbabaababab, abbabbabbaababababab\}$, then $\texttt{HalfSplit}(S) = \{L(S), R, (S), M(S)\}$, where
$L(S) = \{abba, abbaba, abbabbabba\}$,
$R(S) = \{baba, bababa, babababab\}$ and
$M(S) = \{\lambda\}$.

Now, by applying learning algorithm $A_{\mathcal{LT}}$, with $k = 2$ we obtain constructors $\mathcal{H}_L$ and $\mathcal{H}_R$ with $\mathcal{H}_M = \{\lambda\}$ where the equivalence classes constructed by the learning algorithm are the following
$$\mathcal{H}_L = \{[\lambda]_{\equiv_2}, [a]_{\equiv_2}, [ab]_{\equiv_2}, [abb]_{\equiv_2}, [abba]_{\equiv_2}, [abbab]_{\equiv_2}\}$$
$$\mathcal{H}_R = \{[\lambda]_{\equiv_2}, [b]_{\equiv_2}, [ba]_{\equiv_2}, [bab]_{\equiv_2}, [baba]_{\equiv_2}\}$$

After obtaining constructors from a finite sample then we can define different even linear language subclasses. Our motivation is to combine different equivalence classes from the relation $\equiv_k$ that has been obtained during the learning process. It is obvious that the sets that we have obtained from $\texttt{HalfSplit}$ form an input sample for a hidden locally testable regular language.

We will define *synchronicity* among the equivalence classes that we have obtained apart from $L(S)$ and $R(S)$. Synchronicity means that, if we take a string from the input sample $x = x_1 a x_2 \in S$, then the equivalence class obtained for x_1 must be linked to the equivalence class obtained for $(x_2)^r$. So, we can define the relation $\sim_k$ between strings as follows:$(\forall x, y \in \Sigma^*)$ with $|x_1| = |x_2|, |y_1| = |y_2|$, $x = x_1 a x_2$, $y = y_1 a y_2$ and $a \in \Sigma \cup \{\lambda\}$

$$x \sim_k y \Longleftrightarrow v_k(x_1) = v_k(y_1) \wedge v_k(x_2) = v_k(y_2)$$

Definition 6. *We will say that $L \subseteq \Sigma^*$ is k-testable synchronized half-split iff it is the union of some equivalence classes of $\sim_k$. L is locally testable synchronized half-split if it is k-testable synchronized half-split for any $k > 0$.*

We will denote the language class of *locally testable synchronized half-split* even linear languages by $\mathcal{LTSHS}_{ELL}$. Then, we can infer k *locally testable synchronized half-split* even linear languages from constructors by applying the script showed in Figure 4.

Input: A finite sample S and constructors $\mathcal{H}_L, \mathcal{H}_M$ and $\mathcal{H}_R$
Method:

Enumerate $\mathcal{H}_L$ and $\mathcal{H}_R$
/* $card(\mathcal{H}_L) = n$ and $card(\mathcal{H}_R) = m$ */
$N = \{A_{ij} : 0 \leq i \leq n, 0 \leq j \leq m\}$
$S = A_{00}$
$\forall x \in S$
$\quad \forall u, v, w \in \Sigma^* \; a, b \in \Sigma : x = uawbv$ with $|u| = |v|$
$\quad$ /* $[u]_{\equiv_k}$ is the ith equivalence class in $\mathcal{H}_L$ */
$\quad$ /* $[v^r]_{\equiv_k}$ is the jth equivalence class in $\mathcal{H}_R$ */
$\quad$ /* $[ua]_{\equiv_k}$ is the kth equivalence class in $\mathcal{H}_L$ */
$\quad$ /* $[v^r b]_{\equiv_k}$ is the lth equivalence class in $\mathcal{H}_R$ */
$\quad A_{ij} \rightarrow aA_{kl}b \in P$
$\quad$ if $w \in \mathcal{H}_M$ then $A_{kl} \rightarrow w \in P$
Output: $G = (N, \Sigma, P, S)$

Figure 4. *A method to infer languages from* $\mathcal{LTSHS}_{ELL}$.

The identification in the limit of the class $\mathcal{LTSHS}_{ELL}$ can be easily deduced from the convergence of hypotheses $\mathcal{H}_L$ and $\mathcal{H}_R$ by using the algorithm $A_{\mathcal{LT}}$. Observe that the method proposed in Figure 4 is *conservative*, that is, all the classes of relation $\equiv_k$ are combined iff they have any representant in the input sample.

Example 3. Let us take the input sample and constructors of Example 2. Then the hypothesis $\mathcal{H}$ obtained by the method of Figure 4 is the following grammar

$A_{00} \rightarrow aA_{11}b$ $\qquad A_{44} \rightarrow bA_{53}b \mid \lambda$
$A_{11} \rightarrow bA_{22}a$ $\qquad A_{53} \rightarrow aA_{44}a \mid bA_{54}a$
$A_{22} \rightarrow bA_{33}b$ $\qquad A_{54} \rightarrow bA_{53}b \mid aA_{43}b$
$A_{33} \rightarrow aA_{44}a$ $\qquad A_{43} \rightarrow bA_{54}a$

The following result characterizes the grammars that generate the languages of $\mathcal{LTSHS}_{ELL}$.

Property 2. Let $k > 0$ and let $G = (N, \Sigma, P, S)$ be an even linear grammar such that the following condition holds: $(\forall A \in N)$ if $S \overset{*}{\underset{G}{\Rightarrow}} x_1 A y_1$ then $S \overset{*}{\underset{G}{\Rightarrow}} x_2 A y_2$ iff $x_1 \equiv_k x_2$ and $y_1 \equiv_k y_2$. Then, $L(G) \in k - \mathcal{LTSHS}_{\mathcal{ELL}}$

Proof.

Let us suppose that the grammar G holds the condition that the property states. Then, obviously, if we take two different strings of $L(G)$ which can be obtained during a derivation process in the grammar as follows

$$S \overset{*}{\underset{G}{\Rightarrow}} x_1 A y_1 \underset{G}{\Rightarrow} x_1 a y_1$$
$$S \overset{*}{\underset{G}{\Rightarrow}} x_2 A y_2 \underset{G}{\Rightarrow} x_2 a y_2$$

it can be easily proved that, according to the last derivations, $x_1 \equiv_k x_2$ and $y_1 \equiv_k y_2$. The strings of the language $L(G)$ can be obtained by at most $\mathcal{O}(card(N))$ equivalence classes according to $\sim_k$. So, $L(G) \in k - \mathcal{LTSHS}_{\mathcal{ELL}}$ $\qquad\square$

The definition of *non synchronized half-split* even linear languages is quite simple. Here, we do not force every equivalence class to be linked with its correspondent (right or left) equivalence class. We will define the relation $\approx_k$ between strings as follows: $(\forall x, y \in \Sigma^*)$ with $|x_1| = |x_2|, |y_1| = |y_2|, x = x_1 a x_2, y = y_1 a y_2$ and $a \in \Sigma \cup \{\lambda\}$

$$x \approx_k y \iff v_k(x_1) = v_k(y_1) \vee v_k(x_2) = v_k(y_2)$$

Definition 7. *We will say that $L \subseteq \Sigma^*$ is k-testable non synchronized half-split iff it is the union of some equivalence classes of $\approx_k$. L is locally testable non synchronized half-split if it is k-testable non synchronized half-split for any $k > 0$.*

The class of *locally testable non synchronized half-split* even linear languages will be denoted by $\mathcal{LTNSHS}_{ELL}$. Then we can infer k *locally testable non synchronized half-split* even linear languages from constructors by applying the script showed in Figure 5.

> **Input:** A finite sample S and constructors $\mathcal{H}_L, \mathcal{H}_M$ and $\mathcal{H}_R$
> **Method:**
> $\qquad$ Enumerate $\mathcal{H}_L$ and $\mathcal{H}_R$
> $\qquad$ /* $card(\mathcal{H}_L) = n$ and $card(\mathcal{H}_R) = m$ */
> $\qquad$ $N = \{A_{iL} : 0 \le i \le n\} \cup \{A_{jR} : 0 \le j \le m\} \cup \{S\}$
> $\qquad$ $\forall x \in S$
> $\qquad\qquad$ $\forall u \in \Sigma^*\ a \in \Sigma : x = uawv$ with $|ua| \le |v|$
> $\qquad\qquad$ /* $[u]_{\equiv_k}$ is the ith equivalence class in $\mathcal{H}_L$ */
> $\qquad\qquad$ /* $[ua]_{\equiv_k}$ is the kth equivalence class in $\mathcal{H}_L$ */
> $\qquad\qquad$ $\forall b \in \Sigma$
> $\qquad\qquad\qquad$ $A_{iL} \to aA_{kL}b \in P$
> $\qquad\qquad\qquad$ if $w \in \mathcal{H}_M$ then $A_{kL} \to w \in P$
> $\qquad$ $\forall x \in S$
> $\qquad\qquad$ $\forall v \in \Sigma^*\ b \in \Sigma : x = uwbv$ with $|bv| \le |u|$
> $\qquad\qquad$ /* $[v^r]_{\equiv_k}$ is the ith equivalence class in $\mathcal{H}_R$ */
> $\qquad\qquad$ /* $[v^r b]_{\equiv_k}$ is the kth equivalence class in $\mathcal{H}_R$ */
> $\qquad\qquad$ $\forall a \in \Sigma$
> $\qquad\qquad\qquad$ $A_{iR} \to aA_{kR}b \in P$
> $\qquad\qquad\qquad$ if $w \in \mathcal{H}_M$ then $A_{kR} \to w \in P$
> $\qquad$ if $A_{0L} \to w$ then $S \to w \in P$
> $\qquad$ if $A_{0R} \to w$ then $S \to w \in P$
> **Output:** $G = (N, \Sigma, P, S)$

Figure 5. *A method to infer languages from $\mathcal{LTNSHS}_{ELL}$.*

Again, the identification in the limit of the class $\mathcal{LTNSHS}_{ELL}$ can be easily deduced from the convergence of hypotheses $\mathcal{H}_L$ and $\mathcal{H}_R$ by using the algorithm $A_{\mathcal{LT}}$.

Example 4. Let us take the input sample and constructors of Example 2. Then the hypothesis $\mathcal{H}$ obtained by the method of Figure 5 is the following grammar

$$S \to aA_{1L}a \mid aA_{1L}b \mid aA_{1R}b \mid bA_{1R}b$$

$$\begin{aligned}
A_{0L} &\to aA_{1L}a \mid aA_{1L}b & A_{0R} &\to aA_{1R}b \mid bA_{1R}b \\
A_{1L} &\to bA_{2L}a \mid bA_{2L}b & A_{1R} &\to aA_{2R}a \mid bA_{2R}a \\
A_{2L} &\to bA_{3L}a \mid bA_{3L}b & A_{2R} &\to aA_{3R}b \mid bA_{3R}b \\
A_{3L} &\to aA_{4L}a \mid aA_{4L}b & A_{3R} &\to aA_{4R}a \mid bA_{4R}a \\
A_{4L} &\to \lambda \mid bA_{5L}a \mid bA_{5L}b & A_{4R} &\to \lambda \mid aA_{3R}b \mid bA_{3R}b \\
A_{5L} &\to aA_{4L}a \mid aA_{4L}b \mid bA_{5L}a \mid bA_{5L}b
\end{aligned}$$

The following result characterizes the grammars that generate languages of the class $\mathcal{LTNSHS}_{ELL}$.

Property 3. Let $k > 0$ and let $G = (N, \Sigma, P, S)$ be an even linear grammar such that the following condition holds: $(\forall A \in N)$ if $S \overset{*}{\underset{G}{\Rightarrow}} x_1 A y_1$ then $S \overset{*}{\underset{G}{\Rightarrow}} x_2 A y_2$ iff $x_1 \equiv_k x_2$ or $y_1 \equiv_k y_2$. Then, $L(G) \in k - \mathcal{LTNSHS}_{\mathcal{ELL}}$.

Proof. Let us suppose that the grammar G holds the condition that the property states. Then, obviously, if we take two different strings of $L(G)$ which can be obtained during a derivation process in the grammar as follows

$$S \overset{*}{\underset{G}{\Rightarrow}} x_1 A y_1 \underset{G}{\Rightarrow} x_1 a y_1$$

$$S \overset{*}{\underset{G}{\Rightarrow}} x_2 A y_2 \underset{G}{\Rightarrow} x_2 a y_2$$

then, it can be easily proved that, according to the last derivations, $x_1 \equiv_k x_2$ or $y_1 \equiv_k y_2$. The strings of the language $L(G)$ can be obtained by $\mathcal{O}(card(N))$ equivalence classes according to $\approx_k$. So, $L(G) \in k - \mathcal{LTNSHS}_{\mathcal{ELL}}$ □

From properties 2 and 3, we can obtain the following result

Corollary 1. $\mathcal{LTNSHS}_{ELL} \subseteq \mathcal{LTSHS}_{ELL}$

5   Conclusions and Future Works

We have introduced different transformations over input strings of even linear languages in order to characterize several language subclasses that can be inferred from positive sample. The learning algorithms that we have used are those concerning locally testable languages. Obviously, by selecting different learning algorithms for regular languages we can define different subclasses of even linear languages. Under this approach, there have been such reductions as those showed in [Fe99, KMT97, RN88]. We will explore the relationship between the classes of languages defined in such works and our approach by using σ and g.

On the other hand, the reductions that we have used goes in the same direction as the definition of *function distinguishable languages* [Fe00b]. We will explore the relationship between function distinguishability and the reductions that we have proposed.

Finally, we have selected only two learning algorithm concerning local testability. The selection of different learning algorithms for local testability as those showed in [Ru97] (i.e right and left locally testable, piecewise locally testable, etc.) will define new inferrable language classes inside even linear language class. We will explore such direction in order to obtain a complete catalog of inferrable locally testable even linear languages.

Acknowledgements

José M. Sempere is grateful to Erkki Mäkinen for nice comments and corrections made to this work.

References

[AP64] V. Amar and G. Putzolu. *On a Family of Linear Grammars*. Information and Control 7, pp 283-291. 1964.

[An80] D. Angluin. *Inductive Inference of Formal Languages from Positive Data*. Information and Control 45, pp 117-135. 1980.

[An82] D. Angluin. *Inference of Reversible Languages*. Journal of the Association for Computing Machinery. Vol 29 No 3, pp 741-765. July 1982.

[AS83] D. Angluin and C. Smith. *Inductive Inference : Theory and Methods*. Computing Surveys, vol. 15. No. 3, pp 237-269. 1983.

[EST96] J.D. Emerald, K.G. Subramanian and D.G. Thomas. *Learning code regular and code linear languages*. Proceedings of the Third International Colloquium on Grammatical Inference ICGI-96. (L. Miclet, C. de la Higuera, eds). LNAI Vol. 1147, pp 211-221. Springer. 1996.

[EST98] J.D. Emerald, K.G. Subramanian and D.G. Thomas. *Learning a subclass of context-free Languages*. Proceedings of the 4th International Colloquium ICGI-98. (V. Honavar, G. Slutzki, eds). LNAI Vol. 1433, pp 223-243. 1998.

[EST00] J.D. Emerald, K.G. Subramanian and D.G. Thomas. *Inferring Subclasses of contextual languages*. Proceedings of the 5th International Colloquium ICGI 2000. (A. Oliveira, ed). LNAI Vol. 1891, pp 65-74. 2000.

[Fe99] H. Fernau. *Learning of terminal distinguishable languages*. Technical Report WSI–99–23. Universität Tübingen (Germany), Wilhelm-Schickard-Institut für Informatik, 1999.

[Fe00a] H. Fernau. *k-gram extensions of terminal distinguishable languages*. Proceedings of the International Conference on Pattern Recognition ICPR 2000, Vol. 2 pp 125-128. IEEE Press. 2000.

[Fe00b] H. Fernau. *Identification of function distinguishable languages*. Proceedings of the 11th International Conference on Algorithmic Learning Theory ALT 2000. (H. Arimura, S. Jain, A. Sharma, eds.). LNCS Vol. 1968 pp 116-130. Springer-Verlag 2000.

[Ga88] P. García. *Explorabilidad Local en Inferencia Inductiva de Lenguajes Regulares y Aplicaciones*. Ph.D. Thesis. Departamento de Sistemas Informáticos y Computación. Universidad Politécnica de Valencia. 1988.

[GVO90] P. García, E. Vidal and J. Oncina. *Learning Locally Testable Languages in the Strict Sense*. Proceedings of the First International Workshop on Algorithmic Learning Theory. pp 325-338. 1990.

[Go67] M. Gold. *Language Identification in the Limit*. Information and Control 10, pp 447-474. 1967.

[HU79] J. Hopcroft and J. Ullman. *Introduction to Automata Theory, Languages and Computation*. Addison-Wesley Publishing Co. 1979.

[KMT97] T. Koshiba, E. Mäkinen, Y. Takada. *Learning deterministic even linear languages from positive examples*. Theoretical Computer Science 185, pp 63-97. 1997.

[Mä00] E. Mäkinen. *On inferring zero-reversible languages*. Acta Cybernetica 14, pp 479-484. 2000.

[McP71] R. McNaughton and S. Papert. *Counter-free automata*. MIT Press. 1971.

[RN87a] V. Radhakrishnan. *Grammatical Inference from Positive Data: An Efective Integrated Approach*. PhD. Thesis. Department of Computer Science and Engineering. IIT, Bombay. 1987.

[RN87b] V. Radhakrishnan and G. Nagaraja. *Inference of Regular Grammars via Skeletons*. IEEE Trans. on Systems, Man and Cybernetics, 17, No. 6 pp 982-992. 1987.

[RN88] V. Radhakrishnan and G. Nagaraja. *Inference of Even Linear Languages and Its Application to Picture Description Languages*. Pattern Recognition, 21, No. 1. pp 55-62. 1988.

[Ru97] J. Ruiz. *Familias de Lenguajes Explorables : Inferencia Inductiva y Caracterización Algebraica*. Ph.D. Thesis. Departamento de Sistemas Informáticos y Computación. Universidad Politécnica de Valencia. 1997.

[Sa97] Y. Sakakibara. *Recent advances of grammatical inference*. Theoretical Computer Science 185, pp 15-45. 1997.

[SG94] J.M. Sempere and P. García. *A Characterization of Even Linear Languages ans its Application to the Learning Problem*. Proceedings of ICGI'94 (R. Carrasco and J. Oncina, eds.). LNAI Vol. 862, pp 38-44. Springer-Verlag. 1994.

[Ta88] Y. Takada. *Grammatical Inference of Even Linear Languages based on Control Sets*. Information Processing Letters 28, No. 4, pp 193-199. 1988.

Inferring Attribute Grammars with Structured Data for Natural Language Processing

Bradford Starkie

Telstra Research Laboratories, Box 249 Rosebank MDC 770 Blackburn Road Clayton
Victoria, Australia 3168
Brad.Starkie@team.telstra.com

Abstract. This paper presents a method for inferring reversible attribute grammars from tagged natural language sentences. Attribute grammars are a form of augmented context free grammar that assign "meaning" in the form of a data structure to a string in a context free language. The method presented in this paper has the ability to infer attribute grammars that can generate a wide range of useful data structures such as simple and structured types, lists, concatenated strings, and natural numbers. The method also presents two new forms of grammar generalisation; generalisation based upon identification of optional phrases and generalisation based upon lists. The method has been applied to and tested on the task of the rapid development of spoken dialog systems.

1 Introduction

Attribute grammars are a form of augmented context free grammar that can assign "meaning" in the form of a data structure to a string in a context free language [1]. Attribute grammars are commonly used in speech recognition systems, compilers and concept spotting robust parsers.

The motivation for the research was to develop a grammatical inference algorithm as part of an Integrated Development Environment (IDE) for spoken dialog systems. The IDE was intended to increase the speed of application development without sacrificing application quality, as well as to reduce the amount of expertise required by an application developer. The philosophy of the prototype IDE was to combine simple descriptions of desired applications with examples of their behaviour, and to generate working applications. Grammatical inference was a key component of this philosophy and the ideal grammatical inference algorithm for this task needs to be able to learn meaning as well as syntax, and to be able to learn a high quality grammar with a minimal number of training examples.

The work presented here extends previous work on the grammatical inference of attribute grammars [2] to include the ability to infer attribute grammars that can generate complex data types such as structures and lists. In addition the algorithm is enhanced so that the grammars it infers can be used for language generation. Some novel techniques for grammar generalisation are also presented here, which enable a grammar to be learnt with less training examples than would otherwise be needed.

P. Adriaans, H. Fernau, and M. van Zaanen (Eds.): ICGI 2002, LNAI 2484, pp. 237-248, 2002.
© Springer-Verlag Berlin Heidelberg 2002

Firstly an introduction to attribute grammars will be given, followed by a brief description of previous research into the inference of attribute grammars. An introduction to the Lyrebird^{TM} algorithm will then be given, followed by a description of the extensions to the algorithm used to infer grammars that can generate complex data types such as structures, lists and concatenated strings. Finally experimental results will be presented that demonstrate the algorithms ability to infer grammars that produce complex data types.

1.1 Attribute Grammars

Attribute grammars are a specialisation of context free grammars. A context free grammar can be represented by a 4-tuple $G = (N, \Sigma, \Pi, S)$, where N is the alphabet of non-terminal symbols; Σ is the alphabet of terminal symbols such that $N \cap \Sigma = \{\}$; Π is a finite set of productions P of the form $L \rightarrow s_1 s_2 ... s_n$ where $L \in N$ and each $s_i \in (N \cup \Sigma)$; and S is the set of specialised non-terminals called top level non-terminals that can be used as starting non-terminals for the generation of phrases.

Attribute grammars extend context free grammars to incorporate attributes which represent the meaning of utterances. An attribute a consists of a key k and a value v such that $a = (k, v)$ For instance;

$a_1 = (city, melbourne)$

Values can also contain attributes or sets of attributes, enabling the construction of structured attributes, for instance

$a_2 = (time, (hour, 3))$ or $a_3 = (date, \{(month, january), (day, 3)\})$

The attributes of a given utterance are attached to a parse tree for that utterance, such that each nonterminal symbols in the parse tree has associated a finite set A(s) of attributes. The actual attribute sets are determined by a finite set C(P) of attribute copy rules attached to each production rule P. These copy rules define the relationship between $A(L)$ and $A(R)$; where $A(R)$ is the set of attribute sets attached to the right hand side of P; i.e. $A(R) = \{A(s_i)|_{i=1 \rightarrow n}\}$. Copy rules that define a particular element of $A(L)$ from $A(R)$ are known as synthesised copy rules, while copy rules that define a particular element of $A(R)$ from $A(L)$ are known as inherited copy rules. Copy rules that define the relationship between different elements of $A(L)$ are known as agreement copy rules.

1.2 Attribute Grammars for Language Recognition

Figure 1 below shows an attribute grammar capable of being inferred using the method described in this paper. The notation used in this paper is as follows: symbols beginning in upper case are non-terminals while those beginning in lower case are terminals. Top level non-terminals begin with a period.

In our notation a non-terminal "Y" can have a variable "x" attached to it denoted as "Y:x". This represents a reference to the set of attributes $A(s)$ attached to that symbol.

```
.S -> i'd like to fly S2:s {from=$s.from,to=$s.to,
op=bookflight}
S2-> from Location:1 { from=$1.location }
S2-> from Location:11 to Location:12
{from=$11.location to=$12.location }
Location -> melbourne { location=melbourne }
Location -> sydney { location=sydney }
```

Figure 1. Example attribute grammar.

In this notation attribute copy rules are contained within curly braces. The current prototype can only contain synthesised copy rules. These copy rules assign a value to the attribute returned by the rule $A(R)$ either as a constant (e.g. location=melbourne) or by referencing the values of attributes attached to non-terminals $A(s)$ (e.g. from=$1.location). In addition, the value of an attribute can be set to the result of a function that takes one or more arguments that are either constants or the value attached to a non-terminal or the results of other functions (e.g. number=add($n1.number $2.number)).

The grammar in figure 1 is capable of generating and parsing 6 different phrases including the expression;

    i'd like to fly from melbourne to sydney

to which it would attach the attributes :

        { op=bookflight from=melbourne to=sydney}

1.3 Previous Research into the Inference of Attribute Grammars

Although the grammatical inference of attribute grammars has not been widely investigated, some methods that have been applied to the inference of other types of grammars are candidate approaches for the inference of attribute grammars. We will classify these techniques into four broad categories as follows.

a) Model Merging, where a grammar with small grammar coverage is generalised [3][4],
b) Model Splitting, where an overly general grammar is made more specific[5][6],
c) Explanation based learning, where a new phrase is explained (partially parsed) using existing rules [7][8] and
d) Parameter Estimation, where the structure of a grammar is fixed but probabilities are modified. In parameter estimation algorithms, zero probability rules can be deleted to make the grammar more specific[9].

In practice grammatical inference implementations often combine several of these techniques together [3][5] .

Model merging algorithms involve the creation of a starting grammar that generates the training data explicitly. Hierarchical structure is then added to the grammar through a process known as chunking. Chunking involves creating new non-terminals that represent commonly occurring sequences of symbols. The grammar is then generalised by merging non-terminals. Both merging and chunking modify the grammar, but only merging can generalise a grammar.

Stolcke [3] used a form of model merging known as Bayesian Model Merging to infer attribute grammars. In his work, Stolcke extended attribute grammars by including non-deterministic attribute copy rules with a corresponding probability. The limitations of the algorithm as described by Stolcke include its ability to infer non-deterministic grammars and its inability to model hierarchical attributes. Stolcke tested his algorithm on examples where the value of an attribute was consistently correlated with a single word in each phrase. In natural language however this is in no way guaranteed.

Model splitting algorithms [5][6] require a starting grammar, a set of positive examples that the grammar must be able to parse and a set of negative examples which the grammar might parse erroneously, but should not be able to parse. If the grammar is simple enough it can be improved by simply removing those rules that generate the negative examples. In many examples however the removal of bad rules would also reduce the ability of a grammar to parse some good examples. To overcome this problem rules are unfolded, so as to produce a larger set of more specific rules that cover the same phrases as the original grammar. If the unfold is successful it will be possible to delete a rule that generates negative examples without affecting the grammars ability to parse good examples. If the unfold is unsuccessful subsequent rules will need to be unfolded.

Explanation Based Learning [7][8] when applied to grammatical inference involves partial parsing, and the creation of new rules that reference existing rules when possible. The creation of rules by partial parsing is a very fast way to generalise grammars. Problems that need to be overcome include the unwanted substitution of non-terminals in top level rules, and in the case of attribute grammars, deciding how attributes returned by substituted non-terminals should be referenced in the attribute copy rules.

Pearlman [8] used a form of explanation based learning to infer augmented hierarchical n-gram grammars. He also applied the technique to the task of rapidly creating spoken dialog systems by non-experts. The limitations of Pearlman's technique include the inability to infer reversible grammars, and its reliance on keyword spotting that can make the recognition of negative clauses such as "anywhere but adelaide" difficult or impossible. Generalisation of the grammar is also achieved through similar assumptions to the generation of n-grams, which can result in meaningless in-grammar phrases.

2 Inferring Attribute Grammars Using the Lyrebird[TM] Algorithm

In [2] the Lyrebird[TM] algorithm was introduced that infers attribute grammars from tagged positive examples, and optionally a starting grammar and negative examples. Experimental results presented in the paper suggested that the algorithm performed better than Bayesian Model Merging on grammars with inconsistent correlation between words and attributes. The algorithm was also compared to the performance of an experienced human developer in developing grammars for spoken dialog systems. Experimental results showed that the algorithm produced grammars of a similar quality to experienced human developers, but in a reduced amount of time.

2.1 Lyrebird™ and Determinism

The Lyrebird™ algorithm attempts to infer consistent but probabilistic attribute grammars. The inference algorithm is a consistent learner, in that the inferred grammar will always attach the same attributes to a training phrase, which will be the same as they appear in the training phrase. For instance a phrase `"ten past four"` is ambiguous in English because it may refer to ten past four in the morning or ten past four in the evening. One way to model this ambiguity is by returning two possible sets of attributes. The alternative approach as taken by the Lyrebird™ algorithm is to either tag the phrase as ambiguous using an attribute or to leave ambiguous attributes unfilled. The advantage of this approach is that phrases that are ambiguous in natural language are not ambiguous with respect to the attributes they would be assigned. Another advantage is that some forms of overgeneralisation can be detected during the inference process, because they result in alternative meanings (attributes) being assigned to training phrases.

Despite the desired aim to learn consistent grammars, the process of inference often involves uncertainty. The Lyrebird™ algorithm generalises the grammar by a process of transforming it one step at a time. At some points in the inference process there may be more than one alternative way in which the grammar can be transformed. For instance during the process of incorporation, training examples are partially parsed to form new rules that cover not only the training phrase, but also additional unseen phrases. Consider the training phrase;

```
a  circle  is  above  a  circle  {  lm=circle  rel=above
tr=circle}
```

If a rule exists as follows

```
Object circle {object=circle}
```

Then the following two rules are candidates for inclusion into the grammar namely

```
a Object:x1 is above a Object:x2
       { lm=$x1.object rel=above tr=$x2.object}
a Object:x1 is above a Object:x2
       { lm=$x2.object rel=above tr=$x1.object}
```

Given only the training example either rule is likely, but because the attribute grammar needs to be consistent, only one can be added. The approach taken in the Lyrebird™ algorithm is to provide checkpoints at specific points in the inference process where the grammar must be consistent. Between checkpoints however inconsistency can exist. All rules are given a probability, and just prior to a checkpoint, rule probabilities are re-estimated, and zero probability rules are deleted. Rule probabilities are re-estimated considering both positive and negative training data.

2.2 Inferring Reversible Grammars

The grammars inferred by Lyrebird™ are reversible in that they can be used to attach meanings (attributes) to phrases, as well as being able to generate phrases given meanings (sets of attributes). Software has been written that converts the inferred grammar directly into language generation software that can be included in developed applications. Alternatively the inferred grammars can be used as data by language generation software. This is relatively straightforward because the Lyrebird^{TM} algorithm creates only reversible attribute copy rules. Reversible copy rules have the property that they can be represented as either synthesised copy rules, or inherited copy rules.

Consider the general case of a synthesised copy rule with multiple arguments;

$a_i = f_i(A(R))$ where $a_i \in A(L)$ and $f_i(A(R)) = C(P)$ and P:L->R is the rule in question. Here we can see that any particular attribute associated with a rule can be derived from a function that takes as its arguments, the attributes attached to the symbols of the right hand side of the rule.

For the purposes of language generation, it would be ideal if the value of each attribute attached to the symbols of the right hand side of the production rule, could be defined using a function that takes as its argument, the attributes attached to the rule. i.e.

$$a_i(s_j) = f_j(a_i) \text{ where } a_i(s_j) \in A(R)$$

When this is the case, generating a phrase from a set of attributes consists of selecting a rule, and passing to the non-terminals on the right hand side of that production rule, sets of attributes derived using the reversible copy rules. This process can then be repeated until a complete phrase is generated. The process of selecting the correct copy rule is not defined here for brevity's sake.

Two of these six forms of reversible attribute copy rules created by the inference algorithm are shown in table 1.

Table 1. Example reversible copy rules that can be constructed by the Lyrebird^{TM} algorithm

copy rule	action when interpreted bottom up	action when interpreted top down
`y=$x.z`	The attribute 'y' of a non-terminal is set to the value of the 'z' attribute attached to a symbol with the variable $x.	The attribute z of the symbol with the variable $x , is set to the value of the 'y' attribute attached to the non-terminal.
`y[] = insert_end ($x.y[] $z.q)`	The 'q' attribute attached to the symbol with the $z variable is appended to the end of the list y attached to the symbol with the variable $x. The resulting list is then assigned to the y attribute attached to the non-terminal.	The attribute q of the symbol with the variable $z , is set to the last element of the list 'y' attached to the non-terminal. The remainder of the list is assigned to the list y attached to the symbol with the $x variable

2.3 The Lyrebird^{TM} Algorithm

The Lyrebird^{TM} algorithm is a hybrid algorithm in that it combines all four techniques described in section 1.3. The algorithm follows the following procedure.

1. The algorithm is presented with a set of positive tagged training examples. It can also be given a starting grammar and a set of negative examples.
2. The positive examples are incorporated into the starting grammar using partial parsing (Explanation based learning). If the starting grammar is empty, rules are created which generate the examples explicitly.

3. The grammar is then checked for consistency. If any of the positive examples can be tagged differently to the way in which they are tagged in the training set, the alternative representations are added to the negative data set.
4. Model splitting is then applied to remove those rules that generate negative phrases.
5. Model Merging is then undertaken in an attempt to generalise the grammar. Hierarchical structure is added through chunking and generalisation occurs through non-terminal merging.
6. The grammar is then simplified and improved through parameter estimation.
7. After parameter estimation, model merging is repeated. This is because merges that may have been prevented through the inclusion of bad rules, may now be possible. A cost function is used to determine if model merging should cease.

A more detailed description of the Lyrebird^{TM} algorithm can be found in [2]. In addition to generalisation through the merging of non-terminals the algorithm also generalises by identifying optional phrases. Worded simply the bias is; "If a substring is seen to be optional at one part in the grammar, it is likely to be optional elsewhere in the grammar."

Consider the occurrence of two rules

```
X -> Y Z
X -> Z
```

Given these rules, one hypothesis is that the symbol Y is universally optional in the grammar. As a result the algorithm takes the following action;

1. If Y is terminal create the following two rules;
```
Q -> Y
Q ->
```
Then substitute all other occurrences of Y in the grammar with Q.

2. Alternatively if Y is a non-terminal create a rule of the form;
```
Y->
```

The grammars inferred by the Lyrebird^{TM} algorithm are strongly typed in that all rules attached to a particular non-terminal return the same attributes.

Consider the following rules;

```
Y -> house {building=house}
Z -> car {transport=car}
Q -> at Time:x1 on Date:x2
       { time[]=$x1.time[] date[]=$x2.date[]}
Q2 -> at Time:x1 { time[]=$x1.time[]  }
```

Here the non-terminals Y & Z could not be merged as they have different types. The non-terminals Q and Q2 however could be merged. This may lead to the substring 'on Date' being flagged as being optional throughout the grammar.

The remainder of this paper will focus on extensions to the algorithm to enable it to infer attribute grammars that can generate attributes of complex data type.

3 Inference of Structured Data Types

3.1 Inference of Structures

Previous research [2] demonstrated that the Lyrebird™ algorithm was effective at inferring attribute grammars that generated simple types such as enumerated tags. In addition, the algorithm could infer attribute grammars that attached structured attributes provided those structures had a finite depth and a finite number of parameters in each structure. The way in which this was done was to flatten structures into a set of assignment functions. For instance consider a date structure defined using the following "C" code:

```
enum Month {jan,feb,mar, ... , ... ,oct,nov,dec};
struct Date {
        int day_of_month;
        enum Month month;
        int year;};
```

In the Lyrebird™ algorithm an instance of this structure is represented by a set of attributes, that also represent a set of assignment functions to construct the object.

```
date.day_of_month=1 date.month=jan    date.year=1996
```

These assignment functions are then processed as unstructured attributes. The flattened notation can also be used to extend grammars that contain hand written components that can generate structures with an infinite depth and infinite number of elements (lists).

3.2 Inference of Lists

The first structured type that will be discussed is the list. A list can be considered to be a structure with a variable number of elements. As a result the assignment notation can be used to describe list data as well. The Lyrebird™ algorithm uses the same notation to describe lists as the Javascript language uses to assign values to them namely.

```
list[elementnumber]=value
```

In addition an attribute describing the length of the list is added namely;

```
list.length=value
```

To infer lists, the algorithm adds reversible list manipulation copy rules. The first of these copy rules is one rule that assigns one list to another. The notation used is

```
targetlist[]=$variable.assignmentlist[]
```

Its effect is to copy all the attributes attached to the symbol with the $variable , to the attribute set of the rule, while changing the prefix of attribute keys from asignmentlist to targetlist.

In addition two copy rule functions devoted to list insertion have been added namely;

```
y[]=insert_begin($x.y $z.q[])&
y[]=insert_end($x.y[] $z.q)
```

The `insert_end` function was described earlier in section 2.2. The `insert_begin` function is similar with the exception that the new element is added to the beginning of the list when the function is interpreted bottom up. These functions work equally well for lists of simple types as for lists of structures.

A simple set of rules that generates a list structure can thus be defined as follows

```
LOOPX -> X:x1 { x.length=1 x[0]=$x1.x }
LOOPX -> X:x1 LOOPX:x2 { x[]=insert_begin($x1.x $x2.x[]) }
```

These rules are ideal in that they are right-recursive rather than left-recursive. However in English, lists use a conjunction word such as "and" or "or" prior to the last element in the list, thus a rule of the form below is also required.

```
X2 -> LOOPX:x1 and X:x2 { x[]=insert_end($x1.x[] $x2.x) }
```

Identifying list structures in partially inferred grammars is a matter of identifying a sequence of consecutive non-terminals, whose values are used as the elements of a list as is described in the assignment notation. For lists of simple types this is dependent upon interchangeable elements in a list being represented by the same non-terminal. For lists of structured types, a non-terminal needs to exist that represents all of the components of that element.

Inferring attribute grammars that produce lists can thus be performed as follows;

1. The list structures are flattened into a set of simple attributes.
2. The attribute grammar is inferred as per normal. At the end of this process for lists to be successfully inferred a non-terminal needs to exist that represents the list element type.
3. Attribute copy rules are then generalised, by replacing simple assignment rules, by rules that assign lists and use list insertion functions.
4. Sequences of list elements are replaced with a reference to a pair of recursive rules that generate lists of variable length.
5. Rule probabilities are then re-estimated and redundant rules are deleted.

3.3 Inference of Concatenated Strings and Natural Numbers

A concatenated string can be considered to be list of characters. As a result a range of grammars that can convert phrases to concatenated strings can be generated. Provided that there is a sufficient number of training examples to generate a non-terminal that represents the list elements, a grammar can be inferred. It should be noted that one of the more difficult tasks in creating transducers that convert a string in one format to another is identifying the alignment between the lexical units in one string to the lexical units in the other. As this problem has not been adequately addressed in the research the use of inferred attribute grammars is unlikely to rival other techniques such as finite state transducers or HMMs at this point. Despite this, a range of grammars that converted phrases to concatenated strings were successfully inferred including one that could convert natural number phrases to strings of digits .i.e. `twenty seven <-> "27"`

Attribute grammars that parse natural numbers often use arithmetic in their copy rules. Inferring such a grammar would be extremely difficult, and the resulting grammars would not be reversible. In contrast, the natural number grammars inferred using the Lyrebird™ algorithm need only to understand the relationship between concatenated strings and lists. Also the inferred grammars are reversible.

4 Experimental Results

The performance of the algorithm was tested on a range of hand crafted grammars. A number of unique example phrases were generated from the target grammar and divided into a disjoint training set and testing set. The Lyrebird™ algorithm was then trained using the training data to generate an inferred grammar. The percentage of phrases in the test set that were in grammar according to the inferred grammar, with the correct attributes was measured. This measurement is listed in the tables below as the recall, using a similar notation to that used in information retrieval research [11]. Similarly a range of example phrases were generated from the inferred grammar that did not appear in the training set. The percentage of these phrases that were parsed correctly by the target grammar was then measured. This measure is listed as the precision in the tables below. If the inferred grammar was identical to the target grammar its precision and recall would be 100%. High precision and low recall suggests an overly specific grammar, while high recall and low precision suggests an overly general grammar. The results listed in the tables below are crosscorrelated as listed.

Measurements of the time taken to infer the grammar were also collected. In the results below the correlation coefficient of the number of samples and the length of time taken to infer the grammar are listed. This gives an indication of how linear and therefore how scalable the algorithm is.

4.1 Time Grammar

The Lyrebird™ software was then tested on a time grammar. The grammar was chosen because it was a grammar that contained structures, and a grammar with inconsistent correlations of substrings and attributes. For instance consider the following examples;

```
ten past four   { hours=4 minutes=10 }
ten to four     { hours=3 minutes=50}
```

In the first example the word "four" correlates to a value of "4" while in the second it correlates to "3". The grammar also produced phrases that were ambiguous in English, although the tag assignment was unambiguous. The grammar contained 126 rules and could generate 6,559 possible phrases. A comparison was made between the Lyrebird™ algorithm and Bayesian Model Merging (BMM) using the BOOGIE software package, this was achieved by flattening the structure into assignment functions. Unfortunately large training sets derived from this grammar, caused the BOOGIE software to stop halfway through, and thus only the results of runs using 100 training examples can be displayed here. The data in table 2 represents the average of 4 tests. Here we can see the use of the Lyrebird™ algorithm results in over a 10x improvement in Recall and a 30x improvement in precision.

Table 2. Experimental results using time expressions.

Algorithm	# positive examples	Recall	Precision
BMM	100	6.35%	3%
Lyrebird[TM]	100	60.3%	95%
Lyrebird[TM]	700	99.6%	98%

The target grammar could be inferred on some training sets with 100% recall and 99% precision with 500 samples. Where the learnt grammar has less than 100% precision, the learnt grammar was overly general in that it allowed phrases such as "two noon" that had been generalised from the phrase "twelve noon". The correlation coefficient of the time to infer the grammar versus the number of samples was 0.94. It should be noted that both time and date expressions can be tagged as either simple types or structured types. The performance of the inference algorithm is identical either way.

4.2 List Grammar

The algorithm was then tested on a grammar that generated lists. Phrases that could be generated from the grammar include;

```
i like the colours blue green and red
blue red violet orange yellow
i like the colour orange
```

The grammar contained 19 rules and could generate an infinite number of phrases due to recursion. The grammar could generate 294,119 examples of lists that contained 4 or less elements in the list. The data represents the average of 10 tests. In some tests the grammar could be inferred with as little as 50 samples, with 100% recall and precision. The correlation coefficient of the time to infer the grammar versus the sample size was 0.99.

Table 3. Experimental results using sentences with conjunctions.

# positive examples	Recall	Precision	Time (seconds)
100	99%	100%	315

4.3 Natural Numbers

As an example of concatenated strings the algorithm was trained on a examples of natural language number phrases. The target grammar could generate phrases for all integers between zero and nine thousand ninety nine. The grammar contained 51 rules and could generate 10,000 phrases. The data represents the average of 4 tests.

Table 4. Experimental results using natural numbers.

# positive examples	Recall	Precision	Time (seconds)
700	99.3%	97.7%	1281

The target grammar could be inferred on some training sets with 100% and 99% precision with 1100 samples. The correlation coefficient of the time to infer the grammar and the number of samples was 0.94. The less than 100% precision is due to the fact that the inferred grammar could generate phrases such as

```
and nineteen { number="19" }
```

5 Conclusion and Further Work

This paper describes how the Lyrebird™ grammatical inference algorithm described in [2] has been extended to include the inference of attribute grammars that can attach complex data types to natural language phrases. The algorithm has also been extended to infer attribute grammars that are capable of being used in natural language generation as well as language recognition systems. Experimental results demonstrate the algorithm is capable of inferring grammars that can accommodate simple types, structures, lists and concatenated strings. Current work in progress includes the extension of the algorithm to infer attribute grammars that can attach attributes with recursively nested structures. The high linear correlation between the number of training examples and the time taken to infer the grammars, suggests that although the algorithm is not linear in the time it takes to infer grammars with respect to the number of training examples it is reasonably scalable.

References

1. Knuth, Donald E., 1968, "Semantics of context-free languages." Mathematical Systems Theory , 2(2): pp 127-45.
2. Starkie, Bradford C., 2001. Programming Spoken Dialogs Using Grammatical Inference, in *AI 2001: Advances in Artificial Intelligence, 14th Australian Joint Conference on Artificial Intelligence,* pp 449-460, Berlin: Springer Verlag
3. Stolcke, Andreas, 1994, Bayesian Learning of Probabilistic Language Models. Berkely CA: Univeristy of California dissertation.
4. Stolcke, A. and Omohundro, S. 1994, Inducing probabilistic grammars by Bayesian model merging, Grammatical Inference and Applications. Second International Colloquium on Grammatical Inference, ICGI-94 , pp 106-18 Berlin: Springer Verlag.
5. Cancedda, Nicola and Samuelsson, 2000, "Corpus-Based Grammar Specialization", Proceedings of the 4th conference on Computational Natural Language Learning and of the Second Learning Language in Logic Workshop, pp 7-12, Association for Computational Linguistics, New Brunswick USA.
6. Alexin Z., Gyimóthy T., and Boström H., 1997, IMPUT: An interactive learning tool based on program specialization. *Intelligent Data Analysis, 1(4),* October 1997. Elsevier Science Inc
7. Samuelsson, Christer & Rayner, Manny, 1991, Quantitative evaluation of explanation based learning as an optimization tool for a large-scale natural language system. *In Proceedings of the IJCAI-91,*Sydney Australia.
8. Pearlman J., 2000, "SLS-Lite: Enabling Spoken Language Design for non experts",M.Eng. Thesis, MIT, Cambridge, 2000.
9. Charniak, Eugene 1993, Statistical Language Learning, Cambridge, Mass. : MIT Press.
10. Starkie, Bradford C., 1999. A method of developing an interactive system, International Patent WO 00/78022.
11. Salton, Gerard & McGill, Michael J, 1983, Introduction to Modern Information Retrieval, p55, McGraw-Hill Inc.
TM – Trade mark applied for by Telstra New Wave Pty Ltd.

A PAC Learnability of
Simple Deterministic Languages

Yasuhiro Tajima[1] and Matsuaki Terada[1]

Department of Computer, Information and Communication Sciences,
Tokyo University of Agriculture and Technology,
2-24-16 naka-chou, koganei, Tokyo 184-8588, Japan
{ytajima, m-tera}@cc.tuat.ac.jp

Abstract. We show a polynomial time PAC learnability of simple deterministic languages with new defined queries and samples. In this paper,
we define a new query called *hashed membership query*. This query takes
a 3-tuple of words. Then it replies with the membership of the word
which is the concatenation of these three words in addition whether the
3-tuple represents a nonterminal or not in the target grammar. With
this query, the polynomial time PAC learnability is shown by the same
analysis in [2] on the new suggested algorithm in this paper.
Key words : PAC learning, learning via queries, simple deterministic language, representative sample

1 Introduction

We show a polynomial time PAC[8] learnability of simple deterministic languages
with new defined queries and samples. In this paper, we define a new query
called *hashed membership query*. This query takes a 3-tuple of words. Then it
replies with the membership of the word which is the concatenation of these
three words. In addition to the membership, it is answered that whether the
3-tuple represents a nonterminal or not in the target grammar. That is to say,
the learner can obtain a partial structural information by this query. With the
hashed membership query, a polynomial time PAC learnability is shown by the
same analysis in [2] on the new suggested algorithm in this paper. This learning
algorithm takes n_i samples for i-th stage and makes a hypothesis in every stage.
Then, if a hypothesis does not satisfy PAC, we can show that the set of samples
gathered by the algorithm is certainly close to a representative sample. Here, a
representative sample is a special finite subset of the target language[1][7]. When
the learner obtains a representative sample, the target language is laernable
exactly via membership queries[7]. In addition, there exists the representative
sample whose size is bounded by a polynomial of the target grammar. It implies
that the algorithm suggested in this paper terminates in a polynomial time with
a PAC hypothesis.

This paper is organized as follows: In Section2, we note preliminaries and
definitions. Section3 consists of definitions of queries, PAC learning, and related
theorems. In Section4, we describe the learning algorithm of our main result and

P. Adriaans, H. Fernau, and M. van Zaanen (Eds.): ICGI 2002, LNAI 2484, pp. 249–260, 2002.

evaluate the time complexity of this algorithm. Section5 concludes this paper with some future problems.

2   Preliminaries

A *context-free grammar* (CFG) is a 4-tuple $G = (N, \Sigma, P, S)$ where N is a finite set of *nonterminals*, Σ is a finite set of *terminals*, P is a finite set of *rules* and $S \in N$ is the *start symbol*. If P is ε-*free* and any rule in P is of the form $A \to a\beta$ then $G = (N, \Sigma, P, S)$ is said to be in *Greibach normal form*, where $A \in N, a \in \Sigma$ and $\beta \in N^*$. A CFG G is a *simple deterministic grammar* (SDG) [6] iff G is in Greibach normal form and for every $A \in N$ and $a \in \Sigma$, if $A \to a\beta$ is in P then $A \to a\gamma$ is not in P for any $\gamma \in N^*$ such that $\gamma \neq \beta$. In addition, such a set P of rules is called *simple deterministic*.

The *derivation* with $A \to a\beta$ in P is denoted by $\gamma A\gamma' \underset{G}{\Rightarrow} \gamma a\beta\gamma'$ where $A \in N$, $a \in \Sigma$, $\beta \in N^*$ and $\gamma, \gamma' \in (N \cup \Sigma)^*$. We define $\underset{G}{\overset{*}{\Rightarrow}}$ to be the reflexive and transitive closure of $\underset{G}{\Rightarrow}$. When it is not necessary to specify the grammar G, $\alpha \Rightarrow \alpha'$ and $\alpha \overset{*}{\Rightarrow} \beta$ denote $\alpha \underset{G}{\Rightarrow} \alpha'$ and $\alpha \underset{G}{\overset{*}{\Rightarrow}} \beta$, respectively. A *word* generated from $\gamma \in (N \cup \Sigma)^*$ by G is $w \in \Sigma^*$ such that $\gamma \underset{G}{\overset{*}{\Rightarrow}} w$ and the *language* generated from γ by G is denoted by $L_G(\gamma) = \{w \in \Sigma^* \mid \gamma \underset{G}{\overset{*}{\Rightarrow}} w\}$. A word generated from S by G for the start symbol S is called a word generated by G and the language generated by G is denoted by $L(G) = L_G(S)$. For a CFG G_c and an SDG G_s, $L(G_c)$ and $L(G_s)$ are called a context-free language (CFL) and a simple deterministic language (SDL), respectively. Readers would refer to [3] for other basic definitions.

In this paper, $|\beta|$ denotes the length of β if β is a string and $|W|$ denotes the cardinality of W if W is a set. For any SDG $G_1 = (N_1, \Sigma, P_1, S_1)$, there exists an SDG $G_2 = (N_2, \Sigma, P_2, S_2)$ such that $L(G_1) = L(G_2)$ and every rule $A \to a\beta$ in P_2 satisfies that $|\beta| \leq 2$. Such a grammar G_2 is said to be in *2-standard form*. For an SDG $G = (N, \Sigma, P, S)$ and $A \in N$, if there exists a derivation such that $S \overset{*}{\Rightarrow} xAz \overset{*}{\Rightarrow} xyz$ for some $x, z \in \Sigma^*$ and $y \in \Sigma^+$ then A is called *reachable and live*. Throughout this paper, we assume that an SDG is in 2-standard form and all nonterminals are reachable and live. It implies that the target language L_t holds that $L_t \neq \{\}$.

For $w \in \Sigma^+$, $pre(w) = \{w' \in \Sigma^* \mid w'w'' = w, w'' \in \Sigma^*\}$ is called a set of *prefixes* of w. proper_pre$(w) = \{w' \in \Sigma^* \mid w'w'' = w, w'' \in \Sigma^+\}$ is called a set of *proper prefixes* of w.

Assuming an equivalence relation $\sim$ over R, the equivalence class of $r \in R$ is denoted by $B(r, \pi) = \{r' \in R \mid r \sim r'\}$. A classification π over R is defined as the set of equivalence classes $B(r, \pi)$.

We denotes the symmetric difference between L_1 and L_2 by $L_1 \Delta L_2$, i.e. $L_1 \Delta L_2 = \{w \in \Sigma^* \mid w \in (L_1 - L_2) \cup (L_2 - L_1)\}$.

A *representative sample* of the SDG G_t is a special finite subset of $L(G_t)$ such that all rules in G_t are exercised when we generate the subset.

Definition 1. *Let $G = (N, \Sigma, P, S)$ be an SDG. Q is a representative sample of G iff*

- $Q \subseteq L(G)$, *and*
- *for any $A \rightarrow a\beta$ in P, there exists a word $w \in Q$ such that $S \stackrel{*}{\Rightarrow} xA\gamma \Rightarrow xa\beta\gamma \stackrel{*}{\Rightarrow} w$ for some $x \in \Sigma^*$ and $\gamma \in N^*$.*

$\square$

For any SDG $G = (N, \Sigma, P, S)$, there exists a representative sample Q such that $|Q| \leq |P|$. Let k be the *thickness* of G, i.e. $k = \max\limits_{A \in N} \min\limits_{w \in \Sigma^*} (w \in L_G(A))$. Then, the length of the longest word in Q is at least k. Generally, k would not be bounded by a polynomial of the size of G.

Definition 2. *For an SDL L, a finite set $Q \subseteq L$ is a representative sample iff there exists an SDG $G = (N, \Sigma, P, S)$ such that $L(G) = L$ and Q is a representative sample of G.*

$\square$

3   Learning via Queries and PAC Learning Model

Throughout this paper, we assume that L_t denotes the target language and $\mathbf{L}$ denotes the class of target languages.

MEMBER(w) : A membership query for $L_t \in \mathbf{L}$ is defined as follows.
Input : $w \in \Sigma^*$.
Output : "true" if $w \in L_t$ and "false" if $w \notin L_t$.

EQUIV(G_h) : An equivalence query for $L_t in \mathbf{L}$ is defined as follows.
Input : a hypothesis grammar G_h such that $L(G_h) \in \mathbf{L}$.
Output : "false" and a counterexample $w \in L(G_h) \Delta L_t$ if $L(G_h) \neq L_t$ and "true" if $L(G_h) = L_t$.

A counterexample w is called *positive* if $w \in L_t$ and is called *negative* if $w \in L(G_h)$.

Let G_t be a grammar such that $L(G_t) = L_t$. Then L_t is *polynomial time learnable via queries* if there is a learning algorithm which uses some type of queries like the above definition, which guesses a hypothesis grammar G_h such that $L(G_h) = L(G_t)$, and whose time complexity is bounded by a polynomial with the size of G_t and the length of the longest word obtained by queries or a priori samples (like a representative sample). There are theorems about polynomial time query learnability.

Theorem 1 (Angluin[1] Theorem 3). *Given a membership query for a regular set L_t and a representative sample for L_t, $\mathbf{L}$ is polynomial time learnable.* $\square$

Where, a representative sample of a regular set is a set of words which exercise all transition rules in the minimum DFA M such that $L(M) = L_t$. On a similar setting of Theorem1, the learnability of an SDL had been shown.

Theorem 2 (Tajima et al.[7] Theorem 2). *Any SDL L_t is polynomial time learnable with membership queries and a representative sample Q. The polynomial consists of $|Q|$, $\max\{|w| \mid w \in Q\}$, $|N_t|$ and $|\Sigma|$ for any SDG $G_t = (N_t, \Sigma, P_t, S)$ such that $L_t = L(G_t)$.* □

The following theorem is a significant result on query learnability.

Theorem 3 (Angluin[2] Theorem 6). *A regular set is polynomial time learnable with membership queries and equivalence queries. The polynomial consists of the number of states of the minimum DFA which accepts the target language and the length of the longest counterexample obtained by equivalence queries.* □

There are some relations between learning via queries and probably approximately correct (PAC) learning[8]. Readers would refer to [5] for basic definitions about PAC learning.

EX() : The sampling oracle along with the distribution D over Σ^*.
Input : none
Output : $w \in \Sigma$ along with the distribution D, and "true" or "false" corresponding to the membership of w to L_t.

Let **G** be the hypothesis grammar class. We define $P(L(G_1)\Delta L_t)$ for $G_1 \in$ **G** is the probability of difference between $L(G_1)$ and L_t, i.e. the total of the probability for every $w \in L(G_1)\Delta L_t$ on the distribution D.

Then, if there exists a learning algorithm which outputs $G_h \in$ **G** such that

$$Pr[P(L(G)\Delta L_t) \leq \varepsilon] \geq 1 - \delta$$

then L_t is called PAC learnable by **G**. In addition, if the time complexity of the PAC learning algorithm is bounded by a polynomial of ε, δ, the longest length of a word obtained by EX() and sizes of a grammar G_t such that $L(G_t) = L_t$, then **L** is said to be polynomial time learnable by **G**.

Angluin[2] has shown that equivalence queries in a polynomial time query learning algorithm can be converted to a number of EX() calls with PAC learnability. In a converted learning algorithm, an equivalence query is replaced by

$$n_i = \frac{1}{\varepsilon} \left(\log \frac{1}{\delta} + (\log 2)(i + 1) \right)$$

times of EX() when the algorithm makes ith equivalence query. When a hypothesis is guessed, the learner checks itself whether the hypothesis is consistent with n_i samples obtained by EX() instead of an equivalence query. If there is a word w in the samples such that $w \in L_t \Delta L(G_h)$, then the learner treats w as a counterexample. If there is no conflicts between n_i samples and the hypothesis, the learner outputs the hypothesis grammar as the final guess and terminates.

This conversion guarantees PAC learnability because as follows.

– If the PAC learner meets counterexamples in a set of n_i samples for each $i = 0, \cdots, m$ then a correct hypothesis should be guessed by the learner, where m is the number of equivalence queries by which the original query learning algorithm terminates.

- Let p_ε be the total probability that the PAC learner terminates with a hypothesis G_1 such that $P(L(G_1)\Delta L_t) \geq \varepsilon$. Then p_ε is bounded by δ because of $\sum_{i=0}^{n-1}(1-\varepsilon)^{n_i} < \delta$.

In our algorithm, the size of a representative sample bounds the sample complexity instead of the number of equivalence queries.

A learning problem of an SDL with membership queries and equivalence queries are still open. In addition, a polynomial time PAC learnability of an SDL by an SDG is not clear. On the other hand, with the following query, a learnability of an SDL had been shown.

ExEQUIV(w) : An extended-equivalence query for an SDL L_t is defined as follows.
Input : a CFG G_h.
Output : "false" and a counterexample $w \in L(G_h)\Delta L_t$ if $L(G_h) \neq L_t$ and "true" if $L(G_h) = L_t$.

Theorem 4 (Ishizaka[4] Theorem 6). *Any SDL L_t is polynomial time learnable with membership queries and extended-equivalence queries. The polynomial consists of an upper bound on the length of any counterexample provided by extended-equivalence queries, $|N_t|$ and $|\Sigma|$ for any SDG $G_t = (N_t, \Sigma, P_t, S)$ such that $L_t = L(G_t)$.* □

We note that the extended-equivalence query takes a CFG whenever the target language must be an SDL. In general, an equivalence problem between two CFGs is undecidable. However, from the above analysis, an SDL is polynomial time PAC learnable with CFGs via membership queries and samples. In this paper, our algorithm guesses an SDG as a hypothesis.

4   The Learning Algorithm

4.1   PAC Learnability

We describe the idea that how the learning algorithm terminates with PAC hypothesis. Let $\mathbf{G_t}$ be the set of all SDGs which generates L_t, i.e.

$$\mathbf{G_t} = \{G \text{ is an } SDG \mid L(G) = L_t\}.$$

Let $M \subset \Sigma^*$ be a finite set, $G = (N, \Sigma, P, S)$ be an SDG, and $P_{(G,M)}$ be a set of rules by which M is generated, i.e.

$$P_{(G,M)} = \{A \to a\beta \mid S \underset{G}{\overset{*}{\Rightarrow}} \alpha A\gamma \underset{G}{\Rightarrow} \alpha a\beta\gamma \underset{G}{\overset{*}{\Rightarrow}} w, w \in M\}.$$

By a similar analysis of the conversion from equivalence queries to a number of calls of EX(), we can obtain the following strategy for a PAC learning algorithm. Assume that the behavior of the leaning algorithm **A** is as follows.

1. Let M be the set of words of samples obtained ever and $M_+ = \{w \in M \mid w \in L_t\}$.
2. The learner gathers n_i samples by EX(); let the set of words of n_i samples is denoted by M_i and $M_{i+} = \{w \in M_i \mid w \in L_t\}$.
3. When $P_{(G_1,M_{i+})} \subseteq P_{(G_1,M_+)}$ for any $G_1 \in \mathbf{G}_t$, the learner finds out an SDG which is consistent with M_i and outputs it. Otherwise, if there exists a rule which is in $P_{(G,M_{i+})}$ but is not in $P_{(G,M_+)}$ for some $G \in \mathbf{G}_t$, then go back to step 1 with $M := M \cup M_i$.

Now, if $\mathbf{A}$ repeats the above process m times, where $m = |P|$ for $G = (N, \Sigma, P, S)$, one of an SDG in $\mathbf{G}_t$, then M_+ becomes a representative sample of L_t. It implies that we can construct a correct hypothesis SDG from Theorem2.

On the other hand, if $\mathbf{A}$ terminates with M_+ which is not a representative sample for any $G \in \mathbf{G}_t$, we can show that the hypothesis guessed by the learner is PAC by the same analysis in [2].

Thus, we have had a proof of PAC learnability such that the learning algorithm has the above behavior.

4.2   Details of the Learning Algorithm

In this section, we describe details of our learning algorithm and prove that the output of the algorithm satisfies PAC.

In the following of this paper, $G_t = (N_t, \Sigma, P_t, S_t)$ denotes the SDG such that $L(G_t) = L_t$. We define the following query called *hashed membership query*. Throughout the learning algorithm is running, we assume that G_t is fixed and hashed membership queries reply with answers according to G_t.

HMEMBER(p, m, s) : A hashed membership query for L_t is defined as follows.
Input : $(p, m, s) \in \Sigma^* \times \Sigma^* \times \Sigma^*$.
Output : "true" if $pms \in L_t$ and there exists a derivation $S_t \underset{G_t}{\overset{*}{\Rightarrow}} pAs \underset{G_t}{\overset{*}{\Rightarrow}} pms$ for
some $A \in N_t$. "false" if otherwise.

We note that HMEMBER$(\varepsilon, w, \varepsilon)$ is equivalent to MEMBER(w). With this query, the learner can know partial structural information about G_t. We assume that the learner can use HMEMBER() and EX().

We define a *self-evidential CFG G_w* for a specific word $w \in \Sigma^*$ as follows.

$$G_w = (N, \Sigma, P, S)$$
$$N_w = \{(p, m, s) \mid p, m \in \Sigma^+, s \in \Sigma^*, pms = w\} \cup \{(\varepsilon, w, \varepsilon)\}$$
$$P_w = \{(p, a, s) \to a \mid a \in \Sigma, p, s \in \Sigma^*, (p, a, s) \in N\}$$
$$\cup \{(p, am', s) \to a \cdot (pa, m', s) \mid a \in \Sigma, m' \in \Sigma^+, p, s \in \Sigma^*, (p, am', s),$$
$$(pa, m', s) \in N\}$$
$$\cup \{(p, am_1m_2, s) \to a \cdot (pa, m_1, m_2s) \cdot (pam_1, m_2, s) \mid a \in \Sigma, m_1, m_2 \in$$
$$\Sigma^+, p, s \in \Sigma^*, (p, am_1m_2, s), (pa, m_1, m_2s), (pam_1, m_2, s) \in N\}$$
$$S_w = (\varepsilon, w, \varepsilon)$$

Then, it holds that $L(G_w) = \{w\}$. In this grammar, a nonterminal is represented by a 3-tuple. This idea is introduced by Ishizaka[4] and it holds that the following lemma.

Lemma 1 (Ishizaka[4] Lemma 10). *Let $G_t = (N_t, \Sigma, P_t, S_t)$ be an SDG. For any $A(\neq S_t) \in N_t$, there exist $w \in L(G_t)$ and a 3-tuple (w_p, w_m, w_s) such that*

- $w_p w_m w_s = w$, $w_p, w_m \in \Sigma^+$, $w_s \in \Sigma^*$,
- $S_t \overset{*}{\Rightarrow} w_p \cdot A \cdot w_s \overset{*}{\Rightarrow} w$, and
- *it holds that $u \in L_{G_t}(A)$ for $u \in \Sigma^+$ iff*
  - HMEMBER$(w_p, u, w'_s) = true$ *and*
  - *for any $u' \in$ proper_pre(u), HMEMBER$(w_p, u', w'_s) = false$ where w'_s is the shortest suffix of w_s such that $w_p w_m w'_s \in L(G_t)$.*

□

From this lemma, any nonterminal in $G_t \in \mathbf{G}_t$ which is appeared in the derivation $S_t \overset{*}{\underset{G_t}{\Rightarrow}} w$ corresponds to some nonterminals in G_w. In this algorithm, nonterminals of a hypothesis is represented by 3-tuples and an equivalence class over them. To decide whether $P_{(G_t, M_{i+})} \subseteq P_{(G_t, M_+)}$ or not, the learning algorithm constructs a CFG called eCFG and checks them with hashed membership queries.

Construction of eCFG : In the first step of the algorithm, the learner makes a CFG called eCFG. The construction algorithm of eCFG is shown in Fig.1. This algorithm makes union of self-evidential CFGs for every $w \in M$ and defines an equivalence relation $\sim$ over nonterminals. Then, the algorithm deletes conflict rules and output eCFG.

Here, T is a mapping $T : (\Sigma^*, \Sigma^*, \Sigma^*) \times \Sigma^* \to \{0, 1\}$ such that

$$T(r, w) = \begin{cases} 1 \ (if \ \mathrm{HMEMBER}(p_r, w, \mathrm{short}(r)) = true, and \\ \quad for \ all \ w' \in \mathrm{proper\_pre}(w), \mathrm{HMEMBER}(p_r, w', \mathrm{short}(r)) = false), \\ 0 \ (otherwise), \end{cases}$$

here short(r) is the shortest suffix of r_s such that HMEMBER$(p_r, r_m, \mathrm{short}(r)) = true$ for $r = (r_p, r_m, r_s)$.

Definition 3. *Let $r \in R$. Then $row(r)$ is the mapping $f : W \to \{0, 1\}$ such that $f(w) = T(r, w)$ where $w \in W$.* □

The equivalence relation $\sim$ is defined for $r, r' \in R$ as

$$r \sim r' \iff row(r) = row(r'),$$

and π is defined as the classification by $\sim$.

From the definition of $row()$, all members in R which are of the form $(\varepsilon, w, \varepsilon)$ are in the same equivalence class. Suppose that $W_1 \subseteq W_2 \subset \Sigma^*$. Let π_1 and π_2 be the classifications which are made from W_1 and W_2, respectively. Then, it holds that π_2 is finer than or equal to π_1.

Procedure eCFG.construct(INPUT, OUTPUT);
INPUT : M : a set of sample words;
OUTPUT : eCFG : a CFG which satisfies PAC;
begin
   repeat
       $M_+ := \{w \in M \mid w \in L_t\}$;
       /* candidates of nonterminals */
       $R := \{(x,y,z) \mid z \in \Sigma^*, x, y \in \Sigma^+, x \cdot y \cdot z \in M_+\} \cup \{(\varepsilon, w, \varepsilon) \mid w \in M_+\}$;
       /* distinguishing strings */
       $W := \{y \in \Sigma^+ \mid x, z \in \Sigma^*, x \cdot y \cdot z \in M\}$;
       find $T(r, w)$ for all $r \in R$ and $w \in W$;
       construct P_{all}/π;
       delete all rules which satisfy Condition 1 and Condition 2 from P_{all}/π;
       eCFG $= (R/\pi, \Sigma, P_{\text{all}}/\pi, B((\varepsilon, w, \varepsilon), \pi))$;
       $i := i + 1$;
       call n_i times of EX();
       let M_i be the set of sample words obtained in the previous step;
       if $(L(\text{eCFG})$ is consistent with $M_i)$ then
          output eCFG and return;
       else
          $M := M \cup M_i$;
   until (forever);
end.

Fig. 1. The eCFG constructing algorithm

For the following set of rules :

$$P_{\text{suff}} = \{(w_p, w_m, w_s) \to a \mid (w_p, w_m, w_s) \in R, w_m = a \in \Sigma\}$$
$$\cup \{(w_p, aw_m, w_s) \to a(w_p a, w_m, w_s) \mid (w_p, aw_m, w_s), (w_p a, w_m, w_s) \in R,$$
$$a \in \Sigma\}$$
$$\cup \{(w_p, aw_{m1}w_{m2}, w_s) \to a(w_p a, w_{m1}, w_{m2}w_s)(w_p aw_{m1}, w_{m2}, w_s) \mid a \in \Sigma,$$
$$(w_p, aw_{m1}w_{m2}, w_s), (w_p a, w_{m1}, w_{m2}w_s), (w_p aw_{m1}, w_{m2}, w_s) \in R\},$$

The CFG $G_{\text{all}} = (R/\pi, \Sigma, P_{\text{all}}/\pi, S_{\text{suff}})$ is defined as follows.

$$R/\pi = \{B(A_0, \pi) \mid A_0 \in R\},$$
$$P_{\text{all}}/\pi = \{B(A_0, \pi) \to a \mid A_0 \to a \in P_{\text{all}}\}$$
$$\cup \{B(A_0, \pi) \to aB(A_1, \pi) \mid A_0 \to aA_1 \in P_{\text{all}}\}$$
$$\cup \{B(A_0, \pi) \to aB(A_1, \pi)B(A_2, \pi) \mid A_0 \to aA_1A_2 \in P_{\text{all}}\},$$
$$S_{\text{all}} = B((\varepsilon, w, \varepsilon), \pi),$$

where $w \in M$.

Then, the rule set of eCFG is made from P_{all}/π by deleting rules with the following conditions.

Condition 1 for rules which are of the form $A \rightarrow aB$: There exists $w \in W$ such that $aw \in W$ and $T(r_A, aw) \neq T(r_B, w)$ where $r_A \in B(r_A, \pi) = A$ and $r_B \in B(r_B, \pi) = B$.

This condition holds when B can generate w but A cannot generate aw or vice versa.

Condition 2 for rules which are of the form $A \rightarrow aBC$: It holds that one of the following conditions.

- There exists $w \in W$ such that $aw \in W$, $T(r_A, aw) = 1$ and

$$T(r_B, w_1) = 0 \text{ or } T(r_C, w_2) = 0$$

for any $w_1, w_2 \in W$ with $w_1 w_2 = w$. Here, $r_A \in B(r_A, \pi) = A$, $r_B \in B(r_B, \pi) = B$ and $r_C \in B(r_C, \pi) = C$.
In other words, aw should be derived from A but BC cannot generate w.

- There exist $w_1, w_2 \in W$ such that $aw_1 w_2 \in W$, $T(r_A, aw_1 w_2) = 0$ and

$$T(r_B, w_1) = 1 \text{ and } T(r_C, w_2) = 1.$$

In other words, $aw_1 w_2$ should not be derived from A but BC generates $w_1 w_2$.

With the above deletion, eCFG is as follows :

$$\text{eCFG} = (R/\pi, \Sigma, P_{\text{all}}/\pi, B((\varepsilon, w, \varepsilon), \pi)).$$

For this eCFG, the learner checks the consistency with M_i. When there exists a word $w \in L_t \Delta L(\text{eCFG})$ then $M := M \cup M_i$ and loop back to the top of this algorithm.

The following lemma holds for eCFG.

Lemma 2. *It holds that the procedure* eCFG.*construct is a polynomial time PAC learning algorithm.*

Proof. We can prove this lemma by that of similar to Theorem4. If there exists a positive counterexample $w \in M_i$, from Lemma1, there is a rule which is in $P_{(G_t, M_i)}$ but is not in $P_{(G_t, M)}$ for any $G_t \in \mathbf{G}_t$. On the other hand, If there exists a negative counterexample $w \in M_i$, from Lemma7 in [4], there exists a rule in P_{all}/π which satisfies Condition1 or Condition2.

It implies that the number of counterexamples are bounded by a polynomial of the size of G_t. Thus this lemma holds.   □

In the following of this section, let M_i be the set of sample words obtained at the latest stage, $M_{i+} = \{w \in M_i \mid w \in L_t\}$, $M_{i-} = \{w \in M_i \mid w \notin L_t\}$, $M = \bigcup_{j=0}^{i-1} M_i$, $M_+ = \{w \in M \mid w \in L_t\}$, and $M_- = \{w \in M \mid w \notin L_t\}$. Next step, the learner checks whether $P_{(G_t, M_{i+})} \subseteq P_{(G_t, M_+)}$ or not by the following procedure.

Finding a SDG which is consistent with M_{i+} : First, we show the following lemma.

Lemma 3. *It holds that $w \notin L_t \iff w \notin L(G_1)$ for any $w \in M_-$ and for any G_1. Where $G_1 = (N_1, \Sigma, P_1, S_1)$ is a SDG such that $N_1 = R/\pi$, $S_1 = B((\varepsilon, w, \varepsilon), \pi)$ for some $w \in M_+$, and $P_1 \subset P_{all}/\pi$ where P_1 contains at most one rule which is of the form $A \to a\beta$ for every pair of $A \in N_1$ and $a \in \Sigma$.*

Proof. From the procedure eCFG.construct, it holds that $w \notin L(eCFG)$ for any $w \in M_-$. It implies that any $P_1 \subset P_{all}/\pi$ can not generate w.   □

Let S_e be the start symbol of eCFG. For each $A \in R/\pi$ and every $u \in M_{i+}$, let

$$C_{A,u} = \{w \in L_{eCFG}(A) \mid w_1, w_2 \in \Sigma^*, S_e \underset{eCFG}{\overset{*}{\Rightarrow}} w_1 A w_2 \underset{eCFG}{\overset{*}{\Rightarrow}} w_1 w w_2 = u,$$
$$\text{HMEMBER}(w_1, w, w_2) = true\}$$

and

$$C_A = \bigcup_{u \in M_{i+}} C_{A,u}.$$

Let $A \to a\beta$ be a rule in P_{all}/π. For every $v \in \Sigma^*$ such that $av \in C_A$, if it holds that

$$v \in L_{eCFG}(\beta)$$

then we call $A \to a\beta$ "useful".

The learner constructs the SDG by selecting one "useful" rule from P_{all}/π, arbitrarily, for every $A \in R/\pi$ and every $a \in \Sigma$. Such the SDG is denoted by $G_h = (N_h, \Sigma, P_h, S_h)$.

From Lemma 1, if $A \in N_t$ satisfies that $S_t \underset{G_t}{\overset{*}{\Rightarrow}} w_1 A w_2 \underset{G_t}{\overset{*}{\Rightarrow}} w$ for some $w \in M_+$, then there exists $r_A = (p, m, s) \in R$ such that $S_t \underset{G_t}{\overset{*}{\Rightarrow}} pAs \underset{G_t}{\overset{*}{\Rightarrow}} pms$. Inversely, $r \in R$ corresponds to A if there exists a derivation such that $S_t \underset{G_t}{\overset{*}{\Rightarrow}} p_r A s_r \underset{G_t}{\overset{*}{\Rightarrow}} p_r m_r s_r$ for $A \in N_t$. In addition, a rule $B(r_0, \pi) \to aB(r_1, \pi) \cdots B(r_j, \pi)$ in P_{all}/π corresponds to $A_0 \to aA_1 \cdots A_j$ in P_t if $r_0, r_1, \cdots, r_j$ correspond to $A_0, A_1, \cdots, A_j$, respectively.

Lemma 4. *If $P_{(G_t, M_{i+})} \subseteq P_{(G_t, M_+)}$ then the following holds for every rule $A \to a\beta$ in $P_{(G_t, M_{i+})}$ where $\beta \in N_t^*$.*

- *there exists $\beta_1 \in (R/\pi)^*$ and $B(r_0, \pi) \to a\beta_1$ in P_{all}/π which corresponds to $A \to a\beta$. In addition, the rule $B(r_0, \pi) \to a\beta_1$ is "useful".*

Proof. From the assumption $P_{(G_t, M_{i+})} \subseteq P_{(G_t, M_+)}$ and the procedure to construct eCFG, it holds that there exists $\beta_1 \in (R/\pi)^*$ and $B(r_0, \pi) \to a\beta_1$ in P_{all}/π which corresponds to $A \to a\beta$ for any rule in $P_{(G_t, M_{i+})}$.

If $|\beta_1| > 0$, let $\beta_1 = B(r_1, \pi) \cdots B(r_j, \pi)$. We prove that $B(r_0, \pi) \to a\beta_1$ is "useful" by induction of the length of $w \in C_{B(r_0, \pi)}$. If $|w| = 1$ ($w = a \in \Sigma$) then a word contained in $C_{B(r_0, \pi)}$ with a as the first symbol is only w, because

$C_{B(r_0,\pi)}$ is a subset of a SDL L_t. Thus $w \in L_{eCFG}(B(r_0,\pi))$ and $B(r_0,\pi) \rightarrow a$ is "useful".

Assume that this lemma holds for every $B(r_0,\pi) \in R/\pi$ and $w \in C_{B(r_0,\pi)}$ such that $|w| < l$, i.e. for every rule $A' \rightarrow b\beta'$ in $P_{(G_t,M_{i+})}$ and $B(p_0,\pi) \rightarrow b\beta_1'$ in P_{all}/π corresponds to $A' \rightarrow b\beta'$,

- if $bu \in C_{B(p_0,\pi)}$ where $|u| < l-1$ then $bu \in L_{eCFG}(B(p_0,\pi))$ and $u \in L_{eCFG}(\beta_1')$.

Now, we are concerned with $aw \in C_{B(r_0,\pi)}$ such that $|aw| = l$. From the assumption of this induction, $w \in L_{eCFG}(\beta_1)$ holds. Thus $aw \in L_{eCFG}(B(r_0,\pi))$ and $B(r_0,\pi) \rightarrow a\beta_1$ is "useful". This concludes the lemma.   □

The learner outputs G_h and terminates if it holds that

$$w \in L(G_h) \iff w \in M_{i+} \quad \forall w \in M_i.$$

Otherwise, let $M := M \cup M_i$ and go back to the top of this learning algorithm. From Lemma 4, when the learner go back to the top $|P_t|$ times, M_+ becomes a representative sample of L_t. Whereas, the main loop consists the following steps.

1. Constructing eCFG,
2. Finding G_h,
3. Let G_r be the SDG which is a output of the learning algorithm with membership queries and a representative sample[7]. If G_h or G_r is consistent with M_i then output either of them and terminates. Otherwise, update M and go back to 1.

Then the following theorem holds.

Theorem 5. *The class of all SDLs is polynomial time PAC learnable with an SDG via hashed membership queries and samples. The polynomial consists of the maximum length of samples, $|N_t|$ and $|\Sigma|$ for a SDG $G_t = (N_t, \Sigma, P_t, S)$ such that $L_t = L(G_t)$ where L_t is the target language.*

Proof. The time complexity of eCFG construction procedure is bounded by a polynomial because of Theorem 4. For every nonterminal in eCFG, denoted by $A \in R/\pi$, we can find C_A in polynomial time because the size of the self-evidential grammar G_w for any $w \in M_+$ is bounded by a polynomial of the sizes of eCFG, $|M|$ and $\max\{|u| \mid u \in M\}$.

At most P_t times loop is sufficient to terminates the learning algorithm with PAC hypothesis. Then this theorem holds.   □

5   Conclusions

In this paper, we have shown that SDLs are polynomial time PAC learnable with SDGs via hashed membership queries and samples. We can construct the learning algorithm which guesses a PAC hypothesis or collects a representative sample by

EX(). The length of the longest word in a representative sample is not bounded by a polynomial of the size of a SDG which generates the target language, but with the length of the longest sample, it is bounded by a polynomial.

A study of the power of hashed membership queries for other languages is remained as a future work.

References

1. Angluin, D.: A note on the number of queries needed to identify regular languages. Info. & Cont. **51** (1981) 76–87
2. Angluin, D.: Learning regular sets from queries and counterexamples. Info. & Comp. **75** (1987) 87–106
3. Hopcroft, J. E., Ullman, J. D.: Introduction to Automata Theory, Languages, and Computation. Addison-Wesley (1979)
4. Ishizaka, H.: Polynomial time learnability of simple deterministic languages. Machine Learning **5** (1990) 151–164
5. Natarajan, B. K.: Machine Learning : A Theoretical Approach. Morg., Kauf. Publ. (1991)
6. Korenjak, A. J., Hopcroft, J. E.: Simple deterministic languages. Proc. IEEE 7th Annu. Symp. on Switching and Automata Theory (1966) 36-46
7. Tajima, Y., Tomita, E.: A polynomial time learning algorithm of simple deterministic languages via membership queries and a representative sample. 5th Intern. Coll. on Gramm. Inference, LNAI 1891 (2000) 284–297
8. Valiant, L. G.: A theory of learnable. Comm. of the ACM, 27(11) (1984) 1134–1142

On the Learnability of Hidden Markov Models

Sebastiaan A. Terwijn[*]

Vrije Universiteit Amsterdam, Department of Mathematics and Computer Science,
De Boelelaan 1081a, 1081 HV Amsterdam, the Netherlands,
terwijn@cs.vu.nl

Abstract. A simple result is presented that links the learning of hidden
Markov models to results in complexity theory about nonlearnability of
finite automata under certain cryptographic assumptions. Rather than
considering all probability distributions, or even just certain specific ones,
the learning of a hidden Markov model takes place under a distribution
induced by the model itself.

Keywords. Pac-learning, hidden Markov models, complexity.

1 Introduction

Hidden Markov models (HMM's for short) are a widely used tool for describing
processes, ranging from speech recognition to topics in computational biology.
In many situations where a process can be described by a HMM, one tries to
infer from data produced by the process (e.g. spoken text or products from a
chemical reaction) a HMM describing that process. In this paper we address the
computational complexity of such general learning tasks. We will use Valiants
[13] model of pac-learning to talk about efficient learning (see [1,10] for an introduction to this model). In the early 1990's, interesting connections were proven
between assumptions on which the security of public-key cryptography systems is
based and hardness results for pac-learning various natural classes. E.g., Kearns
and Valiant [9] proved that under the Discrete Cube Root Assumption, say-
ing roughly that it is impossible to efficiently invert functions that occur in the
RSA cryptosystem, the class of polynomial size finite automata is not efficiently
pac-learnable. More precisely, let $\mathrm{ADFA}_n^{p(n)}$ denote the class of finite automata
of size $p(n)$ that accept only words of length n. (ADFA stands for acyclic deterministic finite automata.) Then (under suitable cryptographic assumptions)
there is a polynomial p such that $\mathrm{ADFA}_n^{p(n)}$ is not efficiently pac-learnable. Pac-
learnability can be characterized in terms of a measure of complexity of the
concept space, the Vapnik-Chervonenkis dimension (VC-dimension), see Blumer
et al. [4]. A concept class of VC-dimension d can be pac-learned by an algorithm taking samples of size linear in d. So when for a parametrized concept

---

[*] Supported by a Marie Curie fellowship of the European Union under grant no. ERB-
FMBI-CT98-3248. Most of this research was done while the author was working at
the University of Munich.

P. Adriaans, H. Fernau, and M. van Zaanen (Eds.): ICGI 2002, LNAI 2484, pp. 261–268, 2002.
© Springer-Verlag Berlin Heidelberg 2002

class $\mathcal{C} = \bigcup_n \mathcal{C}_n$ the VC-dimension of $\mathcal{C}_n$ is polynomial in n, the class can be pac-learned using polynomial size samples. If such a class $\mathcal{C}$ does not admit an efficient pac-algorithm, irrelevant of how hypotheses are represented (as long as they are polynomial time evaluatable), it is called *inherently unpredictable*. Since the class $\mathrm{ADFA}_n^{p(n)}$ has polynomial VC-dimension the result of Kearns and Valiant shows that it is inherently unpredictable.

Below we will consider in an analogous way classes of polynomial size acyclic HMM's, and link a nonlearnability result for finite automata of Kharitonov to a specific task of learning HMM's. The problem of learning HMM's is defined not in terms of arbitrary probability distributions (as is usual in the pac model, which is therefore sometimes referred to as "distribution free") but in terms of the distributions induced by the HMM's themselves. So we consider a distribution specific learning problem, where every HMM has to be identified from examples generated according to its own likelihood distribution.

We now describe the nonlearnability result for finite automata that we will use. Blum integers are integers of the form $p \cdot q$, where p and q are primes congruent to 3 modulo 4. The cryptographic assumption used in the result is that *factoring Blum integers is hard*. We refer to Kearns [8, p 105-108] for a precise statement and a discussion of this assumption.

The following result follows from Kharitonovs results in [11] using the reductions from Pitt and Warmuth [12], see also [10].

Theorem 1. (Kharitonov [11]) *Assuming that factoring Blum integers is hard, there is a polynomial p such that the class $\mathrm{ADFA}_n^{p(n)}$ is inherently unpredictable under the uniform distribution.*

2   Hidden Markov Models

In this section we discuss hidden Markov models (HMM's). HMM's can be used to describe mechanisms in a diversity of fields. A HMM can be thought of as a probabilistic automaton with a finite number of states, with fixed probabilities for going from one state to another, and in which for every state there are probabilities for outputting certain symbols. Usually, we only see these output symbols, and the states are hidden from us. Over time, the HMM thus generates an infinite sequence of output symbols, adding a symbol at every time step. In the next formal definition we use the notation of Clote and Backofen [6]. It will be convenient to work with the alphabet $\Sigma = \{0, 1\}$.

Definition 1. A hidden Markov model (HMM) is a tuple $M = (Q, \pi, a, b)$, where $Q = 1, \ldots, m$ is a set of states, π is a vector of initial state probabilities, a is a matrix of transition probabilities, and b is a matrix of output probabilities:

$$\pi_i = \Pr[q_0 = i]$$
$$a_{i,j} = \Pr[q_t = j | q_{t-1} = i]$$
$$b_{i,k} = \Pr[o_t = k | q_t = i], \quad k \in \{0, 1\}$$

such that $\sum_{i=1}^{m} \pi_i = 1$, and for every i, $\sum_{j=1}^{m} a_{i,j} = 1$ and $b_{i,0} + b_{i,1} = 1$. Here q_0 is the initial state, and q_t is the state of the system at time t. o_t is the symbol that is output when M is in state q_t. The *likelihood* $L_w(M)$ of a binary word w is defined as the probability that M generates w, i.e. the probability that for every $t < |w|$, in state q_t the output symbol o_t is equal to the t-th bit w_t of w. The likelihood of a sample S is defined as $L_S(M) = \prod_{w \in S} L_w(M)$. The *size* of a HMM M is defined in a straightforward way as $\text{size}(\pi) + \text{size}(a) + \text{size}(b)$. We also allow HMM's to have final states, i.e. states without outgoing transitions. For a polynomial p, denote the class of HMM's of size $p(n)$ that generate only strings of length n by $\text{HMM}_n^{p(n)}$.

We prove two easy lemmas for later reference.

Lemma 1. *Let $T \in \mathbb{N}$ and let $p \in Q^T$ be a fixed path (i.e. p is a sequence of T states in Q). Then $\sum_{|w|=T} \Pr[w|p, M] = 1$.*

Proof. Note that $\sum_{|w|=T} \Pr[w|p, M] = \sum_{|w|=T} \prod_{i=0}^{T-1} b_{p(i),w_i}$. We prove the lemma by induction on T.

$T = 1$: $b_{p(0),0} + b_{p(0),1} = 1$.
$T + 1$:

$$\sum_{|w|=T+1} \Pr[w|p, M] = \sum_{|w|=T} \Pr[w|p \restriction T, M] b_{p(T),0} +$$

$$\sum_{|w|=T} \Pr[w|p \restriction T, M] b_{p(T),1}$$

$$= b_{p(T),0} + b_{p(T),1} = 1,$$

where the second equality follows by the induction hypothesis. □

Lemma 2. $\sum_{p \in Q^T} \Pr[p|M] = 1$.

Proof. Induction on T.

$T = 1$: $\sum_{p \in Q^T} \Pr[p|M] = \sum_{p \in Q} \pi(p) = 1$.
$T + 1$:

$$\sum_{p \in Q^{T+1}} \Pr[p|M] = \sum_{p \in Q^T} \left(\Pr[p|M] \sum_{q \in Q} a_{p(T-1),q} \right)$$

$$= \sum_{p \in Q^T} \Pr[p|M],$$

and this last expression equals 1 by induction hypothesis. □

Every deterministic finite automaton (DFA) G can be represented by a HMM M as follows. Split every state q in G into two states q_0 and q_1. We want to make sure that after every transition labeled with 0 with certainty an output bit 0 in M is output, so for every 0-transition to q in G we make a corresponding transition to q_0 in M, and we give q_0 output probability 1 for 0 and 0 for 1. Similarly, for every 1-transition to q in G we make a corresponding transition to q_1 in M, and we give q_1 output probability 1 for 1 and 0 for 0. If a state in M has two outgoing transitions we give both probability $1/2$, and if it has one it gets probability 1. The start state of G is removed and replaced by suitable initial probabilities in M.

For M defined in this way we have $w \in L(G) \Leftrightarrow L_w(M) > 0$. (Here $L(G)$ is the language associated with G, i.e. the set of words accepted by G.) When we identify H with the set $\{w : L_w(M) > 0\}$ then we see that M represents G. We note that the likelihood $L_w(M)$ is computable in polynomial time by the forward method [5,6]. Since the class of DFA's is inherently unpredictable, irrelevant of which polynomially evaluatable hypotheses representation is used, it follows immediately from the nonlearnability results for finite automata quoted in Section 1 that the class of polynomial size HMM's is not efficiently pac-learnable:

Fact 2 *The class of polynomial size HMM's has polynomial VC-dimension. Hence (under the Discrete Cube Root Assumption) it is inherently unpredictable.*

Below we will prove that a much more specific learning task is not feasible (assuming that factoring Blum integers is hard).

3   Learning Hidden Markov Models

We can associate several learning tasks with the class of HMM's. The first well-known task is to maximize the likelihood:

HMM Likelihood Problem. Given n, the number of states in an unknown HMM M, and a sample S of observation sequences generated by M, determine a HMM H on n states such that $L_S(H)$ is maximal.

The most widely used method to attack the HMM Likelihood Problem is the Baum-Welch method [3], also called the forward-backward method. This algorithm adjusts by iteration the parameters of a given HMM so as to increase the likelihood of an observation sequence. The algorithm works in polynomial time, i.e. every iteration step can be computed efficiently, but no general analysis of its rate of convergence is known.

For a HMM M, define

$$\mathcal{D}_M(w) = L_w(M).$$

For any fixed length n, $\mathcal{D}_M$ is a probability distribution on Σ^n, as the next proposition shows. We will call $\mathcal{D}_M$ the *probability distribution induced by* M.

Proposition 1. *For any n, $\sum_{|w|=n} \mathcal{D}_M(w) = 1$.*

Proof. Using the Lemmas 1 and 2 we have

$$\sum_{|w|=T} \mathcal{D}_M(w) = \sum_{|w|=T} L_w(M)$$

$$= \sum_{|w|=T} \sum_{p \in Q^T} \Pr[w|p, M] \Pr[p|M]$$

$$= \sum_{p \in Q^T} \Pr[p|M] \sum_{|w|=T} \Pr[w|p, M]$$

$$= \sum_{p \in Q^T} \Pr[p|M]$$

$$= 1. \qquad \square$$

HMM Learning Problem. Let p be a fixed polynomial and let $\mathcal{U}$ be the uniform distribution on Σ^n. Given n and $p(n)$, the number of states in an unknown HMM M, $\varepsilon, \delta < 1/2$, and a sample $S \subseteq \Sigma^n$ of observation sequences of length n generated by M, determine a HMM H on $p(n)$ states such that with probability $1 - \delta$, error$(H) < \varepsilon$. Here error$(H) := \Pr_{\mathcal{D}_M}[M - H] + \Pr_{\mathcal{U}}[H - M]$. Here $M - H$ denotes the set of strings in Σ^n that are generated by M but not by H.

Note that this is more specific than in the general pac-model, since each target concept has its own probability distribution, namely the one that it induces. This seems to reflect practical learning situations in a more natural way. After all, when we see the products of some unknown mechanism, we are most likely to see those products that the mechanism is most likely to generate. A solution to the HMM Learning Problem requires a (possibly randomized) algorithm that pac-learns any HMM M on the basis of positive examples only, which are sampled according to the induced probability distribution $\mathcal{D}_M$. The error is measured according to $\mathcal{D}_M$ on the positive examples and to the uniform distribution $\mathcal{U}$ on the negative examples. We note that, if the choice of $\mathcal{U}$ for the negative examples seems too arbitrary, it follows from the results of Kharitonov that we could have chosen any other nontrivial distribution here (see [11] for the definition of 'nontrivial'). The next theorem shows that, although the HMM Learning Problem is much more specific than the general problem of pac-learning HMM's, this problem is still not feasible. That an algorithm L for the HMM Learning Problem runs in polynomial time means that there is a polynomial p such that L runs in time $p(n, 1/\varepsilon, 1/\delta)$, where n is the size of the target concept, and ε and δ are the error and confidence parameter, respectively. Recall that HMM$_n^{p(n)}$ denotes the class of HMM's of size $p(n)$ that generate only strings of length n.

Theorem 3. *Assuming that factoring Blum integers is hard, the HMM Learning Problem is not solvable in polynomial time. (That is, there is a polynomial p such that the HMM learning problem for* HMM$_n^{p(n)}$ *is not solvable in polynomial time.)*

Before proving Theorem 3 we prove two auxiliary results.

Theorem 4. *Let* $\mathcal{C} = \bigcup_n \mathcal{C}_n$ *be a graded concept space, and suppose* $\mathcal{C}_n$ *is not efficiently pac-learnable under the uniform distribution* $\mathcal{U}$ *over* Σ^n *(for both the positive and the negative examples). Then* $\mathcal{C}_n$ *is also not efficiently pac-learnable when we use for every* $c \in \mathcal{C}_n$ *the distribution* $\mathcal{D}_c$ *defined by*

$$\mathcal{D}_c(w) = \begin{cases} 0 & \text{if } w \notin c \\ \frac{1}{\|c\|} & \text{if } w \in c. \end{cases}$$

($\|c\|$ *is the cardinality of* c *), and the error of an hypothesis* h *is defined as* $\mathrm{Pr}_{\mathcal{D}_c}[c - h] + \mathrm{Pr}_{\mathcal{U}}[h - c]$.

Proof. Suppose L is an algorithm that pac-learns every $c \in \mathcal{C}$ under the distribution $\mathcal{D}_c$, with error defined as in the theorem, and that L works in time p for some polynomial p. Then we can pac-learn $\mathcal{C}$ under the uniform distribution as follows. Let ε and δ be the given error and confidence parameters. We sample under the uniform distribution and simulate L on the positive examples. We need $p(n, 1/\delta, 1/\varepsilon)$ hits from c to do this. We show that it is enough to sample $m = (2/\varepsilon)(4\log(1/\delta) + p(n, 1/\delta, 1/\varepsilon))$ examples under the uniform distribution. There are two cases.

Case 1. The weight of c is very small: $\mathrm{Pr}_{\mathcal{U}}[c] < \varepsilon$, and among the m examples there are less than $p(n, 1/\delta, 1/\varepsilon)$ positive ones. Output $\emptyset$. Since $\mathrm{Pr}_{\mathcal{U}}[c] < \varepsilon$ the error is less than ε.

Case 2. $\mathrm{Pr}_{\mathcal{U}}[c] \geq \varepsilon$. When we view the sampling of the m examples as m independent Bernoulli trials, each with success of hitting c at least ε, a suitable Chernoff bound[1] gives us that

$$\mathrm{Pr}[\# \text{ hits in } c < p(n, 1/\delta, 1/\varepsilon)] \leq \mathrm{Pr}[\# \text{ hits in } c < \frac{1}{2}\varepsilon m]$$

$$\leq e^{-\varepsilon m/8}$$

$$\leq e^{-\frac{\varepsilon}{8}\frac{2}{\varepsilon}(4\log\frac{1}{\delta})}$$

$$= \delta.$$

So with probability at least $1 - \delta$, at least $p(n, 1/\delta, 1/\varepsilon)$ of the m examples are labeled positively, and we can simulate L on these examples. This gives with probability at least $1 - \delta$ an hypothesis h with $\mathrm{Pr}_{\mathcal{D}_c}[c - h] + \mathrm{Pr}_{\mathcal{U}}[h - c] < \varepsilon$. Since $\mathrm{Pr}_{\mathcal{D}_c}[c - h] \geq \mathrm{Pr}_{\mathcal{U}}[c - h]$ we have in total that $\mathrm{Pr}_{\mathcal{U}}[(h - c) \cup (c - h)] < \varepsilon$ with probability at least $(1 - \delta)^2$. This shows that $\mathcal{C}$ is pac-learnable under the uniform distribution, since we could have set the confidence parameter δ to δ^2 at the beginning of the proof, thus obtaining the good hypothesis h with confidence at least $1 - \delta$. □

Theorem 5. *For every* G *in* $\mathrm{ADFA}_n^{p(n)}$ *there is an* M *in* $\mathrm{HMM}_n^{O(p(n))}$ *such that for every* $w \in \Sigma^n$ *it holds that* $w \in L(G) \Leftrightarrow L_w(M) > 0$ *and* $L_w(M) > 0 \Rightarrow L_w(M) = 1/\|L(G)\|$.

---

[1] If S is the number of successes in a series of m independent Bernoulli trials with probability of success p, then we use that $\mathrm{Pr}[S < (1 - \gamma)pm] \leq e^{-mp\gamma^2/2}$ for any $0 \leq \gamma \leq 1$.

Proof. Define M from G as in the discussion preceding Fact 2, except for the transition probabilities in M which are defined as follows. Without loss of generality, all paths in G end in an accepting state. We assign to every transition in M going from node q to node q' the probability k/l, where l is the total number of *transitions* that can be followed from q (i.e. its outdegree) and k is the total number of *paths* that can be followed from q'. By induction on the length of the paths, i.e. induction on n, one can check that in this way every path in M defined from a path in G gets the same nonzero probability, and all other paths get probability zero. It is easy to check that M satisfies the statement of the theorem. □

Proof of Theorem 3. Suppose algorithm L solves the HMM Learning Problem in polynomial time. Given a finite automaton G in $\text{ADFA}_n^{p(n)}$, and ε, δ, let M be as in Theorem 5. Then L outputs in polynomial time and with probability $1 - \delta$ an hypothesis H with $\text{Pr}_{\mathcal{D}_M}(M - H) + \text{Pr}_{\mathcal{U}}(H - M) < \varepsilon$. But then, since $\mathcal{D}_M$ is uniform on M, by Theorem 4, we can pac-learn M under the uniform distribution. Now given H and $w \in \Sigma^n$, one can compute in time $O(np(n)^2)$ whether $L_w(H) > 0$ using the forward method (see e.g. [5,6]). This means that, for any polynomial p, we can pac-learn $\text{ADFA}_n^{p(n)}$ under the uniform distribution using the polynomially evaluatable hypothesis class $\text{HMM}_n^{O(p(n))}$. But this contradicts Theorem 1. □

Note that all HMM's used in the proof are polynomial size, so that (by Fact 2) we can say that the nonlearnability is not caused by a nonpolynomial VC-dimension of the class of HMM's under consideration. Also note that we have in fact proved a result about stochastic DFA's (stochastic regular grammars).

Acknowledgment. We thank Peter Clote for introducing us to hidden Markov models and for helpful discussions.

References

1. M. Anthony and N. Biggs, *Computational learning theory: an introduction*, Cambridge University Press, 1992.
2. P. Baldi and Y. Chauvin, *Smooth on-line learning algorithms for hidden Markov models*, Neural Computation 6 (1994) 307–318.
3. L. E. Baum, *An inequality and associated maximization technique in statistical estimation for probabilistic functions of a Markov process*, Inequalities 3, 1972, 1–8.
4. A. Blumer, A. Ehrenfeucht, D. Haussler, and M. K. Warmuth, *Learnability and the Vapnik-Chervonenkis dimension*, J. of the ACM 36(4), 929–965, 1989.
5. E. Charniak, *Statistical Language Learning*, MIT Press, 1993.
6. P. Clote and R. Backofen, *Computational molecular biology: an introduction*, Wiley, 2000.
7. O. Goldreich, S. Goldwasser, and S. Micali, *How to construct random functions*, J. of the ACM 33(4) (1986) 792–807.

8. M. J. Kearns, *The computational complexity of machine learning*, MIT Press, 1990.

9. M. J. Kearns and L. G. Valiant, *Cryptographic limitations on learning boolean formulae and finite automata*, J. of the ACM 41(1) (1994) 67–95.

10. M. J. Kearns, U. V. Vazirani, *An introduction to computational learning theory*, MIT Press, 1994.

11. M. Kharitonov, *Cryptographic hardness of distribution-specific learning*, Proc. 25th ACM Symp. on the Theory of Computing, 372–381, ACM Press, N.Y., 1993.

12. L. Pitt and M. K. Warmuth, *Prediction-preserving reducibility*, J. Computer and System Sci. 41(3) (1990) 430–467.

13. L. G. Valiant, *A theory of the learnable*, Communications of the ACM 27(11) (1984) 1134–1142.

Shallow Parsing Using Probabilistic Grammatical Inference

Franck Thollard and Alexander Clark

EURISE, Université Jean Monnet,23, Rue du Docteur Paul Michelon, 42023
Saint-Etienne Cédex 2, France
ISSCO/TIM, Université de Genève 40, Bvd du Pont d'Arve CH-1211, Genève 4,
Switzerland

Abstract. This paper presents an application of grammatical inference to the task of shallow parsing. We first learn a deterministic probabilistic automaton that models the joint distribution of *Chunk* (syntactic phrase) tags and Part-of-speech tags, and then use this automaton as a transducer to find the most likely chunk tag sequence using a dynamic programming algorithm. We discuss an efficient means of incorporating lexical information, which automatically identifies particular words that are useful using a mutual information criterion, together with an application of *bagging* that improve our results. Though the results are not as high as comparable techniques that use models with a fixed structure, the models we learn are very compact and efficient.

Keywords: Probabilistic Grammatical Inference, Shallow Parsing, Bagging

1 Introduction

Shallow parsing of natural language is the task of dividing sentences into a sequence of simple phrases. Many applications of this can be found. Among them are (i) *indexing web pages*: as users mainly enter noun phrases into internet search engines, detecting noun phrases leads to a better indexing of web pages and (ii) as a *preliminary to full parsing*, *i.e.* building a complete constituent structure tree.

We consider as input a sequence of words together with their part of speech *POS* tags; the task of shallow parsing is then one of adding an additional tag that indicates the beginning and ends of the various types of constituents (Noun Phrase, Verb Phrase, etc.). These tags will be called *Chunk* tags. Initially we shall consider just the mapping from POS tags to *Chunk* tags; later we will consider how to incorporate lexical knowledge.

Our approach is to infer a deterministic probabilistic automaton that models the joint sequence of POS tags and *Chunk* tags. We use a grammatical inference algorithm for this task. We then consider it as a probabilistic transducer that models the mapping from POS tags to *Chunk* tags. This interpretation will be done with the Viterbi algorithm [9]. Since for each word we have one POS tag,

P. Adriaans, H. Fernau, and M. van Zaanen (Eds.): ICGI 2002, LNAI 2484, pp. 269–282, 2002.

and one *Chunk* tag, the resulting transducers are fully aligned which simplifies the algorithms considerably.

We start by presenting the data we will use; we then describe our approach in general terms. The probabilistic grammatical inference algorithms are then introduced. We describe how these automata can be used as transducers, and then present the experimental results we have obtained. We conclude with a brief discussion.

2   The Problem

This task consists in constructing a **flat** bracketing of the sentences. For the sentence *"He reckons the current account deficit will narrow to only # 1.8 billion in September."*, the goal is to insert the following brackets[1] *[NP He] [VP reckons] [NP the current account deficit] [VP will narrow] [PP to] [NP only # 1.8 billion] [PP in] [NP September]* .

The data used are drawn from the Wall Street Journal database [14], a large syntactically annotated corpus. Section 15 to 18 were used as the learning set (211727 words) and section 20 as the test set (47377 words). The most frequent *Chunks* are Noun Phrases (51%), Verb Phrases (20%) and Prepositional Phrases (20%). The data is constructed by taking the words, adding the *Chunk* tags that can be deduced from the parse trees in the corpus, and using POS tags obtained by the Brill tagger [4], not the "correct" POS tags drawn from the corpus. The motivation for this is that it mimics more closely real-world situations. The task then is to identify the *Chunk* tag given the word and its POS tag. The interpretation of the *Chunk* tags is as follows: for a *Chunk* C, B-C will mean Begin *Chunk* C and I-C In *Chunk* C. Beginning a given *Chunk* will automatically ends the previous one. In addition, the symbol O means that the given word is outside any *Chunk*. Different approaches exist to deal with this problem since it was a shared task of the ConLLL 2000 conference [19]. Here is a concrete example:

He	PRP	B-NP		....		
reckons	VBZ	B-VP		billion	CD	I-NP
the	DT	B-NP		in	IN	B-PP
current	JJ	I-NP		Sept	NNP	B-NP
....				.	.	O

3   Our Point of View

The long-term goal is to build a complete system that combines the different levels of structure: the lexicon, the POS, the *Chunks*, and the other levels. This strategy is used for example in [1]. In our approach, each level of representation is dealt with by *one* model. Here we assume we already have the POS tags and concern ourselves with building the POS to *Chunk* model.

---

[1] NP stands for Noun Phrase, VP for Verb Phrase and PP for Preposition.

We will first study the task using just the POS tags to predict the *Chunk* ones. The inclusion of the lexical information is addressed later on in the paper. POS tagging has been widely studied in the literature (see *e.g* [20, 4, 2] for different approches to POS tagging). The problem is then to find a mapping between the POS sequence and the *Chunk* sequence.

If $T_{1,n}$ (resp. $C_{1,n}$) denotes the POS 1 to n, (resp. *Chunks* 1 to n), the goal is to find the most probable set of *Chunks* 1 to n given the POS 1 to n. This can be written:

$$Chunk(T_{1,n}) = \arg\max_{C_{1,n}} P(C_{1,n}|T_{1,n}) = \arg\max_{C_{1,n}} \frac{P(C_{1,n}, T_{1,n})}{P(T_{1,n})}$$
$$= \arg\max_{C_{1,n}} P(C_{1,n}, T_{1,n})$$

The problem is then to estimate the joint probability $P(C_{1,n}, T_{1,n})$. A possible decomposition of $P(C_{1,n}, T_{1,n}) = P_{1,n}$ is:

$$
\begin{aligned}
P_{1,n} &= P(T_1)\ P(C_1|T_1)\ P(T_2|C_1, T_1)\ P(C_2|T_{1,2}, C_1) \times \\
&\quad \ldots \times P(T_n|T_{1,n-1}, C_{1,n-1})\ P(C_n|T_{1,n}, C_{1,n-1}) \\
&= \prod_{i=1}^{n} P(C_i|C_{1,i-1}, T_{1,i})\ P(T_i|T_{1,i-1}, C_{1,i-1}) \\
&= \prod_{i=1}^{n} P(C_i|C_{1,i-1}, T_{1,i-1}, T_i)\ P(T_i|C_{1,i-1}, T_{1,i-1}) \\
&= \prod_{i=1}^{n} \frac{P(C_i, T_i|C_{1,i-1}, T_{1,i-1})}{P(T_i|C_{1,i-1}, T_{1,i-1})}\ P(T_i|C_{1,i-1}, T_{1,i-1}) \\
&= \prod_{i=1}^{n} P(C_i, T_i|C_{1,i-1}, T_{1,i-1})
\end{aligned}
$$

We therefore aim at finding the set of *Chunks* such that the pairs (POS, *Chunk*) are the most probable given the history. We can denote each pair by joining the POS and the *Chunks* in a single symbol.

If we use the "+" symbol as the separator, our learning data will look like:
`PRP+B-NP VBZ+B-VP DT+B-NP JJ+I-NP ...CD+I-NP IN+B-PP NNP+B-NP .+O`

Many models exist to estimate the probability of a symbol given a history. An example is the n-gram model and all the improvements applied to it: smoothing techniques (see [6] for a recent survey) and variable memory models [20, 16].

Another approach would be to infer Hidden Markov Models [21] or probabilistic automata [11, 5, 17, 22]. Among these techniques only four infer models in which the size of the dependency is not bound [21, 5, 22]. The first one is too computationally expensive to be feasible with our data. The others have been used in the context of natural language modeling. We have applied these algorithms to this task but only the best performing one (namely DDSM [22]) will be presented here. Reassuringly, the algorithm that performs best on the natural language modeling task is also the one that performs best on the noun phrase chunking task. We now present formally the model followed by the description of the DDSM algorithm.

4   The Learning Algorithm

We first present the formal definition of the model and the inference algorithm.

A *Probabilistic Deterministic Finite Automaton* (PFA) A is a 5-tuple $(\Sigma, Q^A, I^A, \xi^A, F^A)$ where Σ is the alphabet (a finite set of symbols), Q^A is the *set of states*, $I^A \in Q^A$ is the *initial* state, γ^A is a partial function of probabilistic transitions $Q^A \times \Sigma \to Q^A \times (0,1]$. $F^A\colon Q^A \to [0,1]$ is the probability that the automaton will terminate at a particular state.

We require that for all states q, $\sum_{\sigma \in \Sigma} \gamma^A(q, \sigma) + F^A(q) = 1$, abusing the notation for γ slightly. We assume that all states can generate at least one string with a strictly positive probability. This then defines a distribution over Σ^*.

Let I_+ denote a *positive sample, i.e.* a set of strings belonging to the probabilistic language we are trying to model. Let $PTA(I_+)$ denote the *prefix tree acceptor* built from a positive sample I_+. The prefix tree acceptor is an automaton that only accepts the strings in the sample and in which common prefixes are merged together resulting in a tree-shaped automaton. Let $PPTA(I_+)$ denote the *probabilistic prefix tree acceptor*. It is the probabilistic extension of the $PTA(I_+)$ in which each transition has a probability related to the number of times it is used while generating, or equivalently parsing, the positive sample. Let $C(q)$ denote the count of state q, that is, the number of times the state q was used while generating I_+ from $PPTA(I_+)$. Let $C(q, \#)$ denote the number of times a string of I_+ ended on q. Let $C(q, a)$ denote the count of the transition (q, a) in $PPTA(I_+)$. The $PPTA(I_+)$ is the maximal likelihood estimate built from I_+. In particular, for $PPTA(I_+)$ the probability estimates are $\overset{\wedge}{\gamma}(q, a) = \frac{C(q,a)}{C(q)}$, $a \in \Sigma \cup \{\#\}$.

Figure 1 exhibits a $PPTA(I+)$.

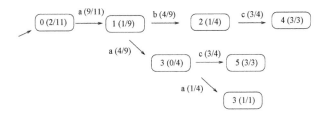

Fig. 1. PPTA built with $I+ = \{$aac,λ, aac, abd, aac, aac, abd, abd, a, ab, $\lambda\}$

We now present the second tool used by the generic algorithm: the state merging operation. This operation provides two modifications to the automaton: (i) it modifies the structure (figure 2, left part) and (ii) the probability distribution (figure 2, right part). It applies to two states. Merging two states can lead to non-determinism. The states that create non determinism are then recursively merged. When state q results from the merging of the states q' and q'', the following equality must hold in order to keep an overall consistent model:

$$\gamma(q, a) = \frac{C(q',a)+C(q'',a)}{C(q')+C(q'')} , \forall a \in \Sigma \cup \{\#\}$$

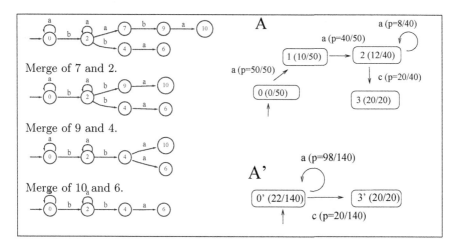

Fig. 2. Merging states.

One can note two properties of the update of the probabilities: first, $\frac{C(q',a)+C(q'',a)}{C(q')+C(q'')}$ is included in $[\frac{C(q',a)}{C(q')}, \frac{C(q'',a)}{C(q'')}]$ which means that, the probability of an after merge transition has a value bounded by the two values of the transitions it comes from. Secondly, $\frac{20+100}{1000+105} = \frac{120}{1105}$ is closer to $\frac{20}{1000}$ than to $\frac{100}{105}$. The merge naturally weights more the probability of the transition that holds the more information.

These remarks hold for each pair of transitions that takes part in the merge. Let us merge states q_i and q_j and define P_{q_i} (resp. P_{q_j}) as the probability distribution defined by considering state q_i (resp. q_j) as the initial state. Since the merge is recursively applied (see figure 2), the probability distribution after merging states q_i and q_j will be a weighted mean between the distributions P_{q_i} and P_{q_j}.

The next section addresses the description of the DDSM algorithm itself.

4.1   The DDSM Algorithm

The DDSM [22] algorithm (algorithm 1) takes two arguments: the learning set I_+ and a tuning parameter α. It looks for an automaton tradeoff between a small size and a small distance to the data. The distance measure used is the Kullback-Leibler divergence. The data are represented by the PPTA as it is the maximum likelihood estimate of the data. While merging two states, the distance between the automaton and the data increases and, at the same time, the number of states and the number of transitions, in general, decreases. Two states will be set compatible if the impact in terms of divergence of their merge divided by the gain of size is smaller than the parameter α.

The DDSM algorithm builds as a first step the $PPTA(I_+)$ and then repeats the following operations: choose two states (states q_i and q_j in the code), and computes the compatibility value (Relative_Divergence in the code) induced by their merge. It then performs the best merge if it is compatible. The ordering in which states are chosen is adapted from the EDSM algorithm, which was the winning algorithm of a non probabilistic grammatical inference competition [13].

Algorithm 1: DDSM $(I+, \alpha)$.

A $\leftarrow$ Numbering_in_Breadth_First_Order($PPTA$);
for $q_i = 1$ to Nb_State (A) do
    best_div $= \infty$;
    for $q_j = 0$ to $i - 1$ do
        if Compatible $(A, q_i, q_j) <$ best_div then
            best_pred $= q_j$;
            best_div $=$ Compatible (A, q_i, q_j);

    if $best\_div < \alpha$ then Merge $(A, q_i, \text{best\_pred})$;
Return A ;

The DDSM algorithm aims at inferring a small automaton that is close to the data. In fact, the bigger α, the more general (and small with respect to the number of states) the resulting automaton should be.

5   Automata as Transducers

In this section, we describe how the automaton can be interpreted as an aligned transducer. Let us suppose that the automaton of figure 3 was inferred by the DDSM algorithm. It can then be considered as a transducer with the same structure which emits symbols on transitions. The transducer transitions are built from the ones of the automaton when taking the POS as the input symbol and the *Chunks* as the output. The transducer is then non-sub-sequential, that is non-deterministic with respect to the input symbols. The automaton of figure 3 can be considered as a fully aligned non sub-sequential transducer.

We can then use the Viterbi algorithm [9] to find out the most probable path given the input POS tags.

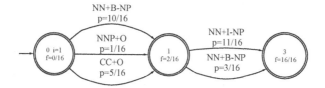

Fig. 3. probabilistic automaton/probabilistic transducer

6   Evaluation

The quality measure used is the F-score based on precision and recall [23]. A given *Chunk* is correct if the starting *Chunk* is correct (*e.g.* B-NP for the NP *Chunk*) and all the inside *Chunks* (I-NP for *Chunk* NP) are proposed correctly.

For a *Chunk* C, the recall is the number of times C is correctly proposed divided by the number of times it should be. Raising the recall can be done easily by proposing a given *Chunk* very often. Conversely, the precision computes the number of times a *Chunk* C is truly proposed divided by the number of times it is proposed. The two criteria are usually combined with the function F_β [23]:

$$F_\beta = \frac{(\beta^2 + 1).Recall.Precision}{\beta^2.Recall + Precision}$$

In the following, we will set $\beta = 1$, as is standard, in order to weight equally the precision and recall.

The original corpus is divided in two sets: the training set (AppTot) (with 8936 sentences and 211727 symbols), and a test set (Test) with 2012 sentences and 47377 symbols. We randomly divided the sentences of the training set into two sets: a training set for the validation step (AppV, 8092 sentences, 191683 symbols) and a validation set (Valid, 844 sentences, 20044 symbols) . AppV contains roughly 90% of the sentences of AppTot. The average number of words per sentence is around 24. The size of the vocabulary (in this case pairs of POS tags and *Chunk* tags) is around 300 (316 for AppV and 319 for AppTot). The PPTA contains roughly 160,000 states when built on the AppV set and 177,000 with AppTot. Our C++ implementation of the DDSM algorithm needs around 30 Megabytes to handle this data. It took from 45 mn (for $\alpha = 0.001$) to 13 hours (for $\alpha = 0.0004$) on a sun ultra 10 with a 333 MHz processor.

The free parameters were estimated on the corpus (AppV, Valid). A final inference was made on the AppTot learning set with the value of α defined during the validation step. The parsing of the test set was then done using the Viterbi algorithm using the parameter values defined on the AppV set.

We now describe the behavior of the machine on the validation set.

7   Validation Set Analysis

This section will deal with the analysis of the different techniques we applied, evaluated on the validation set. We first briefly describe the smoothing technique choosen. We then discuss an adaptation of the bagging technique [3]. Finally we describe an efficient method for using lexical information in the learning process.

The Smoothing Technique The smoothing technique used is inspired by Katz smoothing [10]: a small quantity is discounted from each probability available in the automaton. The probability mass available is then redistributed on the events the automaton cannot handle (*e.g.* parsing NN VP with the transducer of figure 3). The redistribution of the probability mass is made *via* a unigram model to obtain an overall consistent model. The unigram model is built using the same learning set as for the automata inference, extended by an end-of-string symbol. The parsing of the input by a unigram is made using the same technique as for an automaton. The unigram model can also be considered as a one state automaton that contains a loop for each element of the vocabulary.

The discounting value was estimated on the validation set. The discounting is done by subtracting a value from the numerator of the count of each estimated probability. In such a way, the discounted mass gets smaller as the frequency of the transition - and hence the statistical relevance of the probability estimated - increases. The value of this discounting parameter was estimated on the validation set as 0.5. Unlike in other domains such as language modeling, it seems that the tuning of this parameter is not crucial.

The strategy used here smoothes *each* path of the transducer. Even if the best automaton is usually able to parse the input sentence totally, this strategy leads to better results. An interpretation of this phenomenon can be that it is better to trust the choices made at the beginning of the parsing.

Bagging the Density Estimator The bagging [3] technique has been successfully applied in many domains but was reported not to work on this particular task [18]. On the other hand, it was shown to improve the Collins statistical full parser [7]. Moreover, interpolating PDFA has been reported to improve results significantly [22]. Finally, it has been shown that boosting does not perform better than bagging on the full task. We hence use the bagging method here.

The bagging strategy samples the training set in samples (B-sets) of the same size. A model is then inferred from each B-set and a majority vote or an interpolation is done using all these models. Applying this raw technique does not work well since many strings have a very small probability in the original training set. They hence do not appear in the B-sets. In order to get good B-sets, we increse their size up to 50,000 sentences because, with this size, the size of the B-sets PPTA matches roughly the size of the PPTA built from the original training set. Following this strategy, we know that on the one hand, nearly all the input sentences of the original training sample will be present in the B-sets and, on the other hand, the statistical relevance of the main sentences increases.

While bagging the lexicalized training set, we needed to increase again the size of the B-set as going up to 130,000 sentences continue to improve the dev set performances.

Including the Lexical Information Lexical information is known to be quite powerful. For example, Pla et *al.* [15], who use a statistical finite state machine, improve their results by 4%, raising the $F_{\beta=1}$ from 86 to 90. They choose some POS tags and split them with respect to the word they were matching with. A POS tag T_i is then replaced by the symbol W_iT_i for the word W_i they are tagging. The idea behind that is to resolve the ambiguity of a tag T_i when the word can help. As an example, the word *against* always start an B-PP but its POS tag (namely IN) is ambiguous because it can predict a beginning of preposition (B-PP *Chunk* tag) or a beginning of clause with a complementizer (B-SBAR *Chunk* tag). By adding a new POS tag *against-IN* we will be able to save some problem when the POS tag is IN and when the matching word is *against*. The problem then is to choose which POS tag to split and in which way to do it. One obvious idea is to create a new POS tag for each word/POS pair but this will (i) be intractable and (ii) lead to data sparseness. We thus try to determine automatically which POS tag to split and in which way. We will use a criterion based on mutual information.

Choosing the POS tag: we wish to identify which POS tags will be helped by the addition of lexical information. For these POS tags, we would expect there to be a high dependency between the word and the *Chunk* tag. The mutual information between two random variables X and Y is defined as

$$I(X;Y) = \sum_{x,y} P(x,y) \log \frac{P(x,y)}{P(x)P(y)} = H(X) - H(X|Y) \qquad (1)$$

We therefore calculate for each POS tag t the mutual information between the conditional *Chunk* distribution and the conditional *Word* distribution.

$$I(C|T = t; W|T = t) = H(C|T = t) - H(C|W, T = t) \qquad (2)$$

We then select the POS for which this is highest. This is the POS which will give us the greatest reduction in the uncertainty of the *Chunk* tag if we know the word as well as the POS tag.

All the probabilities are estimated using the maximum likelihood. To avoid problems in the estimation of this quantity due to data sparseness, we did not take into account rare combinations of word/*Chunk*, *i.e.* the combinations that appears less than six times.

Splitting the POS tag: the POS being chosen, we need to create a new item (a combination of word and POS tag) according to the ability of the word to predict the *Chunk*. We here again aim at using an information theoretic criterion. Let W_t be the set of words that have t as a POS. Let Π^t be the set of partitions of W^t. We now aim at finding the partition $\pi^t \in \Pi^t$ that leads to the greatest reduction of the uncertainty of the *Chunk*[2]. Obviously, having an exhaustive search of the set of partitions is not computationally possible. Let us define $\pi_i^t = \{\{w_i\}, \{w_1, ..., w_{i-1}, w_{i+1}, ..., w_n\}\}$. We will choose the partition π_i^t that leads to the minimal conditional entropy of the *Chunk* given the partition:

$$\pi_i^t = \text{Argmin}_{\pi_j^t} \, H(C|\pi_j^t) = \text{Argmin}_{\pi_j^t} \, - \sum_{s \in \pi_j^t} \sum_{c_i \in C} p(c_i, s) \log p(c_i|s)$$

We then repeat the procedure until the right number of splits is reached. Figure 4 shows the relationship between the number of splits and the $F_{\beta=1}$ dev set performance. The optimal number of splits as measured on the dev set (see figure 4), seems to be close to 100 which means that only a small amount of POS tag need to be split in order to perform well. This is helpful because it doesn't change significantly the time response of the learning algorithm.

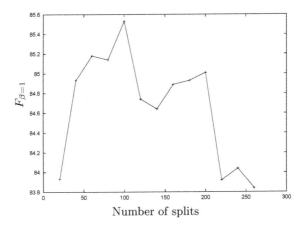

Fig. 4. Number of splits vs dev set F-score

We also experimented with a more global method of optimisation where we searched for an optimal partition of all <word,POS> pairs, but preliminary experiments indicated that this did not perform well.

8   Results on the Test Set

This section describes the results obtained on the test set. The task baseline is performed by a unigram model or equivalently a one state automaton. It provides an overall $F_{\beta=1}$ of 77. Our results are summarized in table 1. They were obtained

---

[2] We actually aim at creating a new item <word,POS>. Since the POS is fixed here, we just need to partition the word set.

on the test set after an inference (on the whole training set) using the value of the parameter α that was optimal on the validation set.

The first column shows the *Chunk*; the remaining columns show the $F_{\beta=1}$ score under various settings: the initial Viterbi technique without lexical information (first column with label I), the results obtained when adding lexical information by splitting the POS tags 100 times, (column L), the bagging technique without lexical information (column B), and finally the results obtained combining the bagging and the lexical information (column LB). The last two columns give some comparable results from other techniques applied to this task, *i.e.* a n-gram model without lexical information [8] and a lexicalized model using Hidden Markov Models [15]. We consider these two techniques relevant, since they use only limited or no lexical information as we do. Techniques that use full lexical information produce results that are substantially higher.

Table 1. Comparison of results on the test set $F_{\beta=1}$

Chunk	I	L	B	LB	ngrm	LMM
ADJP	48	49	58	63	55	70
ADVP	63	69	69	74	70	77
INTJ	33	22	40	67	40	100
NP		85	86	89	89	89	90
PP		87	95	90	95	92	96
PRT	9	55	20	67	32	67
SBAR	15	77	16	81	41	79
VP		86	86	89	88	90	92
ALL		83	86	87	89	87	90

9   Comparison

The n-gram approach (ngrm column) extends the baseline algorithm by using a context sensitive approach instead of using a unigram. A given *Chunk* is chosen with respect to its POS tag context. The context was defined as a centered window around the current POS tag. In the results outlined here a window of 5 POS tags was taken. The author mentioned that the results do not improve significantly while using a bigger window size. The differences between our approach and the n-gram one are that (i) it does not generalize the data and (ii) given the smoothing strategy applied, the method does not provide a true probability.

With regard to (i), it seems that, even if we generalize, we get roughly the same results. However, it is important to note that the generalization provides rather small automata (roughly 200 states and 8,000 transitions), that are significantly smaller than the n-gram models. The item (ii) is not very serious since the measure does not rely on the fact that the model define a true probability distribution. Nevertheless, we note that having a consistent probability distribution will allow us to combine our model with other probabilistic approaches cleanly.

The Lexicalized Markov Model (LMM in table 1) takes the 470 most frequent words of the training data (excluding the punctuation, symbols,proper nouns and numbers) and splits their respective POS tags [15]. They got an overall improvement of 4% of the $F_{\beta=1}$. The main difference with our approach comes from our automatic detection of the POS tags to split. Our method has the advantage of splitting fewer POS tags (100 comparing to 470). Moreover, since identifying proper nouns in large corpora is a research area in itself, having an automatic procedure is preferable. It is also important to note that our study is independant of the grammatical inference algorithm used. The performances should increase as soon as better grammatical inference algorithms will come. Finally, the compactness of our model remains a strong point in favour of our method. To be complete, we need to mention that the best results reported on this data set, with a support vector machine approach [12], are an overall $F_{\beta=1}$ of 93. A number of other approaches have produced similar scores using full lexical information.

10   Conclusion and Further Work

We have presented an algorithm for shallow parsing based on a grammatical inference algorithm; first we build an automaton to model the data sequence, and then we use the automaton as a transducer to recover the optimal sequence of labels.

In addition, we note that it appears possible to get substantial improvements in the performance by using very limited lexical information – in our experiments, it was only necessary to model the effect of 100 words. It seems that bagging can be successfully applied to improve probability density estimators. From our knowledge this is the first application of the bagging technique to probability density estimation.

Nonetheless, we note that the results we present here are not as good as models with a fixed structure. In theory, with sufficient data the grammatical inference algorithms should perform better since they can model dependencies of unlimited length. In practice, as in other natural language processing tasks such as language modeling, the local dependencies account for much of the structure of the sentences.

In future work we will continue our investigations of bagging, particularly examining the use of more bags, and the size of the bags. We will also experiment with some other techniques such as boosting, that we feel could be useful. There are two other directions we will also explore: first, we will experiment with inferring an automaton that models the reversed sequences and combining the predictions of the "forward" and "backward" automata. Secondly, we will experiment with combining our model with other statistical models, *e.g.* to combine the probabilities provided by our model and the one provided by some statistical POS taggers [20, 2].

Acknowledgements: This work was supported by the European Training and Mobility of Researchers (TMR) Network "Learning Computational Grammars".

References

[1] S. Ait-Mokhtar and J.P. Chanod. Incremental finite state parsing. In *Proc. of the 5th Conference of Applied Natural Language Processing*, pages 72–79, Washington, DC, April 1997.

[2] Thorsten Brants. TnT – a statistical part-of-speech tagger. In *Proc. of the 6th Conference on Applied Natural Language Processing*, Seattle, WA, April 2000.

[3] Leo Breiman. Bagging predictors. *Machine Learning*, 24(2):123–140, 1996.

[4] Eric Brill. Transformation-based error-driven learning and natural language processing: A case study in part of speech tagging. *Computational Linguistics*, 21(4):543–565, 1995.

[5] R. Carrasco and J. Oncina. Learning stochastic regular grammars by means of a state merging method. In *Second Intl. Collo. on Grammatical Inference and Applications*, pages 139–152, 1994.

[6] Joshua Goodman. A bit of progress in language modeling. Technical report, Microsoft Research, 2001.

[7] C. John Henderson and Eric Brill. Bagging and boosting a treebank parser. In *NAACL*, pages 34–41, Seattle, Washington, USA, 2000.

[8] Christer Johansson. A context sensitive maximum likelihood approach to chunking. In *CoNLL-2000 and LLL-2000*, pages 136–138, Lisbon, Portugal, 2000.

[9] Daniel Jurafsky and James H. Martin. *Speech and Language Processing: An Introduction to Natural Language Processing, Computational Linguistics, and Speech Recognition*. Prentice Hall, Englewood Cliffs, New Jersey, 2000.

[10] S. M. Katz. Estimation of probabilities from sparse data for the language model component of a speech recognizer. *IEEE Transactions on Acoustic, Speech and Signal Processing*, 35(3):400–401, 1987.

[11] M.J. Kearns, Y. Mansour, D. Ron, R. Rubinfeld, R.E. Schapire, and L. Sellie. On the learnability of discrete distributions. In *Proc. of the 25th Annual ACM Symposium on Theory of Computing*, pages 273–282, 1994.

[12] Taku Kudoh and Yuji Matsumoto. Use of support vector learning for chunk identification. In *CoNLL-2000 and LLL-2000*, pages 142–144, Lisbon, Portugal, 2000.

[13] K. J. Lang, B. A. Pearlmutter, and R. A. Price. Results of the Abbadingo one DFA learning competition and a new evidence-driven state merging algorithm. In *ICGI '98*, volume 1433, pages 1–12. Springer-Verlag, 1998.

[14] M. Marcus, S. Santorini, and M. Marcinkiewicz. Building a large annotated corpus of English: the Penn treebank. *Computational Linguistics*, 19(2):313–330, 1993.

[15] F. Pla, A. Molina, and N. Prieto. An Integrated Statistical Model for Tagging and Chunking Unrestricted Text. In Petr Sojka, Ivan Kopeček, and Karel Pala, editors, *Proc. of the Third Intl. Workshop on Text, Speech and Dialogue—TSD 2000*, Lecture Notes in Artificial Intelligence LNCS/LNAI 1902, pages 15–20, Brno, Czech Republic, September 2000. Springer-Verlag.

[16] D. Ron, Y. Singer, and N. Tishby. Learning probabilistic automata with variable memory length. In *Seventh Conf. on Computational Learning Theory*, pages 35–46, New Brunswick, 12–15 July 1994. ACM Press.

[17] D. Ron, Y. Singer, and N. Tishby. On the learnability and usage of acyclic probabilistic finite automata. In *COLT 1995*, pages 31–40, Santa Cruz CA USA, 1995. ACM.

[18] Erik Tjong Kim Sang. Noun phrase recognition by system combination. In *Proceedings of BNAIC'00*, pages 335–336. Tilburg, The Netherlands, 2000.

[19] Erik Tjong Kim Sang and Sabine Buchholz. Introduction to the conll-2000 shared task: Chunking. In *CoNLL-2000*, pages 127–132, Lisbon, Portugal, 2000.

[20] H. Schütze and Y. Singer. Part-of-speech tagging using a variable memory markov model. In *Meeting of the Assoc. for Computational Linguistics*, pages 181–187, 1994.

[21] A. Stolcke. *Bayesian Learning of Probabilistic Language Models*. Ph. D. dissertation, University of California, 1994.

[22] F. Thollard. Improving probabilistic grammatical inference core algorithms with post-processing techniques. In *Eighth Intl. Conf. on Machine Learning*, pages 561–568, Williams, July 2001. Morgan Kauffman.

[23] C. J. van Rijsbergen. *Information Retrieval*. Butterworths, London, United Kingdom, 1975.

Learning of Regular Bi-ω Languages

D.G. Thomas, M. Humrosia Begam, K.G. Subramanian, and S. Gnanasekaran

Department of Mathematics, Madras Christian College,
Tambaram, Chennai - 600 059, India
kkinfotech@yahoo.com

Abstract. In this paper, we define three classes of languages of bi-infinite words, namely local bi-ω languages, recognizable bi-ω languages and Büchi local bi-ω languages as subclasses of the class of regular bi-ω languages and prove some basic results. We observe that the class of recognizable bi-ω languages coincides with the well-known class of rational bi-adherence languages and show that the class of regular bi-ω languages is the class of morphic images of Büchi local bi-ω languages. We provide learning algorithms for Büchi local bi-ω languages and regular bi-ω languages.

Key words: Learning algorithm, local bi-ω languages, recognizable bi-ω languages, rational bi-adherence languages, Büchi local bi-ω languages, regular bi-ω languages.

1 Introduction

Learning an unknown concept using examples and queries has attracted the attention and interest of researchers in computer science especially in artificial intelligence and has been widely studied in recent research. Knowledge acquisition is modeled as a concept learning process. Concepts may be formal languages, which are typically represented by formal grammars or finite automata. Efficient learning methods for the concepts through their representations are available in the literature [1,2,8]. Gold [8] suggested a learning model called "identification in the limit from positive data" and proved that the class of regular languages of finite words is not identifiable in the limit from positive data. This fact initiated a search for sub-classes of regular languages that are learnable in Gold's model.

Infinite words or ω-words were first considered by Axel Thue and have been investigated systematically in formal language theory [4,12]. Saoudi and Yokomori [11] introduced two sub-classes of regular ω-languages called local and recognizable ω-languages and gave two learning algorithms for these sub-classes. A different approach on learning a subclass of regular ω-languages using prefixes of words is done in [5]. Recently, a learning algorithm for regular ω-languages has been considered in [13].

Bi-infinite words or two-sided infinite words are natural extensions of infinite words and have also been objects of interest and study [6,7,10]. The theory of finite automata has been extended to bi-infinite words by Nivat and Perrin [10] and the study has been continued. Gire and Nivat [7] introduced the notion

P. Adriaans, H. Fernau, and M. van Zaanen (Eds.): ICGI 2002, LNAI 2484, pp. 283–292, 2002.
© Springer-Verlag Berlin Heidelberg 2002

of bi-adherence of languages of finite words whereas equivalent conditions for bi-adherence of regular languages of finite words in terms of finite automata were established [6]. Bi-infinite words are playing important role in 'Symbolic Dynamics' [3] and studied in the theory of codes [9].

In this paper, we extend the concept of local languages to languages of bi-infinite words and define local bi-ω languages. We also define recognizable bi-ω languages. We observe that the class of recognizable bi-ω languages coincides with the class of rational bi-adherence languages. We introduce Büchi local bi-ω languages and provide a learning algorithm for this class using Gold's model of identification in the limit from positive data consisting only ultimately periodic bi-infinite words. We show that every regular bi-ω language is a strictly alphabetic morphic image of a Büchi local bi-ω language. We present an algorithm for learning regular bi-ω languages using positive data and restricted superset queries [2]. Our approach is similar to the one delt in [11].

2   Local Bi-ω Languages and Recognizable Bi-ω Languages

In this section, we recall the notions of bi-ω languages [6]. Then we define local bi-ω languages and recognizable bi-ω languages and obtain few results.

Let A be a finite alphabet. Let A^ω denote the set of all sequences of $\mathcal{N}$ (the set of positive integers) into A. Each element of A^ω is called a right-infinite word. Let $^\omega A$ denote the set of all sequences of Z^- (the set of negative integers) into A. Each element of $^\omega A$ is called a left-infinite word. Let A^Z be the set of all sequences of Z (the set of integers) into A. The shift σ is a mapping $\sigma : A^Z \to A^Z$ defined by

$$\sigma((u_n)_{n \in Z}) = (u_{n+1})_{n \in Z}$$

A bi-infinite word is a class under the equivalence relation $\approx$ over A^Z defined by $u \approx v$ iff $\exists\, n \in Z : v = \sigma^n(u)$. Let $^\omega A^\omega$ denote the set of all bi-infinite words over A. A bi-infinite word u is ultimately periodic if $u = {}^\omega xyz^\omega = ...xxxyzzz...$ for some $x, z \in A^+, y \in A^*$. A bi-ω language is a subset of $^\omega A^\omega$.

A Büchi (finite) automaton M over an alphabet A is $M = (Q, A, E_M, I_{linf}, T_{rinf})$ where

- Q is a finite set of states;
- A is a finite alphabet;
- E_M is a subset of $Q \times A \times Q$, called the set of arrows;
- $I_{linf} \subseteq Q$ is a set of left-infinite repetitive states;
- $T_{rinf} \subseteq Q$ is a set of right-infinite repetitive states.

An arrow (p, a, q) is also denoted by $p \xrightarrow{a} q$. A path in M is a bi-infinite sequence namely $c = \cdots c_{-2} c_{-1} c_0 c_1 c_2 \cdots$. The arrows in the path are consecutive in the sense that $c_{i+1} : q_i \xrightarrow{a_{i+1}} q_{i+1}$ where $i \in Z$. A notation $c : I_{linf} \overset{w}{\ggg} T_{rinf}$ denotes a bi-infinite path c of label w which passes through I_{linf} infinitely often on the left and through T_{rinf} infinitely often on the right. Let $L^{\omega\omega}(M) =$

$\{w \in {}^{\omega}A^{\omega}/\exists(c : I_{linf} \overset{w}{\ggg} T_{rinf})\}$ be the bi-ω language accepted by M. Let $Rec({}^{\omega}A^{\omega}) = \{L \subseteq {}^{\omega}A^{\omega}/\exists$ a Büchi automaton M such that $L^{\omega\omega}(M) = L\}$.

It is known the $Rec({}^{\omega}A^{\omega})$ is the family of all regular bi-ω languages each of which is a finite union of sets of the form
${}^{\omega}XYZ^{\omega} = \{u \in {}^{\omega}A^{\omega}/u = \cdots x_n x_{n-1} \cdots x_2 x_1 y z_1 z_2 \cdots z_{n-1} z_n \cdots, \text{ with } x_i \in X, y \in Y, z_i \in Z(i \geq 1)\}$ where X, Y, Z are regular languages in A^*. The automaton M is said to be deterministic if for every $q, q_1, q_2 \in Q$ and every $a \in A$, $(q, a, q_1) \in E_M$ and $(q, a, q_2) \in E_M$ implies $q_1 = q_2$.

Example : Let $M = (Q, A, E_M, I_{linf}, T_{rinf})$ where $Q = \{1, 2, 3\}$, $A = \{a, b, c\}$, $I_{linf} = \{1\}$; $T_{rinf} = \{3\}$. E_M is given by

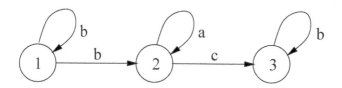

Clearly, $L^{\omega\omega}(M) = {}^{\omega}ba^*cb^{\omega}$, M is non-deterministic.

Definition 2.1 : A local system over A is an ordered pair $S = <A, C>$ where $C \subseteq A^2$. We denote by $L^{\omega\omega}(S)$, the bi-ω language $\{x \in {}^{\omega}A^{\omega}/F_2(x) \subseteq C\}$, where $F_2(x)$ is the set of factors of x of length 2. A bi-ω language $L \subseteq {}^{\omega}A^{\omega}$ is called a local bi-ω language if there exists a local system S such that $L = L^{\omega\omega}(S)$. The set of all local bi-ω languages is denoted by $\mathcal{L}^{\omega\omega}$.

Example 2.2 : We note that when $A = \{a, b\}$,

1. $\{{}^{\omega}(ab^+)^{\omega}\} \cup \{{}^{\omega}b^{\omega}\}$ is a local bi-ω language by taking $C = \{ab, ba, bb\}$. Here $\{{}^{\omega}(ab^+)^{\omega}\}$ denotes the set of bi-infinite strings of the form $...(ab^{n_1})(ab^{n_2})(ab^{n_3})...$ where $n_1, n_2, n_3, ...$ are positive integers.
2. $\{{}^{\omega}aba^{\omega}\}$ is clearly not a local bi-ω language.

Definition 2.3 : A Büchi automaton is a B-automaton if $I_{linf} = T_{rinf} = Q$. Let $DB_\ell = \{L \subseteq^{\omega} A^{\omega}/L = L^{\omega\omega}(M)$ for some deterministic B-automaton $M\}$. Every language in DB_ℓ is called a recognizable bi-ω language.

Theorem 2.4 : $\mathcal{L}^{\omega\omega} \subset DB_\ell$.
Proof : Let $L \in \mathcal{L}^{\omega\omega}$. This implies $L = L^{\omega\omega}(S)$ for some $S = <A, C>$. We now give a construction procedure for a deterministic B-automaton M such that $L = L^{\omega\omega}(M)$.

Algorithm(1)
      Input : $S = <A, C>$
      Output : $M = (Q, A, E_M, Q, Q)$ such that $L = L^{\omega\omega}(M)$

Procedure

  Let $Q = \{[a]/a \in A\} \cup \{[ab]/ab \in C\} \cup \{\$\}$
  for all $q \in Q$ do
    for all $a \in A$ do
    if $q = [b]$ and $ba \in C$ then $\delta([b], a) = [ba]$
    else if $q = [bc]$ and $ca \in C$
        then $\delta(q, a) = [ca]$
        else $\delta(q, a) = \$$.

It is easy to see that $\mathcal{L}^{\omega\omega}$ is properly included in DB_ℓ since $L = \{^\omega ababbaba^\omega\}$ is not a local bi-ω language even though $L \in DB_\ell$.   □

Let A_1, A_2 be two alphabets and $\phi : A_1^* \to A_2^*$ be a morphism. Then ϕ is called strictly alphabetic if $\phi(A_1) \subseteq A_2$.

This definition is applicable to bi-infinite words also.

Theorem 2.5 : If $L \in DB_\ell$ then there exists a strictly alphabetic morphism h and L_1 in $\mathcal{L}^{\omega\omega}$ such that $h(L_1) = L$.
Proof: Let $M = (Q, A, E_M, Q, Q)$ be the deterministic Büchi automaton M such that $L = L^{\omega\omega}(M)$.

Then construct $C_L = \{(q, a, q_1)(q_1, b, q_2)/(q, a, q_1), (q_1, b, q_2) \in E_M\}$. Let $\Gamma = Q \times A \times Q$. Further define $h((q, a, q_1)) = a$ for all $(q, a, q_1) \in \Gamma$. Let $L_1 = L^{\omega\omega}(S_L)$ where $S_L =< \Gamma, C_L >$. Then it is clear that $h(L_1) = L^{\omega\omega}(M) = L$.   □

We now recall the notion of bi-adherence for languages of finite words [6] and show that the class of rational bi-adherence languages coincide with DB_ℓ.

Let $X \subseteq A^*$. The bi-adherence of X is a subset of $^\omega A^\omega$, defined by $Biadh(X) = \{w \in^\omega A^\omega / F(w) \subseteq F(X)\}$ where $F(w)$ is the set of all finite factors of w and $F(X) = \cup_{w \in X} F(w)$.

Let L be a bi-ω language of $^\omega A^\omega$. L is called a rational bi-adherence language if and only if there exists a rational language R of A^* such that $Biadh(R) = L$.

Theorem 2.6 [6]: Let L be a bi-ω language of $^\omega A^\omega$. The following conditions are equivalent.

1. L is a rational bi-adherence
2. There exists an automaton $(Q, A, E_M, I_{linf}, T_{rinf})$ recognizing L and satisfying $Q = I_{linf} = T_{rinf}$
3. There exists a deterministic automaton $(Q, A, E_M, I_{linf}, T_{rinf})$ recognizing L and satisfying $Q = I_{linf} = T_{rinf}$

From this theorem we observe that DB_ℓ is exactly the class of rational bi-adherence languages.

3   Büchi Local Bi-ω Languages

In this section we define Büchi local bi-ω languages and examine their properties. We present an algorithm to identify the class of Büchi local bi-ω languages in the limit from positive data that are ultimately periodic bi-infinite words.

Definition 3.1 : A Büchi local system over an alphabet A is an ordered quadruple $S = (A, C, C', C'')$ where $C \subseteq A^2, C' \subseteq C, C'' \subseteq C$. We denote by $L_{BE}^{\omega\omega}(S)$, the bi-ω language $\{x \in^{\omega} A^{\omega}/F_2(x) \subseteq C, Linf(F_2(x)) \cap C' \neq \phi, Rinf(F_2(x)) \cap C'' \neq \phi\}$ where $F_2(x)$ is the set of all factors of x of length 2, $Linf(F_2(x))$ (resp $Rinf(F_2(x))$) is the set of all factors of x of length 2 which occur infinitely many times in the left (resp. right) in x. A bi-ω language $L \subseteq^{\omega} A^{\omega}$ is called a Büchi extended local bi-ω language if there exists a Büchi local system S over A such that $L = L_{BE}^{\omega\omega}(S)$. The set of all Büchi local bi-ω languages is denoted by $\mathcal{L}_{BE}^{\omega\omega}$.

Example 3.2 : The bi-ω language $L = \{{}^{\omega}b(ab)^n b^{\omega}\}/n \geq 1\}$ over $A = \{a, b\}$ is a Büchi local bi-ω language. Here $C = \{bb, ab, ba\}, C' = \{bb\}, C'' = \{bb\}$.

Note that $\mathcal{L}^{\omega\omega} \subseteq \mathcal{L}_{BE}^{\omega\omega}$, since each $L \in \mathcal{L}^{\omega\omega}$ is such that $L = L_{BE}^{\omega\omega}(S)$ for some $S = (A, C, C, C)$.

The bi-ω language L given in example 3.2 is not a local bi-ω language for, if $L \in \mathcal{L}^{\omega\omega}$, then ${}^{\omega}(ab)^{\omega} \in L$ which is not the case. Therefore $\mathcal{L}^{\omega\omega} \subset \mathcal{L}_{BE}^{\omega\omega}$.

Now, we show that the class of Büchi local bi-ω languages is a proper subclass of $REC({}^{\omega}A^{\omega})$, the class of regular bi-ω languages.

Theorem 3.3 : $\mathcal{L}_{BE}^{\omega\omega} \subset REC({}^{\omega}A^{\omega})$.

Proof : Let $L \in \mathcal{L}_{BE}^{\omega\omega}$. Then there exists a Büchi local system $S = (A, C, C', C'')$ over A such that $L = L_{BE}^{\omega\omega}(S)$. We now give a construction procedure for a deterministic Büchi automaton M such that $L = L^{\omega\omega}(M)$.

Algorithm(2)
Input : $S = (A, C, C', C'')$
Output : $M = (Q, A, E_M, I_{linf}, T_{rinf})$ such that $L = L^{\omega\omega}(M)$
Procedure :
Let $Q = \{[a]/a \in A\} \cup \{[ab]/ab \in C\} \cup \{\$\}$
Let $I_{linf} = \{[ab]/ab \in C'\}$.
Let $T_{rinf} = \{[ab]/ab \in C''\}$.
for all $q \in Q$ do
    for all $a \in A$ do
    if $q = [b]$ and $ba \in C$ then $\delta([b], a) = [ba]$
    else if $q = [bc]$ and $ca \in C$
        then $\delta([bc], a) = [ca]$
        else $\delta(q, a) = \$$.

M is deterministic and $L = L^{\omega\omega}(M)$. Therefore $\mathcal{L}_{BE}^{\omega\omega} \subseteq REC(^{\omega}A^{\omega})$. Since $\{^{\omega}ba^2b^{\omega}\} \in REC(^{\omega}A^{\omega})\backslash \mathcal{L}_{BE}^{\omega\omega}$, the theorem is proved. $\qquad\square$

Proposition 3.4 : $\mathcal{L}_{BE}^{\omega\omega}$ is not closed under (1) union, (2) complement and (3) homomorphism.

Proof :
(1) Let $L_1 = \{^{\omega}(bc)a(bc)^{\omega}\}$ and $L_2 = \{^{\omega}a^{\omega}\}$ be bi-ω languages over $A = \{a, b, c\}$. Then $L_1, L_2 \in \mathcal{L}_{BE}^{\omega\omega}$. But $L_1 \cup L_2 \notin L_{BE}^{\omega\omega}$. For, if $L_1 \cup L_2 \in \mathcal{L}_{BE}^{\omega\omega}$, then $^{\omega}(bc)a^n(bc)^{\omega} \in L_1 \cup L_2$, for all $n \geq 1$.
(2) If $L = \{^{\omega}a^{\omega}\}$ is a bi-ω language over $A = \{a, b\}$, then $L \in \mathcal{L}_{BE}^{\omega\omega}$. $L^c =^{\omega} Aa^*bA^{\omega} \notin \mathcal{L}_{BE}^{\omega\omega}$.
(3) Let $L = {}^{\omega}c\{a, b\}^*c^{\omega}$ be a bi-ω language over $A = \{a, b, c\}$.
Take $C = \{cc, ab, ba, aa, bb, ac, ca, bc, cb\}, C' = \{cc\}, C'' = \{cc\}$.
Then $L \in \mathcal{L}_{BE}^{\omega\omega}$. Let $\Gamma = \{a, b\}$.
Define $h : A \to \Gamma$ by $h(a) = a, h(b) = h(c) = b$.
Then $h(L) =^{\omega} b\Gamma^*b^{\omega}, h(C) = \{bb, ab, ba, aa\}, h(C') = h(C'') = \{bb\}$.
If $h(L) \in \mathcal{L}_{BE}^{\omega\omega}$ then $^{\omega}(b^2a^*b^2)^{\omega} \subseteq h(L)$. Therefore $h(L) \notin \mathcal{L}_{BE}^{\omega\omega}$ proving $\mathcal{L}_{BE}^{\omega\omega}$ is not closed under homomorphism. $\qquad\square$

Note that if L_1, L_2 are Büchi local bi-ω languages over disjoint alphabets, then $L_1 \cup L_2 \in \mathcal{L}_{BE}^{\omega\omega}$.
We now examine learning of Büchi local bi-ω languages. The method is similar to the one presented in [11] for local ω-languages.

Definition 3.5 : Let T be a finite sample of ultimately periodic bi-infinite words. Let $C_T = F_2(T) = \cup_{\omega xyz^{\omega} \in T} F_2(x^2yz^2), C'_T = \cup_{\omega xyz^{\omega} \in T} P_2(x^2), C''_T = \cup_{\omega xyz^{\omega} \in T} S_2(z^2)$ where $x, z \in A^+, y \in A^*$ and $S_2(w), P_2(w)$ are the suffix and prefix of $w \in A^+$, of length 2 respectively and $F_2(w)$ is the set of all factors of w of length 2. $S_T = (A, C_T, C'_T, C''_T)$ is called a Büchi local system associated with T and $L = L_{BE}^{\omega\omega}(S_T)$ is called the Büchi local bi-ω language associated with T.

Definition 3.6 : A finite subset E of $^{\omega}A^{\omega}$ is called a characteristic sample for a Büchi local bi-ω language L, if L is the smallest Büchi local bi-ω language containing E.

If $T = \{^{\omega}x_1y_1z_1^{\omega}, ..., ^{\omega}x_ky_kz_k^{\omega}\}$ is a sample of ultimately periodic bi-infinite words, we denote by T_k, the set $\{x_1^ky_1z_1^k, ..., x_n^ky_nz_n^k\}$.

Proposition 3.7 : $L_{BE}^{\omega\omega}(S_T) = L_{BE}^{\omega\omega}(S_{T_2})$.

By the method of constructing deterministic Büchi automaton M in algorithm(2) we have the following proposition.

Proposition 3.8 : There effectively exists a characteristic sample for any Büchi local bi-ω language.

Now we give a learning algorithm that learns in the limit from positive data an unknown Büchi local bi-ω language.

Algorithm(3)
Input : A positive presentation of an unknown Büchi local bi-ω language L.
Output : An infinite sequence $S_{E_i} (i = 1, 2, ...)$ of Büchi local systems.
Procedure :

$\quad E_0 := \phi, S_{E_0} := (A, \phi, \phi, \phi);$
$\quad$ Repeat (for ever)
$\quad\quad$ Let $S_{E_i} = (A, C_i, C_i', C_i'')$ be the current conjecture
$\quad\quad$ Read the next positive example $w = x^2 y z^2$;
$\quad\quad$ Scan w to compute $F_2(w), P_2(x^2), S_2(z^2)$;
$\quad\quad S_{E_{i+1}} := (A, C_i \cup F_2(w), C_i' \cup P_2(x^2), C_i'' \cup S_2(z^2));$
$\quad\quad E_{i+1} := E_i \cup \{w\};$
$\quad\quad S_{E_{i+1}}$ as new conjecture.

Proposition 3.9 : If $S_{E_0}, S_{E_1}, ...$ is a sequence of conjectures by algorithm(3), then

1. $L_{BE}^{\omega\omega}(S_{E_i}) \subseteq L (i = 0, 1, 2, ...)$ and
2. there exists $r \geq 0$ such that $L_{BE}^{\omega\omega}(S_{E_r}) = L_{BE}^{\omega\omega}(S_{E_{i+r}}) = L$ (for all $i \geq 0$).

Theorem 3.10 : Given an unknown Büchi local bi-ω language L, algorithm (3) learns, in the limit from positive data, a Büchi local system S_E such that $L_{BE}^{\omega\omega}(S_E) = L$.

If N is the sum of the sizes of all positive data $E_n = \{w_1, w_2, ..., w_n\}$ provided (i.e., $N = \sum_{i=1}^n |w_i|$ where $w_i = ^\omega x_i y_i z_i^\omega$ and $|w_i| = |x_i| + |y_i| + |z_i|$) then the time complexity of algorithm(3) is bounded by $O(N)$.

4   Regular Bi-ω Languages

In this section we give a learning algorithm for regular bi-ω languages from positive data and restricted superset queries.

Theorem 4.1 : Every regular bi-ω language is a strictly alphabetic morphic image of a Büchi local bi-ω language.

Proof : If $L \subseteq^\omega A^\omega$ is a regular bi-ω language over A, then there exists a Büchi automaton $M = (Q, A, E_M, I_{linf}, T_{rinf})$ that accepts L. Let $\Gamma = Q \times A \times Q$
$C = \{(q_1, a, q_2)(q_2, b, q_3)/(q_1, a, q_2), (q_2, b, q_3) \in E_M\}$
$C' = \{(q_1, a, q_2)(q_2, b, q_3) \in C/q_1 \in I_{linf}\}$
$C'' = \{(q_1, a, q_2)(q_2, b, q_3) \in C/q_3 \in T_{rinf}\}$

Let $L_1 = L_{BE}^{\omega\omega}(S)$ where $S = (\Gamma, C, C', C'')$. Then $L_1 \in \mathcal{L}_{BE}^{\omega\omega}$.
If $\phi : \Gamma \to A$ is defined by $\phi((q_1, a, q_2)) = a$, then $\phi(L_1) = L$.   □

Example 4.2 : $L =^\omega ba^* cb^\omega, A = \{a, b, c\}, Q = \{1, 2, 3\}, I_{linf} = \{1\}, T_{rinf} = \{3\}$ and $E_M = \{(1, b, 1), (1, b, 2), (2, a, 2), (2, c, 3), (3, b, 3)\}$.
If $\alpha = (1, b, 1), \beta = (1, b, 2), \gamma = (2, a, 2), \delta = (2, c, 3), \lambda = (3, b, 3)$,
let $C = \{\alpha\beta, \beta\gamma, \gamma\delta, \delta\lambda, \alpha\alpha, \gamma\gamma, \lambda\lambda, \beta\delta\}$,
$C' = \{\alpha\alpha, \alpha\beta, \beta\gamma, \beta\delta\}$, $C'' = \{\gamma\delta, \delta\lambda, \lambda\lambda, \beta\delta\}$ and $\Gamma = Q \times A \times Q$.
Let $S_1 = (\Gamma, C, C', C'')$. Then $L_1 = L^{\omega\omega}(S_1) = \{^\omega \alpha\beta\gamma^n \delta\lambda^\omega / n \geq 0\}$.
If $\phi : \Gamma \to A$ defined by $\phi((q_1, a, q_2)) = a$, then $\phi(L_1) = L$.

We now provide the learning algorithm for regular bi-ω languages. Eventhough our method is analogous to the one presented in [11] for recognizable ω-languages, for the purpose of completeness, we recall the notion of restricted superset query and other details.

If L is a regular bi-ω language over A and if L is recognized by a Büchi automaton $M = (Q, A, E_M, I_{linf}, T_{rinf})$, then by Theorem 4.1, there is a Büchi local bi-ω language U over $\Gamma = Q \times A \times Q$ and a strictly alphabetic morphism $h : \Gamma \to A$ such that $h(U) = L$. Consider an ultimately periodic word $^\omega xyz^\omega$ in L and let $w = x^2yz^2 = a_1a_2...a_k$ where each $a_i \in A$. Let $g(w) = (s_1, a_1, s_1')(s_2, a_2, s_2')...(s_k, a_k, s_k')$ be a word over Γ. The word $g(w)$ is said to be a good word for w if $s_i' = s_{i+1}(i = 1, 2, ..., k), s_1(s_{k+1})$ is a left (right) infinite repetitive state. If L is the target regular bi-ω language, the restricted superset query takes as an input a set U and produces as an output "yes" if $U \supseteq L$ and "no" otherwise.

Algorithm(4)
Input : A positive presentation of an unknown regular bi-ω language L.
          $n =$ the number of states of the Büchi automaton accepting L.
Output : A Büchi local system S such that $L = h(L_{BE}^{\omega\omega}(S))$.
Query : Restricted superset query.

Procedure : Initialize all parameters.
                  $E_0 = \phi, C_0 = \phi, C_0' = \phi, C_0'' = \phi$, answer = "no".
Repeat
          while answer = "no" do
              $i = i + 1$
              read the next positive example $w = x^2yz^2$;
              let $G(w) = \{\alpha_1, ..., \alpha_t\}$ be the set of good words for w in $h^{-1}(w)$;
              let $j = 0$
              while $(j < t)$ and answer = "no" do
              $j = j + 1$;
              $E_i = E_i \cup \{\alpha_j\}$
              scan α_j to compute $P_2(\alpha_j), S_2(\alpha_j), F_2(\alpha_j)$;

$$\text{let } S_{E_i} = (\Gamma, C_{i-1} \cup F_2(\alpha_j), C'_{i-1} \cup P_2(\alpha_j), C''_{i-1} \cup S_2(\alpha_j))$$

    be a new conjecture

    let answer = Is-Super set of $(h(L^{\omega\omega}_{BE}(S_{E_i})), L)$

    if answer = "yes" then $S = S_{E_i}$;

    end

until answer = "yes";

output S;

end

Theorem 4.3 : Let n be the number of states for the Büchi automaton accepting the unknown regular bi-ω language L. After atmost $t(n)$ (a polynomial in n) number of queries, algorithm(4) produces a conjecture S_{E_i} such that E_i includes a characteristic sample for a Büchi local bi-ω language U with the property that $L = h(U)$, where $t(n)$ is depending on L.

The proof is similar to that of lemma 15 given in [11].

Theorem 4.4 : Given an unknown regular bi-ω language L, algorithm(4) effectively learns, from positive data and restricted superset queries, a Büchi local system S such that $L = h(L^{\omega\omega}_{BE}(S))$.

Remark : Similar to the learning algorithm(4), we can provide an algorithm that learns recognizable bi-ω languages in the limit from positive data and restricted superset queries through local bi-ω languages using theorem 2.5.

References

1. D. Angluin. Inductive inference of formal languages from positive data. Inform. Control 45 (1980), 117-135.
2. D. Angulin, Queries and concept learning, Machine Learning 2 (1988), 319-342.
3. M.P. Beal and D. Perrin, Symbolic dynamics and finite automata, in : Hand book of Formal Languages (G. Rozenberg and A. Salomaa eds.) Springer, Berlin, Volume 2, Chapter 10, 1997, 463-506.
4. L. Boasson and M. Nivat, Adherences of languages, J. Comput System Sci. 20 (1980), 285-309.
5. C. De La Higuera and J.C. Janodet, Inference of ω-languages from prefixes, Manuscript (2002), see http://eurise.univ-st-etienne.fr/~cdlh.
6. J. Devolder and I. Litovsky, Finitely generated bi-ω languages, Theoretical Computer Science 85 (1991), 33-52.
7. F. Gire and M. Nivat, Languages algebriques de mots biinfinis, Theor. Comp. Sci 86 (1991), 277-323.
8. E.M. Gold, Language identification in the limit, Inform. Control 10 (1967), 447-474.
9. J. Karhumäki, J. Manuch and W. Plandowski, On defect effect of bi-infinite words, Proceedings of MFCS'98, LNCS 1450 (1998), 674-682.
10. M. Nivat and D. Perrin. Ensembles reconnaissables de mots bi infinis, Canadian Journal of Mathematics XXX VIII (1986), 513-537.

11. A. Saoudi and T. Yokomori, Learning local and recognizable ω-languages and monadic logic programs. Computational Learning Theory : Proceedings of Euro COLT'93 (J. Shawe Taylor and M. Anthony eds) Oxford University Press 1994, 157-169.
12. W. Thomas. Automata on infinite objects. Handbook of Theoretical Computer Science (Van Leeuwen ed.), North-Holland, Amsterdam, Volume B 1990, 133-191.
13. S. Gnanasekaran, V.R. Dare, K.G. Subramanian and D.G.Thomas, Learning ω-regular languages, presented in the International symposium on Artificial Intelligence, Kolhapur during December 18-20, 2001. (To appear in the proceedings of the conference).

The EMILE 4.1 Grammar Induction Toolbox

Pieter Adriaans and Marco Vervoort

FNWI / ILLC
University of Amsterdam
Plantage Muidergracht 24
1018 TV AMSTERDAM
The Netherlands
pietera@science.uva.nl
vervoort@science.uva.nl
http://turing.wins.uva.nl/~pietera/ALS/

Abstract. The EMILE 4.1 toolbox is intended to help researchers to analyze the grammatical structure of free text. The basic theoretical concepts behind the EMILE algorithm are expressions and contexts. The idea is that expressions of the same syntactic type can be substituted for each other in the same context. By performing a large statistical cluster analysis on the sentences of the text EMILE tries to identify traces of expressions that have this substitutionability relation. If there exists enough statistical evidence for the existence of a grammatical type EMILE creates such a type. Fundamental notions in the EMILE 4.1 algorithm are the so-called characteristic expressions and contexts. An expression of type T is characteristic for T if it only appears in a context of type T. The notion of characteristic context and expression boosts the learning capacities of the EMILE 4.1 algorithm. The EMILE algorithm is relatively scalable. It can easily analyze text up to 100,000 sentences on a workstation. The EMILE tool has been used in various domains, amongst others biomedical research [Adriaans, 2001b], identification of ontologies and semantic learning [Adriaans et al., 1993].

1   EMILE 4.1

EMILE[1] 4.1 is a program based on the concept substitution in context. Expressions that belong to the same syntactic category can be substituted for each other, without destroying the grammatical structure of the sentence. It attempts to learn the grammatical structure of a language from sentences of that language, without being given any prior knowledge of the grammar. For any type in any valid grammar for the language, we can expect context/expression combinations to show up in a sufficiently large sample of sentences of the language. EMILE

---

[1] EMILE 4.1 is a successor to EMILE 3 .0, written by P. Adriaans. The original acronym stands for Entity Modeling Intelligent Learning Engine. It refers to earlier versions of EMILE that also had semantic capacities. The name EMILE is also motivated by the book on education by J.-J. Rousseau.

P. Adriaans, H. Fernau, and M. van Zaanen (Eds.): ICGI 2002, LNAI 2484, pp. 293–295, 2002.
© Springer-Verlag Berlin Heidelberg 2002

searches for such clusters of expressions and contexts in the sample, and interprets them as grammatical types. It then tries to find characteristic contexts and expressions, and uses them to extend the types. Finally, it formulates derivation rules based on the types found, in the manner of the rules of a context-free grammar. The program can present the grammatical structure found in several ways, as well as use it to parse other sentences or generate new ones. The EMILE 4.1 toolbox is implemented in C and runs on UNIX machines. It is available for research purposes: http://turing.wins.uva.nl/~pietera/ALS/.

The theoretical concepts used in EMILE 4.1 are elaborated on in P. Adriaans articles on EMILE 1.0/2.0 [Adriaans, 1992] and EMILE 3.0 [Adriaans, 2001a]. Note that although EMILE 4.1 is based on the same theoretical concepts as EMILE 3.0, it is not based on the same algorithm. More information on the precursors of EMILE 4.1 may be found in the above articles.

The three most basic concepts in EMILE are *contexts*, *expressions* and *context/expression pairs*.

Definition 1. *A* context/expression pair *is a sentence split into three parts, for instance*

$$John \; (makes) \; tea$$

Here, 'makes' is called an expression, *and 'John (.) tea' is called a* context *(with* left-hand side *'John' and* right-hand side *'tea').*

Definition 2. *We say that an expression e appears with a context c, or that the context/expression pair (c, e) has been* encountered, *if $c_l e c_r$ appears as a sentence in a text, where c_l and c_r are the left-hand side and the right-hand side of c, respectively, and ab denotes the concatenation of a and b.*

Context/expression pairs are not always sensible, as for instance in the sentence

$$John \; (drinks \; coffee, \; and \; Mary \; drinks) \; tea$$

where the expression 'drinks coffee, and Mary drinks' appears in the context 'John (.) tea'. EMILE will find such context/expression pairs and attempt to use them in the grammar induction process, But such pairs are usually isolated, i.e. they are not part of any significant clusters. So EMILE will fail to make use of them, and they will be effectively ignored.

As stated before, we view grammatical types in terms of the expressions that belong to that type, and the contexts in which they can appear (as expressions of that type). As such, we define grammatical types as follows:

Definition 3. *A grammatical type T is defined as a pair (T_C, T_E), where T_C is a set of contexts, and T_E is a set of expressions. Elements of T_C and T_E are called* primary contexts and expressions for T.

The intended meaning of this definition is, that all expressions of a type can appear with all of its the contexts.

The EMILE program also attempts to transform the collection of grammatical types found into a context-free grammar consisting of derivation rules. Such rules generally are of the form

$$[T]s_0[T_1]s_1[T_2]\ldots[T_k]s_k$$

where $T, T_1, T_2, \ldots, T_k$ are grammatical types, and $s_0, s_1, \ldots, s_k$ are (possibly empty) sequences of words. Given a rule with left-hand side $[T]$, and a sequence of word-sequences and grammatical types containing $[T]$, that appearance of $[T]$ can be replaced by the right-hand side of the rule, (concatenating adjacent word-sequences as necessary). Any sequence which can be obtained from another sequence by such rule applications, is said to be derivable from that sequence. The language of a context-free grammar consists of those word-sequences e such that $[0]e$ is derivable, where $[0]$ denotes the type of whole sentences.

Given a rich enough text sample EMILE produces a partial grammar for this sample, in the form of a set of context free rules. If the text is not rich enough to make EMILE converge to a complete grammar it will produce a partial grammar. When applied to natural language texts EMILE will in general find syntactic types with a strong semantic flavor. These semantic types have in some cases proven to be useful in the context of construction of ontologies and knowledge-management[Adriaans, 2001b],[Adriaans et al., 1993].

References

[Adriaans, 2001a] Adriaans, P. (2001a). Learning shallow context-free languages under simple distributions. In Copestake, A. and (eds.), K. V., editors, *Algebras, Diagrams and Decisions in Language, Logic and Computation*. CSLI/CUP.

[Adriaans, 2001b] Adriaans, P. (2001b). Semantic induction with emile, opportunities in bioinformatics. In Vet, P. v. d. e. a., editor, *TWLT19, Information Extraction in Molecular Biology, Proceedings Twente Workshop on Language Technology 19, ESF Scientific Programme on Integrated Approaches for Functional Genomics, Enschede*, pages 1–6. Universiteit Twente, Faculteit Informatica.

[Adriaans et al., 1993] Adriaans, P., Janssen, S., and Nomden, E. (1993). Effective identification of semantic categories in curriculum texts by means of cluster analysis. In Adriaans, P., editor, *ECML-93, European Conference on Machine Learning, Workshop notes Machine Learning Techniques and Text Analysis, Vienna, Austria*, pages 37–44. Department of Medical Cybernetics and Artificial Intelligence, University of Vienna in cooperation with the Austrian Rezsearch Institute for Artificial Intelligence.

[Adriaans, 1992] Adriaans, W. P. (1992). *Language Learning from a Categorial Perspective*. PhD thesis, Universiteit van Amsterdam.

Software for Analysing Recurrent Neural Nets That Learn to Predict Non-regular Languages

Stephan K. Chalup[1] and Alan D. Blair[2]

[1] School of Electrical Engineering & Computer Science
The University of Newcastle, Callaghan, 2308, Australia
phone: +61 2 4921 6034, fax: +61 2 4921 6929
www.cs.newcastle.edu.au/~chalup
chalup@cs.newcastle.edu.au
[2] School of Computer Science & Engineering
The University of New South Wales, Sydney, 2052, Australia
blair@cse.unsw.edu.au

Abstract. Training first-order recurrent neural networks to predict symbol sequences from context-free or context-sensitive languages is known as a hard task. A prototype software system has been implemented that can train these networks and evaluate performance after training. A special version of the (1+1)–ES algorithm is employed that allows both incremental and non-incremental training. The system provides advanced analysis tools that take not only the final solution but the whole sequence of intermediate solutions into account. For each of these solutions a qualitative analysis of hidden unit activity and a quantitative evaluation of generalisation ability can be performed.

1 Introduction

Most studies on training first order recurrent nets to predict non-regular languages report long training times and a low success rate (cf., [Wiles et al., 2001]). The software system described in the present paper is based on the code that was written for the study of [Chalup & Blair, 1999] in which for the first time first-order recurrent neural networks were able to learn to predict subsets of a context-sensitive language. More details about the algorithms and refined experimental results that were obtained with the extended, current version of the system have been included in [Chalup & Blair, 2002]. Compared with feed-forward neural networks, recurrent neural networks typically take longer to train and they are also prone to losing a solution again once it has been found. Recurrent neural networks can be analysed within the framework of dynamical systems.

2 Description of the Software System

The system consists of three main components for the following tasks: (1) training of the networks, (2) evaluation of the trained networks' generalisation ability,

P. Adriaans, H. Fernau, and M. van Zaanen (Eds.): ICGI 2002, LNAI 2484, pp. 296–298, 2002.

(3) analysis of hidden unit activity. The first two tasks have a very high time complexity and the software has been implemented in the programming language C which can be compiled and run on most supercomputers. The third component does not have such high speed requirements and is implemented in MATLAB where it employs visualisation and animation methods. We now address the three components of the system in more detail.

2.1   Training

The system allows for a large variety of network topologies. Each net is represented by a set of connectivity matrices. For example, the well-known simple recurrent networks (SRNs) of [Elman, 1990] have feed-forward and copy-back connections which are active at two consecutive time steps. The system represents a SRN by two connectivity matrices, one for each time step. Networks active on k time steps would be represented by k connectivity matrices. The coefficients of the connectivity matrices are integers which determine whether a link is learnable, frozen or not existing. Associated with each connectivity matrix is a separate weight matrix. The weights were initialised with small random numbers.

The data consisted of sequences of 30 randomly concatenated strings from one of the languages $\{a^n b^n; n \geq 1\}$ (context-free) or $\{a^n b^n c^n; n \geq 1\}$ (context-sensitive). Each symbol was encoded as a vector $a = (-1,1,1)$, $b = (1,-1,1)$ or $c = (1,1,-1)$, respectively. The task was a one-step look-ahead prediction task, that is, the symbols of the sequence are fed into the network one after the other and the network has to predict for each symbol the next symbol in the sequence. As training algorithm the (1+1)–ES of [Rechenberg, 1965] and [Schwefel, 1965] was implemented. It was combined with *data juggling* which is a method that randomly changes the order of the strings in the training sequence after each epoch during training (cf., [Chalup & Blair, 2002]).

2.2   Generalisation Tests

A neural network can generalise if it is able to process data that was not used for training. In the project of [Chalup & Blair, 2002] the networks had two different ways to generalise. One was to generalise to sequences that contained strings of larger depth n. The other possibility was to generalise to sequences in which the strings are concatenated in a different order. The software for the generalisation evaluation takes both aspects into account. Starting with a sequence consisting of low order strings the network's accuracy in processing this sequence is tested on samples of 200 permutations of the test sequence. These tests are repeated and evaluated for sequences containing strings of increasingly larger depth n up to and beyond the maximum depth that was used during training.

2.3   Analysis of Hidden Unit Activity

This component of the software can be used to analyse qualitatively how the network learns. Each network that during the process of weight evolution is able to process the training sequence with 100% accuracy is recorded in a separate file. Then for each of these networks a graph is generated that shows the trajectory of the activity of the three hidden units while the network is processing the string $a^8b^8c^8$. An example graph is plotted below, where the input symbols are encoded as $a1$-$a8$, $b1$-$b8$, $c1$-$c8$ and the output symbols are encoded as $a = \bullet$, $b = \times$, $c = \circ$ and the first b of the string is encoded as $*$.

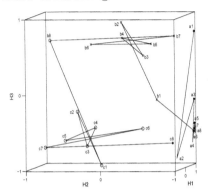

Each training run produces 40–200 of these graphs. Each of them is a frame in one of the movie animations of our software demo. This method can be used to observe bifurcations during training and whether incremental and non-incremental training have different characteristics.

Acknowledgements

The project is supported by the APAC supercomputer grant *Large-Scale Training of Recurrent Neural Networks* and the University of Newcastle ECR grant *Machines Learn via Biologically Motivated Incremental Algorithms*.

References

[Chalup & Blair, 2002] Chalup, S. K. & Blair, A. D.: Incremental Training of First Order Recurrent Neural Networks to Predict a Context-Sensitive Language. Submitted

[Chalup & Blair, 1999] Chalup, S. & Blair, A. D.: Hill Climbing in Recurrent Neural Networks for Learning the $a^nb^nc^n$ Language, Proceedings, 6th International Conference on Neural Information Processing (ICONIP'99),(1999) 508–513

[Elman, 1990] Elman, J. L.: Finding structure in time, Cognitive Science, **14**, (1990) 179–211

[Rechenberg, 1965] Rechenberg, I.: Cybernetic Solution Path of an Experimental Problem, Royal Aircraft Establishment, Library Translation No. 1122, (1965)

[Schwefel, 1965] Schwefel, H.-P.: Kybernetische Evolution als Strategie der experimentellen Forschung in der Strömungsmechanik, Diplomarbeit, Technische Universität Berlin, Hermann Föttinger Institut für Hydrodynamik, (1965)

[Wiles et al., 2001] Wiles, J., Blair, A. and Boden, M.: Representation Beyond Finite States: Alternatives to Push-Down Automata, in A Field Guide to Dynamical Recurrent Networks, Kolen, J. F. and Kremer, S. C. (eds.), , IEEE Press, (2001) 129-142

A Framework for Inductive Learning of Typed-Unification Grammars

Liviu Ciortuz

CS Department, University of York, UK.
ciortuz@cs.york.ac.uk

Abstract. LIGHT, the parsing system for typed-unification grammars [3], was recently extended so to allow the automate learning of attribute/feature paths values. Motivated by the logic design of these grammars [2], the learning strategy we adopted is inspired by Inductive Logic Programming [5]; we proceed by searching through hypothesis spaces generated by logic transformations of the input grammar. Two procedures — one for generalisation, the other for specialisation — are in charge with the creation of these hypothesis spaces.

The work on *typed-unification grammars* can be traced back to the seminal paper on the PATR-II system [7]. Basically, the design of such grammars is underlined by two simple ideas: *i.* context-free rules may be augmented with constraints, generalising the grammar symbols to attribute-value (or: feature) structures; *ii.* feature structures (FSs) may be organised into hierarchies, a very convenient way to describe in a concise manner classes of rules and lexical entries.

Different *logical perspectives* on such a grammar design were largely studied; see [2] for a survey. For the LIGHT system we adopted the Order-Sorted Feature (OSF) constraint logic framework [1].

The *aim* of our work is to explore the usefulness of a logic-based learning approach — namely Inductive Logic Programming (ILP) — to improve the coverage of a given typed-unification grammar: either generalise some (automatically identified) rule or lexical type feature structures (FSs) in the grammar so to make it accept a given sentence/parse tree, or try to specialise a certain type in the grammar so to reject a (wrongly accepted) parse.

The *main idea* of ILP-based learning is to generate (and then evaluate) new clauses starting from those defined in the input grammar. The validation of new "hypotheses" is done using a set of examples and an evaluation function, to rate (and choose among) different hypotheses. The creation of new type hypotheses is done either by generalisation or specialisation. For typed-unification grammars, *generalisation* of FSs amounts to relaxing/removing one or more atomic OSF-constraints, while *specialisation* adds new such constraints to a type FS.

To illustrate a *type feature structure*, Figure 1 presents satisfy_HPSG_principles, the parent of the two (binary) rules used in a simple Head-driven Phrase Structure Grammar (HPSG, [6]) appearing in [8]. The satisfy_HPSG_principles type

P. Adriaans, H. Fernau, and M. van Zaanen (Eds.): ICGI 2002, LNAI 2484, pp. 299–302, 2002.

```
satisfy_HPSG_principles
[ PHON   diff_list,
  CAT    #1:categ,
  SUBCAT #2:categ_list,
  HEAD   #4:phrase_or_word
              [ PHON    diff_list,
                CAT #1,
                SUBCAT #3|#2 ],
  COMP   #5:phrase_or_word
              [ PHON    diff_list,
                CAT #3,
                SUBCAT nil ],
  ARGS   <#4, #5> ]
```

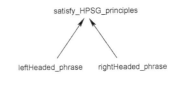

$X : s$ — sort constraint
$X.f = Y$ — feature constraint
$X \doteq Y$ — equational constraint

Fig. 1. A sample type feature structure, a simple sort/type hierarchy, and the atomic OSF-constraints for the logical description of feature structures.

encodes three HPSG principles: the Head Feature Principle, the Subcategorization Principle, and the Saturation Principle.[1] The knowledge embodied in the satisfy_HPSG_principles will be inherited into two rules: leftHeaded_phrase and rightHeaded_phrase.[2]

The *architecture* of the system we implemented for learning attribute path values in typed-unification grammars is designed in Figure 2. The initial grammar is submitted to an Expander module, which propagates the appropriate constraints down into the type hierarchy. The Parser module uses the expanded form of (syntactic) rules and lexical descriptions to analyse input sentences. The ILP/learner module receives (maybe partial) parses produced by the Parser, and — by calling one of two hypothesis generation procedures — it infers either more specific or more general type descriptions for the considered grammar, such that the new grammar will provide a better coverage of the given sample sentences.

The bidirectional arrows in the diagram in Figure 2 are due to the bi-functionality of the Parser and Expander modules. When asked to act in "reverse" mode, the Parser takes as input a parse and tries to build up the FS associated to that parse. If the construction fails, then the LIGHT's tracer component is able to deliver an "explanation" for the failure.[3] This failure "explanation" will be analysed by the ILP/learner module to propose "fixes" to the grammar so that the analysed parse will get accepted. The Expander is also able to work

---

[1] The feature constraint encoding of the three principles is respectively: the Head Feature Principle: satisfy_HPSG_principles.CAT $\doteq$ #1 $\doteq$ satisfy_HPSG_principles.HEAD.CAT, the Subcategorization Principle: satisfy_HPSG_principles.HEAD.SUBCAT $\doteq$ #3|#2 $\doteq$ satisfy_HPSG_principles.COMP.CAT|SUBCAT, and the Saturation Principle: satisfy_HPSG_principles.COMP.SUBCAT $\doteq$ nil.

[2] Actually, the constraints specific to these rules only impose that the *head* argument is on the left, respectively the right position inside a phrase PHON feature value.

[3] This explanation assembles informations on: *i.* the parse operation at which the "derivation" of the FS associated to the input parse was blocked; *ii.* the feature path along which the last (tried) unification failed; *iii.* the (atomic) unification steps which lead to the sort clash causing the unification failure.

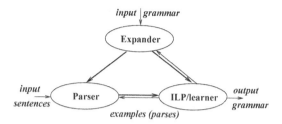

Fig. 2. The *ilp*LIGHT architecture for learning typed-unification grammars.

in "reverse" mode: given as input a type name and an atomic constraint (on a certain path value) contained in the description of that type, the expander will indicate which type in the input (unexpanded) grammar is responsible for the introduction of that constraint in the expanded form of the designated type.

We conducted a series of experiments during which the *ilp*LIGHT prototype system was able to learn by specialisation each of the three HPSG principles, if the other two were present and a (rather small) set of sample sentences was provided. Equally, the system learned by specialisation lexical descriptions, and was able to recover (by generalisation) the definition of the HPSG principles if they were provided in an over-restricted form. In all cases mentioned above, learning took place in a few minutes amount of time.[4]

As *further work*, we are primarily concerned with the elaboration of linguistics-based heuristics supporting the learning of attribute path values in grammars of significant size,[5] and further improving the efficiency of the *ilp*LIGHT prototype.

Acknowledgements: This work was supported by EPSRC ROPA grant "Machine Learning for Natural Language Processing in a Computational Logic Framework". The LIGHT system was developed at the Language Technology Lab of the German Research Center for Artificial Intelligence (DFKI), Saarbrücken.

References

1. H. Aït-Kaci and A. Podelski. Towards a meaning of LIFE. *Journal of Logic Programming*, 16:195–234, 1993.
2. B. Carpenter. *The Logic of Typed Feature Structures – with applications to unification grammars, logic programs and constraint resolution.* Cambridge University Press, 1992.
3. L. Ciortuz. LIGHT — a constraint language and compiler system for typed-unification grammars. In *Proceedings of the 25th German Conference on Artificial Intelligence (KI-2002)*, Aachen, Germany, September 16–20, 2002. Springer-Verlag.

---

[4] For instance, learning the Subcategorization Principle took 4min. 25 sec. on a Pentium III PC at 933MHz running Linux Red Had 7.1, using the sample HPSG grammar in [7] and a set of 14 training sentences.

[5] Note that LIGHT is already able to run the large HPSG grammar for English [4].

4. A. Copestake, D. Flickinger, and I. Sag. *A Grammar of English in HPSG: Design and Implementations*. Stanford: CSLI Publications, 1999.
5. S. Muggleton and L. De Raedt. Inductive logic programming: Theory and methods. *Journal of Logic Programming*, 19,20:629–679, 1994.
6. C. Pollard and I. Sag. *Head-driven Phrase Structure Grammar*. Center for the Study of Language and Information, Stanford, 1994.
7. S. M. Shieber, H. Uszkoreit, F. C. Pereira, J. Robinson, and M. Tyson. The formalism and implementation of PATR-II. In J. Bresnan, editor, *Research on Interactive Acquisition and Use of Knowledge*. SRI International, Menlo Park, Calif., 1983.
8. G. Smolka and R. Treinen, editors. *The DFKI Oz documentation series*. German Research Center for Artificail Intelligence (DFKI), Stuhlsatzenhausweg 3, Sarrbrücken, Germany, 1996.

A Tool for Language Learning
Based on Categorial Grammars
and Semantic Information

Daniela Dudau Sofronie[1], Isabelle Tellier[1], and Marc Tommasi[1]

LIFL-Grappa, Université Charles de Gaulle-Lille3
59653 Villeneuve d'Ascq Cedex, France
dudau@lifl.fr, {tellier, tommasi}@univ-lille3.fr
http://www.grappa.univ-lille3.fr

1 Introduction

Natural language learning still remains an open problem, although there exist many approaches issued by actual researches. We also address ourselves this challenge and we provide here a prototype of a tool. First we need to clarify that we center on the syntactic level. We intend to find a (set of) grammar(s) that recognizes new correct sentences (in the sense of the correct order of the words) by means of some initial correct examples that are presented and of a strategy to deduce the corresponding grammar(s) consistent(s) with the examples at each step. In this model, the grammars are the support of the languages, so, the process of learning is a process of grammatical inference. Usually, in NLP approaches, natural language is represented by lexicalized grammars because the power of the language consists in the information provided by the words and their combination schemas. That's why we adopt here the formal model of a categorial grammar that assigns every word a category and furnishes some general combination schema of categories. But, in our model, the strings of words are not sufficient for the inference, so additional information is needed. In Kanazawa's work [3] the additional information is the internal structure of each sentence as a Structural Example. We try to provide instead a more lexicalized information, of semantic nature: the semantic type of words. Its provenance, as well as the psycho-linguistic motivation can be found in [1] and [2].

2 The Data and the Learning Algorithm

The prototype proposed, conceived in Java, is built in order to be a test instrument of our formal hypothesis concerning the learning of the syntax helped by semantic types. In order to be more precise concerning the notions used, we give here the formal definitions of classical categorial grammars[1] and of semantic types.

---

[1] There exist different classes of categorial grammars depending on the set of combination schemas used: classical categorial grammars, combinatory grammars, Lambek grammars.

P. Adriaans, H. Fernau, and M. van Zaanen (Eds.): ICGI 2002, LNAI 2484, pp. 303–305, 2002.

Let Σ be a finite alphabet and C be a finite set of elementary categories (where S is a distinguished category). C' is the closure of C under the operators "/" and "\", meaning that C' is the smallest set that verifies: (a) $C \subseteq C'$;(b) if $A \in C'$ and $B \in C'$ then $A/B \in C'$ and $B \backslash A \in C'$. A *categorial grammar* G on Σ is any finite relation between Σ and C' ($G \subset \Sigma \times C'$ and G finite). In other words, every word is associated with a corresponding set of categories. A *classical categorial grammar* is a categorial grammar in which the only admissible combination schemas (reduction rules) for all A and B in C' are FA: $A/B . B \to A$ (forward application) and BA: $B . B \backslash A \to A$ (backward application). *The language recognized by a classical categorial grammar* G is the set of sentences (finite concatenations of words from Σ) for which there exists a category assignment that can be reduced to the distinguished category S.

We consider a simple *semantic typing system* in Montague's style, making distinction between *entities* and *facts* and allowing to express the types of *functors*, among which are the *predicates*. The set Θ of every type contains the elementary types $e \in \Theta$ (entities) and $t \in \Theta$ (truth values) and has the following property: if $u \in \Theta$ and $v \in \Theta$ then $\langle u, v \rangle \in \Theta$ (the composed type $\langle u, v \rangle$ is the type of functors taking an argument of type u and providing a result of type v). Between the semantic types and the categories there exists a similarity in construction, but the main difference consists in loosing the direction of application in types expressions, whereas this direction is explicitly indicated by the operators (/ and \) in categories. For example, the categories and the semantic types corresponding with some words of a vocabulary are: "John": category - T, type - e; "man","woman": category - CN, type - $\langle e, t \rangle$; "runs","walks": category - T\S, type - $\langle e, t \rangle$; "fast": category - (T\S)\(T\S), type - $\langle \langle e, t \rangle, \langle e, t \rangle \rangle$; "a": category - (S/(T\S))/CN, type - $\langle \langle e, t \rangle, \langle \langle e, t \rangle, t \rangle \rangle$. The significance of types is not so hard to guess: a proper noun is an "entity"; a common noun is an "one-place predicate" over entities returning a truth value; an intransitive verb is also an "one-place predicate"; an adverb is an "one-place predicate modifier" etc.

The semantic types are considered as previously acquired knowledge, so they are integrated in the sample offered as input as labels of the words. Assuming that a sample of typed sentences is offered to our tool, it will build a set of categorial grammars compatibles with the sample. The categorial grammars we work on have the propriety that the relation between categories and types is an injective homomorphism.

The engine of the whole machinery represents a parse algorithm in the CYK-style that works on the sequence of types attached to each sentence and deduces in the first step all possible parses and some constraints over types. The second step consists in a renaming phase to obtain a set of grammars, by applying the constraints on the expressions of types and thus inferring categories. So, for each sentence we have the set of grammars compatible with it. The entire process is incremental, in the sense that the constraints will be propagated from one sentence in the sample to another. As soon as the processing is finished for a sample, the (set of) grammar(s) inferred will recognize all the sentences in the sample.

Let's consider a simple input sample formed by two typed sentences: $a\langle\langle e,t\rangle, \langle\langle e,t\rangle,t\rangle\rangle$ $man\langle e,t\rangle$ $walks\langle e,t\rangle$. $a\langle\langle e,t\rangle,\langle\langle e,t\rangle,t\rangle\rangle$ $woman\langle e,t\rangle$ $runs\langle e,t\rangle$ $fast\langle\langle e,t\rangle, \langle e,t\rangle\rangle$. The output is a grammar compatible with the input sample: a=((S/A0)/ A1), walks=A0, fast=(A2\A0), woman=A1, runs=A2, man=A1. A generalization occurs here, for example, this output grammar recognizes also the sentence: *a woman walks*.

The interface of the tool proposes two different manners of constructing the input sample. The first consists in a user-sensitive and interactive interface. The user has the possibility to construct himself different sentences with words provided by a vocabulary. The vocabulary is stocked in a file that can be changed at any time, the system restarting with the new added words. When a new word is used in the construction, its type is automatically added, if it is a single-type word; if not, a list of possible types appears and the user has to make a choice. More or less the user must possess a certain knowledge about the semantics of the words (an a-priori semantic acquisition is supposed). As soon as a sentence is finished by a "." the typed sample is ready. The second possibility is to load an already built sample from a file. The sample is then analyzed and the output grammars can be visualized, one grammar in a file. Another functionality of this tool concerns recognizing. With the grammar(s) obtained we can check whether a test sample is or is not recognized. The test sample is charged from a test file, or is built as previously with the words in the same vocabulary.

3   Conclusion

The tool presented is a prototype, it has not been tested yet on large corpora, but the functionalities provided are very flexible: we are allowed to do variations in the vocabulary, by adding or deleting words and also we can choose the grammar and the test sample. Concerning the future extensions to our tool, that needs to be able to process large amounts of data, we shall provide a module that is able to transform a simple corpora labeled in XML format with part-of-speech tags to a typed-corpora. A XML parser will be used and all part-of-speech tags will be replaced by type tags, using a simple table of correspondences. For example: a part-of-speech "intransitive verb" has the type label "$\langle e,t\rangle$". This kind of labelled data are easier to obtain than structural examples needed by Kanazawa, and thus justify our approach.

References

1. Dudau Sofronie, D., Tellier, I., Tommasi, M.: From Logic to Grammars via Types. In: Popelínsky, L., Nepil, M. (eds.): Proceedings of the 3rd Learning Language in Logic Workshop. Strasbourg France (2001) 35–46
2. Dudau Sofronie, D., Tellier, I., Tommasi, M.: Learning Categorial Grammars from Semantic Types. In: van Rooy, R., Stokhof, M. (eds.): Proceedings of the Thirteenth Amsterdam Colloquium. Amsterdam Holland (2001) 79–84
3. Kanazawa, M.: Learnable Classes of Categorial Grammars. The European Association for Logic, Language and Information. CLSI Publications (1998)

'NAIL': Artificial Intelligence Software for Learning Natural Language

Sam Lievesley[1] and Eric Atwell[1]

School of Computing, University of Leeds, Leeds LS2 9JT, England
msczsl@comp.leeds.ac.uk, eric@comp.leeds.ac.uk
http://www.comp.leeds.ac.uk/oop/nail

Abstract. This paper describes NAIL, a software system to learn the semantics of language by relating written English commands to actions and properties in a simple 2D 'blocks world' virtual environment.

1 Introduction

Most Computational Natural Language Learning research on learning semantics (eg [1],[2],[3],[4],[5]) assumes that meanings and meaningful relationships can be inferred from text samples alone. We believe that semantics must be learnt as a mapping between language and an external world. This project aims to demonstrate this principle, on a limited scale: NAIL learns mappings from English words, phrases and sentences to meanings in terms of s simple 2D "blocks world". The software learns about its virtual environment under supervision from a human tutor. The human tutor teaches the computer the meaning of simple language through the use of two interfaces, illustrated in Figure 1.

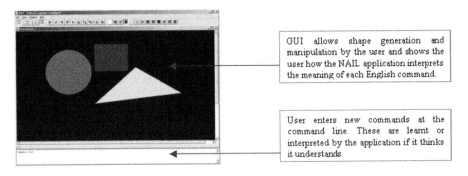

GUI allows shape generation and manipulation by the user and shows the user how the NAIL application interprets the meaning of each English command.

User enters new commands at the command line. These are learnt or interpreted by the application if it thinks it understands.

Fig. 1. Graphical User Interface and Command Line for NAIL

A command line terminal is used by the tutor to enter commands written in English. These commands require the program to manipulate or process information from the 2D virtual environment. The 2D virtual environment is displayed

P. Adriaans, H. Fernau, and M. van Zaanen (Eds.): ICGI 2002, LNAI 2484, pp. 306–308, 2002.
© Springer-Verlag Berlin Heidelberg 2002

in a graphical user interface (GUI). The human tutor uses this to teach the application the meaning of written commands. Teaching is through learning by example; the tutor directly manipulates the environment using the GUI, showing the program what response is required. The GUI also shows the tutor if the program has manipulated the environment correctly in response to a particular command. The two dimensional virtual environment consists of simple shapes that can be created, deleted, moved and selected. The environment is dynamic as the numbers and types of shape may change throughout a session.

2   The NAIL Application

The NAIL application, developed in Java v1.4, was inspired by Winograd's SHRDLU [7]. Unlike SHRDLU the NAIL application does not respond to the user using English, it simply carries out the actions it understands and display the results in the graphical user interface. The application learns new commands by classifying training examples using the WEKA [6],[8] classification tools for machine learning. This will enable further analysis of classification algorithms using any of the WEKA classifiers. The final application will incorporate the most successful classifier from the WEKA package within the program providing real time classification and learning.

NAIL divides the task of learning the meaning of commands between a number of simplified training scenarios. Each scenario trains the system to understand the meaning of a number of simple commands or statements relating to objects in the virtual environment. The training scenarios constrain both the commands that can be entered and the content of the virtual environment. This approach speeds up and simplifies the machine learning process.

2.1   Training Scenario 1: Single Object Properties

The purpose of this training scenario is to learn simple adjectives relating to single objects. Each virtual environment contains a single object or shape. The training set used for classification consists of a number of these environments along with binary classification information. The binary classification information is in the form of an adjective and its negative in order to divide the training examples into two classes.

2.2   Training Scenario 2: Relationship between Two Objects

The purpose of this training scenario is to learn adjectives that compare the properties or spatial relationships between two world objects.

2.3   Training Scenario 3: Relationship between Three Objects

This expands upon training scenario 2 allowing more complicated concepts to be classified. Adjectives such as 'closest' require the comparison of two sets of object property inter-relationships.

2.4   Training Scenario 4: Actions That Modify Object Properties

The purpose of this training scenario is to learn the meaning of verbs that modify the properties of single objects. This scenario is different to the previous examples in that a before and after snapshot of object properties must be analysed.

3   Future Developments: Understanding Complex Commands

After running a number of training scenarios the software should be able to apply what has been learnt to more complicated command sentences. These sentences will consist of a number of words from different training scenarios that will require the software to select and manipulate certain objects in the virtual environment. This will be achieved by using a number of pre-programmed grammars that will convert sentences into ordered processing stages. These processing stages will select and manipulate objects that are classified by a particular sentence, outputting a final selection or modification to the objects in the virtual environment.

References

1. Demetriou, G., Atwell, E.: A domain-independent semantic tagger for the study of meaning associations in English text. In: Bunt, H., van der Sluis, I., Thijsse, E. (eds.): Proceedings of IWCS-4: Fourth International Workshop on Computational Semantics. KUB, Tilburg (2001) 67–80
2. Demetriou, G., Atwell, E., Souter, C.: Using lexical semantic knowledge from machine readable dictionaries for domain independent language modelling. In Gavrilidou, M., Carayannis, G., Markantionatou, S., Piperidis, S., Stainhaouer, G. (eds.) Proceedings of LREC2000: Second International Conference on Language Resources and Evaluation Vol.2. ELRA, Athens (2000) 777–782
3. Escudero, G., Mrquez, L., Rigau, G.: A Comparison between Supervised Learning Algorithms for Word Sense Disambiguation. In: Proceedings of CoNLL-2000: Computational Natural Language Learning. Lisbon (2000)
4. Hartrumpf, S.: Coreference Resolution with Syntactico-Semantic Rules and Corpus Statistics In: Proceedings of CoNLL-2001: Computational Natural Language Learning. Toulouse (2001)
5. Sbillot, P., Bouillon, P., Fabre, C.: Inductive Logic Programming for Corpus-Based Acquisition of Semantic Lexicons In: Proceedings of CoNLL-2000: Computational Natural Language Learning. Lisbon (2000)
6. Waikato Environment for Knowledge Analysis (WEKA), http://www.cs.waikato.ac.nz/ml/weka, last accessed 26/06/2002.
7. Winograd, T.: Understanding Natural Language. Edinburgh University Press (1972)
8. Witten, I., Eibe Frank, E.: Data Mining: Practical machine learning tools and techniques with Java implementations. Morgan Kaufmann (2000)

Lyrebird™: Developing Spoken Dialog Systems Using Examples

Bradford Starkie, Greg Findlow, Khanh Ho, Alvaro Hui, Lawrence Law,
Liron Lightwood, Simon Michnowicz, and Christian Walder

Telstra New Wave Pty Ltd, Box 249 Rosebank MDC 770 Blackburn Road Clayton
Victoria, Australia 3168
{Brad.Starkie, Greg.Findlow, Khanh.Ho, Alvaro.Hui,
Lawrence.Law, Liron.Lightwood,Simon.Michnowicz,
Christian.Walder}@team.telstra.com

Abstract

An early release software product for the rapid development of spoken dialog systems (SDS's), known as Lyrebird™ [1][2][3], will be demonstrated that makes use of grammatical inference to build natural language, mixed initiative, speech recognition applications.

The demonstration will consist of the presenter developing a spoken dialog system using Lyrebird™, and will include a demonstration of some features that are still in the prototype phase.

Using Lyrebird™, developers build a spoken dialog system with the following steps:
1. Firstly the dialog is specified. This is typically developed using a drag and drop GUI that defines a computer directed menu driven application (See Figure. 1). Alternatively a wizard can be used whereby the developer defines the application in terms of slots that need to be filled.
2. The dialog description is then generalised to include mixed initiative input. Starting grammars are automatically created that cover computer directed input.
3. The developer is then prompted for text describing selected phrases that a speaker would use when interacting with the developed SDS (See Figure 2.) Mixed-initiative natural-language grammars suitable for use with a speech-recognition system are then inferred, using grammatical inference.

If desired, the developer can subsequently improve the system under development, using a range of interfaces. For instance:

1. The developer can teach Lyrebird how the speaker will behave using a tool known as the simulator. The simulator enables the user to interact with the application under development using text. (See Figure 3.) Out of grammar phrases are tagged using either robust parsing, or manual input from the developer.
2. The developer can teach Lyrebird how the system should behave using a tool known as the scenario editor (See Figure 4.) Using the scenario editor sample interactions are presented to the developer in a text format similar to that used to

P. Adriaans, H. Fernau, and M. van Zaanen (Eds.): ICGI 2002, LNAI 2484, pp. 309-311, 2002.

describe plays. Users can modify prompts, speech recognition grammars and dialog simply by modifying the scenarios.

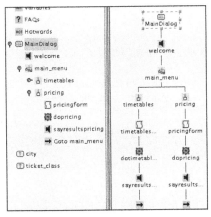

Figure 1. A menu driven dialog description created using Lyrebird™.

```
> Prompt> please say one of timetables or pricing (note please respond with a phrase for
jumping to the timetablesform form)
> Instructions> Please enter a phrase which contains the following slot values:
                 Departure_city : salt lake city
                 Destination_city : helsinki
                 Date : a week from sunday
                 Time : five a m
> Your Input>
> what flights fly from salt lake city to helsinki at five a m on a week from sunday
>
> Grammar Identifier> .Form_timetablesform
> Prompt> please say one of timetables or pricing (note please respond with a phrase for
jumping to the timetablesform form)
> Instructions> Please enter a phrase which contains the following slot values:
                 Departure_city : salt lake city
                 Date : a week from sunday
> Your Input>
> what flights fly from salt lake city on a week from sunday
> commit
>
> Grammar Identifier> .Form_timetablesform
> Prompt> please say one of timetables or pricing (note please respond with a phrase for
jumping to the timetablesform form)
> Hypothetical Response> what flights fly from milwaukee to amsterdam at two fifty nine
> Question> Is this a suitable response?
```

Figure 2. Example phrases being entered into Lyrebird™ by a developer.

```
tags, or select the manual entry option to input the correct tag values yourself.
> PROMPT: welcome to the airline application.
> PROMPT: please say one of timetables or pricing
>
> REPLY   >
> how much does a ticket from melbourne to sydney cost
>
         Please enter the number corresponding to your selected option:
>        0. Re-enter phrase
>        1. Manually enter in attributes
>        2. airline#.Form_pricingform { destination_city="sydney" depature_city="melbourne"}
(p=0.842105)
>        3. airline#.Form_timetablesform { destination_city="sydney"
depature_city="melbourne"} (p=0.157895)
>        4. airline#.Question_operator  (p=3.30838e-48)
>        5. airline#.Quit  (p=2.31587e-48)
>        6. airline#.Question_hello  (p=1.65419e-48)
>        7. airline#.Menu_main_menu_pricing  (p=3.30838e-49)
>        8. airline#.Menu_main_menu_timetables  (p=3.30838e-49)
> YOUR CHOICE >
> 2
> PROMPT: please say the ticket class
>
> REPLY   >
> economy
> PROMPT: a economy flight from melbourne to sydney will cost five hundred dollars
> PROMPT: please say one of timetables or pricing
>
> REPLY   >
```

Figure 3. Example phrases entered into Lyrebird by a developer as seen in the "Simulate and Refine" window of Lyrebird™.

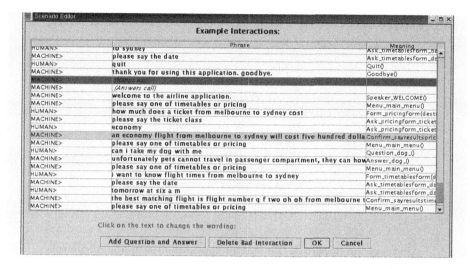

Figure 4. Example behaviours being modified by the developer in Lyrebird™ as seen in the "Scenario Editor" window.

A significant benefit of using Lyrebird™ is that developers don't need to know anything about speech recognition grammars or the underlying VXML used to implement the spoken dialog system. Instead the developers are presented with and present to Lyrebird™, examples of how the application should behave. In this respect Lyrebird can be seen to be a "Programming by Example" system [4]. In addition the use of Lyrebird™ can result in significant reductions in the time required to develop an application [1].

References

1. Starkie, Bradford C., 2002, Inferring Attribute Grammars with Structured Data for Natural Language Processing, in: *Grammatical Inference and Applications. Sixth International Colloquium*, ICGI-2002, pp 1-4 Berlin: Springer Verlag.
2. Starkie, Bradford C., 2001. Programming Spoken Dialogs Using Grammatical Inference, in *AI 2001: Advances in Artificial Intelligence, 14th Australian Joint Conference on Artificial Intelligence,* pp 449-460, Berlin: Springer Verlag
3. Starkie, Bradford C., 1999. A method of developing an interactive system, International Patent WO 00/78022.
4. Cypher, Allen, 1993. *Watch what I do: programming by demonstration*, Cambridge Massachusetts: MIT press.
TM – Trade mark applied for by Telstra New Wave Pty Ltd.

Implementing Alignment-Based Learning

Menno van Zaanen

FNWI / ILLC
Cognitive Systems and Information Processing Group
University of Amsterdam
Nieuwe Achtergracht 166
1018 WV AMSTERDAM
The Netherlands
mvzaanen@science.uva.nl
http://www.science.uva.nl/~mvzaanen

Abstract. In this article, the current implementation of the Alignment-Based Learning (ABL) framework (van Zaanen, 2002) will be described. ABL is an unsupervised grammar induction system that is based on Harris's (1951) idea of substitutability. Instances of the framework can be applied to an untagged, unstructured corpus of natural language sentences, resulting in a labelled, bracketed version of that corpus.
Firstly, the framework aligns all sentences in the corpus in pairs, resulting in a partition of the sentences consisting of parts of the sentences that are equal in both sentences and parts that are unequal. Since substituting one unequal part for the other results in another valid sentence, the unequal parts of the sentences are considered to be possible (possibly overlapping) constituents. Secondly, of all possible constituents found by the first phase, the best are selected.

1 Introduction

The unsupervised grammar induction system Alignment-Based Learning (ABL) has been described extensively in (van Zaanen, 2002). In this article we will only give a condensed overview of the theoretical system and then concentrate on the current implementation of ABL.

The ABL system normally consists of two distinct phases. However, the implementation described here subdivides the first phase into two separate ones. All three phases will be described here briefly.

The *alignment learning phase* finds possible constituents, called hypotheses, by aligning pairs of sentences to each other. Following a reversed version of Harris's (1951) implication (*if parts of sentences can be substituted by each other then they are constituents of the same type*) groups of words that are *unequal* in a pair of sentences are considered hypotheses.

Figure 1 illustrates how ABL finds hypotheses. The first sentence is aligned to the second. The underlined words indicate similar parts in the sentences. The dissimilar parts (*Book Delta 128* and *Give me all flights*) are now considered hypotheses (which is indicated by the pair of brackets).

P. Adriaans, H. Fernau, and M. van Zaanen (Eds.): ICGI 2002, LNAI 2484, pp. 312–314, 2002.
© Springer-Verlag Berlin Heidelberg 2002

$$\underbrace{\overbrace{(_X \quad \textit{Book Delta 128} \quad)_X \underline{\textit{from Dallas to Boston}}}}{}$$

$$\overbrace{(_X \underline{\textit{Give me}} \; (_Y \textit{ all flights })_X \underline{\textit{from Dallas to Boston }})_Y}$$

$$\underline{\textit{Give me}} \; (_Y \qquad \textit{help on classes} \qquad)_Y$$

Fig. 1. Overlapping hypotheses

The system also assigns non-terminal types to the hypotheses. If hypotheses with different non-terminals occur in the same context, then the non-terminals are merged. This is normally part of the alignment learning phase, but the implementation contains a separate *cluster phase* that performs this function.

When the second sentence is aligned to the third, it receives another hypothesis, which overlaps with the older hypothesis. Since the underlying grammar is assumed to be context-free, overlapping constituents are unwanted. The *selection learning phase* eliminates the unwanted, overlapping hypotheses.

2 Implementation

The main programs of the current ABL implementation are written in C++, while some of the support programs are written in Perl. The entire package will be made available soon.

The package has three main entry points. These programs represent the main tasks in a particular project. Firstly, files can be converted to different formats. Secondly, the actual learning takes place and finally, the learned corpus can be evaluated against the original corpus. Each of these three steps is represented by a specific program.

The main programs call many sub-programs, each of which perform a specific task. These programs can also be called by the user directly. The main entry points merely make it easier to handle the different options and data files.

2.1 Conversion

The `abl_convert` program can convert files from and to different formats. The current ABL package recognises the following formats:

plain In this format, the file contains plain sentences only.
gold This is the gold format as used in the EVALB program (Collins, 1997).
abl The abl format is the output of all ABL learning programs.
atis, wsj and ovis The format of the ATIS, Wall Street Journal (Marcus et al., 1993) and OVIS treebanks (Bonnema et al., 1997) can be used as input only.

It converts that file from the input into the wanted output format. Even though this program is not necessarily part of the ABL system, it is a useful addition, since these conversions are often necessary.

2.2 Running ABL

The main program of the package is called `abl_build`. It can be told to do one, two or all three phases of ABL. The user can choose if the output of a phase should be stored for further evaluation or is intermediate and can be discarded afterwards.

Furthermore, one or more different instantiations of each phase can be selected as well as a number of random seeds to be used. This allows the building of several output files (with automatically generated file names) in only one program call.

2.3 Evaluation

The third program of the package, `abl_eval`, takes care of the evaluation. It should be told which files to evaluate and which evaluation metrics should be computed.

Currently, the evaluation program calls the EVALB program to compute most metrics, but the number of learned hypotheses and the number of introduced non-terminal types can also be counted. Additionally, the maximum obtainable scores on all metrics after the cluster phase can be computed by selecting hypotheses only if they occur in the original treebank. This simulates a perfect selection learning phase.

3 Conclusion and Future Work

The current implementation of the ABL grammar induction system, which will become available soon, has three main programs with an easy interface which makes it very user-friendly. A graphical user interface is currently under development. Because it is programmed in C++, it is efficient and easily extendible.

In the near future, we expect to implement new instantiations of all three phases. Special attention will be given to the cluster algorithm. Additionally, a grammar induction phase, which extends the ABL system to a *parseABL* system will be added and finally, we are working on a parallel version of the alignment learning phase, since this is the most time consuming phase of the algorithm.

Bibliography

ACL (1997). *Proceedings of the 35th Annual Meeting of the ACL and the 8th Meeting of the EACL; Madrid, Spain*. ACL.

Bonnema, R., Bod, R., and Scha, R. (1997). A DOP model for semantic interpretation. In ACL (1997), pages 159–167.

Collins, M. (1997). Three generative, lexicalised models for statistical parsing. In ACL (1997), pages 16–23.

Harris, Z. S. (1951). *Structural Linguistics*. University of Chicago Press, Chicago:IL, USA and London, UK, 7th (1966) edition.

Marcus, M., Santorini, B., and Marcinkiewicz, M. (1993). Building a large annotated corpus of English: the Penn treebank. *Computational Linguistics*, 19(2):313–330.

van Zaanen, M. (2002). *Bootstrapping Structure into Language: Alignment-Based Learning*. PhD thesis, University of Leeds, Leeds, UK.

Author Index

Adriaans, P., 293
Antunes, C.M., 1
Atwell, E., 306

Belz, A., 14
Bernard, M., 120
Blair, A.D., 296

Calera-Rubio, J., 199
Cano, A., 28
Carrasco, R.C., 199
Chalup, S.K., 296
Cicchello, O., 37
Ciortuz, L., 299
Clark, A., 269
Costa Florêncio, C., 49

Denis, F., 63, 77
Dudau Sofronie, D., 303
Dupont, P., 77, 149

Esposito, Y., 77

Fernau, H., 92
Findlow, G., 309
Foret, A., 106

García, P., 28, 225
Gnanasekaran, S., 283

Habrard, A., 120
Heeringa, B., 185
Higuera, C. de la, 134, 161
Ho, K., 309
Hui, A., 309
Humrosia Begam, M., 283

Jacquenet, F., 120

Kermorvant, C., 149, 161
Kremer, S.C., 37

Law, L., 309
Lemay, A., 63, 77
Lievesley, S., 306
Lightwood, L., 309

Matsumoto, M., 174
Michnowicz, S., 309

Nakamura, K., 174
Nir, Y. Le, 106

Oates, T., 185
Oliveira, A.L., 1
Oncina, J., 134

Rico-Juan, J.R., 199
Ruiz, J., 28

Seginer, Y., 213
Sempere, J.M., 225
Starkie, B., 237, 309
Subramanian, K.G., 283

Tajima, Y., 249
Tellier, I., 303
Terada, M., 249
Terlutte, A., 63
Terwijn, S.A., 261
Thollard, F., 269
Thomas, D.G., 283
Tommasi, M., 303

Vervoort, M., 293

Walder, C., 309

Zaanen, M. van, 312

Lecture Notes in Artificial Intelligence (LNAI)

Vol. 2333: J.-J.Ch. Meyer, M. Tambe (Eds.), Intelligent Agents VIII. Revised Papers, 2001. XI, 461 pages. 2001.

Vol. 2336: M.-S. Chen, P.S. Yu, B. Liu (Eds.), Advances in Knowledge Discovery and Data Mining. Proceedings, 2002. XIII, 568 pages. 2002.

Vol. 2338: R. Cohen, B. Spencer (Eds.), Advances in Artificial Intelligence. Proceedings, 2002. XII, 373 pages. 2002.

Vol. 2356: R. Kohavi, B.M. Masand, M. Spiliopoulou, J. Srivastava (Eds.), WEBKDD 2002 – Mining Web Log Data Across All Customers Touch Points. Proceedings, 2002. XI, 167 pages. 2002.

Vol. 2358: T. Hendtlass, M. Ali (Eds.), Developments in Applied Artificial Intelligence. Proceedings, 2002 XIII, 833 pages. 2002.

Vol. 2366: M.-S. Hacid, Z.W. Raś, D.A. Zighed, Y. Kodratoff (Eds.), Foundations of Intelligent Systems. Proceedings, 2002. XII, 614 pages. 2002.

Vol. 2371: S. Koenig, R.C. Holte (Eds.), Abstraction, Reformulation, and Approximation. Proceedings, 2002. XI, 349 pages. 2002.

Vol. 2375: J. Kivinen, R.H. Sloan (Eds.), Computational Learning Theory. Proceedings, 2002. XI, 397 pages. 2002.

Vol. 2377: A. Birk, S. Coradeschi, T. Satoshi (Eds.), RoboCup 2001: Robot Soccer World Cup V. XIX, 763 pages. 2002.

Vol. 2381: U. Egly, C.G. Fermüller (Eds.), Automated Reasoning with Analytic Tableaux and Related Methods. Proceedings, 2002. X, 341 pages. 2002 .

Vol. 2385: J. Calmet, B. Benhamou, O. Caprotti, L. Henocque, V. Sorge (Eds.), Artificial Intelligence, Automated Reasoning, and Symbolic Computation. Proceedings, 2002. XI, 343 pages. 2002.

Vol. 2389: E. Ranchhod, N.J. Mamede (Eds.), Advances in Natural Language Processing. Proceedings, 2002. XII, 275 pages. 2002.

Vol. 2392: A. Voronkov (Ed.), Automated Deduction – CADE-18. Proceedings, 2002. XII, 534 pages. 2002.

Vol. 2393: U. Priss, D. Corbett, G. Angelova (Eds.), Conceptual Structures: Integration and Interfaces. Proceedings, 2002. XI, 397 pages. 2002.

Vol. 2394: P. Perner (Ed.), Advances in Data Mining. VII, 109 pages. 2002.

Vol. 2403: Mark d'Inverno, M. Luck, M. Fisher, C. Preist (Eds.), Foundations and Applications of Multi-Agent Systems. Proceedings, 1996-2000. X, 261 pages. 2002.

Vol. 2407: A.C. Kakas, F. Sadri (Eds.), Computational Logic: Logic Programming and Beyond. Part I. XII, 678 pages. 2002.

Vol. 2408: A.C. Kakas, F. Sadri (Eds.), Computational Logic: Logic Programming and Beyond. Part II. XII, 628 pages. 2002.

Vol. 2413: K. Kuwabara, J. Lee (Eds.), Intelligent Agents and Multi-Agent Systems. Proceedings, 2002. X, 221 pages. 2002.

Vol. 2416: S. Craw, A. Preece (Eds.), Advances in Case-Based Reasoning. Proceedings, 2002. XII, 656 pages. 2002.

Vol. 2417: M. Ishizuka, A. Sattar (Eds.), PRICAI 2002: Trends in Artificial Intelligence. Proceedings, 2002. XX, 623 pages. 2002.

Vol. 2424: S. Flesca, G. Ianni (Eds.), Logics in Artificial Intelligence. Proceedings, 2002. XIII, 572 pages. 2002.

Vol. 2430: T. Elomaa, H. Mannila, H. Toivonen (Eds.), Machine Learning: ECML 2002. Proceedings, 2002. XIII, 532 pages. 2002.

Vol. 2431: T. Elomaa, H. Mannila, H. Toivonen (Eds.), Principles of Data Mining and Knowledge Discovery. Proceedings, 2002. XIV, 514 pages. 2002.

Vol. 2443: D. Scott (Ed.), Artificial Intelligence: Methodology, Systems, and Applications. Proceedings, 2002. X, 279 pages. 2002.

Vol. 2445: C. Anagnostopoulou, M. Ferrand, A. Smaill (Eds.), Music and Artificial Intelligence. Proceedings, 2002. VIII, 207 pages. 2002.

Vol. 2446: M. Klusch, S. Ossowski, O. Shehory (Eds.), Cooperative Information Agents VI. Proceedings, 2002. XI, 321 pages. 2002.

Vol. 2447: D.J. Hand, N.M. Adams, R.J. Bolton (Eds.), Pattern Detection and Discovery. Proceedings, 2002. XII, 227 pages. 2002.

Vol. 2448: P. Sojka, I. Kopeček, K. Pala (Eds.), Text, Speech and Dialogue. Proceedings, 2002. XII, 481 pages. 2002.

Vol. 2464: M. O'Neill, R.F.E. Sutcliffe, C. Ryan, M. Eaton, N. Griffith (Eds.), Artificial Intelligence and Cognitive Science. Proceedings, 2002. XI, 247 pages. 2002.

Vol. 2475: J.J. Alpigini, J.F. Peters, A. Skowron, N. Zhong (Eds.), Rough Sets and Current Trends in Computing. Proceedings, 2002. XV, 640 pages. 2002.

Vol. 2479: M. Jarke, J. Koehler, G. Lakemeyer (Eds.), KI 2002: Advances in Artificial Intelligence. Proceedings, 2002. XIII, 327 pages.

Vol. 2484: P. Adriaans, H. Fernau, M. van Zaanen (Eds.), Grammatical Inference: Algorithms and Applications. Proceedings, 2002. IX, 315 pages. 2002.

.e Notes in Computer Science

Vol. 2445: C. Anagnostopoulou, M. Ferrand, A. Smaill (Eds.), Music and Artificial Intelligence. Proceedings, 2002. VIII, 207 pages. 2002. (Subseries LNAI).

Vol. 2446: M. Klusch, S. Ossowski, O. Shehory (Eds.), Cooperative Information Agents VI. Proceedings, 2002. XI, 321 pages. 2002. (Subseries LNAI).

Vol. 2447: D.J. Hand, N.M. Adams, R.J. Bolton (Eds.), Pattern Detection and Discovery. Proceedings, 2002. XII, 227 pages. 2002. (Subseries LNAI).

Vol. 2448: P. Sojka, I. Kopeček, K. Pala (Eds.), Text, Speech and Dialogue. Proceedings, 2002. XII, 481 pages. 2002. (Subseries LNAI).

Vol. 2449: L. Van Gool (Ed.), Pattern Recognotion. Proceedings, 2002. XVI, 628 pages. 2002.

Vol. 2451: B. Hochet, A.J. Acosta, M.J. Bellido (Eds.), Integrated Circuit Design. Proceedings, 2002. XVI, 496 pages. 2002.

Vol. 2452: R. Guigó, D. Gusfield (Eds.), Algorithms in Bioinformatics. Proceedings, 2002. X, 554 pages. 2002.

Vol. 2453: A. Hameurlain, R. Cicchetti, R. Traunmüller (Eds.), Database and Expert Systems Applications. Proceedings, 2002. XVIII, 951 pages. 2002.

Vol. 2454: Y. Kambayashi, W. Winiwarter, M. Arikawa (Eds.), Data Warehousing and Knowledge Discovery. Proceedings, 2002. XIII, 339 pages. 2002.

Vol. 2455: K. Bauknecht, A M. Tjoa, G. Quirchmayr (Eds.), E-Commerce and Web Technologies. Proceedings, 2002. XIV, 414 pages. 2002.

Vol. 2456: R. Traunmüller, K. Lenk (Eds.), Electronic Government. Proceedings, 2002. XIII, 486 pages. 2002.

Vol. 2458: M. Agosti, C. Thanos (Eds.), Research and Advanced Technology for Digital Libraries. Proceedings, 2002. XVI, 664 pages. 2002.

Vol. 2459: M.C. Calzarossa, S. Tucci (Eds.), Performance Evaluation of Complex Systems: Techniques and Tools. Proceedings, 2002. VIII, 501 pages. 2002.

Vol. 2460: J.-M. Jézéquel, H. Hussmann, S. Cook (Eds.), «UML» 2002 – The Unified Modeling Language. Proceedings, 2002. XII, 449 pages. 2002.

Vol. 2461: R. Möhring, R. Raman (Eds.), Algorithms – ESA 2002. Proceedings, 2002. XIV, 917 pages. 2002.

Vol. 2462: K. Jansen, S. Leonardi, V. Vazirani (Eds.), Approximation Algorithms for Combinatorial Optimization. Proceedings, 2002. VIII, 271 pages. 2002.

Vol. 2463: M. Dorigo, G. Di Caro, M. Sampels (Eds.), Ant Algorithms. Proceedings, 2002. XIII, 305 pages. 2002.

Vol. 2464: M. O'Neill, R.F.E. Sutcliffe, C. Ryan, M. Eaton, N. Griffith (Eds.), Artificial Intelligence and Cognitive Science. Proceedings, 2002. XI, 247 pages. 2002. (Subseries LNAI).

Vol. 2465: H. Arisawa, Y. Kambayashi (Eds.), Conceptual Modeling for New Information Systems Technologies. Proceedings, 2001. XVII, 500 pages. 2002.

Vol. 2469: W. Damm, E.-R. Olderog (Eds.), Formal Techniques in Real-Time and Fault-Tolerant Systems. Proceedings, 2002. X, 455 pages. 2002.

Vol. 2470: P. Van Hentenryck (Ed.), Principles and Practice of Constraint Programming – CP 2002. Proceedings, 2002. XVI, 794 pages. 2002.

Vol. 2471: J. Bradfield (Ed.), Computer Science Logic. Proceedings, 2002. XII, 613 pages. 2002.

Vol. 2475: J.J. Alpigini, J.F. Peters, A. Skowron, N. Zhong (Eds.), Rough Sets and Current Trends in Computing. Proceedings, 2002. XV, 640 pages. 2002. (Subseries LNAI).

Vol. 2476: A.H.F. Laender, A.L. Oliveira (Eds.), String Processing and Information Retrieval. Proceedings, 2002. XI, 337 pages. 2002.

Vol. 2477: M.V. Hermenegildo, G. Puebla (Eds.), Static Analysis. Proceedings, 2002. XI, 527 pages. 2002.

Vol. 2478: M.J. Egenhofer, D.M. Mark (Eds.), Geographic Information Science. Proceedings, 2002. X, 363 pages. 2002.

Vol. 2479: M. Jarke, J. Koehler, G. Lakemeyer (Eds.), KI 2002: Advances in Artificial Intelligence. Proceedings, 2002. XIII, 327 pages. (Subseries LNAI).

Vol. 2480: Y. Han, S. Tai, D. Wikarski (Eds.), Engineering and Deployment of Cooperative Information Systems. Proceedings, 2002. XIII, 564 pages. 2002.

Vol. 2483: J.D.P. Rolim, S. Vadhan (Eds.), Randomization and Approximation Techniques in Computer Science. Proceedings, 2002. VIII, 275 pages. 2002.

Vol. 2484: P. Adriaans, H. Fernau, M. van Zaanen (Eds.), Grammatical Inference: Algorithms and Applications. Proceedings, 2002. IX, 315 pages. 2002. (Subseries LNAI).

Vol. 2488: T. Dohi, R. Kikinis (Eds), Medical Image Computing and Computer-Assisted Intervention – MICCAI 2002. Proceedings, Part I. XXIX, 807 pages. 2002.

Vol. 2489: T. Dohi, R. Kikinis (Eds), Medical Image Computing and Computer-Assisted Intervention – MICCAI 2002. Proceedings, Part II. XXIX, 693 pages. 2002.

Vol. 2496: K.C. Almeroth, M. Hasan (Eds.), Management of Multimedia in the Internet. Proceedings, 2002. XI, 355 pages. 2002.

Vol. 2498: G. Borriello, L.E. Holmquist (Eds.), UbiComp 2002: Ubiquitous Computing. Proceedings, 2002. XV, 380 pages. 2002.